CLEVELAND STATE COMMUNITY COLLEGE

The First Fifty Years

1967-2017

B. Spencer Culbreth

TABLE OF CONTENTS

INTRODUCTION

This book was written to celebrate the 50th Anniversary of Cleveland State Community College. It is primarily a compilation of events and people (students, faculty, staff and community members) that contributed to the development of the college. In essence, it is similar to a yearbook that covers fifty years rather than one year. It is divided into years for easy reference by former students. Although it discusses the major international, national, popular cultural and campus-related events from 1967 through 2016, greater detail is provided for the years 1967-2000.

Numerous people have assisted with this endeavor. First and foremost has been my wife, Ann, whose encouragement, patience, computer knowledge and editing skills were instrumental in the completion of the project. Also important were our good friends, Lew and Delores Warren, who shared both their computer expertise and proofreading skills. Brenda Ellis completed the onerous task of formatting the book for publication. This endeavor was greatly appreciated because of the author's lack of knowledge in desktop publishing. These four people have my eternal gratitude for patiently guiding me through the process. A thank you also is extended to Dr. Carl Hite who indicated to me that it would be great if someone would write a history of the college's first fifty years.

Other helpful individuals have been the college library staff: Sarah Copeland, Slade Scoggins, Brianne Yancey, Suzanne Ratcliff, Janet Caruth and Alan Goslen. Numerous other current and former college employees have also been helpful in gathering information. They were: Tracey Wright, Tony Bartolo, Holly Vincent, Jeff Reep, John Dezember, Ron Hammontree, Patricia Weaver, Sherra Witt, Dr. Ann Cunningham, Larry Burns, Barbara Eaves, Linda Everett, Laura Brogden, Gail Greenwood, Martha Lane, Shirley McDaniel, Gail Key, Ann McCoin, Jason Sewell, Mike Policastro, Dr. Frank McKenzie, Dr. Tommy Wright, Susan Webb-Curtis, Doyle Hawkins, Joan Bates, Michelle Jenkins, Karen Wyrick, Dale Yates, Dr. L. E. Wooten, Jim Cigliano, Cele Curtis, Dr. William Seymour, Ashley Raburn, Dwight Williams, Dan Wallen, Janice Casson, Larry Speight, John Cantrell, Bryan Reed, Dr. Neil Greenwood, Dr. Larry Longerbeam, Hugh Walker, Dan Lumpkin, Lee Cigliano, Alisha Fox, Joyce Brock, Dawn Steele, Roger Parsons and David Knopp. Other individuals who have assisted were: Ken Phillips (who gave me useful tips on formatting), Barbara Aderhold, Angela McClure Mathis, Joy Yates, Nancy Casson and Bernadette Douglas.

ORIGINS

They traveled from the cities, towns and communities in the foothills of the Appalachian Mountains of Tennessee. They arrived day and night by automobile, often on two-lane roads. Later Interstate Highway 75 would improve travel for many of them in their movement to and from their destination. Most were recent high school graduates. Others were adults, some married and some with children. Many worked long hours in day and/or night jobs on the farms or in the businesses and industries in the Tennessee Valley. Their goal was to improve their standard of living and quality of life by acquiring knowledge and skills. Since 1967 over 250,000 of them have made the journey. Their destination—Cleveland State Community College.

Significant endeavors can have modest beginnings. Cleveland State Community College exemplifies this assertion. From an initial enrollment of 681 students in 1967, the college enrolled approximately 3,500 students in 2016. The college administration was originally housed in a small, former residence at 623 Broad Street, in Cleveland, Tennessee. Classes for the first quarter (the fall of 1967) were conducted in the educational building of the North Cleveland Baptist Church. Fifty years later the college contained eleven major buildings spread across approximately 82 acres adjacent to Interstate Highway 75.

American colleges, universities and school systems developed from European models. Community colleges, however, are a unique American educational creation. National interest in community colleges was stimulated by the report of the 1947 Truman Committee on Education. Interest in establishing community colleges in Tennessee began in the 1950s, and in 1955 the legislative council of the Tennessee General Assembly authorized research on the issue. The study was conducted under the direction of Dr. Truman Pierce and Dr. A. D. Albright. The Pierce-Albright Report, titled "Public Higher Education in Tennessee," was completed in 1957, and it recommended additional higher education institutions throughout the state. The report noted that three geographic areas were deficient in accessibility to higher education. One of these was the Third Congressional District of Southeast Tennessee (the Chattanooga-Cleveland area), and the other two were the Jackson and the Pulaski-Columbia areas.

On various occasions State Education Commissioner Joe Morgan, other educators and other officials had recommended community colleges as an alternative to additional four-year universities. In 1963 recently elected Governor Frank G. Clement discussed the issue with the new State Department Commissioner of Education, J. Howard Warf. Shortly thereafter, the General Assembly appropriated $100,000 "per annum" for the development of plans for the colleges. A committee, headed by Commissioner Warf, recommended placing the colleges within a fifty-mile radius of every college-age person in Tennessee.

In June 1965 both Warf's committee and Governor Clement recommended to the Assembly that a community college be established in each of the three geographical divisions of the state. Leadership of the colleges was assigned to the State Board of Education, and Dr. Archie Rushton was appointed as the Board's first Executive Dean of Community Colleges. Immediately Cleveland City and Bradley County officials began a lengthy political struggle to have one of the colleges located in Cleveland. Other areas, such as the city of Chattanooga and the counties of Meigs, Marion, Polk and Rhea, also launched political maneuvers to acquire the college. The political struggle is recounted in detail in Community Colleges of Tennessee, edited by Dr. Roy S. Nicks, and in the book, Morning Has Broken, by Sue Little (author) and Walter Presswood (editor). Little and Presswood noted that critical roles were played by Governor Clement's friends, Cleveland Mayor William Fillauer and Eugene Callaway. Instrumental roles were also played by Hallman Bell, the Governor's Bradley County campaign manager; John Dunlap, a state committee member of the Democratic Party; and Frank Manly, an insurance executive and former teacher and principal. Through the combined efforts of Manly, Callaway, Fillauer, Bell, Dunlap, State Senator Ernest Guffey, Nelom Jackson, Grover Ash, Kenneth Tinsley, W. A. Jones, H. M. Fulbright, John Clayton and others, the goal of establishing the college in Cleveland was achieved.

The State Board of Education stipulated three requirements for a location to be considered as a site for the college: (1) a contribution of $250,000, (2) a contribution of 100 acres of land and (3) provision for all utilities at the site. A woodland of over 100 acres was identified by the Bradley County Court as a site for the college. The land had become county property due to unpaid taxes, and the county court and city commission agreed to provide $125,000 each for the enterprise. A committee, consisting of Guffey, Dunlap, Manly, Fillauer, Jones, Fulbright, Clayton and Paul Davis, presented Cleveland's bid to the State Board's selection committee. On June 22, 1965 Cleveland was approved for the site.

On February 11, 1966 the State Board of Education decreed that the name of the college would be Cleveland State Community College, and on July 20, 1966 bids for contracts were activated for the construction of five buildings (containing 130,000 square feet of floor space), to accommodate a projected student enrollment of between 500 and 750. The initial cost of construction, including equipment, was $2,494,000. A groundbreaking ceremony was conducted in September 1966 on the 105-acre campus (by comparison, the area was about the same size as the Vatican in Rome, Italy). Several years later, the college sold approximately twenty-three acres to a housing development.

In January 1967 Dr. David F. Adkisson was named the first President (and first college employee), and in March 1967 temporary offices were opened in the aforementioned former Cleveland residence on Broad Street. Dr. Adkisson had several years of educational administrative experience. A native of Ashland City, Tennessee, he was an elementary and high school teacher, principal, school superintendent, supervisor for 34 East Tennessee counties, director of instruction for the Knox County School Systems and instructor at the University of Tennessee at Knoxville. His degrees were from Austin Peay Normal, Middle Tennessee State University, George Peabody College and the University of Tennessee at Knoxville.

The first employee hired by Dr. Adkisson was Dr. George L. Mathis, Principal of Brainerd High School. In his role as Dean of Students, Dr. Mathis immediately began touring area high schools to recruit students. Dr. Mathis also had vast experience in education. He worked at high schools in Chattanooga and Knoxville prior to World War II. After returning from his wartime service in the Navy, he served as a coach, a teacher and an athletic director at Chattanooga High School. He later served at various times as Principal of Hardy Junior High School, Elbert Long School and Brainerd High School. While recruiting for Cleveland State, his standard comment was, "If you want to go to college, see me, and I'll see that you have the opportunity to get an education at Cleveland State." His efforts were instrumental in attracting large numbers of students to the campus.

Meanwhile, in addition to Adkisson and Mathis, several other administrators were hired. These were: Dr. F. Dean Banta, Dean of Instruction; McKamy Hall, Business Manager; James Cigliano, Director of Admission and Records; and Hayward R. Bond, Director of Continuing Education. Several faculty members were also hired (one of these, Head Librarian David Archer, had faculty status but did not teach) and four non-teaching staff. The faculty members were Ozane Adams, Tom Boles, Joe Guest, John Bradley, Jere Chumley, Irene Millsaps, Josephine Pritchett, Colonel John Smeltzer, Earl Andrews, Joe Crabtree, Elsie Dalton, Helen Ferguson, Patricia Handley, Johar Jogindar, Roy Lillard, Elizabeth P. Munck, Bob Savage and Robert Stone. The initial non-teaching staff included Jane E. Miller, Receptionist/Clerk; Brenda J. Newman, Secretary to the President; Sally N. Philips, Business Account Clerk; and Charlotte Shaver, Secretary to the Dean of Students.

Classes began at Cleveland State in the Fall Quarter of 1967 (registration was conducted on October 2, 1967) in the educational buildings of the North Cleveland Baptist Church. The total student enrollment for the initial Quarter was 681. There were 16 faculty members, 12 programs of study and 65 course offerings. Ninety-eight quarter hours were required for a degree and thirty quarter hours for a certificate. Ten years later (in 1977) there were 3,996 students, 94 faculty members, 29 programs of study and 710 course offerings. In its first catalog, which was printed in August 1967, the college pledged to devote its efforts to fulfill the following objectives: (1) provide courses to prepare students for transfer of two years of college credits to four-year schools; (2) provide technological and pre-professional courses for students entering industry, business and similar professions; (3) provide continuing education courses for those whose goal is professional or personal enrichment; (4) provide counseling and guidance services; and (5) provide both a cultural atmosphere and college facilities for the community. Although the college has added numerous objectives through the years, these initial ones have served as a foundation for fifty years.

THE SIXTIES

– 1967 - 1968 –

The 1960s were interesting times in international affairs. In May 1967 Egypt closed the Straits of Tiran to Israeli ships. Israel attacked military aircraft in Egypt, and this led to the entrance of Syria, Jordan and Iraq into the conflict. On June 10, 1967 the "Six Days War" ended when Israel and Syria agreed to a United Nations mediated cease-fire. Meanwhile, the war intensified in Vietnam in 1967-68. In early 1968 Communist troops launched the "Tet Offensive" by attacking provincial capitals and several major cities. Although the attackers suffered huge losses, the incident increased opposition to the war in the United States. Other international events were: the Soviet Union and other Warsaw Pact nations invaded Czechoslovakia and crushed the "Prague Spring" liberalization movement; the first heart transplant operation was performed in South Africa by Dr. Christian N. Barnard; in a Gibraltar referendum, 99% of the population voted to remain with Great Britain, rather than Spain; the London Bridge was sold for one million dollars and was later re-erected in Arizona; Pope Paul VI banned Catholics from using the contraceptive pill for birth control; France became the fifth nation with nuclear power capability; the first automated teller machine (ATM) opened in Barclay's in London; and the 83-man crew of the USS Pueblo was seized by North Korea in the Sea of Japan and detained for eleven months before being released in December 1968.

The major domestic events in 1967-68 were: the average cost of a new home was $14,250 in 1967 ($14,950 in 1968); the 1967 average income per year was $7,300 ($7,850 in 1968); the average cost of gasoline in 1967 was 33 cents per gallon (34 cents in 1968); the minimum wage was $1.40 in 1967 ($1.60 in 1968); Jack Ruby, the man who shot and killed President John F. Kennedy's assassin, Lee Harvey Oswald, died in a Dallas hospital; the United States Census Bureau's Population Clock revealed (on November 20, 1967) that America had 200 million people; Thurgood Marshall became the first black Associate Justice of the Supreme Court; Secretary of Defense, Robert S. McNamara, announced he was leaving President Lyndon Johnson's cabinet to become President of the World Bank; the space probe Mariner 5 was launched from Cape Kennedy on a flight that sped past Venus; Jimmy Hoffa began an eight-year prison term for defrauding a Union and for jury tampering; the 25th Amendment, which explained the order of succession to the Presidency, was ratified; interracial marriage was declared constitutional; civil rights-related riots erupted in Newark, Detroit and Cleveland (7,000 National Guardsmen were sent to restore order in Detroit); approximately 50,000 anti-war protesters marched on Washington, D. C.; Martin Luther King, Jr. was assassinated in Memphis by James Earl Ray; Senator Robert F. Kennedy was assassinated in Los Angeles by Sirhan Bishara Sirhan (Ray was sentenced to 99 years in prison and Sirhan's death sentence was later commuted to life in prison); former first lady Jacqueline Kennedy married the Greek shipping magnate, Aristotle Onassis; the Gateway Arch in St. Louis was dedicated by both Vice President Hubert Humphrey and Interior Secretary Stewart Udall; the nation's first emergency telephone system (using number "911") was inaugurated in Haleyville, Alabama; the first "Big Mac" was sold by MacDonald's restaurant; three college students were killed by highway patrolmen during a civil rights protest in Orangeburg, South Carolina; clashes between police and antiwar demonstrators occurred at the Democratic National Convention in Chicago; President Lyndon B. Johnson ordered a halt to all bombing of North Vietnam in an attempt to influence more meaningful peace negotiations (Johnson also announced he would not run for President in 1968); Vice-President Hubert Humphrey and independent candidate George C. Wallace were defeated by Richard Nixon for the Presidency; and Apollo 8 orbited the moon during a five-day mission.

The campus community endured the hectic times of the 1960s but was obviously affected by the turmoil. Commuter-oriented community colleges seldom stimulated excitement for organized protests or mass support for crusades. About 200 students did respond to a February 1968 poll (for students only), conducted by the campus History Department, on the issue of a cease-fire in Vietnam. The poll asked, "Should there be a cease-fire in Vietnam?" Of those responding, 83% replied "Yes" and 17% replied "No."

Although the news was often filled with depressing events, college students, like others, found relief in popular culture. Rowan and Martin's "Laugh-in" premiered on NBC-TV; singer Marvin Gaye released "I Heard it Through the Grapevine;" the counterculture musical "Hair" opened on Broadway; and producer/director Stanley Kubrick's film, "2001: A Space Odyssey," had its world premiere. The winners of the 1967 motion picture Oscars were: "In the Heat of the Night," best picture; Rod Steiger, best actor for "In the Heat of the Night;" and Katharine Hepburn, best actress for "Guess Who's Coming to Dinner." In 1968 the best picture was "Oliver," the best actor was Cliff Robertson in "Charity," and the best actresses were Katharine Hepburn in "The Lion in Winter" and Barbara Streisand in "Funny Girl." The 1967 Emmy Award for best television comedy was awarded to "The Monkees" (NBC), and "Get Smart" won the award in 1968. The 1967 and 1968 Emmy for best drama was presented to "Mission: Impossible" (CBS). The 1967 Grammy Award for the record of the year was presented to the 5th Dimension for "Up, Up and Away," and Simon and Garfunkel's "Mrs. Robinson" won the award in 1968. The Beatles won the 1967 Grammy for album of the year for "Sgt. Pepper's Lonely Hearts Club Band," and Glen Campbell's "By the Time I Get to Phoenix" won the award in 1968. In October 1967 folk singer Woody Guthrie died at the age of 55, and in December singer Otis Redding and six others were killed when their plane crashed in Wisconsin's Lake Monoma.

In sports news Muhammad Ali was stripped of his boxing world championship for refusing induction in the Army. UCLA won the NCAA basketball title in both 1967 and 1968, and the Green Bay Packers won both the first and second professional football Super Bowls in 1967 and 1968. St. Louis won the 1967 baseball World Series, and Detroit won in 1968.

From its inception to the present day, community support has played a vital role in the success of the college. In the first crucial months the following organizations and individuals pledged important monetary gifts: Cleveland Bank and Trust, Cleveland Coca-Cola Bottling, M. C. Headrick Supermarkets, Brown Stove Works, Cleveland Kiwanis Club, Manufacturer's Soap and Chemical, March of Dimes Foundation, Burlington Industries, W. J. McReynolds, Hardwick Stove, Bendix, Mallory Battery, Lions Club, American Uniform, Eugene Callaway, Central Drug, Dr. Wayne McCulley, Veterans of Foreign Wars and Arthell Clark of A&C Amusement. A transportation gift of a station wagon was made by Cletus Benton of Benton Pontiac-Buick, and later he donated a car which was the prize in a fund-raiser for the college.

Although many students had part-time, or even full-time jobs, several immediately began scheduling events and creating organizations for extra-curricular activities. Walter Presswood was elected President of the first Student Government Association (SGA). Other officers were Tommy Fuller, Vice-President; Sandra Kirk, Secretary; and Betty Rominger, Treasurer. The group's advisor (for the next 6 years) was Roy Lillard, a faculty member of the History Department. Students serving on the editorial staff of the first newspaper were Don Crye, Hope Geren, Judy Johnston, Walter Presswood, Bill Lander, Gail Moore, Susan Brooks, Ed Gill and Pam Terry. Dr. George Mathis and Hal Munck, a local newsman, served as advisors for the paper. The first issue, printed on December 13, 1967, lacked a name. Three choices for a name were offered in the first issue, and space was provided for a write-in choice. The choices were "The Cleveland State Courier," "The Cleveland State Prowler" and "The Cougar's Prowl." Suggestions were also gathered from faculty and staff. The suggestions were submitted to a committee composed of the editor, Dr. D. F. Adkisson, Dr. George L. Mathis, Roy G. Lillard and Hal Munck. The name selected was The Cherokee Signal (because of the local area's connection with Cherokee history).

A college motto (or seal) was adopted--"obstinatus sed aequus"--which means "firm but fair." The original seal was spelled incorrectly because of an error by the printer (it read "obstinat us sed aequus"). It was finally corrected in 1977. Blue and white were chosen by the students as the college's colors, and "Cougars" became the athletic nickname. The members of the first athletic team (men's basketball) were Bob Lackey, Mike Fitzgerald, Don Weiss, Bob Petrone, Tony Beard, Gary Barham, Harry Smith, Gary Davis and Jackie Liner. Barham scored the first two points in the christening of the new gym (in February 1968) when Cleveland State defeated Johnson Bible

College, 75-71. The first coaches were Athletic Director Joe Crabtree and Assistant Coach Ed Coates. The basketball team ended the 1967-68 season with nine wins and sixteen losses. The baseball program began on April 12, 1968. The Cougars defeated Cumberland College at Fulbright Field by a score of 12-6. The winning pitcher was "southpaw" Stan Goodwin, and the first extra-base hit was a double by Mike Fitzgerald. Ed Coates was the baseball coach during 1968-1974.

The first campus club, Circle K, was a service organization. It was organized by three members of the Cleveland Kiwanis Club, Willis Moore, Gerald Hoskins and Ray Davis. The club's student officers were Walter Presswood, Grant Cobb, Donnie Wyatt and Terry Townsend. Bob Boragaine was the advisor. Work on these and other college endeavors was interrupted by the sad news of the death of Barbara McClanahan, the Secretary for the Dean of Instruction.

When the 766 students arrived on the new campus for the 1968 Winter Quarter, four buildings had been completed -- the administration building, the science building, the student center and the library. The gymnasium was completed soon thereafter. An official dedication ceremony was held on April 29, 1968. Approximately 2,500 people were present at the ceremony which featured Governor Buford Ellington, State Education Commissioner J. H. Warf and several college and local officials. An unusual campus structure was the fallout shelter. It was actually a tunnel, wide enough to accommodate the passage of a large truck, which extended under the gymnasium, library, student center and science buildings. The Cleveland-Bradley County Civil Defense organization stocked it with emergency supplies for 2,696 people. By comparison, the gym held 2,500 people for a ball game and 3,500 for other events. Several years later the tunnel was transformed into a storage facility.

The college's budget, for the fiscal year 1968-69, was $1,146,850 (it was $741,032 for 1967-68). Of that amount, $26, 350 was designated for student activities and athletics, $35,000 for utilities, $119, 568 for supplies and materials, and $15,000 for communications. The estimated receipts were $183,700 from student fees, $900,000 from state and federal funds, $183,750 from organized educational activities (mainly athletics), $3,000 from gifts and grants, $97,200 from auxiliary enterprises (mainly the bookstore) and $13,5000 from student activity fees. The student registration fee for a Tennessee resident taking 10 or more hours of coursework was $50 (plus a five-dollar activity fee).

– 1968 - 1969 –

In campus news the construction of the sixth edifice (the Humanities Building) began, and the college was designated as a center for the General Education Development Test (GED). The year was also characterized by the formation of numerous student clubs, elections of officers, presentations of cultural events and athletic contests. Among these were the following: The first Mr. and Miss Cleveland State (in 1968) were David Cunningham and Janet McCamish (McCamish was married shortly thereafter and she was succeeded by Gail Moore); the first Spring concert was directed by Thomas Boles and the accompanist was Mrs. George Lessig; the Baptist Student Union was organized, and Terry Townsend was the Student President; the Nursing Technology Association was formed, and the officers were Pete Tapley, Bob Richey, Elizabeth Anstey and Geraldine Kelly; the first Nursing "Capping" ceremony was led by the Director of Nursing Education, Helen Ferguson; a Music Club was created, and the officers were Judy Crawley, Fran Eaglehouse, Sharon Geren and Faye Snyder; and a Spanish club (named La Tertulia) was organized, and Bonnie Thomas, Sandra Cochran, Betty Rominger and Ken Martel were the officers. The Spanish instructor, Roberto Rojas, was the advisor.

A few of the staff members in 1968-69 were: Dr. Adkisson, President; Dr. Mathis, Dean of Students; Dr. F. Dean Banta, Dean of Instruction; James Cigliano, Director of Admissions; and F. McKamy Hall (and later, Ron Mason) Business Managers. A few other staff members were: Colonel John Smeltzer (both staff and faculty), Paul Boynton, Elvis Brandon, Hal Munck, Donald Hill, Robert Boragaine, Brenda Newman, Bradley Evans, Kay Graham, Norma Davis, Linda Logan, Judy Geren, Beverly Joye, Dianne Harrison, Wanda Lawson and Gail Dodd. Judy Munger was the college nurse; David Archer was the librarian; and Marie F. Boragaine and Helen Chang were the assistant librarians. A few of the faculty members were Patricia Rainey, Elsie Dalton, Buford Guy, Joe Guest, Francis L. Williams, Clair Scott, Dr. T. P. Mathai, Josephine Pritchett, John Barnes, Nancy Dupree, Roy Lillard, Joseph Suppinger, Jerome Taylor, Rebecca Mobbs, Joe Crabteee, Ozane Adams, Ed Coates, Fred Martin, Irene Millsaps, Alleyna Ellis, L. D. Brooks, Sarah Bruner, Michael Dorset, Donald Fairbairn, Jay Williams, Luther Williams, Patricia Handley, Elizabeth Munck, Jean Poe, James Perry, Bob Savage, Dolly Maley, Jean Poe, Mary Barker, Larry Speight, Phyllis Dickinson, David Straits, Marilyn Fillers, James Allen and Lorraine Fulbright. Maintenance and Grounds personnel were: Jake Newman (Supervisor), Robert Edgemon, Horace Hall, Ida Hitson, Jim Lane, James Passmore, Mollie Smith, James Teague and Irene Whitaker.

In activities the March of Dimes Talent Show was won by Judy Crawley, and Sandra Paul and Harry Rymer led the March of Dimes campus fund-raising drive (and surpassed their goal of $3,000). A Student Government Association (SGA) Election was conducted and the officers were: Douglas Smith, President; Betty Rominger, Vice-President; Tana Cofer, Secretary; and Linda Brewer, Treasurer. Several other student government positions were created: Director of Activities, Mike Lee; Secretary of Exterior (off-campus student affairs), John Hannah; Secretary of Interior, Larry Phillips; Director of Public Information, Cecilia Edgemon; Secretary of Campus Culture and Entertainment, Frances Eaglehouse; and Election Commissioner, Walter Presswood. The Sophomore Class Officers were Fred Rhodes, President; Jean Yates,

Vice-President; Sandra Kirk, Secretary; Loretta Cate, Treasurer; and Shelia Morgan, Class Representative. Mr. and Miss Cleveland State were Terry Townsend and Linda Brewer, and the Homecoming Queen was Gail Moore.

An entertaining joint college and community play, "The Odd Couple," was presented at the Knights of Columbus Theater. The cast included John Bradley, Sarah Bruner (both members of the English Department) and Carolyn Clark Bennett. Jeanne Turner, a reporter for the <u>Cleveland Daily Banner</u>, wrote that Bradley's Performance was "more professional than some on Broadway." Turner also noted that "Sally Bruner and Carolyn Clark Bennett, as the Pigeon sisters, sparkled on stage and sparkled right off again much too soon."

Four tennis courts were completed by the fall of 1969, and the first team compiled a 2-2 record. The coach was John Smeltzer (also a Counselor and Psychology instructor) and the team members were Lee Scheel, Pat Hanks, Reed Bacon, Glen Davis, Tom Varnell, Al Kuykendall, Robert Easterly and Houston Brown. The men's basketball team compiled a 10-15 overall record and 5-11 in the conference. The team members were Ken Byrd, Charles Queener, John Eldridge, Tommy Haun, Gary Barham, Rex Bearden, Joe Axley, Levi Scott, Mike Fitzgerald and Eddie Thacker.

The 1968-69 <u>Student Handbook</u> contained amusing suggestions for proper attire at college events. When attending teas and semi-formal events, women should wear an "after-five" dress and heels, and men should wear a white shirt, tie and suit. For formal events women were to wear long or short formals and men a dinner jacket, tuxedo or dark suit. When attending classes and/or intercollegiate games, women were to wear a dress or a skirt and blouse with flats and men a white shirt and tie or slacks and a sport shirt. At informal occasions women were to wear Bermuda shorts, a shirt and flats and men Bermuda shorts and a sport shirt. How closely this suggested dress code was followed in the free-spirited 1960s is open to conjecture.

Humor has always been a part of campus life. The comedian Phyllis Diller, for example, had several entertaining quotes that were popular around the campus during the 1960s and 1970s. A few were: "A smile is a curve that sets everything straight; Housework can't kill you, but why take a chance; The best way to get rid of kitchen odors is to eat out; I'm eighteen years behind in my ironing; His finest hour lasted a minute and a half; My photographs don't do me justice—they look just like me;" and "You know you are old if they have discontinued your blood type." Puns were also a favorite of several faculty and staff. A few were: "How does Moses make tea? Hebrews it;" "A cartoonist was found dead in his home. Details are sketchy;" I used to be a banker, but then I lost interest;" "When chemists die, they barium;" "I'm reading a book about anti-gravity. I just can't put it down; and "I didn't like my beard at first. Then it grew on me."

Enrollment records continued to be shattered every quarter as students came to the campus from Anderson, Knox, Roane, Loudon, Rhea, Meigs, McMinn, Monroe, Polk, Hamilton and Bradley Counties. The Fall Quarter enrollment for 1968 was 1,365 students (1020 day and 345 evening students). Male students in the day classes outnumbered female day students two to one (686-337). By the fall of 2015 the gender analysis had altered so much that, of the 3,509 students, 2,088 (60%) were females and 1,421 (40%) were males. The Student Handbook recommended that a first quarter college freshman take 17 hours of course credit (18 hours for a student with an overall B or above average) and 12 hours for a student on academic probation.

The Cherokee Signal staff featured Walter Presswood, Editor; Cecilia Edgemon, News Editor; Charlotte Stuman, Make-up and Layout Editor; and Ron Eberhardt, Sports Editor. A yearbook, named "The Statesman," was planned for completion in 1969. Linda Richard was the Editor, and the Business Manager was Frances Eaglehouse. Other section editors included: Hope Geren, Class Editor; Doug Smith and Grant Cobb, Sports; Ricky Quine, Introduction; Sharon Freeman, Activities; Dennis Cannon, Faculty and Administration; Sandra Croft, Index; and Ron Eberhardt, Photographer. Hal Munck (a local news reporter) and Dr. George Mathis were the advisors. The Cheerleaders were Debbie Roberts (Captain), Gail Moore, Jennifer Murphy, Tricia Garrison, Patsy Moore, Bill Hambaugh, Steve Smith, Roger Stewart and Darlene Chambers. The existing student organizations in 1968-69 were the Baptist Student Union, the Cheerleading Squad, the Circle K Club, the Alumni Association, the Music Club, the Student Nurses Association, the Spanish Club and the Student Government Association.

– 1969 - 1970 –

Astounding headlines filled the newspapers, magazines, televisions and radios in 1969. Astronaut Neil Armstrong, commander of the Apollo 11 mission, became the first person to set foot on the moon; two manned Soviet Soyuz spaceships became the first vehicles to dock in space and transfer personnel; President Nixon announced a "Vietnamization" policy for the war in Vietnam, and a steady withdrawal of the 543,400 American forces began in July 1969; the revelation of a massacre of South Vietnamese villagers, by American troops, at My Lai, South Vietnam, heightened the tension connected with the war; Golda Meir, of Milwaukee, Wisconsin, became the Prime Minister of Israel; and the first test flight of France's Concorde was conducted.

The major domestic events were: the average cost of a house was $15,550; the average income was $8,550; the average cost of gasoline was 35 cents per gallon; the new President was Richard Nixon; a car driven by Senator Edward M. Kennedy plunged off a bridge on Chappaquiddick Island, and his passenger, Mary Jo Kopechne, drowned; actress Sharon Tate and four other people were brutally slain by cult leader Charles

Manson and his group of followers; the Woodstock rock music festival, near Bethel, New York, attracted 300,000 to 500,000 people; Hurricane Camille, a Category 5 hurricane that hit the Mississippi coast, killed 256 people; anti-Vietnam War demonstrations were held in numerous cities (one in Washington D. C. attracted 250,000 marchers); the trial of the Chicago Seven (for inciting a riot at the 1968 Democratic National Convention) began (they were found guilty in 1970 but the decision was later overturned by a Court of Appeal); Earl Warren retired and Warren Burger became the new Supreme Court Justice; President Dwight Eisenhower died at the age of 78; actress-singer Judy Garland died at the age of 47; and the U. S. Government held its first draft lottery since World War II.

Meanwhile, information about the Vietnam conflict, drug abuse, airplane hijackings, rising crime rates, environmental pollution, legalized abortion, minority rights, women's rights and fears of world overpopulation were constantly in the news. During all of these developments the atmosphere at Cleveland State remained stable. Many students had part-time jobs, and/or families, and this did not provide time for extra-curricular activities. As already noted, commuter schools did not lend themselves to the formation of large, organized movements. On two different occasions, however, a one-day "Moratorium for Peace" was held on the campus, and a "rally" was conducted by two small groups of students. During the "moratorium" a few students wore peace symbols to proclaim their opposition to the war while others wore miniature flags to show support for the war. At the "rally" one small group wore black armbands to indicate their opposition to the American invasion of Cambodia and their support for the four students who were killed by National Guardsmen at Kent State. Another small group wore white armbands and supported the National Guard's use of force at Kent State. These developments, and others, were debated and discussed at length in numerous classrooms across the campus. Students were made aware of the pros and cons of issues and this created a healthy learning environment.

Entertainment and athletics provided a respite from the year's domestic turmoil. A few events were: the popular kids' show, "Sesame Street," was launched on public television; Kurt Vonnegut Jr.'s famous book, Slaughterhouse Five, was published; the Academy Award winning movie for 1969 was "Midnight Cowboy;" the best actor award for 1969 was John Wayne ("True Grit"); the best actress Oscar for 1969 was awarded to Maggie Smith ("The Prime of Miss Jean Brodie"); the Grammy Award for best record of the year was won by the 5th Dimension for "Aquarius/Let the Sunshine In," and the best album of the year was Blood Sweat and Tears, "Blood, Sweat and Tears;" the Emmy Award for TV's best comedy was won by "Get Smart" (NBC), and the best drama was "NET Playhouse"(NET); UCLA won the NCAA college basketball championship; the Super Bowl was won by the New York Jets; and the World Series was won by the New York Mets.

Sixty-nine degrees were awarded during the college's first graduation ceremony in 1969. Elizabeth Jane Anstey received the first degree and Walter Presswood received the Outstanding Student Award (an Outstanding Faculty member Award was added in 1973). Enrollment increased to 1,576 for the Fall Quarter of 1969 (972 day and 604 evening division students). The college offered 104 day and 52 evening courses taught by a total of 59 instructors. The 1969-70 Student Handbook noted that the average cost of books and supplies for a student was approximately $35 per quarter. Mrs. Norman Greason, Admissions Secretary and Director of Veterans" Affairs, reported that the number of military veterans had increased from 28 in 1967 to 118 students in 1970 (68 of these were full-time students).

By 1969 the college was a member of the American Association of Junior Colleges (AAJC), the Tennessee College Association (TCA), the Southern Association of Junior Colleges (SAJC), the National Education Association (NEA), the Tennessee Education Association (TEA) and the Tennessee Junior College Athletic Association (TJCAA). Most importantly, it also received accreditation by the Southern Association of Colleges and Universities (it was later renamed the Southern Association of Colleges and Schools-SACS). A college could not receive accreditation until it graduated its first class. After the accomplishment of this feat, Dr. F. Dean Banta and Dr. George Mathis attended the SACS meeting in December of 1969 and received the credentials for accreditation.

The day after the college was awarded with accreditation a student called Dot Cantrell, the switchboard operator, and inquired if classes were being held that day. The student heard that the college would be taking a holiday to celebrate receiving accreditation. Much to his chagrin, he was informed that, although receiving accreditation was an honor, classes would be meeting as usual.

The 1969-1970 academic year was filled with numerous developments. These were: construction on the Humanities Building continued; the library experimented with Saturday hours; Ronald N. Mason succeeded F. McKamy Hall as Business Manager (the latter resigned to assume a position at Charleston Hosiery Mill); a Cougar Athletic Booster Club was organized; and seventeen new faculty members were hired. The new faculty members were Dorothy Davis, Emmett Forbes, James Howard, Charles Laws, William Longley, Delmus Ledford, Betty Ledford, Steve Longley, Frances Moore, Matt Reiser, Edwin Rowlee, Leslie Wooten, Jr., David Vandiver, Alex Nichols, Katharine Trewhitt, Richard Vail and Bill Roberts. Department Heads were now a part of the college's organizational structure. These were: Donald Hill, Evening Division and Continuing Education; Matt Reiser, Technology; Roy Lillard Social Sciences and Business; Irene Millsaps, Science and Math; Elizabeth Wooten, Humanities; Joe Crabtree, Health, Physical Education and Recreation and Education; and Jake Newman, Maintenance.

Another first for the college occurred in 1969. "Aria Da Capo" was the first dramatic presentation held on campus. Directed by John Bradley, the cast members were David Curry, Lettice Jones, William Spinger, Les Underwood and Richard Finnell. New student officers assumed the helm of several organizations. The new SGA officers for 1968-1969 were: David Stiles, President; Melinda Hester, Vice-President; Rusti Hunt, Secretary; and Sherry Lowe, Treasurer. The officers for 1969-1970 were: David Stiles, President; Kay Ballew, Vice-President; Wanda Cook, Secretary; and Brenda Kirk, Treasurer. The new staff members of The Cherokee Signal were: Editor, Jennifer Wattenbarger Murphy; Business and Circulation Manager, Mike Wortman; Layout Editor, Kinch Exum; Copy Editor, Pat Davis; Sports Editor, Mitchell Parkinson; Assistant Sports Editor, Chuck Brown; Social Editor, Rusti Hunt; and Photographer, Phil Pritchard. The advisors were Dr. George Mathis and Bob Robinson.

Officers for the newly formed Junior Engineering Technological Society were: Ed Stanberry, President; Jim Killebrew, Vice-President; Julian Beavers, Secretary; David Clark, Treasurer; and Frank Bailey, Station Trustee. James Allen was the faculty sponsor. Members of the Spelunkers club elected the following officers: Zeke Baxter, President; Robert Torbet, Vice-President; Brenda Breeden, Secretary; and Brenda Kirk, Treasurer. Tricia Garrison was Captain and Bill Hambaugh was co-Captain of the Cheerleading squad. Other cheerleaders were Roger Stewart, Cathy Wilson, Valerie Hyberger and Jennifer Murphy. Ozane Adams was the sponsor. Circle K officers were: Bob Kirkpatrick, President; Ray Collins, Vice-President; Ken Adams, Secretary; David Stiles, Treasurer; and Jim McCallie, Project Chairman. Joyce Smith was elected President of the campus chapter of the Tennessee Association of Student Nurses. Betty Cardin was Vice-President, Shirley Turvey, Secretary and Marilyn Murphy, Treasurer. The Future Secretaries Association elected Reba Hudgins, President, Linda Bishop, Vice-President, Beverly Wood, Secretary and Jean Bramlett, Treasurer. Nancy Dalton was crowned Homecoming Queen, and Patrick Binkley and Denise Wilson were named Mr. and Miss Cleveland State.

The college's academic offerings continued to keep pace with the changing times. Technology courses offered were Business and Accounting, Secretarial Science, Computer Programming, Engineering Design and Graphics, Industrial Management and Inhalation Therapy. A new addition to the academic program was an Associate Degree in Law Enforcement. New courses were offered in Journalism, Drama, Tennessee History and Abnormal Psychology. Don Hill (Director of the Evening Division) and Les Cox (Instructor) joined with the Chattanooga Community Action Agency in coordinating a training program for nurses, recreational directors and instructional assistants for teachers.

Requests were made for composing an Alma Mater for the college. Frances Eaglehouse (a student) submitted one, but apparently it was never officially adopted by the college. It was:

"Cleveland State, our Alma Mater,
May honor ever grace thy name.
May laurels crown thee,
Victory hail thee,
Everlasting be thy fame.
May God direct thine every pathway,
Wisdom keep thee ever free.
Cleveland State our Alma Mater--
Hail to thee!"

In athletics two performances by the men's 1969-70 basketball team (a Ladies' Team was organized in 1974) were outstanding. The Cougars defeated Dyersburg State 109-51 and Morristown 124-56. In this game Gene Meadows scored 21 points; Ed Thacker, 19; Steve Williams, 17; Freddie Rice, 14; Ken Byrd, 13; Danny Jones, 12; and Mike Myers, 12. Meadows scored 46 points in another game and ended the season with 463 points and 305 rebounds. Steve Williams had 164 assists for the season and averaged 13.1 points per game. Meadows averaged 18.1 points per game, Ken Byrd averaged 14.7 points per game and Eddie Thacker averaged 13.6 points per game. Other players, in addition to those listed above were Larry Johnson, John Shuey, Tim Vaughn, Ken Hurrek, William Evans, Raymond Foster, Roddy Roark, Gay Powell, Anthony Hall, Reginald Davis and Harry Smith. The team ended the season with an 18-8 overall record and 9-5 in the conference. In post-season play, the team captured third place in the NJCAA Regional Tourney.

The baseball team members for the 1969-70 season were Larry Scott, Steve Williams, Charlie Morrow, Lee Midgett, J. T. Lemons, Dan Jenkins, Steve Harbison, Joe Kerr, Ronnie Hughes, Tom Lane, Rodney Hannah, Richard Neal, Danny Hutsell, Eddie Thacker, Freddie Rice and Mike Myers. Hutsell led the TJCAA with a .473 batting average, and the team ended to compiled an 8-18 record.

The college's first golf team won their first match against Hiwassee College 11-1. They finished third in the TJCAA golf tournament and ended the season with a 4-2 record. The team members were: Richard and Mitchell Parkinson, (brothers), David and Larry Forrester (brothers), Hardin Murdock, Paul Stancil, Jim Pemberton and Danny Crowe. Donald Fairbairn was the coach of the team. The tennis team (coached by Colonel John Smeltzer) compiled a 2-2 record and the players were Lee Scheel, Pat Hanks, Reed Bacon, Glen Davis, Tom Varnell, Al Kuykendall, Robert Easterly and

Houston Brown. There was also an unofficial track team, and team member Bob Wade performed well in the Knoxville Relays. The annual All Sports Banquet presented awards to Teresa Garrison and Bill Hambaugh for cheerleading, Tom Lemons and Danny Hutsell for baseball, Eugene Meadows for basketball and Richard Parkinson and Danny Crowe for golf. Ed Thacker was named athlete of the year.

Travel to state, regional and/or national organizations enabled faculty and staff to keep abreast of the latest developments in their disciplines and learn the latest techniques in teaching and administrative endeavors. Budgets for travel were always minimal and often the majority of expenses for travel were paid by the individual faculty and staff members. Most out-of-state travel was limited to once a year. The college President and the administrators for academics, finance, student affairs and athletics attended quarterly statewide meetings every year. Faculty members, Fred Martin and Larry Speight, attended Biology institutes during the summer of 1969. The former attended a six-week session at Oregon State, and the latter attended a twelve-week institute at North Carolina State. Roy G. Lillard (History faculty member) visited several Scandinavian countries on a National Education Association tour during the summer. Lillard and Jerome Taylor (History faculty member) also attended a meeting of the East Tennessee Historical Society in Knoxville.

The majority of the English faculty attended the Southern Modern Language Association meeting in Atlanta. Alleyna Ellis (Nursing) was a panel member at a Knoxville meeting sponsored by the Tennessee Nurses Association. She also was present at a meeting of Deans and Directors of Nursing Schools in Knoxville, Tennessee, and later, at a meeting of the Southern Regional Education Board in Atlanta, Georgia. Two other Nursing Faculty, Lorraine Fullbright and Betty Garver, attended a symposium on the "Management of Diabetes," at Vanderbilt University.

Jere Chumley (Art) attended the Tennessee College Art Council meeting in Memphis and several faculty and staff members attended the East Tennessee Education meeting in Knoxville. Among them were Dr. D. F. Adkisson, Dr. George Mathis, Dr. F. Dean Banta, Paul Boynton, Josephine Pritchett and Elsie Dalton. Dr. Mathis, and Coaches Joe Crabtree and Ed Coates, participated in the annual meeting of the Tennessee Junior College Athletic Association (TJCAA) at Martin College in Pulaski, Tennessee. Dr. Banta and Matt Reiser attended a three-day seminar in Washington, D. C. on the subject of available federal programs for community colleges. Dr. Adkisson, Dr. Banta and Ronald Mason (Business Manager) attended the meeting of the Southern Association of Schools and Colleges in Atlanta.

THE SEVENTIES

– 1970 –

The major international events in 1970 were: the Treaty of Non-Proliferation of Nuclear Weapons was inaugurated (43 nations signed it); the People's Republic of China launched its first satellite; Palestinian guerillas seized and blew up four jetliners on the ground (fortunately, no hostages were harmed); in April American and South Vietnamese forces crossed the border into Cambodia to attack enemy bases; Egyptian leader Gamal Abdel Nasser died; and American astronauts James A. Lovell, Fred W. Haise and Jack Swigert splashed down safely in the Pacific Ocean after a ruptured oxygen tank ended their moon mission.

In domestic affairs the Vietnam War continued to divide America. As noted earlier, in May Ohio National Guardsmen killed four students and wounded nine others during a protest at Kent State University. Two weeks later two black students at Jackson State College in Mississippi were killed when police opened fire during a student protest. In addition a van was blown up by anti-war extremists at the University of Wisconsin, killing a 33-year old researcher. Other news events were: the average cost of a house was $23,400; the average income was $9,350; the average cost of a gallon of gas was 36 cents; the Environmental Protection Agency began operations; and California became the first state to adopt a "No Fault Divorce Law."

In the realm of popular culture the major developments were: National Public Radio was incorporated; the Mary Tyler Moore Comedy Show began on CBS-TV; the Broadway Play, "Hello Dolly," closed after 2,844 performances; Soviet author Alexander Solzhenitsyn won the Nobel Prize for literature; Rock Music lost two popular stars when Jimi Hendrix and Janis Joplin died; the Academy Award for the best movie was "Patton;" the best actor award was given to George C. Scott for the movie, "Patton" (he refused the award); the best actress award was presented to Glenda Jackson for the movie, "Women in Love;" the Emmy Award for Best TV Comedy was won by "My World and Welcome to It" (NBC); the Emmy for Best Drama was awarded to "Marcus Welby, M.D.;" and the Grammy Awards for Best Record and Best Album were won by Simon and Garfunkel for "Bridge Over Troubled Water."

In sports Monday Night Football made its debut on ABC-TV with the Cleveland Browns defeating the New York Jets, 31-21; UCLA won the NCAA college basketball championship; the Kansas City Chiefs defeated the Minnesota Vikings in the Super Bowl; and Baltimore defeated Cincinnati in the World Series.

In campus news, several faculty and staff traveled to meetings in the spring of 1970. They were: Josephine Pritchett (Secretarial Science) attended the Southeastern Regional Meeting of the American Business Communications Association in Gatlinburg; Pritchett and Nancy Dupree (Secretarial Science) attended the National Business Education Association Conference in Chicago, Illinois; Frances Moore (Guidance Counselor) visited Gatlinburg for the annual convention of the Tennessee Personnel and Guidance Association; the Southeastern Section Meeting of the Mathematics Association met at Clemson University, and Irene Millsaps (Mathematics) represented the college at that event; and Roy Lillard (History) was one of 200 individuals invited to attend a National Foreign Policy Conference at the Department of State in Washington, D. C.

Other personnel attending conferences were: Jerome Taylor (History) traveled to Louisville, Kentucky, for the Southern Historical Association Meeting; David Archer (Librarian) attended the meeting of the Southeast Library Association in Atlanta, Georgia; Nancy Boyd and Josephine Pritchett (Secretarial Science instructors) attended a workshop on Office Administration at the University of Tennessee at Knoxville; Ozane Adams (Physical Education) attended the Southern District Convention of the American Association of Physical Education in Columbia, South Carolina; Elsie Dalton (English) was in Philadelphia for the National College Reading Association Conference; Paul Boynton (Student Personnel) was in New Orleans for the Convention of American Personnel and Guidance Association; and Alex Nichols (Data Processing) attended an eight-week summer institute at the University of Missouri to study computing and programming.

Others who represented the college at meetings were: James Cigliano (Admissions) attended the Southern Association of Admission Counselors' Conference in Atlanta and the meeting of the American Association of Collegiate Registrars in New Orleans; Judy Munger (the College Nurse) and Alleyna Ellis (Nursing Faculty) attended the Tennessee League for Nursing's annual convention in Chattanooga; Dr. F. Dean Banta traveled to Appalachian State, in Boone, North Carolina, for the Conference on Two-Year College Personnel; Elvis Brandon (Financial Aid Director) attended the meeting of the Association of Financial Aid Administrators in Atlanta, Georgia; Marilyn Fillers, Mary Barker, John Bradley and Elizabeth Wooten (English Faculty) attended the Southeastern Conference on Teaching English in the Two-Year College in Washington D. C.; and Wooten, Paul Boynton (Student Personnel) and Jo Pritchett (Secretarial Science) attended a Tennessee Education Workshop on Professional Rights and Responsibilities (in Cleveland, Tennessee).

Accomplishments and/or recognitions were achieved by the following: Buford Buy (Physics) published an article in the Physics Teacher titled, "The Full House Demonstration," and he was a speaker at the Tennessee section of the American Association of Physics' Teachers in Memphis. Pat Rainey (Psychology) had an article published in The Creative Teacher titled, "Teaching Personality Theory to High School and College

Students" and another article titled, "Sometimes It's a Bird, Sometimes It's an Antelope," was published in Today's Education. The same article was referred to in the August 15th issue of Saturday Review. Roy Lillard (History) wrote a book review for the Journal of Southern History on C. A. Weslager's book, The Log Cabin in America: From Pioneer Days to the Present. Lillard was also elected Chair of the Tennessee Baptist Historical Society and served as President of the John Sevier Memorial Association. He was also a former President of the East Tennessee Historical Society.

The campus received sad news upon learning that John R. Barnes (Marketing Instructor) died at his home in Chattanooga. He was married with two children and was an eighteen-year Army veteran with the rank of Lieutenant Colonel. He received both his Bachelor's and Master's Degrees from the University of Tennessee at Chattanooga.

Students were also active during the spring of 1970. Eight Nursing students—Nancy Allen, Gwen Andrews, Martha Clinton, Carolyn Ingram, Geraldine Johnson, Sam Norman, Connie Norris, and Sonja White—represented the college's Nursing Department at the annual National Student Nurses Convention in Miami, Florida. In student elections Mike Wortman was President of the SGA; Linda Williams, Vice-President; Pat Davis, Secretary; and Frankie Logan, Treasurer. Sophomore Class Officers were: President, Marion Arbuckle; Vice-President, Sandy Lowery; Secretary, Carolyn Davis; and Treasurer, Janice Gibson. The President of the Freshman Class was Lee Midget, and the Vice-President was Rita Haddock. The new co-editors of The Cherokee Signal student newspaper were Bill Gomes and Deborah Williams. The Business Manager was Mike Wortman; the Photographer was Phil Pritchard; and the advisors were Dr. George Mathis and Bob Robinson. Students in Nancy Boyd's Secretarial Science class conducted a fashion show, and students in Jim Allen's "Design and Drafting" class demonstrated the use of surveying equipment as part of a class exercise.

The college kept the community informed of its offerings via radio shows. At 12:15 p. m. on Sundays, Political Science students, with the assistance of their advisor, Roy Lillard, interviewed local government and business leaders on WBAC. At two p. m., on Sundays, in a program on WCLE called "This Is Cleveland State," faculty and staff members discussed opportunities at the college. Cultural events were also offered to both students and the community. The musical, "Oklahoma," was conducted in May 1970 under the direction of Tom Boles and John Bradley. Dr. Ruth Stephens, UTK Professor Emeritus of Political Science, delivered a speech on current political affairs titled, "This Fascinating and Frightening Era."

When students returned to campus, after the April 1970 Easter vacation, a new $584,777 Humanities classroom building was available for them. Approximately 1,600 students had enrolled in the Fall Quarter of 1969, and the college needed additional space. In addition to classrooms and faculty offices, the new building housed the departments of English, Language, Reading, Chemistry, Physics and Nursing. Two building expansions were planned for the fall of 1970 that would double the sizes of the library and the student center. The Federal Department of Health, Education and Welfare approved a $255,000 grant for the library expansion. Classrooms were to be constructed on the ground level and additional library facilities built on the second level. Both floors contained a total of 42,000 square feet.

Commencement was held in June 1970, and the address was given by Dr. Joseph Morgan, President of Austin Peay State University. During the ceremony the Outstanding Student Award was presented to David Stiles.

– 1971 –

The major events in international affairs in 1971 were: the People's Republic of China was awarded a seat on the United Nations Security Council; India supported East Pakistan's (later named Bangladesh) successful bid for independence from Pakistan; women finally gained the right to vote in Switzerland; Hafez Assad was confirmed as President of Syria; Qatar was granted independence from Great Britain; and Idi Amin seized power in Uganda.

In domestic affairs the major events were: the average cost of a new house was $25,250; the average income was $10,600; the cost of a gallon of gasoline was 40 cents; the passenger service Amtrak began operations; the microprocessor was invented; the Walt Disney Resort opened in Florida; Federal Express began operations; cigarette advertising was banned from television; in an effort to control inflation, President Nixon announced a 90-day freeze on wages and prices; the classified Pentagon Papers were released to the public; Charles Manson and three of his followers were convicted of murder in the slayings of seven people; NASDAQ, the world's first electronic stock exchange, held its first trading day; Texas Instruments released the first pocket calculator; the first soft eye contact lens were released; Apollo 14 astronauts Alan Shepard and Edgar Mitchell landed on the moon in the first of two lunar excursions; the occupation of Alcatraz Island in San Francisco Bay by American Indian activists ended; a hijacker known as D. B. Cooper parachuted from a NW Orient Airlines 727 in the northwestern United States (after receiving $200,000 in ransom); the Kevlar polymer (five times stronger than steel, weight by weight) was released to the market; and President Richard Nixon signed the 26th Amendment, which lowered the minimum voting age from 21 to 18.

The major events in cultural affairs were: "All in the Family" premiered on CBS-TV; the music program "Soul Train" made its debut as a nationally syndicated TV program; Stanley Kubrick's controversial movie, "A Clockwork Orange," premiered; Jazz musician and singer Louis Armstrong died at the age of 69; singer Jim Morrison of "The Doors" died at the age of 27; and the humorist poet, Ogden Nash, died at the age of 68. In the movie industry, "The French Connection" won the Academy Award for best picture, Gene Hackman ("The French Connection") was named best actor and Jane Fonda best actress for the movie "Klute." The Grammy Award for record (single) of the year was presented to Carole King for "It's Too Late," and the Grammy for album of the year was also presented to Carole King for "Tapestry." "All in the Family" (CBS) won the Emmy for best comedy, and "The Bold Ones: 'The Senator'" (NBC) won the Emmy for best drama. In athletics the Baltimore Colts defeated the Dallas Cowboys (16-13) in the Super Bowl; the Pittsburgh Pirates defeated the Baltimore Orioles in the World Series; and Joe Frazier defeated Muhammad Ali, in what was billed as "The Fight of the Century," in Madison Square Garden in New York.

Meanwhile, Henny Youngman was becoming a hit in comedy and his jokes proliferated around the campus. A few of his jokes were: "He lives by his wits—which accounts for the half-starved look on his face; He has concrete opinions—thoroughly mixed and permanently set; He has an open mind—it should be closed for repairs; He has a mechanical mind—too bad some of the screws are loose; He took her for better or worse--she took him for everything;" and "He lights up a room when he leaves it."

A major highlight for the college was the establishment of a scholarship Foundation. The purpose of the Foundation was to raise funds "that would provide academic scholarships and short-term loans to students on the basis of academic performance and/or financial need." The Foundation was a joint enterprise among civic, business, community leaders and college officials. Those playing instrumental roles in the organizational meeting were: Dr. D. F. Adkisson, William Fillauer, Roy Lillard, Ronald Mason, Dr. George Mathis, Eugene Callaway, Frank Manly and Henry Barkley. By 1983 the assets of the Foundation were over $500,000, and by 1987 Cleveland State became the first Tennessee community college Foundation to raise one million dollars.

In other campus news a 1971 college report indicated the 1970 fall quarter student enrollment was 1,960. Of these, 657 were evening division students, and the counties with the largest number of students attending were Bradley (841) and Hamilton (515). In other news President Adkisson was named Chairman of the Higher Education Division of the East Tennessee Education Association; Elvis Brandon became the Supervisor for Financial Aid and Auxiliary Services; and Robert Robinson was appointed as the Supervisor of Public Relations and Information. New faculty and staff members were: Chlora Dunn, Efrain Guillen, David Watts, Frederick Wood, Lynn Hogin, Walter Harrison, Byung Moo Lee, Penny Overend, Josephine Troxel and Kay Huddleston.

The Cherokee Signal staff members were: Pat Davis, Editor; Tom Finnell, Business Manager; Barry Burnett and Janice Pendergrass, Advertising Managers; and Lana Hatcher, Features Editor. Freshman class officers were: Frank Harper, President; Sandy Miller, Vice-President, Janey Pendergrass, Secretary; and Carlene Carter, Treasurer.

In September 1971 the first executive committee of the Foundation was appointed. Those named to the committee were Dr. D. F. Adkisson, Ronald Mason, Frank Manly and Eugene Callaway (it was decided that the Chairman of the State Board of Education would also be a member). Those present at the meeting were: Dr. Adkisson, Harold Almond, Henry Barkley, Kenneth Brown, Eugene Callaway, George Castings, W. K. Fillauer, Roy G. Lillard, Wayne McCulley, Frank Manly, Dr. George Mathis, Ronald Mason, Pearson Mayfield, Will McReynolds, W. C. Thomason, George Thorogood and Pledger Wattenbarger. By 1971 businesses, individuals and local foundations had endowed 232 scholarships amounting to $200,000 in financial assistance for students.

Another important event in 1971 was a "Self-Study" by the college. The Southern Association of Colleges and Schools (SACS) mandated that a five-year self-study should occur once the college existed for five years. The members of the Purpose Committee for the self-study were: Mary Barker, English; Larry Speight, Biology; L. E. Wooten, Sociology; Tom Harrison, Accounting; Fred Martin, Biology; Renate Hufft, French; Ed Howard, Economics; Ray Coleman, Evening Division; and Jo Pritchett, Technology. Pritchett chaired the Steering Committee and the other members were Marilyn Fillers, English; Joe Guest, Mathematics; Steve Longley, Physical Education; Jerome Taylor, History; and Frank Harper, Student Government Association President. By offering degrees in three general areas-- Associate of Science, Associate of Arts, and Certificate Programs—the college planned to accomplish the following objectives:

1. Provide academic programs that prepare students to transfer to senior colleges and universities.
2. Provide career programs that prepare students to transfer to senior colleges and universities.
3. Provide evening classes and offer courses of a community-service nature.
4. Provide remedial and developmental courses.
5. Provide counseling, guidance and testing services for both current and prospective students.
6. Provide a cultural atmosphere and promote good citizenship by making college personnel and facilities available to the community.

Several activities filled the calendar in 1971. Jerry Lee Lewis appeared at the gymnasium on March 18, 1971 for a benefit show sponsored by McDonald School. Another event was arranged by the Public Relations Office through contact with NASA. A lunar sample, about the size of a baseball, was exhibited in the front portion of the gym from March 2 through March 5. It was the first lunar display at any college or university in Tennessee, and large numbers of college and community people viewed the display. A marketing movie titled, "The Cleveland State Story," was produced by the college and aired on WDEF-TV, Chattanooga, on March 9, 1971. The sound track also aired on nine area radio stations. In May the play "Carousel" had a six night run. It was directed by John Bradley (Speech/English) and had a cast of 35 members. Numerous female patrons appeared at the production in the new clothing fashion--pantsuits. Nursing students began wearing the attire and so did other faculty and students.

Student activities were also abundant in the spring semester of 1971. Rusti Hunt was elected as the Homecoming Queen, and Jim Simmons and Miss Carolyn Brewer were Mr. and Miss Cleveland State. A new student club, known as the "K-ettes," was formed, and Penny Overend (English) served as the faculty advisor. The club was organized under the direction of Glen Thornton, the President of the Circle K Club. The President of the "K-ettes"was Carolyn Davis; the Vice-President was Sandra Lowery; the Secretary was Patti Creasman; and the Treasurer was Kay Farmer. The men's basketball team won the conference with a 24-4 overall record and a 16-2 conference record. Coach Joe Crabtree was awarded co-recipient of "Coach of the Year" honors from the Tennessee Junior College Athletic Association (TJCAA). Crabtree's Assistant Coach was Ed Coates; the manager was Ronnie Stegner; the statistician was Will Womack; and the bookkeeper was Frank Harper. Team members were Gay Powell, Larry Johnson, Jimmy Meadows, Junior Collins, Paul Walker, Scotty Tipton, Willie Evans, Larry Belk, Maxie Garrett, Norman Cole, Alvin Massey, Mike Green, Donald Willoughby and Mike Cole.

Several faculty members continued to hone their teaching skills by participating in numerous meetings and workshops. These were as follows: Jo Pritchett (Secretarial Science) served on an office occupations research project committee in Nashville; National Science Foundation (NSF) Grants were awarded to Larry Speight (Biology) and Alex Nichols (Data Processing); Speight spent a portion of the summer in Arizona studying flora and fauna through a program organized by Arizona State University at Tempe; Nichols studied computer science for eight weeks during the summer at the University of Missouri at Rolla; Buford Guy (Physics) received two NSF summer grants for the study of solid state and radiation physics at the University of South Carolina; Business instructors John Cantrell, Tom Harrison and Bill Roberts attended a Junior College Business Instructor's meeting in Gatlinburg; Katharine Trewhitt (English) attended the National Humanities Association meeting in Racine, Wisconsin; Renate Hufft (French and German Language instructor) traveled, with three Cleveland students, to Germany during the summer, and they toured much of Europe by car; Elizabeth Wooten (Head of the Humanities Division) participated in a seminar in Los Angeles conducted by the Association of the Departments of English; and Mike Dorset (Biology) and Larry Speight (Biology) attended a meeting in Memphis of the Commission on Undergraduate Education in the Biological Sciences.

Other faculty members received important recognitions. These were: Joseph Semak became the new coordinator of the Allied Health Program; Tom Harrison (Accounting) was one of four nominated for the Cleveland Jaycees Distinguished service award; Roy Lillard (History) reviewed the book, Neutralization and World Politics (written by Cyril Black), in the October issue of the journal, Military Affairs; Elizabeth Wooten

(Humanities Division Chair) was one of twelve heads of English Departments in the nation chosen to serve on the Executive Council of the Modern Language Association's Departments of English; Fred Wood (English) was appointed regional judge for the National Council of Teachers of English Achievement Awards Program for 1971; and Wood, in addition to other faculty members across the nation, evaluated the writing skills and literary awareness of 7,000 selected students who were enrolled in their junior year of high school.

One hundred and thirty-seven students graduated in the spring of 1971, and the commencement speaker was Tennessee's Education Commissioner, E. C. Stimbert. During the graduation ceremony, the Outstanding Student award was presented to Pat Davis. In the fall of 1971, 2,283 students registered for day, evening and non-credit courses. It was the 16th consecutive term that the college had broken previous enrollment records. An especially noteworthy event for the college and the city of Cleveland was the announcement that the Humanities Division received a grant (for the second consecutive year) from the National Woodrow Wilson Fellowship Foundation. Cleveland was one of 70 towns selected for the grant (from over 500 applicants) which was used to sponsor a series of humanities programs led by professional actors and actresses. The programs traced the dreams, purposes and values that shaped American History. They were conducted on the Cleveland State campus and at area civic and social clubs. Co-Chairs of the college committee for the programs were Elizabeth Wooten and Katharine Trewhitt of the Humanities Department. The Department also was selected to host the Southeast Regional Conference on English in February of 1972. The conference was held in Chattanooga and over 300 delegates from eight states attended the three-day affair. Another major event occurred at the college on November 18, 1971, when 70 representatives from area schools attended a High School Principal and Counselor workshop.

In other fall activities John N. Popham, Managing Editor of the <u>Chattanooga Times</u> newspaper, made a speech, on October 19, 1971, on recent and projected technological developments which had an impact on society. The next month nine former drug addicts presented a drama in which they described the activities of "Marathon House." It was actually five houses in the New England area that rehabilitated drug addicts. A different type of drama featured both college and community actors and actors. It was a dinner-theater play held at the Knights of Columbus. Titled "The Rainmaker," it was directed by John Bradley (Speech/English faculty member), and the cast was composed of Bill Gatlin, Robin Whitehead, Dan Disharoon, Scott Bell, Jim Wilson, Perry Skates and Peter Moisan.

Among many students who excelled academically were Carolyn Ashe, Evangeline Le Noir and David Rogers. They were part of a two-month study-travel program in Europe. The program was designed for students to study French Language and French Civilization for four weeks at the University of Paris while other students studied

German Language and German Civilization at the University of Vienna during the same time period. The last four weeks were spent touring Europe by car. As noted previously, Renate Hufft (German and French Language instructor) joined the three for that portion of the trip. Three other students—Frank Harper, Glen Thornton and Mike Wortman—attended the Tennessee Student Legislative meeting in Nashville. Five students attended the 16th Annual Circle K International Convention in Chicago. They were: James Moody (Circle K Club President); Max Fuller (Circle K Club Treasurer); Carolyn Humberd ("K-ette" Club President); Kathy Murray ("K-ette" Club Treasurer); and Connie Tarpley ("K-ette" Club member).

Student officers serving in 1971-72 were: Frank Harper, SGA President; Kathy Kleinfeldt, SGA Vice-President; Gayle Wood, SGA Secretary; and Kay Farmer, SGA Treasurer. Sophomore Class officers were: Max Fuller, President; Ron Wallace, Vice-President; Janey Pendergrass, Secretary; and Frances Hubbard, Treasurer. Freshman Class Officers were: Dwight Henry, President; Beverly Payne, Vice-President; Janice Oxford, Secretary; Becky Greene, Treasurer; Harlena Odom, Senator; and Janet Loftis, Senator. Special elections were held later to elect five student senators, three from the student body as a whole and two from the Sophomore Class. Those elected were Gay Trotter, Ed Richelson, Charles Nolan, Will Womack and Bill Gilmore.

Several students also served either as contributors to the student newspaper, The Cherokee Signal, or as cheerleaders for athletic events. The newspaper staff members were: Carolyn Humberd and Russell Coward, Co-editors; Nyoka Warren, Business Manager; Dwight Henry, Assistant Business Manager; Lamone Lowery and Will Womack, Sports Editors; Martin Athearn, Copy Editor; Jay Branum, Head Photographer; Jay King and Ed Richelson, Staff Photographers; and Carlene Carter, Astrology Editor. The Cheerleaders were: Bridget Berry (Co-Captain); Charlotte Hess (Co-Captain); Debbie Studer; Carolyn Brown; Barbara Kelly; Charlotte Rominger; Glenda Black; Kenneth Buchanan; Ray Chadwick; and Bertha McDonald. Alternate cheerleaders were Libby McAmis, Jane Brooks, Pat Anderson, Johnny Miller and Charles Nolan.

– 1972 –

There were a number of significant international political events in 1972. A few of these were: on January 30, Roman Catholic civil rights marchers were killed by British soldiers in Northern Ireland on what became known as "Bloody Sunday;" the U. S. Senate ratified the Anti-Ballistic Missile Treaty with the Soviet Union (the U. S. withdrew from the treaty in 2002); the North Vietnamese launched attacks across the demilitarized zone; the U. S. resumed heavy bombing of North Vietnamese targets; Ceylon became a Republic and changed its name to Sri Lanka; Cameroon gained its independence from France and Great Britain; America's Bobby Fischer defeated Russia's Boris Spassky to become the World Chess Champion; and 11 members of the

Israeli Olympic team and a German police officer were killed by a terrorist group (Black September) in Munich (five of the eight terrorists were killed in a rescue attempt). The other three were arrested and later released in an airliner hostage exchange. These three, in addition to several collaborators, were eventually killed by Israel's Mossad.

The major national events were: President Richard M. Nixon made an historic eight-day visit to China; Army Lieutenant William L. Calley, Jr. was convicted of murdering 22 Vietnamese civilians in the My Lai massacre (he served three years under house arrest); Apollo 16 astronauts John W. Young and Charles M. Duke, Jr. explored the surface of the moon; Polaroid introduced its SX-70 folding camera, which ejected self-developed photos; FBI Director J. Edgar Hoover died in Washington at the age of 77; Governor George C. Wallace and three others were shot and wounded in a Maryland shopping center by Arthur Bremen (Bremen received a 63-year sentence for the shootings); the Environmental Protection agency ordered a ban on the pesticide DDT; five burglars were arrested inside the Democratic National Headquarters in the Watergate complex in Washington D. C.; President Richard Nixon was re-elected over George McGovern; the Dow Jones Industrial Average closed above the 1,000 level for the first time; and former President Harry S. Truman died in Kansas at the age of 88.

A few noteworthy athletic events in 1972 were: the Boston Marathon allowed women to compete for the first time; Mark Spitz won seven gold medals at the Munich Olympics; UCLA won its sixth straight NCAA college basketball tournament (81-76 over Florida State); the Dallas Cowboys defeated the Miami Dolphins 24-3 in the Super Bowl; the Oakland Athletics defeated the Cincinnati Reds in the World Series; the American League adopted baseball's designated hitter rule on an experimental basis (which eventually became a permanent development); and baseball's Hall of Fame member and breaker of the racial barrier, Jackie Robinson, died in Connecticut at the age of 53.

The major cultural events in 1972 were: the musical "Grease" opened on Broadway; the situation comedies, "Maude" and "Mash" premiered on CBS-TV; the family drama "The Waltons" premiered on CBS-TV; Bernardo Bertolucci's controversial film, "Last Tango in Paris," premiered in Rome and Paris; the premium cable TV network Home Box Office made its debut; author and poet Ezra Pound died in Italy at the age of 87; and the video arcade game "Pong" was created. The Academy Award for best picture was won by "The Godfather." Although he refused to accept it, the Best Actor Award was won by Marlon Brando for "The Godfather," and the Best Actress Award was won by Liza Minnelli for "Cabaret." The Grammy Award for record (single) of the year was won by Roberta Flack for "The First Time Ever I Saw Your Face," and the album of the year award was won by George Harrison and friends for "The Concert for Bangladesh." The Emmy for TV's best comedy was won by "All in the Family" (CBS), and the award for best drama was won by "Masterpiece Theatre: Elizabeth R." (PBS).

During the spring construction continued on the CSCC library and student center. Approximately 17,000 additional square feet was added to the student center and 22,000 to the library. Webb and Sons were the contractors for the student center, and T. U. Parks Construction Company was the contractor for the library. Harrison Gill Associates were the architects on both projects. These additions increased the workload for the maintenance department. The members of the department in 1972 were: Jake P. Newman, James L. Passmore, L. A. Smith, Fletcher Goforth, Fred Anderson, Malcolm Hall, R. E. Edgmon, John Hudgins, Jim Lane, Steve Wayman, Tony Teague, Ida Mae Hitson, Clarice Bonine, Mollie Smith, Matilda Evans and Horace Hall. Newman was the Superintendent of Buildings and Grounds from 1967 to 1974, when he was succeeded by Passmore.

The first official meeting of the college's Foundation occurred in April of 1972. Those present were: Harry Dethero, Kenneth H. Brown, Dr. Wayne McCulley, Pearson Mayfield, George Thorogood, Pledger Wattenbarger, Lloyd Callaway Jr., John Besse, Roy G. Lillard, Clarence E. Gregg, Harold Almond, Eugene Callaway, Will McReynolds, George Castings, Frank Manly, Clarke Stamper, Henry Barkley, W. K. Fillauer, Dr. George Mathis, Jim Morris and Dr. D. F. Adkisson. Dr. Adkisson was elected as the Foundation President, and he retained that position until 1985. Although total enrollment (including non-credit courses) had exceeded 2,000 before this time, the credit course headcount of 2,270 was a first for the college. This led to a budget increase of $1.7 million from the previous year. The fiscal year budget for 1971-1972 therefore, was $2,294,000.

In other activities six German Language students, accompanied by the Language Instructor Renate Hufft, attended a special movie production of Johann Wolfgang von Goethe's "Faust" at the University of Tennessee at Chattanooga (UTC). The students were Robert Wilson, Jan Thompson, Gay Robertson, Lee Hines, Elizabeth Edwards and Barbara Hansen. Several students also accompanied Instructor Hufft on another visit to UTC to view reproductions of the art of Albrecht Durer. Students on the trip were: Verlinda Couch, Gay Robinson, Barbara Lawson, Connie Tarpley, Dan Disharoom, Claude Freitas, Ann Byers and Janice Thompson.

Four dramatic productions were conducted in the spring of 1972. The first one was the musical comedy, "Paint Your Wagon." It was directed by John Bradley and Tom Boles. The cast was composed of John Shuey, Debbie Newell, Joe Taylor, Jerry Rymer, Kenneth Buchanan, Lamone Lowery, Becky Rogers, Cathy Lee, Larry Hughes, Gary Samples, Lee Gordon, Barbara Larsen, Fred Anderson, Jim Dent, Bob White, David Jenkins, Jackie Heston and Betsy Langley. The annual Kiwanis Club Variety Show was also conducted on the campus in the spring. The title of the performance was "Give My Regards to Keith Street," and it was directed by John Bradley. Tom Boles sang a solo, and in a humorous skit, Dr. L. E. Wooten (Sociology) starred as the Mayor of Cleveland in the Year 2002. In the third play, John Bradley and Bill Gatlin (Staff) were the only two cast members. It was the Edward Albee one-act drama titled, "The Zoo Story." John Bradley also directed the fourth play, "My Three Angels," which featured cast members Allan Ledford, Becky Larsen, Debbie Newell, Bill Gatlin, Scott Bell, Dwight Henry, Dale Newman, John Shuey, Gay Robinson and Frank Harper.

In other news Betty Bull (Reading Faculty) was named as a consultant on "Systems Approaches in Reading" by the Houghton-Mifflin Publishing Company; Judy Munger, the college's nurse from 1968 to April 1972, resigned to accept a similar position at American Uniform Company, and she was replaced by Brenda Geren (a graduate of the college's Nursing Program); Elizabeth Wooten, Head of the Humanities Division, was elected Chair of the Executive Committee of the Southeastern Conference on English in the Two-year College; Colonel James Stubbs, Director of the Law Enforcement Program, was named to the Advisory Committee of the Tennessee Law Enforcement Planning Commission; Patricia Rainey's (Psychology) book, <u>Journey Into Perception</u>, was published by the Linnet Book Company of Homewood, Illinois; Ron Mason resigned as Business Manager and was replaced by James Morris; Joseph Semak became the new coordinator of the Allied Health Program; and Roy Lillard was named historian of the John Sevier Memorial Association.

A unique event that has continued annually was the inauguration of the Tennessee Wildlife Resources Agency's Hunter Education and Firearms Safety Program. The program was enacted by the State of Tennessee in 1972 and CSCC was among the first institutions to support the program (as of the year 2012, over 3,500 students had received the training). All students were required to be nine years old at the beginning of the class and any prospective hunter, born after January 1, 1969, was required to complete the course. Certification included twelve hours of instruction, four hours of live firing and successful completion of an examination. Classroom topics included ethics, responsibility to land owners and wildlife, archery equipment, muzzle-loading black powder equipment, modern firearms, first aid, survival and wildlife management. Additional support for the free program was provided by the Cleveland Hunting Rifle and Pistol Club and numerous volunteer instructors. The original instructors were Dennis Daniels, Sam Rogers and Gary Martin. Other volunteer instructors were Ted Keirn, Ben Davis, Brandon Lee, James L. Carman, Jack C. Adkisson and Dr. Don E. Robinson.

Classroom activities were not always intellectually serious. In one of this author's classes, much-needed humor occurred concerning the lecture on the 1832 Presidential Election. A major event in the election was the introduction of a national nominating convention by the nation's first third party (the Anti-Masonic Party). A student asked what system had been used in the past, and he was given an explanation of the caucus system. The next part of the lecture concerned the three major candidates (four actually received electoral votes) and the issues in the election. Another student, obviously inattentive, bored and eager to hear the results of the election, asked, "So did President Caucus win the election?" The class erupted with laughter.

Another incident occurred when a student in one of Dr. Larry Longerbeam's English classes asked, "Professor Longerbeam, is it okay if we call you coach?" Professor Longerbeam politely declined to accept the suggested new title. Once when asked "What is your favorite lecture," Longerbeam replied jokingly, "The Semicolon: Its Uses and Misuses."

Numerous students were involved in extracurricular activities in 1972-73. The officers of the SGA were: Dwight Henry, President (he had also been elected as Chairman of the Junior College Division of the Southern University Student Government Association (SUSGA); David Marr, Vice-President; Janet Loftis, Secretary; and Linda Dixon, Treasurer. The Sophomore Class Officers were James Griggs, President; Ed Richelson, Vice-President; and Lisa Lively, Secretary. The co-editors of The Cherokee Signal were Carolyn Humberd and Russell Coward; the Homecoming Queen was Vicki Coffey; and Mr. and Miss Cleveland State were Dwight Henry and Bertha McDonald.

By 1972 the number of Student Clubs had expanded to sixteen. A recent addition was the Black Student Association. It was formed to promote Afro-American heritages and an appreciation of black culture. The officers were: Nicholas Cox, President; Jackie King, Vice-President; Linda Saddles, Secretary; James Sears, Treasurer; and Charles Johnson, SGA representative. Other clubs were the Baptist Student Union, the CSCC Alumni Association, the CSCC Legal Society, Chi Beta Chi Fraternity, the Church of Christ Student Union, the Circle K Club, the Future Secretaries's Association, the Music Club, the Nurses's Association, Phi Beta Lambda, Phi Sigma Chapter of the Jets Club, the Spanish Club, the Spelunker's Club, the Young Democrats and the Young Republicans. Many of the clubs engaged in fund-raising activities for charities and other events that supported civic events. For example, Chi Beta Chi raised money for children in Tennessee stricken with leukemia.

In campus athletics a noteworthy event was a guest speaking performance by the legendary Kentucky basketball coach, Adolph Rupp. The golf team, coached by Steve Longley, won the state's TJCAA Tournament and ended the year with a 20-3 won-lost record. The team members were Tom Maupin, Jim Walden, Hank Tiller, Ed Gowan, Steve Mills, Winston Prince and Glen Willoughby. The baseball team was coached by Ed Coates and the Assistant Coach was Steve Longley. The team members were: Shug Hutson, Eddie Ingle, Sid Derrick, Gerald McConkey, Rusty Melvin, Tommy Hyler, Mike Smith, Mike Murphy, Al Amburn, Charles Blevins, Will Harris, Jody Montgomery, Wayne Combs, Larry Smith, Sonny Woodcock, Maxie Garrett, Jim Carson, John Stair, Jerry Steadman and Mac Coly. The tennis team was coached by Colonel John Smeltzer and the players were: Norman Cole, Charles Harris, Mike Cole, James Griggs, Benny Parker, Randall Sharp, John Mulluttee, John Shuey and Pat Hanks (team manager). The basketball team lost the services of several players late in the season. Only seven members were left and only four played in the final minutes of a game with the Tennessee Tech Freshman team. The team members were: Scott

Hayes, Rick Goree, Scott Tipton, Don Willoughby, Alvin Massey, Leon Ballard, Johnny O'Neal, Ronnie Smith, Joe Rutherford, Danny Hardin, Henry Hudson, Charlie Patton and Jerry Banks. The coaches were Joe Crabtree and Ed Coates.

The commencement address, in June of 1972, was delivered by the President Emeritus of the University of Tennessee at Knoxville, Dr. Andrew David Holt. Degrees were awarded to 172 students, and the Outstanding Student Award was presented to Vicki Coffey. Enrollment for the fall of 1972 was 2,229 students. Another construction project, a Technology Building, was approved by the state government. When completed, the 40,725 square foot building was three stories in height and had 10 classroom/lab rooms, two conference and audio-visual rooms, 25 offices for instructors, four restrooms and a printing lab.

An important administrative event in 1972 was the Tennessee General Assembly's creation of the State Board of Regents. All facets of the government, management and control of the State University and Community College System were assigned to the State Board of Regents. The Board consisted of sixteen members (later eighteen). Four of the members were ex-officio--the Governor, the Commissioner of Education, the Commissioner of Agriculture and the Executive Director of the Tennessee Higher Education Commission (THEC). Eleven public members were appointed by the governor--one from each congressional district and three at-large members from the different geographical areas of the state. The immediate past Commissioner of Education also served as a member. The first Chancellor of the system was Dr. Cecil C. Humphreys, President of Memphis State University.

Numerous faculty and staff members attended conferences in 1972. These were: Elizabeth Wooten (Head of the Humanities Division) and Renate Hufft (Foreign Language Instructor) attended the South Atlantic Modern Language Association meeting in Jacksonville, Florida; Adeline Baskett (Head Librarian) and Byung Moo Lee (Library Staff) attended the Southeast Library Association Convention in New Orleans, Louisiana; Alleyna Ellis (Nursing Faculty) attended the meeting of the Council for Nursing Education of the Southern Regional Education Board (SREB) in Atlanta, Georgia; Paul Boynton (Student Personnel) attended the Tennessee College and University Personnel Officers meeting at Middle Tennessee State University (MTSU); Jim Cigliano (Admissions) and Elvis Brandon (Financial Aid) attended the Alumni Development and Placement meeting at MTSU; Cigliano also attended the Association of College Admissions Counselors meeting in San Antonio, Texas; Matt Reiser (Head of the Technology Division) attended the Southeastern meeting of the American Technical Education Association in Atlanta, Georgia; Chlora Dunn (Media Center Coordinator) visited the Georgia Medical Center in Augusta to study their personalized instruction system; Quentin Lane (Director of Institutional Research) attended the meeting of the Association for Institutional Research at Miami Beach, Florida; the college bookstore had grown large enough to merit the appointment of a Bookstore Manager (Loren

Boehm); and Elizabeth Wooten was a guest speaker at the Conference on Composition and Communication in Boston, Massachusetts.

In campus affairs Tennessee Governor, Winfield Dunn, visited the college and presented the Tennessee Handicapped Citizen of the Year Award to Bill Talley, Coach at Cleveland High School. Lamar Baker and Howard Sompayrac, candidates for the Third District Congressional seat, visited the campus and exchanged their political views in a debate. A Maintenance Building was completed and a building permit was issued by the City Planning Commission for the construction of a private dormitory for ladies adjacent to the campus. A group of citizens, living in the vicinity of Norman Chapel Road and Blair Drive, opposed the building, believing it would decrease property values and would not provide safety for the students. They also believed there would be inadequate student parking, an absence of fire escapes and would create sewage problems.

The City Planning Commission upheld the issuance of the building permit and construction of the edifice was completed. Thereafter, it was generally known as "Cougarette" Hall. Being a privately owned structure, dormitory residents were separate from the college and considered as tenants in an apartment building. The number of tenants varied but there were generally around 50 female students living in the dormitory. Shortly after its completion, the student residents were complaining about the facilities and there was a continuing controversy about the dormitory during its early months of existence. The college maintained applications for the dormitory and occasionally recommended it to students. In early 1973, however, the college severed all connections with the private dormitory.

A few students were displeased with the final exams conducted at the end of a quarter. The Student Government Association (SGA) conducted a poll of the students concerning the issue. The poll questionnaire asked the following questions: (1) was a final exam harmful to the final grade; (2) was there too large of a percentage of the final grade determined by the final exam; and (3) did the mental pressure caused by a final exam affect overall performance in a course? Affirmative responses on the three questions averaged 201 and negative responses averaged 23. The issue was debated at length by the faculty and the students. A major factor in the discussion was the State Board of Education's requirement that teachers were required to give a final exam and that a copy of the exam must be filed in the office of the college's Dean of Instruction. The issue was finally resolved in January 1973. The final exam week would be retained, but the discretion of how to use the time would be left to the individual faculty member.

The SGA also altered their student constitution during 1972. For a few years, they experimented with a county representation concept. The new approach was designed to increase representation in the SGA. Each county received one representative for the first 100 students attending Cleveland State and one representative for each additional 150 students. Based on the 1972 enrollment, Bradley County had seven representatives,

Hamilton four, McMinn two and Polk one. There were three at-large representatives to be elected for those counties with less than 100 Cleveland State students (pertaining primarily to Monroe and Meigs County).

Elections for several student offices were conducted in October 1972. Freshman Class officers were: Lisa McMahan, President; Jack Cain, Vice-President; Terri Trusley, Treasurer; and Debbie Davis, Secretary. The student county representatives were: Hank Tiller, James Daugherty, Michael Dobo and John Morgan represented Hamilton County; Vickey Simpson and Dinky Waters represented McMinn County; Michael Armour, James Crawford, Sharon Hart, Patti Patterson, Hoyle Baker, Brenda Fain and Bob Johnson represented Bradley County; Bill Moats represented Polk County; and Tom Collins, Tommy Reese, and Craig Vincent were the three at-large representatives. In addition two vacant student government positions were filled by Bertha McDonald, Treasurer and Pat Draper, Secretary of Exterior (for off-campus student concerns).

In November 1972 two students were selected by the "Experiment in International Living" (EIL) organization to study in Europe during the summer of 1973. They were Connie Tropley and Gay Robinson. Tropley was selected to visit the University of Vienna to study German Language and Culture, and Robinson was selected to visit the Sorbonne in Paris to study French Language and Culture. The EIL, with its headquarters in Vermont, was a private, non-profit organization supported by donations from individuals and foundations. It enabled approximately 1,500 high school and college students to visit about 30 countries in the summer months. EIL college students were required to return to their college for three quarters and be available for speeches to local civic and educational groups.

Four students attended the Circle K International Convention in Denver, Colorado. The event was sponsored by the Cleveland Kiwanis Club and those attending were: James Crawford (President of the college's Circle K Club); Gary Samples (Lieutenant Governor of the Lookout Mountain Division); and alternates Franklin Maples (the college's club Treasurer) and Bryan Coffer (club member). Twelve students were selected as cheerleaders for the college. They were: Barbara Kelly, Diane Williams, Georgia Woodruff, Debbie Studer, Mart Raulston, Valerie Geren, Carolyn Brown, Bertha McDonald, Vicki White, Charlotte Rominger, Janet Atkins and Janet Loftis.

– 1973 –

The international events that received headlines in 1973 were: the United States and China agreed to establish liaison offices; a Peace Treaty ended American involvement in South Vietnam; the Bosporus bridge was completed linking Europe and Asia in Istanbul; a military coup in Chile was led by General Augusto Pinochet; both Belize and the Bahamas received independence from Great Britain; the last American combat troops left South Vietnam; the first release of American POWs from the Vietnam conflict occurred; the American bombing of Cambodia ceased; war erupted in the Middle East as Egypt and Syria attacked Israel during the Yom Kippur holiday; the Organization of Petroleum Exporting Countries (OPEC) restricted the oil flow to countries supporting Israel; a recession began in Europe due to OPEC's restrictions and oil price increases; Great Britain, Ireland and Denmark joined the European Economic Community (EEC); the Sydney Opera House opened in Australia; Israel's first prime minister, David Ben-Gurion, died at the age of 87; and artist Pablo Picasso died at the age of 91.

The major national events were: the average cost of a new house was $32,500; the average income was $12,900; gasoline was 40 cents per gallon; acting FBI Director L. Patrick Gray resigned after it was revealed he had destroyed files related to the Watergate scandal; President Nixon announced the official end of the military draft; Nixon also announced the resignation of his aides, H. R. Haldeman and John D. Ehrlichman, and the firing of White House Counsel John W. Dean III; charges against Daniel Ellsburg for his role in the printing of the Pentagon Papers case were dismissed; a special Senate committee began televising hearings into the Watergate scandal; Tom Bradley was elected the first black mayor of Los Angeles; Vice President Spiro T. Agnew, accused of accepting bribes, pleaded no contest to federal income tax evasion and resigned his position; the so-called "Saturday Night Massacre" led to the dismissal of special Watergate prosecutor Archibald Cox and the resignations of Attorney General Elliot L. Richardson and Deputy Attorney General William B. Ruckelhaus; the twin towers of New York's World Trade Center were dedicated; Congress overrode President Nixon's veto of the War Powers Act, which limited the President's ability to wage war; Nixon's personal secretary, Rose Mary Woods, stated that she had accidentally erased part of the 18 and one-half minute gap in a Watergate related tape; in the Roe vs. Wade case, the Supreme Court ruled, in a 7-2 vote, that a fetus was not a person with constitutional rights and that the right to privacy protected a woman's decision to have an abortion; the Supreme Court also ruled that states may not ban abortions during the first three months of pregnancy and may regulate, but not ban, abortions during the second trimester; two hundred Oglala Native American members of the American Indian Movement (AIM) occupied Wounded Knee (from February until May) to protest broken treaties; the Endangered Species Act was approved; Skylab, the nation's first space station, was launched; the Mariner 10 Spacecraft was launched to probe the planet Mercury; after the outbreak of the Arab-Israeli War, a total ban on oil exports to America was imposed by the Arab oil-producing nations (the ban lasted from mid-October 1973 until mid-May 1974); and the Senate confirmed Gerald R. Ford as the new Vice-President.

A few major athletic events in 1973 were: the Miami Dolphins won the Super Bowl (by defeating the Washington Redskins 14-7); George Foreman upset heavyweight boxing champion Joe Frazier in their match in Kingston, Jamaica; UCLA won the NCAA Division I Basketball Championship (by defeating Memphis 87-66); the Oakland Athletics won the World Series (by defeating the New York Mets); and Secretariat became the first triple crown winner in horse racing since Citation in 1948.

The 1973 Academy Award for best movie was "The Sting." Jack Lemmon received the Best Actor Award for "Save the Tiger," and Glenda Jackson received the Best Actress Award for "A Touch of Class." The Grammy Award for the best record (single) of the year was presented to Roberta Flack for "Killing Me Softly With His Song," and the Grammy for album of the year was awarded to Stevie Wonder for "Innervisions." The Emmy Award for the best TV Comedy was won by "All in the Family" (CBS), and the best drama award was won by "The Waltons" (CBS).

A campus academic highlight of 1973 was the inauguration of a Legal Assistant Program. Cleveland State was the first college in the State of Tennessee to receive approval for the program by the American Bar Association. As of 1973 Cleveland State was the only public-supported college to offer the program. Legal Assistant students received training to assist lawyers much as para-medics were trained to assist doctors. A graduate, among other things, received an Associate of Science degree and instruction as how to gather facts, draft deeds and wills, research questions of law and trace property titles. A student could opt to take a program of study to become a Legal Secretary or to attain a Legal Secretary Certificate.

An unfortunate event, in early 1973, led to the resignation of two Nursing instructors. The instructors gave "D" grades to three nursing students. According to an unwritten policy of the Nursing Division, if a student received a "D" in any nursing course, regardless of the student's overall grade point average (GPA), the student would be dropped from the program. This conflicted with college policy which stated that a student could graduate if they maintained a "C" average in their overall GPA. College policy was adhered to and the two instructors resigned in protest because they believed there were already enough unqualified nurses who graduated with an overall "C" average. The college policy was later altered to allow an exception to the grade policy by Nursing, and the Division included this in their written policies.

In activities the college's music department, under the direction of the Music Instructor, Tom Boles, presented a spring musical performance of "On Stage." Sketches included music from such Broadway shows as "Carousel," Fiddler on the Roof," "Camelot" and "Oklahoma." Three former students, Tim Dent, John Shuey and Paula Duff, were invited to present solos. Other soloists were: Lee Gordon, Susan Hamilton, Charles Mason, Gayle McLain, Sandi Moody and Becki Rogers. Two dance routines were presented by Amanda Cate and Paula Duff. Members of the combined Chamber Choir and Chorus were: Scott Alverson, John Brock, Kenny Buchanan, Milteen Cartwright, Amanda Cate, Brenda Chestnutt, Emily Jane Cline, Elizabeth Edwards, Brenda Fain, Larry Fain, Mike Gann, Victoria Hamby, Linda Diane Harper, David Harrison, Robbie Haynie, Charlotte Hixson, Ray Hooper, Mike Kaylor, Jay King, Partick Mahon, Joy Parham, Emily Penney, Gary Samples, Vicky Simpson, Jesse Swafford, Scott Tipton, Karen Trent and Melva Nyoka Warren. The narrator was Dwight Henry, and the musical accompanist was Leal R. Cate.

An unusual event occurred in the Humanities Building Courtyard. On March 15, 1973 an unusual event occurred in the Humanities Building Court. Debbie Keith and Larry Kelly were married by Reverend Ronald Sorah, Pastor of the First Baptist Church of Calhoun. In other activities Mary Price Ayton (English Faculty) recruited guest speakers from the community in the fields of religion, ecology, media, mental health and city and county government. The college, in conjunction with the Kiwanis Club and the Bradley Bar Association, launched a series of speeches on legal issues such as consumer protection laws, no-fault insurance, employer-employee relations and income tax returns. Dr. Ruth Stephens, a former Professor of History and Political Science at UTK, made another visit to the campus and delivered a speech titled, "Watergate and the Washington Situation."

Another event, that had a positive effect on enrollment increases, concerned an avenue of transportation. A major section of Interstate 75 was completed on January 23, 1973. The completed section ran from highway 60 in Cleveland to approximately three miles from Charleston. It was announced that the interstate would be completed to Knoxville later in the year. Unfortunately, it would be several years before a bridge was built that increased traffic flow from Cleveland to Dayton via Highway 60. That trip involved a five-minute ferry ride across the Tennessee River. The ferry service had been operating for over 100 years. Known as Blythe Ferry, in 1973 the business was owned by the corporation of Brady and Associates. The ferry pilot was Wilford Caraway and his assistant was Mike Matthews. One hundred years ago the charge was ten cents per person and twenty cents per animal. In 1973 the charge was $1.25 per car. Apparently, ferry rights for most animals no longer existed.

The ferry transportation requirement made it difficult for Rhea County students to attend Cleveland State. Another event also impacted the college's attraction for Chattanooga students. In April 1973 Governor Winfield Dunn signed a bill creating a Community College in Chattanooga (approximately 25 miles from Cleveland State). Cleveland State Faculty members were obviously concerned about their future job security. Dr. Quentin Lane, the college's Director of Research and President of the Higher Education Division of the Tennessee Education Association, played a key role in securing passage of a resolution in the State Department of Higher Education. The resolution ensured that if a faculty member lost their job because of an enrollment decline at Cleveland State (due to the creation of Chattanooga State), all Tennessee Community Colleges should give special consideration to hiring these faculty members. Fortunately, the impact was not as great as anticipated, and Cleveland State continued to grow, although at a somewhat slower pace than previously.

In October 1973 the college had the honor of hosting the Board of Regents' meeting. It was the first meeting of the Regents at a community college. Other accomplishments were the designation of the college library as a depository of United States Government Publications, the creation of a new College Learning Skills Center and the addition of three new programs in the Technology Division—Dental Lab Technician, Health Care Management and Food Service Management. The Director of the Learning Skills Center was Martha Newman and its purpose was to assist students in the development of study skills, provide assistance with difficult courses (especially Math and English) and teach students how to take tests. The Dental program was designed to train students in fabricating crowns and bridges, arranging artificial teeth on dental appliances, processing plastic materials and working with dental ceramics, gold castings and non-precious alloys. In personnel news, Ray Coleman was named the Director of Continuing Education and the Evening Division.

Another development that affected the college was the federal 1973 Rehabilitation Act. It stated that, "…except under the most unusual circumstances, handicapped persons must be permitted to go to the same schools and the same classrooms as non-handicapped students." This led to the college's construction of ramps and the installation of elevators and other conveniences for disabled people.

In 1973 the athletic department suffered through a year of controversy concerning the hair length of athletes. The Athletic Director, Joe Crabtree, believed male athletes should keep their hair cut above the ears, and in another issue, that the coach should select team captains and not the players. Others disagreed and the positions of two coaches were later vacated because of the brouhaha.

The basketball team ended the season with a record of 8 wins and 22 losses. The team members were: Ronnie Sharpe, Raymond Smith, Perry McCowan, Frank Martin, Ronnie Smith, Chuck Sanders, Jerry Richt, Charles Patton, Daniel Hardin, Mike Seals, Rick Smith and Rody Tucker. The coach was Joe Crabtree. The golf team members were: Steve Willis, Tom Maupin, Rick Sisson, Mike Benson, Jim Collins, Mike Wallace, Gary Hammons and Larry Garner. The coach was Steve Longley. The tennis team won 4 and lost 6 matches but placed four players in the semi-finals at the state tournament. The team members were: James Gibson, Don McFall, Norman Cole, Benny Parker, James Griggs, John Mallot, Tom Williamson, Bill Neal, Bill Anderson and Lynn Griffith. The coach was Colonel John Smeltzer.

The 1973 baseball team had a successful year. They won 23 games and lost 9 (with a 17-7 conference record) and finished second in the conference. Coached by Ed Coates and Steve Longley, the team members were: Denny Williams, Doug Odom, Mac Coly, Ronnie Sharpe, Ronnie Gowan, Charlie Blevins, Bobby Lett, Dennis Byrd, Russell Blakely, Larry Garner, Jerry Steadman, Mike Murphy, Jewel Brock, Mike Smith, Wadie Davis, Rodney Amburn, Ron Spangler, Terry Apple, Dale Goodwin and Alvin Amburn. The student newspaper, The Cherokee Signal, named Jerry Steadman the athlete of the year. He played both baseball and basketball and his two-year pitching record was 11 wins and 3 losses. In November 1973 the college was selected as the site for the NJCAA Region VII Basketball Tournament for March 4-9, 1974. The event was sponsored by the Cleveland Chapter of the Knights of Columbus, and the co-chairs of the tournament committee were Ed Coates and Jim Cigliano.

The college was also selected to host the Southeastern Conference on English in the Two-Year College. Although Cleveland State was the host, the site for the conference was in Jacksonville, Florida. Elizabeth Wooten was named Chairperson of the conference, and the 24-member college choir, directed by Tom Boles, provided entertainment at a conference banquet in Jacksonville's Robert Meyer Hotel. The other college members attending the conference, in addition to Boles and Wooten, were Walter Presswood, Mary Barker, Marilyn Fillers, Ann Norman, Harry Dean, Fred Wood and Fred McDonald.

Several other faculty and staff members traveled to meetings in 1973. These were: Ray Coleman and Dr. Quentin Lane attended a federal workshop on Developmental Education at Jacksonville, Florida; Matt Reiser attended a conference of the American Vocational Association in Nashville; Jo Pritchett, Technology, Bill Roberts, Business and Education, and Ed Howard, Economics, attended the UTK Conference for Community and Junior College Business teachers; Dr. Adkisson and Dr. Banta were among 3,000 delegates that attended the American Association of Community and Junior Colleges in Anaheim, California; and Paul Boynton, Director of Personnel Services, attended the Regional Conference for Academic Affairs Administrators at the University of Florida in Gainesville.

In May 1973 Fred Wood (English) edited the college's first literary magazine titled, "Image." The magazine contained short stories and poems as well as illustrations submitted by the Art Department. Its name was later changed to "Frontage Road" and subsequent editors were English instructors, Harry Dean and Julie Fulbright. The publication continued to be printed every year. That same year, Dr. Lane became Dean of Instruction, Dr. Banta became Head of the Division of Education, Health, Physical Education/Recreation and Psychology and Alleyna Ellis resigned as Head of Nursing. Ellis had been Head of Nursing from July, 1968 to February, 1973. She remained with the college as a Nursing faculty member.

Several students received recognitions in 1973. Amanda Cate was awarded a $1,000 European International Living Scholarship (EIL), and she spent one month studying in Italy. Rebecca Rogers won the title of Miss Cleveland, and the college's Homecoming Queen was Kay Anderson. Those elected to SGA offices were: David Henry, President; Hoyle Baker, Vice-President; Vicky Simpson, Secretary; and Joy Parham, Treasurer. James Griggs was elected Central Committee Chairman of the Tennessee Students Association (the highest office in the TSA). Sophomore Class officers were: Dinky Waters, President; Bill Moats, Vice-President; Debbie Davis, Secretary; and Pattie Patterson, Treasurer. The leaders of The Cherokee Signal in 1973 were: Melva Nyoka Warren, Editor; Brenda Fain, Editorial Editor; and Dwight Henry, Business Manager. Later that year, as was customary, a new Signal staff was appointed for the fall. These were: Brenda Fain, Editor; Vaughn Riley, News Editor; Scottie Holder, Sports Editor; Sue Little, Editorial Editor; and Walter Presswood, Faculty Consultant.

Other contributors to the newspaper were Ray Hooper, David Henry, Allen Hudson, Pat Mahon, Alan McCosh and Barbara Ward. Vaughn Riley did an outstanding job in reporting and eventually became the owner/president of Graphic Impressions Printing in Chattanooga.

Freshman class officers, elected in late 1973 for the following fall, were: Lisa McMahan, President; Melody Plemons, Vice-President; and Julie Penney, Secretary-Treasurer. County representatives were: Jerry Clark and George Melton (Bradley); Azalea Buroughs (Hamilton); Sherry Estes, Mary Hughes and Emily Patton (McMinn); Becky Morehouse (Polk); and Nancy Love and Joe Merchant were the two at large representatives for counties having less than 100 students enrolled in the college. Cheerleaders selected in late 1973 were returnees, Jan Best, Diana Weir, Emily Penney and Vicky Veal, and the newly elected members were Renee Madden, Julie Penney, Diana Williams, Diane Bryant, Elaine Toney and alternate, Melissa Toney. All four of the returning cheerleaders attended a National Cheerleading Camp at East Tennessee State University, and they won two outstanding awards and one superior award at the camp.

An important event in 1973 was the inauguration of the Omega Omicron Chapter of Phi Theta Kappa (PTK). PTK was an honor society especially for two-year colleges. The Society emphasized the four "Hallmarks" of Scholarship, Leadership, Service and Fellowship. The Hallmark Awards competition was conducted annually and recognized both chapter and individual member achievements. The top twenty chapters scoring the highest received a Distinguished Chapter Award. Individual and chapter awards were judged on essays, letters of recommendations, scholarship and service to the community. The charter members of the college's honor fraternity were Jim Gibson, Bill Kimbrough, Rosalie Kimball, Robert White and Amanda Cate. The faculty sponsor was Frances Layne. A new campus organization, The Veterans' Club, was also organized, and the first President was Mike Millsaps. The commencement address in June of 1973 was given by Dr. John K. Folger, the Executive Director of the Tennessee Higher Education Commission (THEC). During graduation exercises, the Outstanding Faculty Member Award was presented to Dr. David Watts (Biology) and the Outstanding Student Award was presented to Gary Samples.

An interesting controversy occurred during the year concerning the Homecoming Queen contest. A male student said one's sex should not play a role in the election. The qualifications stated that one must be a full-time sophomore student, be enrolled the previous quarter and present a petition with 100 signatures. The male student fulfilled these requirements (although there was a possibility that some of the signatures were not those of full-time students) and decided to enter the competition. He later withdrew, however, citing a desire to avoid creating animosity between the SGA and the college administration. Another controversy concerned police officers who were students. Should they carry weapons while attending classes on the campus? The decision was that the officers could wear their weapons (either uncovered or concealed).

– 1974 –

The major international events in 1974 were: most of the Arab oil-producing nations ended their oil embargo; Isabella Peron (Evita), Juan Peron's third wife, became President of Argentina but was ousted in a military coup in 1976 (she was exiled to Spain in 1981); the world's population reached four billion; worldwide inflation occurred due to gas shortages and price increases; the Irish Republican Army exploded bombs in the Tower of London, the Houses of Parliament and in various pubs throughout Great Britain; the Soviet Union launched the Salyut-4 Space Station; Turkey invaded northern Cyprus; India detonated a nuclear weapon (becoming the sixth nation to develop nuclear weapons); and "Lucy," a hominid skeleton over three million years old, was discovered by Paleontologist Donald Johanson in Ethiopia.

The major developments in domestic affairs were: the average cost of a house was $34,900; the average income was $13,900; the price of a gallon of a gas was 55 cents; the Sears Tower in Chicago became the world's tallest building; in an energy saving development, President Richard Nixon signed legislation requiring states to limit highway speeds to 55 miles per hour (the law was abolished in 1995); as a result of the energy crisis, daylight saving time began four months early; students, many of whom held part-time jobs, were obviously pleased by the minimum wage increase to $2; the House Judiciary Committee opened impeachment proceedings against President Nixon when he refused to surrender Watergate-related tape recordings and documents subpoenaed by the Senate Watergate Committee; the Supreme Court ruled that Nixon had to turn over 64 tapes of White House conversations, and in July 1974 the House Judiciary Committee recommended three articles of impeachment against Nixon for conspiracy to obstruct justice in the Watergate cover-up, for abuses of power and for defiance of committee subpoenas; in August former White House Counsel John W. Dean III was sentenced one to four years in prison for obstruction of justice (Dean served only four months); that same month, Nixon announced his resignation, and in September President Gerald R. Ford granted an unconditional pardon to the former President; Nelson Rockefeller became Vice-President; Ella T. Grasso (of Connecticut) became the first woman to win a gubernatorial office without succeeding her husband; Karen Silkwood, a union activist at the Oklahoma Kerr-McGee Cimarron plutonium plant, was killed in a car crash; and newspaper heiress, Patricia Hearst was kidnapped in California by the Symbionese Liberation Army.

In the entertainment industry the Oscar for the best movie of 1974 was awarded to "The Godfather, Part II." Art Carney won the best actor award for "Harry and Tonto," and Ellen Burstyn won the best actress award for "Alice Doesn't Live Here Anymore." The Grammy for the best record of the year was awarded to Olivia Newton-John for "I Honestly Love You," and the Grammy for album of the year was awarded to Stevie Wonder for "Fulfillingness' First Finale." In athletics North Carolina State defeated

Marquette in the NCAA Basketball Championship; the Miami Dolphins defeated the Minnesota Vikings in the Super Bowl; and the Oakland Athletics defeated the Los Angeles Dodgers in the World Series. A highlight of the baseball season occurred when Hank Aaron of the Atlanta Braves broke Babe Ruth's record when he hit his 715th career home run. In boxing Muhammad Ali regained his heavyweight title after defeating George Foreman.

Meanwhile, the continuing energy crisis affected the college. C. C. Humphreys, Chancellor of the State University and College System, called for a 15% energy reduction in all colleges. Ray Coleman, Director of Continuing Education and Chair of the college's Energy Conservation Committee, submitted a plan to the Chancellor which complied with the Chancellor's decree. The plan included measures such as adjusting thermostats, conserving gasoline and reducing electricity usage. Student access to the college was further enhanced by the extension of Interstate 75 to Loudon, Tennessee, and instruction was assisted by the completion of a closed circuit television system which made possible live programs that could be produced and broadcast throughout the campus.

Classes were made more accessible to students as a result of a petition, signed by approximately 200 students, requesting Wednesday night classes. At that time the college only offered night classes on Monday, Tuesday and Thursday nights because, for some people, Wednesday evening was a church activity. This prohibition rendered it impossible for evening students to take the twelve hours of courses that were necessary to be a full-time student. Seven Wednesday night classes (five on the campus and two in Athens) were added to the 1974 Fall Quarter schedule. Educational opportunities were also enhanced by the completion of an Astronomical Observatory. Buford Guy, the Physics Instructor, used the facility, which officially opened in the summer of 1975, to supplement his courses in Astronomy. He also directed small tours for Tiger Scouts, Cub Scouts, local schools and other organizations.

Other campus activities were: thirteen area high schools participated in Phi Theta Kappa's spring High School Quiz Bowl; in May "Flash Cadillac and the Continental Kids" performed and many attendees dressed in 1960s attire; and the play, "South Pacific" was also held in May. The play was directed by Tom Boles and John Bradley and the six main characters were Dennis Cannon, Vicky Hamby, Rob Robinson, Sabra Maples, Robert Wilson and Larry Fain. A paperback annual, titled "Personality," was published. The student staff for the annual included Peggy Byrne, Janice Hodgson, Debbie Kress, Bill Moats, Vicky Simpson and Terri Trusley. The faculty advisor for the publication was Bob Robinson.

A student, Robert White, received accolades for his TVA Research Intern Report titled, "Cherokee Indian Removal from the Lower Hiwassee Valley." Students elected to SGA offices were Randy Eaves (President), Melody Plemons (Vice-President) and

Diane Bryant (Secretary-Treasurer). Sophomore class officers were Sharon Armstrong (President), Karen Armstrong (her twin sister—Vice-President) and Ruth Wilson, Secretary-Treasurer. Staff for The Cherokee Signal were: Barbara Ward, Editor; Alan McCosh, Editorial Writer; Allen Hudson, Sports Editor; Jeffrey DeLude, Business Manager; and Walter Presswood, Faculty Consultant. Later, Buffy Hoge became the Picture Editor and Bill Miller the News Editor. Jim Gibson and Amanda Cate were elected Mr. and Miss Cleveland State and Vicky Veal was chosen Homecoming Queen.

In spring sports the 1974 golf team won the State and Region VII championships and represented the college at the NJCAA Golf Championship in Fort Myers, Florida. It was the first college athletic team to participate in a national event. By winning the region tournament, Cleveland State represented Tennessee, Kentucky and Mississippi in the national event. Winston Prince was the medalist at the Region VII Tournament with a two-round score of 143. Coached by Steve Longley, the team members, in addition to Prince, were Steve Allen, Rick Sisson, Mike Benson, Rick Cutcher, Steve Sisson and Johnny McGee. The tennis team also compiled an impressive record of nine wins and two losses. Coached by Joe Crabtree, the team members were Jim Gibson, Lynn Griffith, Donnie McFall, Danny Cooper, Tony Cavett and Fred Walker. Another winning record was achieved by the baseball team (29-10). The team won the Eastern Division of the state conference, and its members were Tim Baxter, Russ Blakely, Jewell Brock, Dennis Byrd, Wadie Davis, Larry Garner, Dale Goodwin, Ron Gowan, Doug Barnes, Rodney Amburn, Ron Spangler, Ray Sheets, Ron Sharpe, Terry Self, Mike Seals, Rick Melvin, Sam West, Bobby Lett, Denny Williams and Gus Harmon. The coach was Steve Longley.

In April 1974 unwelcome excitement was generated by a tornado that ripped through the Cleveland area and elsewhere. Fortunately, it missed the college but it did much damage throughout the college's surrounding area. The weather was calmer by graduation time when 284 students received their diplomas. The Commencement speaker was Mildred Doyle, Superintendent of Knox County Schools. The Outstanding Faculty Award was presented to Spencer Culbreth (History) and the Outstanding Student Award to Jim Gibson.

By the fall of 1974 fourteen new faculty had been added and enrollment was 2,834 (1,284 of these were evening students). Mary Barker became Head of the Humanities Division, and Dr. Quentin Lane was the new Dean of Instruction. A few years later, the Gymnasium was named for Lane, and several years later, the Humanities Building was named for Barker. Meanwhile, Lonas Construction Company had completed new sidewalks and steps at the north end of the student center, an outdoor handball court, four new tennis courts beside the baseball field and a new student parking lot at the campus entrance. The City of Cleveland bestowed an honor upon the college President by naming the street in front of the college, "Adkisson Drive."

Instruction was enhanced by a new TV studio, a new program in Communications and the completion of the one million dollar Career Education Building. The new Writing Lab was supervised by three English instructors, and the Communications Program added Graphic Arts and Journalism as options to the program. The new Career Building accommodated 1,000 daytime and 600 evening students.

During this time, a humorous event occurred in Dr. Larry Longerbeam's English class. At the beginning of classes, he was often unable to find chalk or erasers. He was forced to leave the classroom and find the departmental secretary for assistance in locating replacements. After a week or so, he encountered a maintenance employee who noted that he had found a pile of erasers and chalk on the ground, outside the classroom window. Obviously, a student had been "displacing" the items for the purpose of delaying the beginning of class. Perhaps it was the same student who wanted to call him coach rather than professor.

Meanwhile, an additional enhancement to instruction was the purchase of forty color monitors located in the classrooms. These were wired to the TV studio and wall phones were installed in the classrooms for communication with the studio. An information channel was added on closed circuit TV that transported messages throughout the campus to fourteen black and white TV monitors. Support for these endeavors, and others, was provided by the operating budget of $2,862,437. The 1974-75 college payroll, for a total of 175 employees, was $1,894.727.

In personnel actions, Ray Coleman became the new Dean of Administrative Services. A few years later, the campus Auditorium Building was named for him. Succeeding Coleman as the Director of Continuing Education and the Evening Division was Al Fine. Jim Cigliano became the Director of the Financial Aid Office, when Elvis Brandon resigned to become the Chief Deputy of the Bradley County Sheriff's Office, and Charles Coblentz became the new head of the Respiratory Therapy Program. The 1974 Board of Trustees consisted of Harold Almond, Mrs. Walter Presswood, Henry Barkley, George Castings, W. K. Fillauer, W. J. McReynolds, Mayor Harry Dethero, Earl McGhee, Mrs. Joel Parrott, Eugene Callaway, Frank Manly, Pearson Mayfield, Dr. Wayne McCulley, Pledger Wattenbarger, Wayne Feehrer, Bill Thomason, Clarke Stamper, Ben Longley, James Morris, George Mathis and Dr. David Adkisson.

Several faculty and staff attended meetings, or achieved accomplishments during the summer and fall of 1974. Judy Cox (Biology faculty) was among twenty-five faculty from colleges across the nation to attend a two-week seminar on energy and radiation that was sponsored by the Atomic Energy Commission and held at the University of Kansas. Buford Guy and Jim Allen co-authored an article that appeared in the Physics Teacher and was titled, "Velocity of Sound by Reasonances." Guy also wrote another article for the same journal titled, "Let's Hang Those Meter Sticks."

Two students spent much of the summer in Europe as part of the Experiment in International Living (EIL) program. Kim Butler traveled to Unterkuin, Switzerland, and Ellen Brewer to Vasteras, Sweden. In the elections for the Freshman Class officers, Wes Martz was chosen as President, Charlie Ericson as Vice-President and Sheila Martin as Secretary-Treasurer. The new cheerleaders were Terry Tilly, Lavonne Headrick, Janice Hensley, Diane Bryant, Alisa Adams, Valeria Tate, Marlene Johnson, Renee Madden and Joyce Rymer. The mascot was Missy Longley.

Several personnel changes occurred in athletics. Steve Longley succeeded Ed Coates as head baseball coach. Coates became the new Athletic Director, Basketball Coach and Baseball Coach at Tusculum College in Greeneville, Tennessee. Longley had played baseball at UTK for two years. He then signed a professional contract for the Cincinnati Reds and spent two years with that organization until an injury cut short his career. Longley had been serving as an Assistant Baseball Coach, Physical Education instructor and Golf Team Coach at Cleveland State. Hugh Walker, former girl's basketball coach at Calhoun High School for eight years, became the Ladies' basketball coach and Dr. Joe Dzikielewski (Health and Physical Education) became the new tennis coach and director of intramural sports.

– 1975 –

In comparison with other years, international affairs in 1975 were relatively calm. The major events were: Angola gained its independence from Portugal; King Faisal of Saudi Arabia was assassinated; the Suez Canal was re-opened after being shut down during the Six-Day War of 1967; Juan Carlos was proclaimed King of Spain; Margaret Thatcher was elected leader of Britain's Conservative Party; Japanese climber Junko Tabei became the first woman to reach the summit of Mount Everest; President Gerald Ford declared an end to the "Vietnam Era;" the South Vietnamese government officially surrendered to North Vietnam on April 30, 1975; the American merchant ship, the Mayaguez, and its crew of 39 members was seized by Cambodian forces in the Gulf of Siam; and American marines attacked Tang Island, planes bombed the air base and Cambodia released the ship and crew.

The major national events were: the average cost of a house was $39,900; the average income was $14,400; the average cost of a gallon of gasoline was 44 cents; three new inventions were the personal computer, a digital camera and a laser printer; former Attorney General John Mitchell and ex-Presidential advisors H. R. Haldeman and John Ehrlichman were found guilty of the Watergate cover-up; Jimmy Hoffa, the ex-Teamster Union boss, disappeared and was never seen again; construction of a trans-Alaskan pipeline began; an American Apollo spaceship docked with a Russian Soyuz spacecraft in orbit in the first superpower link-up of its kind; and newspaper heiress

Patricia Hearst was apprehended by the FBI nineteen months after being kidnapped by the Symbionese Liberation Army (she later served two years of a seven-year sentence for armed robbery).

The Academy Award for the best picture of the year was "One Flew Over the Cuckoo's Nest." The movie also earned the Best Actor Award (Jack Nicholson) and the Best Actress Award (Louise Fletcher). The Grammy Award for the best single record of the year was Captain and Tennille's, "Love Will Keep Us Together." The Emmy Award for the best comedy was the "Mary Tyler Moore Show" (CBS), and the Emmy for the best drama was "Masterpiece Theatre: Upstairs, Downstairs" (PBS). In sports UCLA won the NCAA Basketball Tournament; the Cincinnati Reds defeated the Boston Red Sox in the World Series; the Pittsburgh Steelers defeated the Minnesota Vikings in the Super Bowl; and Arthur Ashe became the first black man to win a Wimbledon singles title.

Meanwhile, the college was making its own history. On January 10, 1975, Mrs. Paula Phillips registered for a pharmacology course at the college. She was the 3,000[th] student to register for that winter quarter. It was the first time Cleveland State had enrolled 3,000 students for one quarter. Mrs. Phillips, who had two sons attending the college, later received her Associate of Science Degree in Nursing from Cleveland State and was employed by Bradley Memorial Hospital.

The community was invited to see the college's progress when the first "Open House" event since 1968 was conducted. A few months later, a workshop at the college for high school teachers, sponsored by the American Revolution Bicentennial Commission, was attended by 150 people. In other construction a Graphic Arts Lab was added to the Print Shop, and a Cleveland/Bradley Career Park was completed. The latter would be utilized by the city and county secondary school systems.

By 1975 the Cooperative Education Program (established in 1973) was blossoming. The program had assisted 111 students in obtaining full or part-time employment with approximately 52 employers in the college's service area. The average pay was generally about $2.39 per hour, and the average number of hours worked was sixteen per week. The money earned by the students was paid by the employer, and students earned up to 12 credit hours toward their degree. Credit was also earned by students who were already employed.

Several faculty and staff were active in the early part of 1975. Charles Coblentz (Respiratory Therapy) was elected as the Vice-President of the Tennessee Respiratory Therapy Association. Several others were program participants at the Tennessee Education Council Meeting at Volunteer State Community College. They were: Matt Reiser, Director of Career Education; Mary Ann Green, Cooperative Education Coordinator; Joe Semak, Allied Health Coordinator; and David Vandiver, Industrial Management Instructor. Dr. Quentin Lane was elected as President of the MTSU

National Alumni Association, and he also served as President of the Phi Delta Kappa honor fraternity in Chattanooga.

Several students also made the news. Four students (only males applied) spent two and one-half months in the summer working in a Swedish bakery and touring Europe. The jobs were arranged by Renate Hufft (Foreign Language Instructor), and the students were Keith Nye, Philip Prichard, Tom Cormany and Clint Lothorp. The Experiment in International Living (EIL) recipients, chosen by the National EIL Board in Vermont, were Tomme Trikosko and Kin Baker. Trikosko studied anthropology in Mexico, and part of her seven weeks was spent with a family. Baker toured six European countries and studied European Art and Architecture. Ann Norman (English Instructor) was in charge of the program.

In the SGA elections Wes Martz was President, Betty Wilson, the Vice-President and Vickie Ballew the Secretary-Treasurer. Freshmen class officers were: Sharon Armstrong, President; Melody Plemons, Vice-President; and Julie Penny, Secretary-Treasurer. Sophomore Class officers were: Dinky Waters, President; Bill Moats, Vice-President; Debbie Davis, Secretary; and Patti Patterson, Treasurer. Mr. and Miss Cleveland State were Steve Casada and Melody Plemons. The Commencement speaker was Dr. James A. Barksdale, the former State Commissioner of Education. The Outstanding Faculty Member Award was won by Walter Presswood, and the Outstanding Student Award was presented to Judy Velva.

In Athletics the Cougar Club reached a membership of 351 supporters. Founded by Dr, George Mathis and Jim Cigliano, its purpose was to contribute to athletic advancement and to foster a closer identity with the people of the college's service area. The officers in 1975 were: President, Woody Ratterman, Cleveland Insurance Company Executive; Vice-President, Hank Smith, MacDonald's Corporation Executive; Tom Wheeler, Cleveland Utilities Administrator; and Jackie Liner, Cleveland State College Accountant. The organization's first two members were Eddie Cartwright (Cleveland City Commissioner) and Dr. L. Quentin Lane (the college's Dean of Instruction).

A major occurrence in 1974-75 was the inauguration of the Lady Cougars Basketball Team. Coached by Hugh Walker, their sensational season began on November 18, 1974 and continued through the Winter Quarter of 1975. Led by Liz Hannah, Karen Armstrong and Kay Green, they finished 7th in the NJCAA and compiled a record of 13 wins and 5 losses. They were one of 16 teams invited to the national tournament. They won two and lost two in the double elimination national finals in Overland Park, Kansas. Liz Hannah was the first Cleveland State athlete named to an All-American Team. The team members were Karen Armstrong, Sharon Armstrong, Kay Green, Linda Davis, Liz Hannah, Debbie Varner, Dianna Lovelace, Emily Penney, Sharon Sliger and Annettee Seals. The managers were Melody Plemons, Ruth Wilson and Betty Wilson. The Cherokee Signal named Liz Hannah and Mike Seals (baseball) as co-recipients of the Athlete of the Year Award.

The men's basketball team ended their season with a 10-16 record and they set a new scoring record when they defeated Morristown 128-88. The team members were: Jerry Belcher, Michael H. Byrd, Frank Campbell, Thomas Eugene Hilton, Frank Martin, Rudy Ownbey, Jerry Richt, Chuck Sanders, Mike Seals, Ronnie Sharpe, Raymond Smith, Rick Smith, Mark Stinnett and Ricky Lynn Torbett. The coach was Joe Crabtree. An interesting footnote to the basketball season was the husband and wife team of Mike and Annette Seals. He played forward for the men's team, and she played guard for the ladies' team.

The 1975 Baseball Team duplicated its 29-10 won-lost record of the year before. Their Eastern Division Conference record was 21-3 compared with 18-6 in 1974. The team won the Eastern Division but lost to Columbia State in the TJCAA Championship playoffs. Standouts were Stan Loy (with a .398 batting average), Will Harris (with a .333 batting average), Gus Harmon (with four home runs), Ray Sheets (with a two-year pitching record of 14-3), Larry Liebe, Randy Trusley, Mike Seals and Tim Baxter. Mike Moore, a freshman, compiled a 3-1 pitching record and was named to the NJCAA All-American team. He was also the first baseball player in Cleveland State history to be drafted by a professional team. He was drafted by the Baltimore Orioles for their "farm team" in Miami. Moore, however, declined the offer and continued playing in his sophomore year.

The Golf Team also excelled that year. They won both the TJCAA and the Region VII Tournament. They compiled a 13-2 record and five of the players were ranked in the top seven of the TJCAA. They were the second golf team to attend the national playoffs that were held in Hutchinson, Kansas, that year. The coach was Jim Allen, and the players were Steve Myers, Rick Crutcher, Kenny Ames, Ron Waters and Joe Joyner. Myers was the medalist at both the State and the Region VII Tournament. He had a 36-hole aggregate score of 148 in the Region playoffs, and he averaged 73.0 for the season. The site of the national tournament was approximately 17 miles from the geographic center of the continental United States. A homeowner in the area, with a sense of humor, had a sailboat with a huge mast in his yard. He displayed it as a joke because he contended his home was further away from an ocean than anyone in the continental United States.

Another record enrollment occurred in the fall when 3,583 students registered. Alex Nichols, Head of the Computer Center, announced that several new computer terminals would soon be operational. The Media Center announced that videotaping of courses was available, and they would begin taping Math and Physics courses. In addition the college purchased an Optical Mark Reader that graded an objective exam (True-False and Multiple Choice questions) and provided an analysis of student responses to each question. A concert was held in the gym on November 13 as part of the Cleveland/Bradley Community Concert association program. Titled "The Broadway Hit Parade," it featured the popular singer, Dorothy Collins.

Several members of the faculty and staff continued to be active in receiving honors, attending meetings to learn the latest developments in their specialties and participating in community activities. John Bradley was chosen as President-Elect of the Tennessee Theater Association at a meeting in Memphis. He became the President at the meeting in Gatlinburg in October 1976. He also played the lead role of Jeeter Lester in Erskine Caldwell's play "Tobacco Road" (performed at the UTK Carousel Theater). Roy Lillard was selected as Chairman of the Cleveland-Bradley American Revolution Bicentennial Commission and was appointed to a second three-year term on the Board of Advisors for Carson-Newman College. He also wrote several articles that appeared frequently in the Cleveland, Athens, Dayton and Polk County newspapers.

Tom Boles was one of 38 people to visit Sweden, Poland, Yugoslavia, Czechoslovakia and England as part of a "People-to-People" Goodwill Mission. A television crew from the Southeast Tennessee Area Health Education Center came to the campus to film a video on Charles Coblentz's Respiratory Therapy Laboratory. The video was included in a WCTE television program on allied health training in Southeast Tennessee. It was also distributed to 1,700 educational television stations. In October Dr. Quentin Lane, Mary Barker, Ann Morelock, Adrian Strother (Student Activities Counselor), Martha Newman, Al Fine and Dr. Irene Millsaps attended a "Non-Traditional Learning" Symposium at MTSU. Dr. Millsaps was a guest speaker at the meeting, and her subject was the unique audio-tutorial math lab at Cleveland State. Additional college positions had been added to various areas during the previous couple of years. These were filled by Janice Matthews, Joyce Scoggins, Kay Graham and Lois Howe. James Morris was the Business Manager and others in that area were Jacky Liner, Hugh Robinson, Beverly Evans, Reba Hudgins, Mitzi Hooper, Mary Jane Carter and Brenda McBrayer. Ray Coleman was in charge of Institutional Research; Al Fine was in charge of the Continuing Education and Evening Division; Martha Newman was Director of the Learning Skills Center; Chlora Dunn (assisted by Sam Neas) was head of the Media Center; and Brenda Geren was the College Nurse.

Other staff, faulty and student achievements, in the fall of 1975, were: Ann McCoin passed the Tennessee Bar exam, giving the college two licensed attorneys (the other one was Colonel Marcus Stubbs); Mary Ann Geren's article on cooperative education appeared in the October issue of the Tennessee Technical Education Council's Newsletter; Jim Johnson, Dental Lab Instructor, attended a dental porcelain clinic in Atlanta; Mary Barker attended the Conference for English Teachers in Memphis; Jerome Taylor attended a History Conference in Boston; Jere Chumley (Art) had two paintings selected for the 22nd Chattanooga Area Painting Exhibition (they were displayed in the Hunter Art Museum); Norman West became the Director of Student Activities; Buffy Hoge was elected President of the Sophomore Class and Ronnie Bright, Secretary-Treasurer; Donna Casto was elected President of the Freshman Class and Karen Sneed, the Secretary-Treasurer.

– 1976 –

International events in 1976 were characterized by the usual mix of both good and bad news. The most significant events were: Britain and France opened trans-Atlantic Concorde supersonic transport service to Washington, D. C.; the Canadian National Tower was completed in Toronto (at that time, at 1,815 feet high, it was the tallest free-standing structure in the world); the world's first recorded Ebola virus epidemic began in the Sudan; riots occurred in Soweto, South Africa; Mao Tse-tung, the founder of the Chinese Communist Party and Chinese ruler, died; Israeli commandos raided the Entebbe airport in Uganda and rescued the majority of passengers and crew of an Air France plane that had been seized by Palestinian hijackers; and the UN General Assembly approved resolutions condemning apartheid in South Africa.

In domestic affairs the major events were: the average cost of a new house was $43,400; the average income per year was $16,000; the average cost of a gallon of gasoline was 59 cents; it was America's celebration of its 200th "birthday;" Apple Computer was founded by Steve Jobs, Steve Wozniak and Ronald Wayne; the reclusive billionaire, Howard Hughes, died in Houston at the age of 70; in New York City, the "Son of Sam" began a series of violent attacks that terrorized the city for a year; Legionnaires disease affected 4,000 American Legion delegates in Pennsylvania; the two dollar bill was issued; America's Viking I robot spacecraft made a successful, first ever landing on Mars; Viking II landed a few months later and photographed scenes from the planet's surface; and James Earl Carter defeated Gerald R. Ford in the Presidential Election.

The Oscar for the year's best movie was awarded to "Rocky," the Best Actor Award was presented to Peter Finch ("Network'), and the Best Actress Award was won by Faye Dunaway ("Network"). The Emmy Award for TV's best comedy was the "Mary Tyler Moore Show" (CBS), and the award for the best drama was "Police Story" (NBC). The Grammy Award for the best record was George Benson's, "This Masquerade," and the award for the best album was Stevie Wonder's, "Songs in the Key of Life." In sports the NCAA Basketball Champion was Indiana; the Pittsburgh Steelers defeated the Dallas Cowboys in the Super Bowl; the Cincinnati Reds defeated the New York Yankees in the World Series; and Nadia Comaneci of Romania won three gold medals at the Montreal Olympics with seven perfect scores.

At the conclusion of registration at CSCC, for the Winter Quarter in January 1976, the headcount enrollment was 3,420 as compared with 2,967 in the winter of 1975. By 1976, several types of financial aid were available for students. The major ones were Basic Educational Opportunity Grants (BEOG), Supplementary Educational Opportunity Grants (SEOG), National Direct Student Loans (NDS), Law Enforcement Educational Program Grants (LEEP), Nursing Grants and Nursing Loans and Cleveland State Institutional Scholarships. In addition, non-credit courses on subjects such as dancing, small engine repair, food canning, golfing, basic woodworking and auto mechanics were continually expanding. Funding from the state, however, was based only on credit courses. The funding formula was linked to the number of students taking at least twelve hours of credit. Categorized as full-time equivalency (FTE) students, the number for the 1976 Winter Quarter was 1,939 as opposed to 1,777 in the winter of 1975. Funding from the state was increased or decreased depending upon the FTE number.

The major campus news in 1976 was the announcement by Dr. George Mathis (Dean of Students) that he would be retiring at the end of June. He was honored on June 30 with a surprise retirement party and by the news that the Student Center would be named in his honor by the State Board of Regents. Another noteworthy event was the announcement of the completion of a new book titled, The History of Bradley County. The general editor was Roy G. Lillard. Other college personnel on the editorial board were Katharine Trewhitt and Walter Presswood. In the spring the college conducted a campus on the mall event. Faculty and staff exhibited a large variety of items related to instruction and finance at the Bradley Mall. The college also hosted the first annual Future Secretaries of America Convention, and approximately 140 delegates attended. In another development, thirty Tennessee Valley Authority public safety officers received certificates for completing a three-week training course at the college.

Students made the news when the Tennessee Intercollegiate State Legislature (TISL) passed a decree requiring all police officers to check their weapons, immediately upon arriving at a campus, with the campus security office. The goal was to have gun-free campuses. The bill was written by two Cleveland State students, but it was not endorsed by the State Legislature.

In February 1976 the national Buckley Amendment was passed which denied the release of certain types of student information (for those students over the age of 18) without the consent of the student. Known as "The Family Educational Rights and Privacy Act," it denied any educational institution federal funds if it did not follow the guidelines of the amendment.

In personnel news the college was saddened by the death of Colonel John Smeltzer. A Psychology instructor, he had assisted in establishing the college counseling department, in forming the General Education Diploma (GED) Testing Center and in organizing a tennis team. He was a retired Air Force Chaplain with the rank of Colonel. In other developments Joe Crabtree announced his resignation, for health reasons, as Athletic Director and men's basketball coach. Crabtree remained at the college in a teaching position. Jerome Taylor was named the Vice-President of the East Tennessee Historical Society, Ed Howard (Economics) retired, and Dale Yates (Accounting) became the new Business Department Coordinator. Fred Wood (English) was appointed as Tennessee's representative on the Advisory Committee for the Southeast Conference on English in the Two-year College. Appointees to other positions were: Robert Vogler was named the new Director of Nursing; Colonel James Stubbs became the Head of the Criminal Justice and Legal Assistant Programs; Dr. Mary Barker was now Head of both Humanities and Social Sciences; and Dr. Dean Banta was in charge of Education, Psychology, Health and Physical Education/Recreation.

A lengthy discussion about grading resulted in the retention of the "F" grade. In a faculty vote of 51-18, the grade was retained and the "W" grade was altered to permit withdrawal from a course up to the end of the sixth week. A "no-credit" (NC) grade was added to permit students, making satisfactory progress, to withdraw from a course.

In athletics the women's basketball team improved on their excellent performance of 1975. They compiled an impressive 28-3 won-lost record and won the State and the Region VII Tournament, which was held at the Cleveland State gym. They finished fourth in the 1976 NJCAA tournament in Overland Park, Kansas. Liz Hannah was named to both the All-American first team and the All-Tournament team. She was also selected to the Tennessee women's all-star team, which later played a team from Russia, and she was invited to participate in the Olympic tryouts at Nashville, Tennessee. Zandra Montgomery received Honorable Mention for her play in the national tournament, and Hugh Walker was named Coach of the Year by the TJCAA. Walker was also named Tri-State Coach of the Year by the Chattanooga Times newspaper.

The baseball team, coached by Steve Longley, also excelled. They won the Tennessee State championship and finished 2nd in the Eastern District Tournament of the NJCAA (which was held at Cleveland State May 21-23). It was the first state championship for the baseball team. Ted May was the leading hitter with a .384 batting average and 43 RBIs. He had two grand slam home runs in one game, and he led the NJCAA with 14 home runs. He later transferred to a Florida Junior College. Outstanding pitchers were: Bobby Petitt, with four wins and two losses and a 1.64 earned run average; Mitch Trotter, with 3 wins and 0 losses and a 2.36 earned run average; and Steve McLaughlin, with 4 wins and 3 losses and a 3.77 earned run average.

The men's basketball team ended their season with a 6-23 record, and the golf team, coached by Jim Allen, won a third consecutive Tennessee State Championship. The golf team members were: Steve Myers, Steve Hill, Jimmy Sharp, Kenny Ames, Ron Waters, Allen Rudd and Buster Goins. The Tennis Team, coached by Dr. Joe Dzikielewski, hosted the state tournament and tied for fourth in the regional tournament. The team members were Ralph Buckner, Robin Hayes, David Houser, Phil Howard, Ron Kuhns, Wayne Mathis and Steve Richey. Phil Howard received the first annual George L. Mathis Scholastic Athletic Award at the spring sports banquet.

In other news Jo Beverlee Wilson and Kathy Ann Hooven were selected as the ambassadors for the Experiment in International Living (EIL) program. Wilson traveled to Switzerland and Hooven to Holland. Another student, Margaret Lee Gamble, financed her own trip to Canada. The college hosted the 3rd annual High School Bowl Quiz, which was won by Cleveland High School. The college also formed a Quiz Bowl Team that finished 5th in the Berry College Invitational Junior College Bowl. Patty Moisan was awarded a scholarship for being an outstanding participant. The team advisor, Frances Layne, also noted that the team captain, Tomme Trikosko, performed well in the contest. In addition to Trikosko and Moisan, the team members were John Anderson, Scott Parkinson, Ed Clark and Joe Finnell.

In the SGA elections, Don Loftis was elected President, Tony Twarzynski, Vice-President and Ronni Bright, Secretary-Treasurer. In the Sophomore Class elections, John Campbell was elected President, Bettye Patterson, Vice-President and Roseann Godbehere, Secretary-Treasurer. Later that year (1976) Andrew Skipper was elected President of the Freshman Class. The spring staff members for The Cherokee Signal were: Steve Holland, Editor; Carl Wright, News Editor; Allen Hudson, Sports Editor; Tom McGill, Editorial Editor; and Janis Johnson, Makeup Editor. In the fall, the staff members were: Barbara Ward, Editor; Sue Little, Editorial Editor; Allen Hudson, Sports Editor; Mike Fitzgerald, News Editor; and Bill Clark, Business Manager. The faculty advisor was David Suttles. Mr. and Miss Cleveland State were Don Loftis and Margaret Cheek. The commencement speaker was Dr. Roy Nicks, Chancellor of the State Board of Regents. Joe Allen (Biology) was the recipient of the Outstanding Faculty Member Award, and Tomme Trikosko received the Outstanding Student Award.

Another highlight of the year occurred on September 24, 1976 when the State Board of Regents voted to name the college's Administration Building in honor of Dr. David Adkisson. It was the first time a community college facility had been named for one of its Presidents. Another record enrollment was achieved when 3,710 students registered in the fall. The first of several Iranian students were among the enrollees. By 1979 nineteen of them had enrolled at the college. Apparently, an incentive for enrolling in American colleges was the beginning of a military draft system in Iran as differences between that country and Iraq increased the likelihood of war. In construction news the announcement was made that a new Community Service and Continuing Education building would be completed by 1977. The architect was James R. Franklin of Chattanooga and the building would contain 11,600 square feet at an estimated cost of $750,000. The structure, which included a 400-seat auditorium, would be used for community events, cultural programs, lectures, seminars and conferences. It was later named the Coleman Building in honor of Ray Coleman who would later hold several different administrative positions at the college. In December the third annual Christmas Party for disabled children was held at the college. Co-sponsors were the Cleveland Kiwanis club and the Cleveland Civitan Club. Campus organizers were Bertha Goldston, Joyce Scoggins, Jim Cigliano, Katharine Trewhitt, Carolyn McDole, Wanda Trewhitt, Al Fine and Norma Davis.

Additional personnel changes also occurred in the mid-1970s. James Cigliano was named the new Dean of Student Personnel Services. He had been Director of Admissions. Cooperative Education and Job Placement were combined under a new coordinator—Rosemary Den Uyl of Athens. Bill Gatlin, a former Cleveland State graduate, became the new Veterans' Coordinator. Marcia Fair was hired as a counselor, having been a physical education coordinator at Waterville Elementary School. Other counselors were Paul Boynton, Frances Layne, Adrian Strother and Hugh Walker. Secretaries in the department were Marty Allen and Verna Moore. Dr. Quentin Lane was the Dean of Academic Affairs and Dr. David Watts was the Assistant Dean. Staff members in the Office of Admissions and Records were: Dianne Harrison, Norma Davis, Gail Key, Sherry Miller, Dorothy Mowery and Vivian Rapier. The Library staff members were: Adeline Baskett (Head Librarian), Janet Caruth, Byung Moo Lee, Martha Allison, Marie Humphrey, Norma Patterson, Elizabeth Scott and Robbie Quinn. A few other staff members were: Alex Nichols, Computer Center; Mary Ann Green, Health Services; Martha Newman, Learning Skills Center; Sam Neas, Coordinator of the Media Center; Al Fine, Director of Continuing Education and the Evening Division; Walter Presswood, Director of Community Relations and Development; and Robert Vogler, Head of Nursing.

In other personnel news Byung Moo Lee, Library Cataloguer, became a citizen of the United States. Originally from Seoul, Korea, he moved to America in 1965 and was employed at Cleveland State in 1971. Josephine Pritchett was selected by the Tennessee Business Education Association as their first recipient of the Tennessee Teacher of the year award in Business Education. Dr. Ozane Adams received her doctor's degree from MTSU in Elementary Education, Health, Physical Education and Recreation. Jerome Taylor was appointed to the State Historical Records Advisory Board for the National Historical Publications and Records Commission.

Faculty and staff attending meetings were: Bernadette Sutherland, Pat Crews, Shelby Millsaps and Elaine Rochelle (Nursing Faculty members) attended a Clinical Evaluation Workshop in Nashville; Mary Barker, Harry Dean, Fred Wood and Renate Hufft (English and Foreign Language instructors) attended a meeting of the South Atlantic Modern Language Association in Atlanta, Georgia; Gayle Wood (Registrar) and Frances Layne (Director of Admissions) attended the meeting of the Southern Association of Collegiate Registrars' and Admissions' Officers in Jackson, Tennessee; Adeline Baskett (Head Librarian) attended the Southeastern Library Association Meeting in Knoxville; Mary Barker and Al Fine attended the Tennessee Commission for Humanities meeting at Henry Horton State Park; Dr. Matt Reiser and David Vandiver attended the national Conference of Career Education in Houston, Texas; John Bradley attended the 9th Annual Tennessee Theater Conference in Gatlinburg; Jim Cigliano and Walter Presswood attended a meeting of the Tennessee Intercollegiate Student Legislature in Nashville; Roy G. Lillard, Jerome Taylor and Spencer Culbreth (History faculty members) attended the meeting of the Southern Historical Association in Atlanta; Bob Vogler (Head of Nursing) attended a meeting of the Tennessee Higher

Education Commission (THEC) Task Force on Nursing in Nashville. Dr. Ozane Adams and Dr. Joe Dzikielewski (Health and Physical Education) attended the Tennessee Association of Health, Physical Education and Recreation Convention in Memphis; and Dr. Mary Barker, Penny Overend, Harry Dean and Fred Wood (English faculty members) attended the Southeastern Conference on English in the Two-Year College at Columbia, South Carolina.

During the year the college welcomed Tom Losh as the new head coach for basketball. Losh had been a standout player at UTC and former head baseball and assistant basketball coach at his alma mater. The assistant coach was Charles Cogdill and the team members were Doug Armstrong, Jeff Buchanan, Gerald Crutcher, Tony Davis, David Ellis, Reginald Golson, Bobby Harper, Terry Henley, Dale Kennedy, Tim Lockhart, Mike Lowry, Jerry Parks, Jimmy Rawn, Terry Reedy, Kenny Short and Lorenzo White. The cheerleaders were Kathy Blevins, Kathy Guess, Teri Hargis, Debbie Harris, Susan Holloway and Devonda Pierce. The sponsor was Carolyn McDole.

– 1977 –

International events in the year continued to be a mixture of triumph and tragedy. Important incidents were: France created an international uproar by releasing Abu Daoud (a Palestinian Liberation Organization official behind the massacre of Israeli athletes at the 1972 Munich Olympics); Egyptian President Anwar Sadat became the first Arab leader to visit Israel; Quebec adopted French as its official language; Pakistani President Zulfikar Ali was overthrown by Muslim extremists; and Menachem Begin became Israel's Prime Minister.

Important domestic developments were: the average cost of a new house was $49,300; the average income was $15,000; the average cost of a gallon of gasoline was 65 cents; the minimum hourly wage was $2.30; Jimmy Carter assumed the office of President; convicted murderer Gary Gilmore was shot by a firing squad at Utah State Prison (the first U. S. execution in a decade); President Carter pardoned virtually all of the Vietnam Conflict draft evaders; the space shuttle Enterprise, sitting atop a Boeing 747, had its maiden flight above the Mohave Desert; the trans-Alaska oil pipeline was completed; John N. Mitchell became the first former Attorney-General to serve a prison term for his role in the Watergate cover-up (he was released 19 months later); a New York City power failure (known as the "Blackout") lasted for 25 hours and resulted in looting and disorder; the first Apple II computers were sold; Elvis Presley died at his Graceland estate in Memphis at the age of 42; thirty-nine people were killed when the Kelly Barnes Dam burst, sending water through Toccoa Falls College in Georgia; the World Trade Center in New York was completed; the Energy Department, a new federal government cabinet, was created; and the city of New Orleans elected its first black mayor, Ernest "Dutch" Moral.

The Academy Award for the best movie was "Annie Hall." The best actor award was won by Richard Dreyfuss for "The Goodbye Girl," and the best actress award was presented to Diane Keaton for "Annie Hall." George Lucas produced his first "Star Wars" film. The TV miniseries, "Roots," aired on the ABC network, and it won nine Emmy Awards and one Golden Globe Award. The Emmy for best comedy was won by the "Mary Tyler Moore Show" (CBS), and the best drama award was given to "Masterpiece Theatre: Upstairs, Downstairs" (PBS). The Grammy for best record was presented to the Eagles for "Hotel California," and the Grammy for album of the year was awarded to Fleetwood Mac for "Rumors."

In athletics Marquette won the NCAA Basketball Championship; the Oakland Raiders defeated the Minnesota Vikings in the Super Bowl; and the New York Yankees defeated the Los Angeles Dodgers in the World Series. In thoroughbred horseracing, Seattle Slew became the 10th Triple Crown champion by winning the Kentucky Derby, the Preakness Stakes and the Belmont Stakes.

The 1977 Winter Quarter at CSCC began with a headcount enrollment of 3,585. A national study indicated that the average cost for tuition, fees, books and supplies at a public two-year college was $579 per year. This compared with $4,113 for a private two-year college. The American Bar Association approved the college's Legal Assistant Program, and Cleveland State became the 22nd college in the nation to receive such certification. Colonel James Stubbs played an instrumental role in this achievement.

A campus administrative reorganization of instruction occurred in the summer of 1977. Dr. Lane, the Dean of Academic Affairs, announced that the goal was only three Divisions: (1) Arts and Sciences, (2) Community Services and Continuing Education and (3) Career Education. Instructors of history, political science, economics and sociology were assigned to the new Humanities and Social Sciences Division. Accounting instructors were assigned to the Math and Science Division, and Business instructors were assigned to the Career Education Division.

A scholarship endowment fundraising campaign, with a goal of $200,000, was launched in 1977. One of the supporting efforts for it was a car fund-raiser. One-dollar tickets were sold for a raffle on a 1977 Buick Regal donated by Benton Enterprises. Another supporting activity was a gigantic yard sale from items donated by the faculty, staff and students. Smaller activities, such as a student car wash, were also conducted. The goal was met and exceeded within a few months. The response to the campaign was indicative of the enthusiastic support for the college that existed in its service area.

An important event was the college hosting of a Conference on the Governor's Committee on Employment of the Handicapped. David Suttles and Judy Scoggins assisted with the planning, and Congresswoman Marilyn Lloyd gave the keynote address. Her speech was titled, "Legislation for the Betterment of the Handicapped."

Suttles was named regional co-coordinator for the Southeastern Tennessee Region of the Governor's Committee on Employment of the Handicapped. The other co-coordinator was Dr. Theodore C. Mercer, President of Bryan College in Dayton, Tennessee. In another activity the faculty and staff conducted a campus on the mall exhibit at the Bradley Mall. This became an annual event for the next few years. Astronaut Paul Weitz, who served as the pilot on a Skylab II mission in 1973, was a guest speaker at the college. While working with Astronauts Charles Conrad Jr. and Joseph Kerion, he logged 28 days and 404 orbits of the earth during the 1973 Skylab Mission.

The college faculty and staff continued to upgrade their skills by attending conferences. These were: Nancy Boyd, Benita Harris and Dr. Frank McKenzie attended a Business Education Conference at UTK; Matt Reiser attended a TN Technical Education Council meeting in Memphis; Jerry Berman (Photography) attended a Conference of the School of Communications at MTSU; Bruce Busby, Marilyn Fillers, Ann Morelock, Penny Overend and Fred Wood attended the Southeastern Conference on English in the Two-Year College in Williamsburg, Virginia; Adeline Baskett and Janet Caruth (Library) attended the College and University Section meeting of the Tennessee Library Association at MTSU; and Jim Cigliano, Bill Gatlin and Dianne Harrison attended a Sub-Council for Student Affairs meeting in Murfreesboro. A 1972 Nursing Graduate of Cleveland State, Dale Jones, became the new college nurse. Jones, who was also a certified piano teacher, had worked at Campbell Clinic in Chattanooga and at Bradley Memorial Hospital.

As usual, humor continued to be a part of campus life. Puns were an ongoing source for campus lexophiles. A few of these were: "To write with a broken pencil is pointless; When fish are in schools, they sometimes take debate; A thief who stole a calendar got twelve months; When the smog lifts in Los Angeles, U. C. L. A.; With her marriage, she got a new name and a dress; A boiled egg is hard to beat; A bicycle can't stand alone—it is 'two' tired; He had a photographic memory which was never developed; and "Acupuncture is a jab well done. That's the point of it."

The college's athletic teams had another outstanding year. The golf team, coached by faculty member Jim Allen, won both the State and Region VII tournaments for the fourth consecutive year. Their victories earned them an invitation to the National Tournament in Fort Myers, Florida. The team members were Jerre Mosley, Jerry Burrell, Rick Barnette, Ricky Watson, Billy Gilliland, Buster Goins and Bob McIntire. Watson was the medalist at the State Tournament and Gilliland was selected to the all-state team. The tennis team, coached by faculty member Ken Newton, compiled a 12-6 won-lost record and tied for 2nd in the TJCAA State Tournament. Standout players were Chris Powers, Robin Hayes, Rick Hunt, Phil Traylor and Kevin Byars. Powers and Hayes won the state tournament number one doubles competition and advanced to the National Tournament in Arizona.

The baseball team, coached by Steve Longley, tied for the Eastern Conference lead with Motlow State. The men's basketball team, coached by Tom Losh, ended the season with 17 wins and 11 losses (8-6 in the conference). Terry Reedy set a career scoring record with 803 points (the record had formerly been held by Gay Powell). For the season, Jerry Parks averaged 16.9 points, Dale Kennedy 14, Reedy 13.9 and David Ellis 13.6.

The ladies' basketball team had another great year. They won the State Tournament but lost in the Region VII Playoffs (which were held at Cleveland State). The team was 28-4 overall and 16-1 in the conference. At one point during the season, they were ranked 3rd in the NJCAA. The coach was Hugh Walker, and the team members were Debbie Allmon, Leisa Bates, Kim Borden, Data Caldwell, Donna Caldwell, Pam Dugan, Carol Green, Debbie Hendricks, Denise Henry, Kim King, Zandra Montgomery, Cindy Moore, Leslie Shamblin, Debbie Shipley, Cathy Simonds, Cathy Sisson and Kathy Chastain Smith. Cindy McRae and Cindy Lovelace were the team managers. Data Caldwell led the team in scoring average (18.7) and rebound average (10). Caldwell was named to the TJCAA and the Region VII All-Star teams.

Once again Cleveland State had a recipient of an EIL award. Jeanne Marshall was selected as an "ambassador" to Great Britain. The new staff members for The Cherokee Signal were: Jane Williams, Editor; Glenn Harbison, News and Sports Editor; Cindy Underwood, Feature Editor; and Cindy Hicks, Visuals Editor. An "International Club" was formed to foster good relations between foreign students and American students and another college bowl team was also organized. Its members were Ed Clark, Mike McCloung, Becky Jones, Tom Eldredge, Steve Walker, John Feuerbacher, Tony Trawzynski, Diane Garen, Joe Finnell, Scott Perkinson, Pattie Moisan and Kin Baker. The team was coached by Penny Overend and Bruce Busby. Grant Caywood and Barbara Osment were selected as Mr. and Miss Cleveland State, Donna Caldwell was the Homecoming Queen, and another Cleveland State student, Sabra Maples, was crowned Miss Cleveland.

The Commencement address was delivered by C. C. Bond, the Assistant Superintendent for Student Personnel Services for the Chattanooga City Schools, a member of the State Board of Regents and a former Principal of Howard High School. The average age of the 320 members of the graduating class was 27. The first ten-year Service Awards were presented to: Dr. Adkisson, Dr. Mathis, Dr. Banta, Janie Arms, Tom Boles, Jim Cigliano, Jere Chumley, Norma Davis, Joe Guest, Roy Lillard and Molly Smith. Zandra Montgomery was awarded the Outstanding Student Award, and the Outstanding Faculty Member Award was presented to Dr. Charles Wheeler (Physics).

The fall registration official enrollment headcount was 3,910. Dr. Adkisson planned to retire in June 1978, and this necessitated the formation of a search committee for a new president of the college. Dr. Roy S. Nicks, Chancellor of the State University and Community College System, appointed a committee composed of two faculty members, one student and one administrator from the college, one representative from the community and one administrator from the State Board of Regents (SBR) staff. The members were: Nancy Boyd, Associate Professor of Office Careers; Dr. Spencer Culbreth, Assistant Professor of History; Mimi Lindner, President of the SGA; Henry Smith, President of the Cleveland-Bradley Chamber of Commerce; and Dr. Wray Buchanan, Vice-Chancellor for Academic Affairs at the SBR.

The Foundation continued to remain active in dispensing scholarships. Several new trustees were added in 1977. These were: Bob Easterly, Cleveland Postmaster; M. F. Finfrock, General Manager of Cities Service Company of Copperhill; Scott Mayfield, President of Mayfield Dairy Farms of Athens; Don Russell, Plant Manager of Westvaco; Bill Markiewicz, Cleveland Kiwanis Club President; Jimmy Goddard, President of Benton Banking Company; Allen Rhea, President of People's Bank of Polk County; Ruth Hynes, Cleveland Women's Club; Ed Richelson, CSCC alumnus; Carl E. Painter, Jr., President of Ducktown Banking Company; Michael Callaway, Cleveland Attorney; Jimmy Cooke, President of Cooke Manufacturing Company; Eddie Botts, President of Cleveland Evening Lions Club; and Robert Varnell Jr., President of Cleveland Rotary Club. They joined the current members, Beecher Hunter, Pledger Wattenbarger, Dr. L. Quentin Lane, Roy G. Lillard, James Morris, Dr. George L. Mathis and Sheila Presswood. The new officers were: Dr. D. F. Adkisson, President; Henry Barkley, Treasurer; Frank Manly, Secretary; and W. K. Fillauer, Member of the Executive Committee at Large.

The college received sad news when David Vandiver died in a plane crash. He was an Assistant Professor of Management, Director of the Bradley-Cleveland Vocational Center and was instrumental in developing the college's aviation program. In other news Buffy Hoge, a former CSCC student, became the first female campus security officer. She worked with Paul Cagle, a cheerful and humorous officer who was popular with students and staff. Cagle was also a vocalist who loved opera music and admired Enrico Caruso.

Four students, Judy Lansford, Vivian Thomasson, William Phillips and Pat DiGennaro, accompanied by instructor Dr. Frank McKenzie, attended the Students in Free Enterprise (SIFE) meeting in Nashville. Charles Layne, a voice student, won a statewide audition sponsored by the Music Teachers National Association of Chattanooga (his accompanist was Tracy Sesler). The new student cheerleaders were Susan Elliott, Elyn Dodd, Mary Callahan, Jenny Gregg, Kim Johnson, Karen Seto, Pattie Rogers, Terri Clark and Cindy Johnson. Mimi Lindner was the new SGA President and the members of The Cherokee Signal staff were: Adelia Lambert, Editor; Don Bower, News Editor; Sheryl Brown, Features Editor; Karen Loudermilk, Editorial Editor; and Denise Masengil, Visuals Editor. The new Sophomore Class officers were: Tom Carroll, President; Kim Hayes, Vice-President; Katie Suits, Secretary-Treasurer; and Roger Wright, Speaker of the Senate. New Freshman Class Officers were: Sandy Cross, President; Keith Colloms, Vice-President; Cecil Stansberry, Secretary-Treasurer; and Jack Harrison, Senator.

– 1978 –

The major international events during the year were: in a meeting at Camp David, Maryland, Israeli Prime minister Menachem Begin and Egyptian President Anwar Sadat signed a framework for a peace treaty (both men were later named as winners of the Nobel Peace Prize); 1978 was the year of three Popes as Pope Paul VI and John Paul I died shortly after taking office and John Paul II succeeded them; the first trans-Atlantic balloon flight ended as Maxie Anderson, Ben Abruzzo and Larry Newman landed their Double Eagle II outside Paris; Sweden became the first nation to ban aerosol sprays which were believed to damage the earth's protective ozone layer; in Guyana over 900 followers of cult leader Jim Jones obeyed his instructions to commit suicide by taking poison; Volkswagen suspended production of the "Beetle" car; Rhodesia's Prime Minister, Ian Smith, agreed to accept majority rule in future elections; and the first test tube baby was born in Great Britain from "in vitro fertilization."

In domestic events President Jimmy Carter and Panamanian leader Omar Torrijos signed documents of ratification for the Panama Canal treaties. Approved by the Senate, the treaty called for control of the waterway to be awarded to Panama on the last day of 1999. Other developments were: the average cost of a new house was $54,800; the average income was $17,000; the average cost of a gallon of gas was 63 cents; the hourly minimum wage was $2.65; Sally Ride was selected as America's first woman in space; Guion S. Bluford Jr. became the first black astronaut in space (neither Ride nor Bluford made flights until 1983); Karl Wallenda, the seventy-three old patriarch of the family high wire act, fell to his death while attempting to walk a cable between two hotel towers in San Juan, Puerto Rico; the Supreme Court ordered that Allan Bakke (a white man) be admitted to the University of California-Davis Medical School because he was a victim of reverse discrimination; serial killer David Berkowitz (known as "the Son of Sam") was sentenced to 25 years to life in prison; movie director, Roman Polanski, fled to France hours before he was to be sentenced for rape and other crimes against a child; although not circulated until 1979, the Philadelphia mint began minting the Susan B. Anthony dollar; and the cellular mobile phone system was introduced.

In popular culture news the Academy Award movie winner was "The Deer Hunter." Jon Voight won the award for best actor for the movie, "Coming Home," and Jane Fonda won the best actress award for the same movie. "All in the Family" (CBS) won the Emmy for best comedy, and "The Rockford Files" (NBC) won for the best drama. The Grammy for the best record was awarded to Billy Joel for "Just the Way You Are," and the Grammy for album of the year was won by the Bee Gees for "Saturday Night Fever." In sports Kentucky won the NCAA Division I Basketball Championship; the Dallas Cowboys defeated the Denver Broncos in the Super Bowl; and the New York Yankees defeated the Los Angeles Dodgers in the World Series.

In campus news Dr. Adkisson received a new truck from friends and employees on his last day as President (June 30, 1978). Dr. Quentin Lane became the college's new President. He graduated at an early age (19) from MTSU and taught in Chattanooga for several years. He received his Master's Degree from George Peabody College and his Doctorate from UTK. He was the youngest of seven brothers. His Mom died when he was four years old and his twenty-three year old brother became the head of the family. All the brothers worked together running the family farm. Four of his brothers obtained Master's degrees and three were school Principals in Hamilton County. He was Assistant Principal of Brainerd High School and later the Principal of Elbert S. Long School. He arrived at CSCC in 1971 as the Director of Continuing Education. Later, he was the Director of Research and the Dean of Instruction.

An advisory committee, was formed to select a new Dean of Academic Affairs to replace Dr. Lane. The committee was composed of Ray Coleman, Dean of Administrative Services; Dale Yates, Accounting instructor; Fannie Hewlett, Psychology instructor; Benita Harris, Office Careers Instructor; and Dr. Spencer Culbreth, President of the CSCC Education Association. Dr. Lane concurred with their recommendation, and Dr. Galen McBride was named the new Dean of Academic Affairs. McBride earned a Bachelor's degree from East Texas Baptist College and a Master's and a Doctorate from the University of Texas at Austin.

A few additions to the staff were: Janice Matthews was the President's Secretary; Ray Coleman was in charge of Administrative Services, and the secretary was Kay Graham; Billie Dupree was the Secretary in Academic Affairs, and Dr. David Watts was the Assistant Dean; Bill Gatlin was in charge of both Admissions and Records and Veterans' Affairs; Lyn Gulliford was the Director of the Computer Center, and he was assisted by Curtis McNeely, Charles Riedel, Ryna Shamblin and Bertha Goldston; John Cook was the new coordinator of Criminal Justice (he earned a law degree from the University of South Carolina and had 27 years of experience with the FBI), and the office secretary was Glendon Belk; and Al Fine was the Director of Community Services and Continuing Education and was assisted by Carolyn McDole and Pamela Abels. Other staff personnel in the late 1970s were: Mitzi Hooper, Joyce Scoggins, Adrian Strother, Dianne Harrison, Norma Davis, Verna Moore, Hugh Robinson, Dennis Cannon, Wanda Green, Joann Gregg, Brenda Ledford, Karen Tipps, Gayle Wood, Martha Lane, Irene Rice, Joyce Ferguson and Marty Allen.

In other news the Bradley/Polk Vocational Center, located on the campus, reverted to the college on July 1, 1978. The state government's partial funding of the center ceased at that time. In personnel changes Alex Nichols, the former Director of the Computer Center, returned to the classroom as a fulltime instructor in Data Processing. Shelby Millsaps replaced Robert Vogler as the new Head of the Department of Nursing Education. Millsaps had been a Nursing Education faculty member since 1974. She received her Master's in Nursing from the Medical College of Georgia and was a former Instructor and Recruiter for the Baroness Erlanger Hospital School of Nursing.

Two of the college's faculty members, Roy G. Lillard and Katharine Trewhitt, announced their plans to retire. Lillard had been at the college since its inception in 1967. He was an Associate Professor of History and Political Science. He was Head of the Social Sciences and Business Division, an advisor to the SGA for over six years and an advisor to the Baptist Student Union for eleven years. He was also the Editor of The History of Bradley County, Chair of the Bicentennial Committee of Cleveland/ Bradley County, Co-Chair of the Bicentennial Committee of Polk County and Chair of the CSCC Bicentennial Commission. In addition, he was a former President of the East Tennessee Historical Society, the Polk-Bradley County Historical Society, the John Sevier Memorial Association and the Tennessee Baptist Library Association. Trewhitt, an Associate Professor of English, was affiliated with education for 45 years. She worked with both Cleveland City and Bradley County Schools. She began teaching at CSCC in 1969. She developed several new courses—Children's Literature, two courses in the Bible as Literature and two courses in Southern Mountain Heritage. Trewhitt was also a charter member and former President of the local chapter of Delta Kappa Gamma (an international honorary society for women teachers), a lifetime member of the National Education Association and a former President of both the Cleveland Education Association and the CSCC Education Association.

Winter and spring activities included a Music Department presentation of the play, "Shenandoah," at the Bradley High School Little Theater, a campus on the mall display at Bradley Mall and a performance of the play, "Vanities," at the Knights of Columbus clubhouse. The latter was co-directed by John Bradley and Bill Gatlin and the main performers were Connie Cox, Kim Butler and Suzanne Allen. In athletics the Lady Cougars basketball team compiled a 20-8 record and won the State Championship. They lost by only one point to East Mississippi in the finals of the Region VII Tournament (56-55). Data Caldwell and Tracey Dixon Walker made the All-Tournament Team, and Caldwell set a CSCC career record with 566 rebounds. The team was ranked 19th in the final season poll of the NJCAA. The Men's Basketball team was led by Rodney Benson, with an average of 19.9 points per game and 12.8 rebounds. Other standouts were Sylvester Ware, with an average of 19 points, and Keith Miller, with an average of 14.2 points per game. The members of the Golf team were Jerry Burrell, Jerre Mosley, Billy Gilliland, Rick Barnette, Bob McIntire, Scott Hicks and Craig Green. The team compiled a 9-14-1 record. The Tennis team members were Tim Walker, Rebble Johnson, Jerry Stout, Steve Clark, David Lee and Kevin Maxwell. The team ended the season with a 4-9 record. Although not an officially recognized sport, a Soccer "Club" was organized by Don Turner and sponsored by Ed Leech. The team, composed primarily of Iranian students, was led by Davood Borhani who averaged three goals per game.

The baseball team finished second in the Eastern Division with an overall record of 27 wins and 11 losses. Impressive hitters were Mark Hooper (.358), Joey Grubb (.337), Tony Ridge (.330) and Mitch Trotter (.306). Bobby Petitt led the pitchers with a 9-3 record and a 2.64 earned run average. Pitchers Mitch Trotter, Steve McLaughlin and

Benny Culpepper also excelled. Donny Garner had 18 of 19 base steals, and both he and Joey Grubb were Eastern Division All-Stars. Other players were Lamar Queen, Rob Elsea, Larry Simcox, Ricky Lewis, Danny Rue, Steve Lawson, Phillip Munck, Mark Hooper, Jimmy McGowan, Ricky Bryan, Rusty Bowden, Tony Ridge, Mario Trujillo, Paul Burnette, Randy Starkey, George Johnson and Tim Kuhns. During the season Coach Longley won his 100th game, and this gave him a CSCC career record of 114-47.

In an article for The Cherokee Signal, Sports information Director Ed Grief presented a brief history of college sports history. He noted that Joe Crabtree coached men's basketball for nine years and compiled a 108-143 record. The current coach, Tom Losh, had a two-year record of 31-21, and Hugh Walker's current record, as coach of the Lady Cougars, was 98-17. Grief also identified several former outstanding baseball players—David Rogers, Scotty Bell, Mark Boggs, Ted May, Steve McLaughlin and Rob Elsea. By 1978 the college had three All-Americans from the Lady Cougars—Liz Hannah (1975-76), Zandra Montgomery (1976-77) and Data Caldwell (1977-78).

For the fourth consecutive year the college was represented at the Berry College Quiz Bowl. Sophomore Chauncey Mapes won a scholarship to Berry College, and Freshman Danny Davenport received honorable mention. Others on the team were Cecil Stanberry, Cindy McLain and alternates Debbie Cox and Mimi Lindner. The coaches were Dr. Bruce Busby and David Suttles. Danny Davenport was the college's EIL recipient and he traveled to Germany during the summer of 1978. The Spanish instructor, Efrain Guillen, led Cleveland State students and interested community members on a trip to Mexico. The Homecoming Queen was Robin Roberts; Becky Blackburn was elected as President of the SGA; Tom Carroll was Mr. Cleveland State; and Mimi Lindner was Miss Cleveland State. The Cherokee Signal staff members were: Adelia Lambert, Editor; Karen Loudermilk, Editorial Editor (and later also the Editor); Don Brower, News Editor; Joe Turner, Sports Editor; and Allen Mincey, Advertisements Editor.

The Commencement address was delivered by Dr. Sam Ingram, the Commissioner of Education for Tennessee. Three hundred and fifty-nine students graduated, and for the first time at CSCC, a father and son graduated--Billy Cole Sr. and Billy Cole, Jr. All six of the Cole family members had attended CSCC. The recipient of the Outstanding Faculty Award was Dr. Bruce Busby, and the winner of the Outstanding Student Award was Charles Layne.

The 1978 fall enrollment was 4,088. An analysis of registration indicated that students represented 43 different Tennessee Counties and that 52 students represented states outside of Tennessee. Bradley County was the home for 2,171 students, Hamilton for 623, McMinn for 578, Polk for 284, Monroe for 99, Meigs for 87 and Rhea for 51. Saturday classes were offered for the first time, and by November construction of the new auditorium was completed.

A fifteen-member college "Stage Band" was formed under the direction of Robert Horton, the owner of the Music Center in Cleveland. Team members for the basketball teams were announced and their seasons were launched. Members of the Lady Cougars were Tammy Bates, Tracey Walker, Liz Atchley, Tammy Murphy Dunn, Debbie Clark, Tina Hall, Venetia Goins Smith, Carla Yount, Renee Grizzle, Pam Arnwine, Neasy Barrett, Cinday McMahan, Teresa Millsaps and Melinda Shell. The team members for the men were Rodney Benson, Keith Miller, Sylvester Ware, Artis Knox, Lawanza Crutcher, Eddie Cooper, Brian Howard, Don Burton, James Williams, Mike Stiles, Tobin Davidson, Eric Beck, Kin Farner, Tim Jones and Jimmy Webb.

In other student news the new editorial staff members of The Cherokee Signal were: Joe Turner, Editor; Linn Goins, News Editor; Richard Murray, Sports Editor; Allen Mincey, Business Manager; Katy Little, Editorial Editor; Sharon Jones, Head Photographer; Ronnie Rhea, Photo Editor; Polly Fowler, Typesetter; and David Suttles, Faculty Consultant. The Cheerleaders were Teresa Norris, Elyn Dodd, Noreen Yuki, Pam North, Janet Townsend and Sonya Green. Karen Gibson was the Faculty Advisor for the team.

– 1979 –

The major international events during the year were: Ayatollah Ruhollah Khomeini seized power in Iran, and 66 Americans (and 24 others) were taken hostage at the American Embassy in Teheran; the Iranian Shah, Mohammed Reza Pahlavi, had departed Iran, seeking asylum in the United States, then in Panama, and finally in Egypt, where he died in 1980; Adoph Dubs, the US ambassador to Afghanistan was kidnapped in Kabul by Muslim extremists and killed in a shootout between his abductors and police; Idi Amin was deposed as President of Uganda; Conservative party leader Margaret Thatcher was chosen to become Britain's first female prime minister; Sandinista rebels captured the Nicaraguan capital of Managua; NASA's Voyager I space probe flew past Jupiter and sent back to earth photos of the planet and its moons; the Soviet Union attacked Afghanistan; in Rhodesia the first black-led government in 90 years assumed power and the country's name was changed to Zimbabwe; Pope John Paul II became the first Pope to visit a communist country when he made a trip to his native Poland (he also became the first Pope to visit the White House); Saddam Hussein came to power in Iraq; China instituted the one child per family rule; Lord Mountbatten (the uncle of Prince Philip) and three others were assassinated by the Irish Republican Army; four hundred armed Sunni Islamic Muslims seized the Grand Mosque in Mecca; and President Jimmy Carter and Soviet President Leonid Brezhnev signed the SALT II strategic arms limitation treaty in Vienna.

The major domestic developments were: the average cost of a new house was $58,100; the average income was $17,500; the average cost of a gallon of gasoline was

86 cents; the hourly minimum wage was $2.90; President Carter proposed a ten-year 140 billion dollar program to reduce dependence on foreign oil; former Vice-President Nelson Rockefeller died in New York at the age of 70; the US House of Representatives began televising its daily business; America's worst commercial nuclear accident occurred at the Three Mile Island plant near Middletown, Pennsylvania; and former first lady Mamie Eisenhower died in Washington D. C., at the age of 82.

In popular culture the academy award-winning movie was "Kramer vs. Kramer," and the best actor award was presented to Dustin Hoffman for the same movie. Sally Field won the best actress award for the movie, "Norma Rae." The Grammy award for the best record was won by the Doobie Brothers for "What a Fool Believes." The best album was Billy Joel's "52nd Street." The Emmy award for the best comedy was won by "Taxi" (ABC), and the best drama was "Lou Grant" (CBS). The major sports events were: Michigan State won the NCAA Division I Basketball Championship; the Pittsburgh Steelers defeated the Dallas Cowboys in the Super Bowl; the Pittsburgh Pirates defeated the Baltimore Orioles in the World Series; and ESPN began operation on cable television.

On campus the $650,000 auditorium was officially opened. It contained a 392-seat auditorium, a lobby, a kitchen, four classrooms and office space. Al Fine, Director of Community Services and Continuing Education, announced that it would be a meeting place for community groups, a center for dramatic and cultural events and a location for college classes. An important event for simplifying registration occurred with the advent of computer-assisted registration in the spring of 1979.

The college supported employment issues by providing a district office for a federal government initiative known as the Comprehensive Employment and Training Act (CETA). CETA was a federal law enacted by Congress and signed by President Nixon in 1973. It existed until 1982 when it was replaced with the Job Training Partnership Act (JTPA). CETA was designed to offer work to those with low incomes and the long-term unemployed (as well as summer jobs to low income high school students). Full-time jobs were provided for 12 to 24 months in public agencies or private "not for profit" organizations. The intent was to impart a marketable skill that would allow participants to move to an unsubsidized job. One of Hitch's tasks was to find jobs for students that related to their field of study. Students were required to complete 15 hours of classes per quarter and maintain a 2.0 grade point average. Students also worked for a minimum wage ($2.90 in 1979) for 10 hours per week and 10 cents per mile for travel expenses and free tuition and books.

In activities, a musical comedy, "Bye Bye Birdie," was held in the new auditorium in March. Over 40 people were involved under the overall direction of Don Thomas and assistant director, Barry Kidwell. Tom Boles directed the music with assistance from Tracy Sesler. Randy Davis played the lead, and a few of the other cast members were Aaron Gibson, Cindy Glaze, Becky Greene, Gayla Henry, Keith Colloms, Marian Douglas, Steve Clark, Kent Gill, Darrell Henry, Linda Harris, Cindy Harris, Kellye Hicks, Rhonda Bishop and Rex Calfee. A Youth Enrichment Program was also started in 1979. Initially for gifted children, it later became a summer camp for any interested children. The program offered a variety of courses such as Tennis, Aviation, Architectural Design, Computers, Heroes and Villains, Mythology, Stunts and Tumbling, Reading and Math. An intriguing guest speaker--Dr. Kark Heinze, a NASA astronaut--presented a lecture in April.

A series of lectures about life in Iran were presented by a college employee, Paul Boynton. He and his family lived there for six years. His lectures also featured several of the college's Iranian students who were invited to make presentations on current events in Iran. The College President, Dr. Lane, complimented CSCC's Iranian students (there were 19 of them in the fall of 1979) on their maturity. Lane stated that, "While Iranian students across the country demonstrated for the overthrow of the Shah, none of the Cleveland State students were involved in anything except their education." Faculty member Jim Allen (Architecture) noted that one of his best students was a 26-year old Iranian named Behrouz Azarnoush. In an interview for the college's Employee Newsletter, Azarnoush stated that, "the people in Cleveland are very friendly—the hospitality is best here. The students are very nice. But I feel bad. I don't like fighting. I wish the world could be friendly and the situation now would finish. I wish gas would be cheap and students could continue coming here for a good education."

Another event, in the fall of 1979, was the appearance of the Atlanta Symphony in the gymnasium. Conducted by Robert Shaw and Louis Lane, the symphony brought 89 musicians to perform works by Beethoven, Dvorak, Ives and Tchaikovsky. Dr. Mary Barker, Head of the Division of Arts and Sciences, coordinated the event which was attended by approximately 500 spectators. John Bradley also directed the play "Picnic" in the fall. The drama featured a combination of student and community participants. Among these were Charlotte Lear, Laura Franklin, Katie Suits, Maurine Nichols, Mike Bagwell, Connie Cox, Bill Gatlin, Tim Hooker, Rhonda Richmond, Jo Ann Gann and Scott Bell.

In personnel news Karen Gibson became the new Financial Aid Director and Roy Lillard's (Emeritus Faculty member) books on Bradley and Polk Counties were selected as part of a compilation of books by Memphis State University Press. The project consisted of a multi-volume history of Tennessee's 95 counties. A vital part of any campus is the maintenance staff. In 1979 they were Bill Pettit (Supervisor), Helen McCleary, Matilda Evans, Helen Piersaul, Lou Thompson, David Hamilton, Dexter Jenkins, Tom Green, Levi Brown, Larry Pritchett, Leon Smith, Paul Miller, Paul Underwood, Lillie Woods, Ida Mae Hitson, Clarice Bonine, Patsy Woods, Ricky Walker, Henry Helton, Paul Clowers, Fred Anderson (night foreman) Benton Shelton, Tom Griffis, N. W. Rayfield and Marvin Green. Other administrative support staff members throughout the campus were: Wanda Cartwright, Peggy Lowe, Gretchen Coppinger, Marilynn Johnson, Glen Wilbanks, Lois Howe, Janet Caruth, Norma Hicks, Martha Allison, Doris Henderson, Elizabeth Scott, Denise Tate, Robbie Quinn, Bill Clark, Betty Berry, Jean Salter, Evonne Drown, Jane Arms, Brenda Elliott, Darlene Rush and Beverly Evans.

In campus athletics Tom Losh resigned as the men's basketball coach to become the college's Coordinator of High School Relations. He attained a 43-30 record as head coach from 1976-79. The team compiled 17-11, 14-10 and 12-9 won-lost records during those three years. His assistant coach, Charles Cogdill, became the new head coach. The Lady Cougars, coached by Hugh Walker, ended the season with a 19-6 record (11-3 in the conference) but failed to win the state championship for the first time in four years. The baseball team, coached by Steve Longley, compiled a 29-10 record and finished second in the TJCAA. Standouts were Ted Carson, Tobin Davidson, Greg Geren, Dale Scott, Ricky Lewis, Larry Simcox, Steve Green, Wes Ivey, Donny Garner, Randy Starkey, Rusty Bowden, Mike Jordan and Mario Trujillo. The tennis team (coached by Dr. Spencer Culbreth) won 11 and lost 3 and finished 3rd in the TJCAA. The players were Sean Glaser, Jeff Hoge, Robbie Ray, Bill Rush, Rohn Poe, Kevin Rogers and Tim Henderson. The golf team (coached by Dr. L. E. Wooten) finished 3rd in the state and sent two players (Al Miller and Jay Goza) to the National Tournament in Odessa, Texas.

The coaches in 1979 had interesting backgrounds. Steve Longley was a graduate of Baylor High School where he lettered in football, baseball and basketball. He attended UTK on a baseball scholarship. After two years at UTK, he signed with the Cincinnati Reds and played baseball on their farm teams for three years. A back and pelvis injury forced him to retire. He coached at Darlington High School in Georgia for a year prior to his arrival at CSCC as an assistant baseball coach. He also coached the golf team for three years prior to becoming the Head Baseball Coach. By the fall of 1979 his baseball record was 143-56, and his golf record was 65-15. His golf teams won two state championships, one region championship, and the team made one trip to the national tournament. He was a golf TJCAA Coach of the Year for three years and baseball coach of the year for the Eastern Division for three years. By 1979 his baseball teams had won three division titles and one region title, and 25 of his players had made All-Conference teams.

Hugh Walker attended high school at Knoxville Central. While there he lettered in football, basketball and track. He received a college basketball scholarship from Tennessee Wesleyan. His college degree was from Wesleyan, and his Master's degree was from UTK. He coached golf, baseball and women's basketball at Calhoun High School. He arrived at CSCC in 1974. In five seasons his Lady Cougars compiled a 118-25 record. His CSCC teams were state champions from 1975 through 1978, region champions in 1975 and 1976, 4th in the national tournament in 1976, 3rd in the final

NJCAA poll in 1977, 5th in the NJCAA poll in 1978 and 19th in the NJCAA final poll of 1979. He was also TJCAA coach of the year in 1976 and a nominee for NJCAA coach of the year in 1978.

Charles Cogdill succeeded Tom Losh as coach of the Men's basketball team. In high school, at Marion County, he lettered in football, basketball and baseball. He was All-Conference, All-District, All-Region and All Tri-State in basketball. Cogdill received his Bachelor's degree from Tennessee Wesleyan and his Master's from Tennessee Tech. His coaching career began at Marion County High School in 1971. He later coached at Sequatchie County and Manchester. He was assistant coach at CSCC for two years, head coach at Motlow State Community College for one year and then back at CSCC as Head Coach.

Dr. L. E. Wooten, Sociology Professor and the golf coach, attended high school in Rossville, Georgia. He received his Bachelor's degree from UTC, his Master's degree from MTSU and his Doctorate from Mississippi State. He arrived at CSCC in 1969. His first golf team lost only one conference match and was 2nd in the state and the region tourney. Wooten continued to serve in a dual role as an instructor and a coach.

Dr. Spencer Culbreth, History Professor, Chair of the Department of Social Sciences, and the tennis coach, received his Bachelor's degree from Wofford College, Master's degree from the University of North Carolina at Chapel Hill and Doctorate from MTSU. His first tennis team was 4-9 and the second one was 11-3. Like Wooten, Culbreth also continued to perform his academic duties in addition to being a coach.

An important announcement in 1979 was that the college would start a ladies' softball team in 1980. Bob Taylor, a Physical Education instructor, would also assume duties as the team's coach. Taylor was from Salisbury, Maryland, and, in high school, he lettered in wrestling, soccer and baseball. He received his Bachelor's degree from Salisbury State College and his Master's from UTK. Taylor was a member of the track team at Salisbury State and he later coached track, soccer and cross-country track at Columbia Military Academy. He also taught at T. C. Bower Elementary School before arriving at CSCC. After serving several years at Cleveland State, he left to become a Principal at Michigan Avenue Elementary School, and later, Superintendent of Bradley County Schools.

The commencement address in June of 1979 was delivered by Lamar Alexander, the Governor of Tennessee. An unusual feature of the event was the graduation of Sheri Trotter, the first deaf graduate of the college (her twin sister, Teri Trotter, was also a CSCC student). The first deaf recipient of a GED was Johnny Groomes. The interpreter for Trotter was Connie Baker, and the interpreter for Groomes was Barbara Ballinger. Dr. Jerome Taylor (History) received the Outstanding Faculty Award, and Pam Cole received the Outstanding Student Award.

The 1979 Fall Quarter headcount enrollment was 4,140 (a huge increase from the original 681 in 1967). The steady increase reflected the national trend. A 1979 study revealed that over one-third of the nation's 11 million college students attended community colleges. The college Foundation announced that 33 full scholarships, totaling $11,336, had been awarded for the 1979-80 academic year. The Financial Aid Department noted that $331,500 had been disseminated for the academic year of 1978-79. The tuition cost for taking 12 or more quarter hours was $90 for an in-state student and $334 for an out-of-state student.

Another first for the college was the introduction of the four-day workweek. The college operated from 8 am until 9 pm Monday through Thursday. The purpose of the initiative was to conserve electrical energy, natural gas, and gasoline. An estimated savings of $175,000 in gasoline was expected per year. Two campus visitors, from Volunteer State Community College (VSCC), Dr. Pat Lebkuecher and Dr. Jim Woods, praised the success of the four-day week at their college. It improved the evening division's effectiveness because campus offices remained open later, and more faculty members were available to assist students. Electricity consumption was reduced at VSCC by 43% and natural gas consumption by 44%.

An interesting proposal related to the four-day week was made by Bristol United Corporation of Chattanooga. The company proposed a van pooling operation for those students with a long distance daily commute. The van pool would be open to any student, faculty or staff member who lived within specified areas. The average commuter student traveling from Chattanooga or Ootlewah spent about $7.74 a day, not including wear and tear on their automobile. The company planned to charge about $3 to $3.50 per day to ride in one of their 9-passenger vans. A student driver would be in charge of the van and would receive a free ride. The van schedule would be set by the students involved. Everyone would meet in a designated area (or perhaps door-to-door pickup would be arranged). Drivers would include the van on their insurance as a second car, and gas would be paid from a portion of passengers' fares. The driver would be required to perform routine maintenance on the van. Although it was an innovative proposal, interest was not enough to merit its implementation.

A November 1979 survey revealed that 89.8% of the students responding supported he four-day week, 6.5% opposed it and 3.7% had no opinion. Of those responding, 82.3% had no scheduling problems. Those favoring the four-day week among the remainder of the campus population were as follows: faculty, 71%; administrative and support personnel, 76.9%; clerical, 60.5% and custodial and maintenance, 95.5%. Of all employees therefore, 73.1% supported the four-day week. A later estimate indicated that gas consumption by students was reduced by 2,085 gallons per week and employee gas consumption was reduced by 296.5 gallons per week.

The survey prompted another one concerning why students attended CSCC. The top six reasons, in rank order, were: proximity (close to home); course offerings; affordability; academic reputation; parental influence; and the athletic program. The college marketing strategy cited low tuition, quality instruction, modern equipment and the personal atmosphere (caring faculty, and strong tutoring and counseling services) as the major benefits of a community college.

A major emphasis for the year was improving campus facilities for the disabled. A grant of $75,000 enabled the college to construct wheelchair ramps from the Humanities Building to the Student Center and from the Administration Building to the Library, the Student Center and the Science Building. In addition wheelchair stalls were constructed in restrooms, and lower water fountains were installed in campus buildings. In other initiatives college employees attended a workshop to enable them to work more effectively with deaf students; a one-year certificate program was implemented to train interpreters for the deaf; and fifty students were enrolled in the first Basic Sign Language class.

In its efforts to meet the needs of area students, the college continued to teach classes in off-campus sites in Athens, Dayton, Chattanooga, Copperhill, Crossville and Etowah. Twenty-eight classes were offered in these locations in the fall, and numerous other courses were offered in plants and industries. On campus, the media center, which was housed beneath the main floor of the library, assisted instruction by the videotaping of classes, dramas, musicals, sporting events, dancing classes, visiting lecturers and other community events. Students viewed tapes of classes they had missed and they were able to witness their strengths and weaknesses in Speech classes. In addition computer terminals, connected with the computer center, were installed in the learning skills center of the library to enable both students and instructors to enhance the learning process.

In student news the EIL recipient was Clare Boland. She was unable to travel however, and alternate Carla Stalvey was her replacement. During the summer Stalvey traveled to the Netherlands and spent four weeks with a family in the city of Heerenveen. Tracey Walker, an All-State and All-Region basketball player, was crowned the Homecoming Queen, and the following students received CSCC music scholarships: Julie Roberts, piano; Robbi Presswood, piano; Clare Boland, voice; Charles Mason, voice; Linda Harris, voice; Jann Warren, voice; Melanie Harris, voice; Yvette Holmes, voice; and Brenda Goodwill, voice. In other music-related news, Vicky Stewart Edging, one of Tom Boles' music students, wrote a piano method for pre-school children that later became a publication. Joe Taylor, a former CSCC student, joined with his wife in launching a career as a gospel singer. Taylor was a former member of the "Regeneration" touring group and a former choir director of a Knox County Baptist Church. Three other former CSCC music students were: Ron Galloway, a

McMinn County High School teacher and music Director at Antioch Baptist Church; Pam Wright, a graduate of Tennessee Wesleyan and a piano teacher in Athens; and Charles Layne, a music and business major at Belmont College.

Jerry Sadler, the President of the SGA, and students Annette Horne (Vice-President of the SGA) and Sandy Mantooth, attended the Tennessee Intercollegiate State Legislature meetings in Nashville. The new staff members of The Cherokee Signal were: Rick Melvin, Editor; Rebecca Flanigan, News Editor; Ken Brown, Photo Editor; Rickey Hooper, Sports Editor; Kelley Brown, Student Activities Editor; Tammy Stewart, Business Manager; Phyllis Miller, Design Editor; Polly Fowler, Typesetter; and David Suttles, Faculty Advisor. The new cheerleaders were Carrie Brank, Teresa Norris, Michelle Hassen, Sherry Davis and Robin White. Instructor John Bradley (Speech and Drama) reported that alumnus Robin Whitehead was serving an internship as assistant manager of the Burt Reynolds Dinner Theater in Tallahassee, Florida, while also working on her Master's degree at Florida State. Another alumnus, Mary Lou Sorrells, received a Bachelor's degree from TN Tech and played Dulcinea, the female lead in the drama, "Man from La Mancha."

THE EIGHTIES

– 1980 –

The year's major international events were: six US diplomats, who had avoided capture at their embassy in Tehran, flew out of Iran with the help of Canadian diplomats; the US launched an unsuccessful attempt to rescue American hostages in Iran (eight American soldiers died when a helicopter collided with a transport plane); Israel's Knesset passed a law reaffirming all of Jerusalem as the capital of the Jewish state; former Soviet Premier Alexeii Kosygin died at the age of 76; and Queen Juliana of the Netherlands abdicated and was succeeded by her daughter, Beatrix.

The major domestic events were: Herman Tarnower, author of the Scarsdale Diet, was killed by his former lover Jean Harris (she was convicted of murder and served 12 years in prison); a Chicago jury found John Wayne Gacy, Jr. guilty of murdering 33 men and boys (he was executed in May, 1994); the Mount St. Helens volcano in Washington exploded, killing 57 people; at the request of President Carter, the US Olympic Committee voted to boycott the Moscow Olympics in protest of the Soviet invasion of Afghanistan; draft registration began in the US for 19 and 20-year old men; actor Steve McQueen died in Mexico at the age of 50; 87 people died in a fire at the MGM Grand Hotel in Las Vegas, Nevada; rock star John Lennon was shot to death outside his NY City apartment building by an apparently deranged fan; and Ronald Reagan was elected 40th President of the US.

By the 1980s computer acronyms such as "CPU," "ROM," "RAM," "Cursor" and "Diskette" were part of the vocabulary of many individuals. In popular culture "Ordinary People" won the Academy Award for best picture; Robert DeNiro received the Best Actor Award for "Raging Bull;" and Sissy Spacek received the Best Actress Award for "Coal Miner's Daughter." The Emmy Award for the best comedy was won by "Taxi," (ABC) and the best drama award was won by "Lou Grant" (CBS). The Grammy Award for the best record was presented to Christopher Cross for "Sailing," and the Grammy for the best album was Christopher Cross for "Christopher Cross." In athletics, at Lake Placid, New York, the US Winter Olympic hockey team upset the heavily favored Soviet team 4-3. The US team also won the gold medal. The University of Las Vegas won the NCAA Division I Basketball Championship; the Pittsburgh Steelers defeated the Los Angeles Rams in the Super Bowl; and Philadelphia defeated Kansas City in the World Series.

Although the college's fall quarter headcount enrollment was large (4,565 students), 1980 was a year of budget cuts. Governor Lamar Alexander announced that approximately $11.3 million must be cut from Tennessee college budgets. This measure reduced the CSCC budget by $234,000. The college decided to discontinue tennis and golf (after the 1980 spring season), increase class size (CSCC's average class size of 20 was the smallest in the state), reduce the travel budgets for faculty and staff and reduce the equipment budget. Statewide, college tuition was increased by 13.5%. An Institutional Self-study, completed in 1983, indicated that revenues for 1980 were $4,608,197.85 and expenditures were $4,525,614.75. The 1980 average salaries were $16,147 for the 88 full-time faculty, $28,816 for the seven executive/administrative personnel and $7,864 for the 50 clerical/secretarial personnel.

Fortunately, students had a plethora of financial aid programs available to them. The major ones were: Middle Income Assistance Act; CSCC Foundation Scholarship Endowment Fund; Basic Educational Opportunity Grant (BEOG); Supplemental Education Opportunity Grant (SEOG); Tennessee Student Assistance Award; National Direct Student Loan (NDSL); Guaranteed Federally Insured Student Loan; CSCC Work-Study Program; Law Enforcement Education Program (LEEP); Nursing Student Loan Program and Nursing Scholarships; G-I Bill; War Orphan Program; Vocational Rehabilitation Program; Social Security Educational Benefits Program; and the State Board of Regents Scholarship Program.

An innovation for the year was the creation of a college Alumni Association. Dr. Lane appointed a six-member steering committee to formulate objectives for the organization. Those appointed were Wes Martz, David Henry, Walter Presswood, Millie Sue Millican, Grant Cobb and Linda Kennet. Those who volunteered to recruit members were: Jenny Burchfield and Pat Sylvester of Chattanooga, Wes Martz of Knoxville and Betsy Lawson (who also agreed to contact alumni in the Athens area). Dr. Lane, the keynote speaker, announced that the purpose of the association would be to provide support (moral and financial) to the college, to provide fellowship opportunities for alumni and to maintain contact and interest in the college. Among those attending the inaugural meeting, in addition to those named above, were Mitzi Hooper, Janice Matthews, Sherry Estes, Judy Henry, Mike Bagwell, Sheila Presswood, Carolyn McDole, Dr. D. F. Adkisson, Jim Cigliano, Roy Lillard, Dr. George Mathis, Peggy Lowe, Sue Little, Frank Lawson, David Suttles, Ernie De Shield and Dr. David Watts. The Association introduced a new publication titled, "Update." Five hundred issues of it were mailed to alumni, schools, organizations, government offices, donors and others throughout the college's service area. Its purpose was to acquaint Southeast Tennesseans with the college's programs and activities.

The tradition of early America's town meetings was revived by the college in February, March and April. Area citizens were invited to participate in a series of forums with the theme of "Energy and the Way We Live." The college was one of

450 community colleges in the nation holding the forums to examine the nation's energy crisis. The coordinator of the program was the college Physics and Astronomy instructor, Buford Guy. The series was partially funded by the American Association of Community and Junior Colleges, the National Endowment for the Humanities and the Department of Energy. Several local officials also participated in the program. Among these were: Fran Day, Managing Director of the Associated Industries (CAI) of the Cleveland/Bradley County area; Joe Beavers, General Manager of Cleveland Utilities; Craig Bivens, the Cleveland City Planner; and Nelom Jackson, President of the local Chamber of Commerce.

Several local organizations also helped sponsor the forums. These were: Bradley/ Cleveland Community Services Agency; Cleveland Associated Industries (CAI); Cleveland Board of Realtors; Cleveland Daily Banner; Cleveland Public Library; Cleveland Rotary Club; Cleveland Sertoma Club; Cleveland Utilities; Cleveland Woman's Club; Cleveland Community Development; the Magnolia Garden Club; and Radio Stations WBAC and WCLE/WQLS. The CSCC Faculty and Staff Committee members were Diana Bach, Dr. Mary Barker, Adeline Baskett, John Bradley, Ray Coleman, Dr. Spencer Culbreth, Mike Dorsett, Buford Guy, Al Fine, Renate Hufft, Dr. Quentin Lane, Dr. Galen McBride, Dr. Matt Reiser, Dr. Irene Millsaps, Sam Neas, Walter Presswood, Dr. Jerome Taylor, Dr. Arun Venkatachar and Dale Yates.

The first forum had approximately 200 attendees, and it was held in the college auditorium on February 20, 1980. Tom Rowland, News and Program Director of WCLE (AM) and WQLS (FM) radio, was the moderator. The panelists were: Dr. William H. Peterson, Director of the Center for Economic Education at UTC; Dr. John Partridge, former president of the World Energy Conference; Dr. Ernest G. Silver, Assistant Director of Advanced Planning for the National Nuclear Standards Management Center; Dr. Robert Lundy, Pastor of Cleveland's Broad Street Methodist Church; and Dr. David Alaniz, Director of External Information, the US Department of Energy. The second forum, in March 1980, featured a videotaped lecture by noted author and physicist, Dr. Albert Bartlett. It was followed by a panel discussion composed of several of the faculty/staff forum committee (listed above) as well as the following: Patsy Bettis, Magnolia Garden Club; Joe Cate, Cleveland Community Development Office; Grant Cobb, Cleveland Board of Realtors; Tom Wheeler, Cleveland Utilities; Mrs. Leonard Hamm, Cleveland Women's Club; Joe Guest, Math Faculty; and Edwin Rowlee, Chemistry Faculty. The first two forums dealt with problems created by the world's dwindling energy resources, world population growth, alternate fuels such as hydrogen and alcohol and recycling issues.

The third and final forum, held in April, dealt with local energy issues and was led by six panelists. They were: Tish B. Jenkins, Nuclear Engineer and District Administrator of TVA; Fran Day, Managing Director of CAI; Wesley Johnson, Executive Director of the Tennessee Energy Authority; Joe Beavers, Manager of Cleveland Utilities; Craig

Bivens, Cleveland City Planner; and Nelom B. Jackson, Executive VP of the Cleveland/ Bradley Chamber of Commerce. The discussion centered on local energy needs and the effects of energy planning, growth and development. Other topics were the impact of oil and gas prices on the local economy, the growing use of nuclear energy, the impact of local population growth on the infrastructure and how increasing energy costs affected local families and workers.

Numerous college activities occurred in the winter and spring of 1980. In January, travel opportunities were planned for students, and in some instances, for the community as well. Renate Hufft coordinated trips to Germany; Efrain Guillen organized trips to Mexico; and Ann Morelock coordinated the EIL program. The EIL scholars in 1980 were Robbi Presswood and Cindy Anderson. Presswood traveled to Denmark and Anderson to Switzerland. In February the musical group, Regeneration, appeared at the college auditorium. In April the Kiwanis Club conducted their customary musical comedy in the Coleman Community Services Auditorium. In a campus event Walter Presswood made a series of speeches about his recent journey to India. His trip was part of an exchange program sponsored by Rotary International. He also visited Bangkok, Honolulu and Hong Kong during his eight-week excursion. Six of the eight weeks were spent in India. One of the highlights of his sojourn to India was attending a speech by the Nobel Peace Prize recipient, Mother Teresa. Shortly after his return, he announced that he did not want to eat peas or cheese casseroles for at least two years.

An interesting cultural event was a musical recital presented by Dr. Mary Barker and Fred Wood. Barker, the Head of the Arts and Sciences Division, attended the New England Conservatory of Music where she earned a Bachelor's degree. She also completed a Master's and a Doctorate in English. Wood earned a Bachelor's and Master's degree in English and studied music at the Cadek Conservatory in Chattanooga. Barker, accompanied by Wood on the piano, sang a variety of classical songs in German, Italian and English. Among others, she performed works by Brahms, Mozart, Puccini, Massenet and Niles. Wood performed piano solos by Ibert, Kabalevsky and Debussy. The purpose of the program was to express appreciation to college President Dr. Lane, Business Manager Jim Morris, the Cleveland Kiwanis Club and the Cleveland Jaycees for the purchase of a Steinway Model L 6-foot grand piano for the college.

The college's annual High School Bowl Quiz was conducted in April and the winning team was Cleveland High School. Baylor was second, Ootlewah third and Bradley fourth. A winner's trophy was presented by Reverend and Mrs. Glenn Moore in memory of their son, Tim. Tim, a CSCC student and the President of Phi Theta Kappa, died in March, 1980. His Mom, Verna Moore, was a Secretary in Student Personnel Services. A Memorial Scholarship was started and spearheaded by David Paul Wagner, a family friend and former CSCC student. On campus, David Wilbanks, the Printshop Supervisor, led the campaign among college employees. Other committee members were Jean Salter, Wanda Cartwright, Kay Graham, Dot Cantrell, Mitzi Hooper, Bill

Clark, Norma Davis and Walter Presswood. The requisite scholarship funds were raised by May 1981.

The college's Bowl Quiz team won third place in the two-day Berry College competition for Junior Colleges. The team won seven rounds and lost four. The winning team was Calhoun State Junior College with a 10-1 record. Calhoun's only loss was to CSCC. The team members, coached by David Suttles, were Jerry Sadler, Dennis Grape, Kelley Brown, Sandy Mantooth, Rachel Green, Tammy Stewart, Becky Flanigan, Melinda Hillman and Mike Bagwell. Bagwell won a scholarship to Berry College as a result of his outstanding performance at the bowl.

Meanwhile, two other musical performances were featured at the college. Three performances of the musical play, "Brigadoon," were performed in the spring of 1980. The play was directed by Tom Boles and John Bradley, and Kellye Hicks provided the choreography. The cast included Greg Jones, Jeff Carroll, Katherine Patterson, Robbi Presswood, Rhonda Richmond, David Orr, Jerry Sadler, Dennis Grape, Tim Hooker, Barry Kidwell, Susie Breton, Kenneth Phillips and Mark Raulston. Another concert was directed by Tom Boles, with accompanist Ray Calfee. Special performances were by Ann Waldrop, Kathy Davis and Brenda Goodwill. A highlight of the concert was a rendition of "What Price Freedom" featuring Brenda Goodwill, Carole Veal, Frank McMeen, Greg Jones, Katherine Patterson, Cindy Harris, Rhonda Richmond and David Orr.

Another feature during the year was a nine-part seminar series titled, "Our Cultural Heritage: The Reality of the Past in Contemporary Society." Coordinated by Dr. Mary Barker, the program discussion leaders were: Dr. Duane King, Director of the Museum for the Cherokee Indian in Cherokee, North Carolina; Gary Lawson, Head Ranger of Red Clay State Park; Wilma Dykeman, author of Tennessee: A Bicentennial History; Katharine Trewhitt, retired CSCC English instructor; Roy G. Lillard, retired CSCC History instructor; various representatives from the colleges of Lee, Tennessee Wesleyan, Southern Missionary and Tomlinson; the Dayton Theatrical Group directed by Cal Zethmayr; and designated representatives from Copper Basin and Mayfield Dairy. Topics that were discussed were the contributions of the Cherokee Indians, folk traditions in Southeast Tennessee and Bradley County, the Civil War (as revealed through diaries, letters and journals), the cultural and educational contributions of area colleges, local architecture and businesses and industries established by local families.

By 1980 the Youth Enrichment Program was operational. Created by Dr. Jackie Wattenbarger of Cleveland City Schools, the program was designed for young students (mostly from the ages of 8 to 14) who desired educational activities not usually included in the regular school curricula. The administrator of the program was Carolyn McDole, the Coordinator of CSCC's Community Services and Continuing Education Office. Originally, the courses were taught on Fridays from 10 am until noon. Later, the program was expanded to other school systems, and classes were taught on Saturdays and/or during the summer months. The courses were taught by CSCC faculty members and included subjects such as "So You Want to Learn to Fly," "35 mm Photography," "Introduction to Computers," "Heroes and Villains in History," "Introduction to French," "Electronics and Radio," and "Your Body: The Magnificent Machine." A few of the first instructors were Eric Reiser, Jerry Berman, Dr. Spencer Culbreth, Renate Hufft, Warren Plemmons and Larry Speight.

In other news Dale Jones, R. N., resigned as the college nurse to become a supervisor at Cherokee Park Hospital. She was succeeded by a CSCC graduate, Debra Mooneyham, R.N. Mooneyham was employed at Bradley Memorial Hospital and attended UTC and UTK. Dr. David Watts was appointed Associate Dean of Academic Affairs. Watts was an Associate Professor of Biology at the college and earned a Bachelor's degree from Tennessee Tech, a Master's from UTK and a Doctorate from Oklahoma State University.

By 1980 the college's General Education Development (GED) program was growing. During World War II hundreds of young men left for war without completing their high school education. The Army responded by instituting the GED program to assist veterans in furthering their education. Designed as an alternative to a high school diploma, graduates of the program could enter college, join the military, become eligible for a job, improve their chances of a promotion or achieve personal satisfaction. The college offered the GED Exam twice every month, and CSCC also offered a non-credit preparation course to assist anyone wanting help preparing for the exam. The course covered material related to writing skills, social studies, reading skills, science and math. Paul Boynton, the coordinator of the program, noted that in the early years the college averaged about 168 enrollees per year. In recent years the number increased to an average of about 1,000 per year. Approximately 60% passed the exam. Anyone over the age of 18 could take the exam, and if one failed it twice, there was a waiting period of six months before it could be taken again.

The year 1980 was a banner one for athletics at the college. Nationwide recognition was achieved by the baseball team when they finished second in the NJCAA Tournament in Grand Junction, Colorado. In route to the national finals, the team won the TJCAA State Tournament and the Eastern District Tournament. At one point the Cougars won 22 straight games and finished the regular season with a 29-4 record. After the District Championship, the team's record was 36-5. The team members were Wes Ivey, Roger Crawford, Willie Williams, Steve Simmons, Jeff Davis, Tim Hatfield, Gary Rominger, Mike Jordan, Jeff Campbell, Keith Sloan, Bill Butler, Rick Saunders, Dale Scott, Greg Geren, Bob Oliver, Gene Wade, Mike Connelly, Tobin Davidson, Ted Carson, Mike Whaley, Stuart Jump, Curtis Shaw, Chris Corbin and Mark Cowart. The team manager, Mark Smith, later became President of the Cougar Club and a strong supporter of the CSCC athletic program.

The Eastern District Championship, held at CSCC, was especially exciting. In the double elimination tournament, the Cougars defeated Spartanburg Junior College 3-0 and lost to Louisburg 3-7. One more defeat and the Cougars would be eliminated. They rallied to the occasion by defeating Spartanburg again (6-4 in 10 innings) and by defeating Louisburg twice, 8-1 and 5-2. CSCC played three games in one day and Tobin Davidson pitched 13 innings on that day. Unfortunately, ace pitcher Ted Carson injured his throwing arm while "high-fiving" a teammate and was unable to pitch during the national tournament. In spite of this handicap, the Cougars finished 2nd out of eight teams that competed in Colorado. Play was made difficult for all of the competitors by nighttime temperatures of 26 degrees in the Rocky Mountain atmosphere. Billy Butler was named to the All-American team and Greg Geren set a NJCAA Tournament record with 17 RBIs. Geren was named the Most Valuable Player of the tournament and Butler, Geren, Wes Ivey and Keith Sloan were named to the All-Tournament team. Coach Steve Longley was named Region VII Coach of the Year for the second time in his CSCC career. He was one of only 15 coaches in the nation to receive this honor.

An unexpected development was the amazing record of the new Lady Cougar softball team. Coached by Bob Taylor, the rookie team won the Region VII NJCAA championship with a season record of 30-6. The team members were Carrie Brank, Rose McCallie, Deidra Bates, Jan Wilson, Jo Crowder, Jill Ross, Lisa Hawpe, Neasy Barrett, Connie Parker, Anita Myers, Vicki Leonard, Marseta Elkins, Vicki Gobble, Debbie Millsaps and Norma Mangrum. Paul Underwood, a college maintenance department employee, was the team's bus driver and a loyal fan.

Equally impressive was the college golf team. Coached by Dr. L. E. Wooten, the team captured the 13th spot in the nation in junior college golf. It was the first time a golf team from the region made the cut in the NJCAA golf tournament. The team members were Al Miller, Jay Goza, Mike Johnson, Stan Sherlin, Jeff Ballantine, Darrell Beaton and Bobby Rice. The team recorded a 24-5 record and won both the State and Region VII championship.

The Lady Cougar basketball team, coached by Hugh Walker, also excelled in 1980. Standouts were Melinda Shell, Anita Myers, Teresa Millsaps, Cindy McMahon and Neasy Barrett. The other team members were Pam Arnwine, Renee Grizzle, Deidra Bates, Jo Cowden, Faye Hughes, Lisa Partain, Jill Ross, Kim Hampton, Rose McCallie and team manager, Nancy Gorghis. The team won the state championship and the Eastern Division TJCAA title. Shell was chosen as an NJCAA All-American. She was the 4th Lady Cougar basketball player in the college's history to achieve this status. The tennis team, coached by Dr. Spencer Culbreth, also had a successful season with a record of 11-2. The team members were Jim Srite, Sean Glaser, Rohn Poe, Jeff Hoge, Kevin Rogers, Ray Rose, Gerald Martin, Tim Henderson and Joe Whitson. The men's basketball team ended the season with a 4-20 record. Coached by Charles Cogdill, the team members were Tobin Davidson, Jimmy Webb, Mike Styles, Keith Hutchinson,

Andy Ervin, Stan Sherlin, John Hill, Keith Cartwright, Eric Lane, Broderick Owens, Jimmy Hicks, Hal Landrith and team manager, Mike Callahan. Although not an athletic contest, by 1980 the Spring Fling had become an annual event to relieve the pressure of preparing for the upcoming final exam period. So-called "krazy kontests" were held such as a water balloon toss, a back-to-back banana eating contest, a nerf ball between the legs contest, a nose-pushing peanut contest, a nerf ball chin pass relay race and a slam dunk contest.

Other students were also excelling in 1980. Connie Ogle, Clarence Partin, Sally Finnell, Rita Holt and Harold Hutsell won a $200 award for the college for submitting the "Most Outstanding Entry for Community Colleges" at the Students in Free Enterprise (SIFE) competition in Knoxville. Dr. Frank McKenzie was the advisor for the group. Ray Brewer, Millie Sue Millican, Sally Finnell and Gail Cunningham, accompanied by faculty advisor, Sherra Reynolds, attended the Phi Beta Lambda State Conference in Gatlinburg. Cunningham won 1st Place in the Accounting I competition and Brewer received 3rd Place in the Economics competition. Two new banking courses were also offered during the fall. Through the combined efforts of Dr. McKenzie and Georgia Gann, a 1973 graduate of CSCC, the courses received the approval of the American Institute of Banking. Gann was an Assistant Vice President, Branch Manager and Loan Officer of the Walker Valley Branch of the Cleveland Bank and Trust Company.

Five students represented the college in Nashville at an event with the lengthy title of the "2nd Annual Tennessee Society for Medical Technology's Medical Laboratory Technician Student Bowl." The students were Judy Howell, Teresa Sluder, Tamara Hateley, Vicki Knopp and Linda Riemenschneider, and the team coach was Assistant Professor, Bob Stewart. Tommy Ensley, a Medical Technician at Bradley County Memorial Hospital, was an assistant coach and overall coordinator of the Lab. The Head of the Allied Health Department was Dr. Joe Semak. Meanwhile, the Dental Lab Technology Program was accorded full accreditation by the American Dental Association. It was the only fully accredited program in the state, and of the 58 dental lab programs in the nation, it was one of only 34 that was fully accredited.

Other students receiving recognition were those listed in the National Dean's List publication. Available in 1980, the 1978-79 edition honored over 37,000 outstanding students from 1,200 nationwide colleges and universities. Those listed from CSCC were Milteen Cartwright, Mitzi D. Jones, Susan Loggins, Jewell E. Wilson, Teresa K. Millsaps, Janice F. Waldrop and Cynthia L. McMahan. By 1980 the Student Hosts' program was fully operational. The students served as ushers for college events, informational guides for campus visitors and ambassadors for the college. Those serving for 1980-81 were Jennifer Dixon, Jeff Johnson, Paula McDole, Donna Hooker, Linda Pickler, Scott Shafer, Katie Bagwell, Don Littrell, Sarah Moore, Brad Benton, Ron Boyd and Rhonda Knight. In the discipline of photography, instructor Jerry Berman noted that he had many outstanding students, but one of the most talented was Sue Summers.

Appointments and elections of other students in 1980 were: Pamela J. Arnwine, a basketball player, was crowned Homecoming Queen during halftime of the homecoming game; Sherry Davis and Jerry Sadler were named Miss and Mr. Cleveland State; and the President of the SGA was Sandy Mantooth. The spring staff members of The Cherokee Signal were: Rebecca Flanigan, Editor; Kelley Brown, News Editor; Rickey Hooper, Sports Editor; Bill McConnell, Photo Editor; Tammy Stewart, Business Manager; Michael Bagwell, Features Consultant; Polly Fowler, Typesetter; and David Suttles, Faculty Advisor. In November, the new staff members were: Stevie McVie, Editor; Karyn Daugherty, News Editor, Denny England, Sports Editor; Melinda Hillman, Photo Editor; Debbie Hamilton, Business Manager; Polly Fowler, Typesetter; and David Suttles, Faculty Advisor.

The commencement address, in June of 1980, was delivered by the former President of the college, Dr. David F. Adkisson. The Faculty Merit Award was presented to Dr. Hugh Vroman (Biology), and the Outstanding Student Award was awarded to Mike Bagwell.

Fall registration was so successful that the college ranked first in credit headcount enrollment among state community colleges. The Foundation awarded a record of 52 full scholarships. Unfortunately, dramatic cuts in statewide funding for colleges continued because state revenues did not meet income projections. About 45% of the impoundment at the state level came from public higher education colleges and universities. Dr. Lane believed the impoundment was unfair because it should have been proportionate for all state agencies.

A major issue in the fall was a mandated State Board of Regents study of the college courses that qualified as either upper division or lower division. An upper division classification meant the course was designed for the junior or senior year of college. The lower division level equated with freshman or sophomore level courses. The universities claimed that community colleges were offering too many courses from the upper division level. Upper level courses received greater funding than lower level ones, and courses taken at the lower level were not duplicated by students at the upper level (which could adversely affect the jobs of faculty and others at the upper level). CSCC, for example, offered method courses for local teachers for recertification purposes. The universities claimed these were actually upper level courses. CSCC argued that if these courses were disallowed at the community college level, it would force teachers to travel greater distances, at greater expense, to take courses. They would need to travel to colleges such as UTC and/or UTK for their recertification courses. The universities had the upper hand in the dispute because they had been in existence longer than community colleges, and they had previously designated courses as either upper or lower level. The community colleges were required to peruse their curricula and classify each course as either transfer, terminal (career) or other. As a result, community colleges were required to change several of their course designations and CSCC lost about 20 courses in the process.

Several staff and faculty members were in the news in the fall of 1980. Dr. Frank McKenzie, Head of the Business Careers Department, and Georgia Lowrance, Instructor of Data Processing Technology, co-authored a journal article titled, "Data Processing for Managers." It appeared in the July 1980 issue of the Journal of Data Processing. In other news Dr. Lane was selected as the President of the Cleveland/Bradley Chamber of Commerce; John Bradley was named Communications Director for the Tennessee Theater Association for 1980-81; and Wanda Cartwright became the new bookstore manager (following the retirement of Loren Boehm).

An important event in the fall of 1980 was the request by Governor Lamar Alexander that the State Board of Regents compile a report on all state college athletic programs. Jim Cigliano, the college's Dean of Student Personnel Services, was appointed to the committee. Other members were: C. Scott Mayfield, Chair and member of the SBR; Kenneth P. Ezell, SBR member; Johnella H. Martin, SBR member; Sam H. Ingram, President of MTSU; Harold S. Pryor, President of Columbia State Community College; and John D. Miller, Director of Athletics at Austin Peay State University. The committee's major task was to examine college sports financing. In 1980 the six universities received $300,000 each year from the state, and the 10 community colleges received $60,000 each year. The committee was requested to research the amount of money spent and the revenue generated by the athletic programs. In addition the committee researched the number of athletes, their academic standing, the type of financial aid they received, the salary amounts of athletic personnel, the cost of recruiting, the use of athletic equipment and facilities and the average attendance at sports events.

Although the bulk of athletic contests occurred in the spring, the basketball teams started their seasons in the fall. The Lady Cougar basketball team was coached by Hugh Walker, and the team members were Avis Wilkerson, Gina Hall, Julie Baker, Jill Ross, Rose McCallie, Gean Ervin, English Cartwright, Robin Eldridge, Anita Myers, Avis Smith, Tammy Barrett, Julie Newman, Lisa Partain, Deidra Bates and Jo Cowden. The men's basketball team was coached by Charles Cogdill, and the team members were Keith Cartwright, Andy Ervin, John Hill, Eric Lane, Stan Sherlin, Jeff Brown, Frank Hubbard, Phillp Knight, Feeny Mabry, Gene McCroskey, David Risenhower, Rod Scott, Alex Watkins and Merle Williams. The cheerleaders were Paulina Albornoz (captain), Darlene Belk, Marisa Scoggins, Sharon Rogers, Amy Seymour, Dee Dee Stevens and Tip Hogue.

The college completed a student profile analysis in 1980 which revealed that the average ACT (American College Testing) of CSCC freshmen was 18.9 (the national average was 18.7). Fifty-five percent worked while attending college, 65% received financial aid and 44% planned to pursue a four-year degree. The average age of the students was 27.

Two former CSCC students were in the news. Lawana Taylor, an art graduate, decided to return to CSCC and enroll in the Nursing program. Meanwhile, she won second place in the traveling Tennessee Community College Art Competition, and Mick Gray, another art graduate, won the Teacher Merit Award in the same competition. Another award was captured by the college's Data Processing Team. Coached by Georgia Lowrance, they won first place over 18 other teams in a Chattanooga competition. Kim Carroll Teague demonstrated academic excellence with her score at the American Society of Clinical Pathologist Board of Registry national examination. Her score placed her in the top one percent in the nation of those taking the exam. Other academic standouts in 1980 were Dennis Grape (Criminal Justice), Peter Oliver (Accounting) and Lyda Oliver (Nursing).

An exceptional student was David Griffith. A paraplegic because of an auto accident, David was a full-time student with a family and a full-time job. He worked at the Polk County Ambulance service as a dispatcher. He drove to the campus from Copperhill and majored in Architecture. He said, "my instructors have been very helpful . . . I am very happy at Cleveland State. I would definitely encourage other handicapped students to enroll here."

Two other exceptional students were David and Pat Johnson. They were examples of the nationwide trend toward lifelong learning. David was a statistician at Bowater Southern Paper Corporation and Pat was a former kindergarten teacher's aide. They enrolled as part-time students at the college. Their two children, Mike and Myra, also attended CSCC. In addition, their daughter-in-law, Dianna, their son-in-law, Michael Sanson, and David's brother and wife, Ralph and Linda Johnson, also attended CSCC.

– 1981 –

International events in 1981 were: the 52 Americans held hostage by Iran for 444 days were released and arrived in the United States in January; Pope John Paul II was shot and seriously wounded in St. Peter's square by Turkish assailant Mehmet Ali Agca; Israeli military planes destroyed a nuclear power plant in Iraq (a facility that Israel claimed could produce nuclear weapons); Lady Diana Spencer married Charles, the Prince of Wales; Andrew Lloyd Webber's musical, "Cats," opened in London; the US spacecraft Voyager 2 photographed and gathered data about Saturn; Egyptian President Anwar Sadat was assassinated by extremists while reviewing a military parade; a nuclear-powered Soviet satellite plunged through the earth's atmosphere and scattered radio-active debris over parts of northern Canada; and Israel annexed the Golan Heights, which it had seized from Syria in 1967.

The major domestic events were: approximately two million New Yorkers were present for a ticker tape parade honoring the freed American hostages from Iran;

President Ronald Reagan was wounded in an assassination attempt by John W. Hinckley, Jr.; America's first operational space shuttle, the Columbia, successfully completed its test run with a landing at Edwards Air Force Base in California; the Senate confirmed the appointment of Sandra Day O'Connor as the first female Supreme Court Justice; Mark David Chapman was sentenced to 20 years to life in prison for murdering John Lennon; members of the Professional Air Traffic Controllers Organization went on strike and were eventually dismissed by President Reagan for defying a back-to-work order; singer Harry Chapin was killed in a car accident in New York; the rock music video channel MTV made its debut; and actress Natalie Wood drowned in a boating accident in California.

In popular culture "Chariots of Fire" won the Academy Award for best picture. Henry Fonda, for "On Golden Pond," won the best actor award, and Katharine Hepburn, for "On Golden Pond," won the best actress award. "Taxi" (ABC) won the Emmy Award for best comedy, and "Hill Street Blues" (NBC) won the Emmy for best drama. Kim Carnes, for "Bette Davis Eyes," won the Grammy award for best record, and John Lennon and Yoko Ono, for "Double Fantasy," won the Grammy for best album. In sports Indiana won the NCAA Division I Basketball Championship; the Oakland Raiders won the Super Bowl; and the Los Angeles Dodgers won the World Series.

In college news the 1981 fall quarter headcount enrollment was 3,757, and the Foundation, with assets of $364,241.59, celebrated its 10th anniversary. The Foundation officers for 1981 were: Dr. D. F. Adkisson, President; Dr. George Mathis, Secretary; Eugene Callaway, Vice-President; Dr. L. Quentin Lane, Member-at-Large; Henry Barkley, Treasurer; and W. K. Fillauer, Member-at-Large. The charter trustees with ten years of service were recognized at a tenth anniversary dinner at the college on October 19, 1981. They were: Dr. Adkisson, Dr. Mathis, Callaway, Barkley, Fillauer, Pearson Mayfield, Clarke Stamper, Dr. Wayne McCulley, Roy Lillard, George Castings, Harold Allmond, State Senator Ben Longley, Jack Hoskins, Cletus Benton, Pledger Wattenbarger, Will McReynolds, Bill Thomason and George Thorogood. Dr. Lane and Dr. Adkisson thanked the trustees for their support of the college, and Dr. Adkisson praised Dr. Mathis for his role in organizing the Foundation in 1971 and for the countless number of students he assisted with his own money. The trustees also paid homage to the late Frank Manly for his role in having the college located in Cleveland. A state resolution honoring Manly was presented by State Senator Longley, and Trustee W. K. Fillauer presented a memorial award to Manly's wife, Elizabeth, and daughter, Jeanette Schlaeger. Trustees reappointed to three-year terms were: Henry Barkley, Cletus Benton, Arch Fitzgerald, W. K. Fillauer, Dr. Wayne McCulley, Will McReynolds, Kenneth Rayborn, Walt Robinson, Henry F. Smith, Clarke Stamper, George R. Taylor, Bill Thomason and Lynn Turpin. Terry McGuire was appointed to a new three-year term, and those appointed to one-year terms were: Mark Gibson, Lou Patten and Ruth Hynes.

In other news events the college's employees exceeded their United Way fund goal of $500,000 by raising $5,227.68. Officers for the newly established alumni organization were: Jenny Burchfield, President; Linda Kennett, Vice-President; Millie Sue Millican, Secretary; Pat Sylvester, Treasurer; and Georgia Gann, Member-at-Large. Others attending the spring meeting were Sue Little, Paul Cagle, Sandy Mantooth, Peggy Lowe, Katie Bagwell, John Stanberry, Sherry Davis, Walter Presswood and Dr. George L. Mathis.

The Alumni Association decided that their first project would be to raise $5,000 to establish a John Smeltzer Memorial Scholarship. The association's publication, "Update," was successful in tracking a few alumni. Judy Sullivan Holliday ('74), R.N., was a supervisor at East Ridge Hospital; Billy E. Jacks ('78), R. N., was a therapist with Humana Corporation; Jenny Burchfield ('76), R. N., Shirley Bourn Roberson ('78), R. N., Carolyn Ross ('79), R.N., Connie McConnell ('79), R. N., Lisa McDaniel Atchley ('79), R. N., and Juanita Maynard Griffith ('79), R. N., were all employed by East Ridge Hospital; Timmy Carson (who attended CSCC in 1973-74) was working as a body guard for the Charlie Daniels' band; Vicki Maxwell McIntosh ('77) was employed at Memorial Medical Center in Niagara Falls; J. Scott Perkinson ('77) was working and studying at the Marshall University School of Medicine; Susan Masingill Walker ('75) was an instructor of a medical program at a Knoxville Junior College; Nancy Smith Selvoy ('79) was employed at the Pathology Center of Omaha, Nebraska; and Dr. Aleene Hixson ('69) was a Cleveland, Tennessee, Optometrist.

A highlight of 1981 was the 75th anniversary of Phi Delta Kappa (PDK). The organization was a professional association for educators who excelled as leaders, thinkers and "doers" in the profession. Its vision was to cultivate great educators for tomorrow while continuing to ensure high-quality education for today. Founded in January 1906, it was united by the belief that "the public schools, colleges, and universities share in the conditions affecting all social institutions." Tennessee Governor Lamar Alexander conducted a ceremony honoring the organization on its Diamond Jubilee Celebration. Governor Alexander noted that PDK promoted "high quality education with particular emphasis on publically supported education as essential to the development and maintenance of a democratic way of life." Dr. L. Quentin Lane, the coordinator of the PDK chapters for the state, was present at the ceremony honoring the educational organization.

The college participated in numerous activities during the year. An elaborate musical production was presented by the joint choirs of CSCC and Broad Street United Methodist Church. They collaborated for a presentation of "Messe Solennelle" (Solemn Mass), by Charles Gounod, at the Cleveland church. Thomas R. Boles, the college's Associate Professor of Music, directed the 70-member voice choir. Joyce Higgins, Director of Music at the Broad Street Church, served as organist, and Ray Calfee served as pianist for the production. Soloists were Jeanne Sawyer, soprano, (Voice Instructor at CSCC and Broad Street Choir member), Don Brakebill, tenor (an instructor at Maryville College) and Charles Layne, bass (a CSCC graduate and student at Belmont College). Another musical was performed by the CSCC Choir featuring selections from a variety of Broadway Shows. It was directed by Tom Boles and John Bradley and accompanied by Ray Calfee. Highlights were a piano solo by Jeff Johnson, a dance by Robbi Presswood, and solos by Ann Waldrop, Kathy Davis, Brenda Goodwill, Tammie Roberts, Frank McMeen, John Bradley and Tom Boles. Waldrop, Davis and Goodwill also performed a trio selection.

In other college-related activities the play, "Man of La Mancha," was performed at the Knights of Columbus Hall. Connie Cox was the director, John Bradley played the lead role of Don Quixote, and Georgia Cigliano (the wife of Jim Cigliano and the first graduate of the college's Architecture Program) played the female lead of Aldonza. In another play at the same venue, Bradley played the lead role in the play, "Harvey." The Kiwanis Club performed their annual musical at the college auditorium and featured songs from the past 25 years. The college was also the location for the 1981 Tennessee Community College Art Competition. Guest speeches were made at the campus by Storyteller Sally Kell and State Senator Anna Belle Clement O'Brien. Kell addressed Katharine Trewhitt's Southern Mountain Heritage class, and O'Brien spoke at a chapter meeting of Phi Delta Kappa. In another event, a "Tennessee Mountain Music Night" was presented in the college auditorium by the Ootlewah High School Chorus under the direction of Michael Lees.

The college's 8th Annual High School Bowl Quiz occurred in April 1981. Twelve High School teams were contestants. They were Baylor, Bradley Central, Charleston, Cleveland, Copper Basin, McMinn County, Ootlewah, Polk County, Red Bank, Rhea County, Soddy-Daisy and Tellico Plains. Bradley Central, coached by Shirley McIntyre, won first place and CSCC scholarships were awarded to Tom Gibson (Cleveland), Janet Shadden (Ootlewah), Roger Sisson (Polk County) and Gordon Stanfield (Soddy-Daisy). Baylor placed second, Polk County third and Cleveland fourth.

The Nursing Program achieved another success in 1981. CSCC graduates ranked 2nd in the state on the State Board Examinations. They attained a 100% passage rate in four areas and a 97.5 average in one area of the five-part exam. The five exam sections included medical, psychology, obstetrics, surgical and nursing. The two-day exams, in accordance with standard annual procedure, were administered in all 50 states on the same day. Students were eligible for the exam after successful completion of the prescribed courses in the nursing program and after they received their Associate of Applied Science Degree. The state exam was the final requirement for becoming a licensed registered nurse. The administrators of the program in 1981 were Shelby Millsaps, Head of the Nursing Education Department, and Dr. Matt Reiser, Associate Dean for the Career Education Division. Pat Crews was the Sophomore Team Coordinator, and

Elizabeth Eiswerth was the Freshman Team Coordinator. Crews received her B. S. N. degree from the University of Alabama and her Master's from UTC. Eiswerth received her R.N. from St. Mary's School of Nursing in Rochester, New York, her Bachelor's from Western Kentucky University and her Master's from Vanderbilt University. Two other Nursing faculty members, Nancy Moore and Sheila Hales, received all of their degrees from the same schools. Their Nursing degrees were from the Georgia Baptist School of Nursing and their B. S. N. and M. S. N. degrees were from the Medical College of Georgia.

Meanwhile, the Medical Laboratory Technology Program received acclaim. A recent survey indicated that 77% of the program graduates, from 1975 through 1980, were working full-time, 19% were working part-time, and 4% were full-time students at other colleges. Of those who responded, 85% were satisfied with their career advancement. Dr. Joe Semak, Head of the Allied Health Department, noted that the survey revealed that CSCC graduates were working throughout Tennessee and as far away as Nebraska, New York and West Virginia.

Faculty and staff members were active in 1981. Dr. Jerome Taylor was elected President of the 1,000 member East Tennessee Historical Society. He also received the Marshall Wingfield Annual Award for the best article published in The West Tennessee Historical Society Journal. The article was titled, "Upper Class Violence in Nineteenth Century Tennessee." He also had an article published in the spring issue of the Tennessee Historical Quarterly. It was a review of James C. Dick's book, Violence and Oppression. Taylor joined the CSCC History Department in 1968. He received his Bachelor's and Master's degrees from UTK and his Doctorate from MTSU. Dr. Mary Barker, Chair of the Arts and Sciences Division, was one of 21 educators in the nation to participate in a foreign exchange program. Sponsored by the National Education Association's Office of International Relations, she spent three weeks with a family in Feldkirchen, Germany. Photography instructor, Jerry Berman, received the 3rd Place Bronze Award in the United Way of America's 25th National Communication Contest. It was a slide photo of three-year old Mandi Colloms, a poster girl for Cleveland United Way. Berman's slide was selected from more than 1,000 entries. Several years later, Colloms was a graduate of CSCC.

Other noteworthy developments were: Gayle Wood, a counselor, co-authored a book titled, Good News Among Black Youth; President Lane became the 39th President of the Cleveland/Bradley Chamber of Commerce; Dr. Charles Tollett was named the new Dean of Academic Affairs; Dr. Matt Reiser visited the Naval Air Technical Training Center in Memphis: Dr. Larry Longerbeam, Dr. David Watts, Ken Newton, Larry Speight and Alex Nichols attended the Tennessee Education Association's Department of Higher Education meeting in Nashville (Nichols was elected as the community college representative to the Department); Dr. Jerome Taylor and retired faculty emeritus, Roy Lillard, were named as "Colonel Aides de Camp" to Governor

Lamar Alexander's staff (both Taylor and Lillard also contributed articles to the newly issued East Tennesse Encyclopedia); Dr. Mary Barker and David Suttles participated in the 16th annual Southeast Conference for Teaching English in the Two-Year College in Biloxi, Mississippi (both presented lectures and Barker introduced the keynote speaker); Dr. Barker and Dr. Spencer Culbreth served on the evaluation team for the Southern Association of Colleges and Secondary Schools' evaluation of Tyner High School; Delmus Ledford (History Faculty), Dr. Jerome Taylor and Dr. Spencer Culbreth attended the Tennessee Conference of Historians' meeting at MTSU and the guest speaker was United States Senator George McGovern; Sue Rhodarmer (Psychology Faculty) attended the Family Therapy Seminar in Knoxville and the guest speaker was Virginia Satir, a renowned family therapist and author; Marcia Fair (Counselor), Coach Hugh Walker and Dr. Rodney Fitzgerald (Director of the Learning Skills Center) attended the Tennessee Professional Guidance convention in Nashville; Karen Gibson (Financial Aid), attended the Tennessee Association of Student Financial Aid Conference at Fairfield Glade; Paul Boynton attended the annual meeting of the GED in Nashville; the college nurse, Deborah Hannah, accepted another position and the college decided to discontinue employing a nurse; and the Tennessee Valley Authority (TVA) completed its 10th year of having an on-campus Basic Training Course for Public Safety Officers.

The college's Employee Newsletter occasionally wrote profile articles about college employees. Janice Lawrence was the subject of one of these. She was the Secretary for Dr. Frank McKenzie, the Head of the Department of Business Careers. Lawrence was also the lead soloist of a 22-member choir known as the "Hallelujah Chorus." She was also one of three evangelists with the group. Gayle Wood was the subject of another profile article. As noted above, she co-authored a book (Good News Among Black Youth) with her brother, Reverend Robert Wood. The book was a project of the Presbyterian Church and it provided principles and strategies for black youth evangelism. The authors planned to conduct workshops in Texas, California, Alabama and Pennsylvania.

Another profile was of Levi Brown, the college's maintenance electrician. Brown was from Smokey Row, near Reliance, Tennessee. He sang in a church choir and was a member of a singing group known as "The Old-Timers." Two of his children worked for the college. Jan, a 1979 CSCC graduate, worked as a Secretary in the Associate Dean of Academic Affairs Office. Joan, also a CSCC graduate, was a Secretary in the Nursing Department and later became the Director of Human Resources at the college. Dr. T. P. Mathai was featured in another Employee Newsletter profile. Mathai, a Chemistry Professor, was from Kerala, India. He received his Bachelor's and Master's degrees from Madras University, the oldest Jesuit institution in India. He taught at St. Joseph's College in India—a college operated by French missionaries. He received his Doctorate from St. Louis University in 1968 and arrived at CSCC that same year. His course specialty was Organic Chemistry—a course taken by students in Pre-Medicine, Pre-Dentistry, and Pre-Veterinary Medicine.

In November 1981 Colonel James M. Stubbs announced that he would be retiring in January 1982. During his ten years at the college, Stubbs had served as the Coordinator of the Criminal Justice and Legal Assistant Program and as the college's Personnel/ Affirmative Action Officer. He was from Lanier, Georgia and a graduate of Vanderbilt Law School. He was an Air Force Lawyer for ten years and achieved the rank of Lt. Colonel. The Employee Newsletter noted that among the notable graduates of the Criminal Justice Program were: Tom Kennedy, Chattanooga Police Chief; Arnold Botts, Cleveland Police Chief; and Sidney Matthews, Athens Police Chief. Other retirees in 1981 were Penny Overend (English Faculty) and James Passmore (Maintenance Supervisor).

The college lost a popular professor when John E. Cook died in August 1981. Cook, the successor of Colonel James Stubbs, had been the Coordinator of the Criminal Justice and Legal Assistant Programs since 1976. Cook was born in Columbia, South Carolina and received his jurisprudence degree from the University of South Carolina. He was wounded in action while serving in the United States Army in the Pacific Theater in World War II. He was a special agent for the Federal Bureau of Investigation (FBI) from 1949 until 1976. A Cook Scholarship Steering Committee was formed consisting of Dr. L. E. Wooten, Dr. Jerome Taylor, Ann McCoin (Professor and Lawyer Faculty member) and Dr. Spencer Culbreth. In addition, a large advisory committee was also formed to assist the Steering Committee. Its members were Colonel James Stubbs, the college's Personnel/Affirmative Action Officer; Pat Lennon, FBI agent in Cleveland; Walter Smart, Chattanooga Commissioner of Police and former FBI agent; Tom Kennedy, Chattanooga Chief of Police; Arnold Botts, Cleveland Chief of Police; Sidney Matthews, Athens Chief of Police; Robert Lawson, Bradley County Sheriff; H. Q. Evatt, Hamilton County Sheriff; Jim Rush, Director of the Buckner-Rush Funeral Home; Charles Reilly, retired FBI agent; Gene Roberts, Commissioner of Safety for Tennessee; Wally Still, retired FBI agent; Steve Cole, TBI agent; and Van Deacon, Assistant District Attorney. Their efforts achieved speedy results and a scholarship was created in Cook's name.

A humorous incident occurred in the spring when Dr. Lane visited the campus Community Relations Office. He had been invited to sample a coconut cake prepared by Verna Moore. There were two coffee pots in the office and no one noticed that Dr. Lane poured a cup from a pot that had been sitting for several days. The expression on his face, after taking a sip, made everyone aware that he had served himself from the wrong pot. He was invited back the next day to sample a fresh cup of coffee and homemade cake.

In college athletics the Lady Cougar Softball Team had another good year. Although they lost in the Region VII Tournament, they finished the season with an 18-3 record, and four sophomores, Lisa Partain, Jo Cowden, Deidra Bates and Jill Ross, were named to the All-Region Team. Other team members were Tammy Barrett, Kathy Maxwell, Lisa Hawpe, Lisa Partain, Marseata Elkins, Carrie Brank, Lisa Cross, Robin Eldridge and Gina Hall. The coach was Bob Taylor. Hugh Walker, the Lady Cougar basketball coach, was named Director of Region VII of the NJCAA. The region consisted of community colleges in Tennessee, Kentucky and Mississippi. Walker's coaching record at CSCC was 161-36 and his overall record was 318-111. His teams won four state championships, made two trips to the national tournament and produced four NJCAA All-Americans.

In other sports-related activities Ralph Underhill, Head Basketball Coach at Wright State University, was the guest speaker at the college's annual athletic banquet. Underhill had been an assistant coach under Ron Shumate at UTC, and two former CSCC players, Rodney Benson and Keith Miller, played on Underhill's team. Meanwhile, Baseball Coach Steve Longley resigned and returned to the classroom to teach Physical Education. His replacement, Wayne Norfleet, had been the coach at Tennessee Wesleyan for the last six years. Norfleet had a Bachelor's degree from Austin Peay State University and a Master's from Florida International University. Approximately 160 basketball players participated in a High School "Scrimmage Session" in October 1981. In November the college hosted the "Area High School Jamboree" and conducted the "CSCC High School Classic Invitational Tournament" in December. The college hosted numerous annual High School Basketball Tournaments for many years.

The year 1981 was another busy one for several students. Sandy Mantooth, the SGA President, was elected State President of the Student Teachers Education Association. In Knoxville, the Future Secretaries Association (FSA) of the college won first place honors (over 14 other Tennessee FSA chapters) in the scrapbook competition. Sponsors of the organization were Nancy Boyd and Sherra Reynolds. The award was presented to Barbara Brownfield, an Office Careers major, who won the college's annual award for the Outstanding Office Careers Student. Among those who worked on the scrapbook were Brownfield, Cathy Towe, Kim German, Kelly Price, Kim Keith, Sandi Green, Rebecca Nelson, Renelle Spagnoletti, Rose McCallie and Sherry Whitener. The scrapbook cover was made in walnut by Ron Howell who also hand-carved an FSA symbol on the cover.

Donna Reed, a student with the same name of a famous actress, was featured in a profile article in the Employee Newsletter. She was one of the first female students to major in Industrial Technology with a concentration in electricity/electronics. She also played both basketball and softball at CSCC. She planned to attend UTK and, after graduating, work in Chattanooga with the construction firm of Mabry and Associates.

Another profile was of Stephen Addison. Addison, a retiree, had been a textile engineer and a plant manager. He attended Georgia Tech and Army flight school. He served in World War II and was a navigator and navigation instructor. Addison enrolled in several special interest courses while at CSCC. He loved Civil War History and possessed a huge collection of artifacts in his private museum. He had authentic civil war caps, soldiers' diaries and letters and gorgets (a protective pendant for the throat worn by soldiers). Among his collection of Indian relics were spears, lances and beads. He also collected stamps and coins. He exemplified a national trend toward lifelong education.

Dennis Grape was featured in another profile. He was a "work study" student in the college print shop and he worked part-time with the Southeast Tennessee Legal Services. He completed his A. S. degree in Criminal Justice from CSCC in 1980. He also had an A. A. degree from Platte College in Geneva, Nebraska. Other jobs held by Grape were: a Deputy Sheriff in Platte County; a Chief of Police for Silver Creek, Nebraska; an Assistant Chief of Police for Newman Grove, Nebraska, and a law enforcement officer at Theodore Roosevelt National Park in North Dakota. He also performed in plays and toured with a choral group.

Associate Professor Jere Chumley's art students were also newsmakers. Tom Sain and Michael Valcarel won awards in the 1981 Tennessee Community College Art competition. Three graduates also made the news. First, Jeff DeLude had two paintings on exhibit at the Two Plane Feet Studio in Chicago. DeLude was recognized by a Houston Post art critic as one of Houston's outstanding young artists. Secondly, Steve Rucker exhibited works in clay in New York City. Rucker taught art at Loyola University in New Orleans and was featured in an international magazine, Ceramics Monthly. Thirdly, Belinda Elrod exhibited selections of her art at the college. A 1978 graduate, Elrod received her Bachelor's degree from MTSU and was an Art teacher in the Jackson City School system in Jackson, Tennessee.

Gail Cunningham placed second in the Data Processing II competition at the Phi Beta Lamba State (PBL) Leadership Conference in Nashville. She won first place in the 1980 Accounting I competition at the conference, served as the President of the CSCC chapter of PBL and was elected Vice-President of the state PBL Alumni Chapter. Gail Randolph also participated in the state competition. In addition to being a student, Randolph was also a real estate leaser/bookkeeper. Both students planned to become computer programmers after graduation from CSCC. The new officers of the Business Honorary Society, elected in 1981, were: Bud Goza, President; Mark Abernathy, Vice-President; Dee Dockery, Publicity Chair; Martha Calfee, Secretary-Treasurer; and the faculty sponsors were Bill Roberts and John Cantrell.

Another student, Hal Jernigan, was memorialized in a perpetual scholarship in his name. He had been a student at CSCC in 1973-74 and he died in an automobile accident in 1979. He graduated from UTK with a degree in Communications and was employed with a Knoxville radio station. He was active in dramatic and musical productions while at CSCC.

Several other students were newsmakers in 1981. In May Katie Bagwell became the new SGA President and Michael Presswood the new SGA Vice-President. The

<u>Cherokee Signal</u> staff included the following: Lawana Taylor, Editor; Angela Roper, News Editor and Chief Photographer; Denny England, Sports Editor; Debbie Hamilton, and later, Robin Hybarger, Business Managers; Polly Fowler, Typesetter; and David Suttles, Faculty Advisor. In May Denest England became the new Editor, Angela Roper the News and Sports Editor, and Cathy Holmes the Editorial Editor. The 1981 officers of the Black Student Association were: Michael Whaley, President; Carlos Drake, 1st Vice-President; Vanessa Sharp, 2nd Vice-President; Donna Davis, Secretary; Sylvester Harris, Treasurer; Curtis Drake, Parliamentarian; Ricky Cowan, Chaplain; and Gayle Wood, Sponsor.

In other news Sharon Farmer was the Homecoming Queen, and Beecher Hunter, Editor of the <u>Cleveland Daily Banner,</u> was the Commencement Speaker. The Faculty Merit Award was presented to Dr. L. E. Wooten, and the Outstanding Graduate Award was presented to Mitzi D. Jones.

– 1982 –

A major international news event, in April 1982, was the invasion of the Falkland Islands by Argentine troops. By June the British had retaken the islands. In other events: Israeli troops invaded Lebanon to eliminate the Palestinian Liberation Organization's threat to Israel's northern border; in August American, French and Italian troops arrived in Beirut as a peacekeeping force; In Italy, Italian forces rescued American Brigadier General James L. Dozier 42 days after he had been captured by the Red Brigades; Soviet leader Leonid Brezhnev died at age 75; Yuri Andropov was elected to succeed Brezhnev as General Secretary of the Soviet Communist Party's Central Committee; Princess Grace of Monaco, formerly actress Grace Kelly, died at the age of 52 of injuries from a car crash; and Academy Award winning actress Ingrid Bergman died in London on her 67th birthday.

Major national events were: Klaus von Bulow was found guilty of trying to kill his comatose wife with insulin (he was acquitted later in a retrial); groundbreaking ceremonies were held in Washington D. C. for the Vietnam Veterans Memorial; the World's Fair, in Knoxville, Tennessee, was opened by President Ronald Reagan; the trial of John Hinckley Jr., who had shot four people, including Resident Reagan, ended with Hinckley's acquittal by reason of insanity (Hinckley spent the next 34 years in a mental hospital); the Equal Rights Amendment, sent to the states in 1972, was defeated when the deadline for ratification passed with only 35 of the necessary number of 38 states supporting the amendment; comedian John Belushi died from a drug overdose at the age of 33; and actress Eleanor Powell died at the age of 69.

In popular culture "Gandhi" won the Academy Award for the best movie, and Ben Kingsley won the award for best actor in the same film. Meryl Streep won the award for best actress in the movie, "Sophie's Choice." The Emmy award for best television comedy was presented to ABC's "Barney Miller," and the best drama award was won by NBC's "Hill Street Blues." A first for television was the debut of the Weather Channel. The Grammy for record of the year was won by Toto for "Rosanna," and the Grammy for album of the year was presented to Toto for "Toto IV." In other news singer Michael Jackson's "Thriller" was released, and the situation comedy, "Family Ties," premiered on NBC. The first commercially produced compact discs appeared; a recording of ABBA's "The Visitors" was developed at a Philips factory near Hanover, West Germany; and Sony began selling the first commercial compact disc player, the CDP 101, in Japan.

In sports the highlights were: the National Football League's strike ended after 57 days when players and team owners reached a settlement; in an amazing finish, the University of California football team used five laterals to score a winning touchdown on the last play of a game against Stanford; the NCAA Division I Men's Basketball Championship was won by the University of North Carolina; the inaugural NCAA Division I Ladies' Basketball Championship was won by Louisiana Tech; the Super Bowl was a victory for the San Francisco 49ers over the Cincinnati Bengals; and the St. Louis Cardinals defeated the Milwaukee Brewers in the World Series.

An interesting study was completed in 1982 for the Tennessee Board of Regents. Researched and compiled by the Memphis State University Bureau of Business, the study indicated that Tennessee's sixteen state colleges and universities generated more than $1.5 billion in business volume within the state. As Chancellor Roy S. Nicks noted, "the institutions' contributions to the state economy far exceed the cost of their support." CSCC contributed over $36 million in business volume within the local economy during 1980-81. Over $20 million came from college expenditures and dollars spent by faculty, staff, students and college visitors.

The total student headcount for the fall quarter of 1982 was 4,229, and 88 students received scholarships from the Cleveland State Foundation. The Foundation officers for 1982 were: Dr. D. F. Adkisson, President; Eugene Callaway, Vice-President; Arch Fitzgerald, Treasurer; Dr. George Mathis, Secretary; W. K. Fillauer, Member-at-Large and Dr. L. Quentin Lane, Member-at-Large. Other members were Harold Almond, Representative Steve Bivens, Ron Braam, Charles Brown, George Castings Sr., Ronald Clough, Horace Coffey, Sam Colbert, Carl Cooke, J. F. Corn, Jr., Ben Crox, Mayor Harry Dethero, Bill Ewing, Wayne Feehrer, Fred Hayes, B. F. Hyde, Ruth Hynes, George Johnson, Summerfield Johnston Jr., Jim Jones, Howard Lay, Senator Ben Longley, Jack Mayfield, Steve Miller, Ben S. Moore, Bob Sain, Clarence Streetman, George Thorogood Sr., Leonard Thurman, Representative Clyde Webb and C. G. White. New members were George Calfee, Lucille Headrick, Wilson A. Ledford, Bill Lonas, Joe McGinty, C.W. Newton III, Jim Williams, Jim McClanahan and Martha Shugart.

On May 3, 1982 the late Frank Manly and Elizabeth Cate Manly were honored at a memorial tribute at the college auditorium. Jeanne Sawyer of Cleveland, a part-time music instructor at the college, presented a vocal recital as a gift to their memory. Sawyer studied at Cadek Observatory, Converse College and Southern Mississippi University. She had several students in her college voice classes and was an annual performer with the MacDowell Music Club of Chattanooga. Manly had been an insurance executive, a public school teacher and a Principal. As noted earlier, he played an instrumental role in the political quest for placing the college in Cleveland. He later served as a founding trustee and was the first secretary of the college's Foundation. His wife was a teacher in the city and county schools. She was also a life member of the Cleveland Music Club, and she taught piano for several years in Cleveland.

Meanwhile, nursing students continued to excel. The 1982 graduates had a 100% passage rate on the State Board Licensure Exam (all 46 students passed) and the 1981 graduates had a 97.5% passage rate. Shelby Millsaps, Head of the Nursing program, said, "We have a well-qualified staff with expertise in many fields, and we have highly motivated students." In addition the graduates of the 1982 Medical Laboratory Technology Program also achieved a 100% passage rate on the American Society of Clinical Pathologists' Board of Registry Exam (all ten students passed).

In other academic developments several new courses were added to the curriculum—Microcomputers, Electronics Fabrication, Computer-Assisted Inventory Management, Word Processing, Risk Management and a Child Development course via television. Several other courses were also offered by closed circuit television for the first time at the college. The Industrial Technology Program was altered to allow students to select an area of specialization in either aviation, commercial photography, industrial electronics, industrial maintenance, industrial management, industrial metals, or trade and industry. Certificate programs were also added in electronics, maintenance welding, management and photography and in a ten-week concentrated mini-secretarial program. The Office Education Association placed nationally in several competitive events, and the Future Secretaries Association won the International FSA Award for Outstanding Accomplishments and achieved 1st Place in the Tennessee FSA Division scrapbook category. Meanwhile one academic-related program was ended due to the lack of funding renewal. Known as the FACE II program, it was designed to provide a new beginning for women who suddenly entered, or re-entered the job market due to the death, divorce, separation or disability of a husband. FACE was an acronym for "Facilitate, Advocate, Counsel and Educate."

For several years the college participated in a course sponsored by the Foreign Policy Association known as "Great Decisions." The course was taught every winter quarter and it coincided with national radio and television programs on a series of issues related to foreign affairs. Generally, about 150,000 citizens throughout America participated in it each year. On campus, although the instructors varied, the usual leaders of the lecture/discussions were Delmus Ledford, Dale Yates, Judy Watts, Efrain Guillen, Harry Dean, Dr. Mary Barker, Dr. Jerome Taylor, Dr. L. E. Wooten and Dr. Spencer Culbreth.

An unusual event in 1982 was a donation of $3,500 to the college by an individual indicted for shoplifting (a few years earlier) in several Bradley County stores. The individual fled after being released from custody on bail. Arrested later for similar crimes in several states, the individual served a ninety-day jail term in Bradley County, performed public service in another state, paid restitution to the stores and began a new life. The donation was presented as a symbol of the individual's reformation.

Meanwhile several faculty and staff members were making news. Nancy Boyd, Sherra Witt and Dr. Frank McKenzie attended the Southern Business Association Convention in Nashville. McKenzie led a discussion group on the question of "Can we define computer literacy for the post-secondary level?" At the meeting Witt was elected to a term on the Tennessee Board of the Association. In other achievements Dr. L. E. Wooten was elected as a representative of the faculty to the State Board of Regents Faculty Sub-Council for 1983-84, and Jere Chumley was a judge for the 5th Annual High School Art Competition at UTK. Dr. Jerome Taylor was re-elected as President of the East Tennessee Historical Society and also served as President of the Bradley County Historical Society. The Legal Assistant Program, led by Coordinator Ann McCoin, received renewal of its accreditation, Dr. Mary Barker was named to a three-year term on the Board of Directors of the Tennessee Committee for the Humanities, and Herbert and Elizabeth Disney were recipients of the annual Cougar Club Award for their support of CSCC athletics.

A new employee, John Cassidy, was hired to run the Print shop. His wife was a former secretary for Colonel James Stubbs and their two children were students at CSCC. Joan Brown, secretary for Dr. Charles Tollett, and Evonne Drown, secretary to Dr. Matt Reiser, received their Certified Professional Secretary (CPS) designation. The CPS exam was given annually in May, in approximately 350 exam centers, by the Institute for Certifying Secretaries (which was a department of Professional Secretaries International). The two-day exam featured questions concerning business, economics, management, accounting, communications' applications, business law, office administration and technology.

Paul Boynton, Dr. George Mathis and Norma Davis were featured in Employee Newsletter profiles. Boynton became head of the GED Program in 1968. He said, "I could tell stories all day long about the success of GED graduates. And that is what has made my job so rewarding." Boynton was born in Panama, the son of missionary parents. He earned degrees from Colledgedale Academy, Andrews University and UTK. He taught eleven years at Southern Missionary College and in the Chattanooga Public School system. He and his wife spent seven years (1945-52) in Iran. He supervised educational systems in several Middle Eastern countries, and his wife taught at an elite elementary school in Iran.

As noted earlier, Dr. Mathis, the former Dean of Students, was instrumental in recruitment efforts during the formative years of the college, and he led the drive to establish a permanent scholarship endowment fund by the College Foundation. He was one of the original board members of the Hiwassee Mental Health Association, served on the Board of "HERMES" (an association to assist those with mental problems), was a member of the Title XX Human Services Region 3 Advisory Board, a trustee of Moccasin Bend Psychiatric Hospital, a member of Kiwanis, a member of the American Legion, a member of the Elks Club and a member of City Farmers. In addition he was Past President of the Brainerd Kiwanis Club and Lt. Governor of the Division III Kentucky-Tennessee District of Kiwanis. After retiring from the college, he was Director of Public Relations for the Johnston Coca-Cola Bottling Company for about six years. He and his wife, Irene, had two children.

Norma Davis, a popular campus personality, was one of the college's early employees. She worked in the Admissions Office and the Student Personnel Services Office. A former cheerleader, she advised the college cheerleaders for several years and was a frequent concession stand worker for ball games. Two of her daughters, Sherry and Jean Marie, graduated from CSCC, and Sherry was Miss Cleveland State of 1980.

A new part-time instructor for the Dental Lab Technology Program had a famous name--Roy Rogers. A former CSCC student, Rogers owned a local dental lab. While in military service in Colorado, he visited a dentist. After giving his name, the dentist said, "You're not going to believe this, but do you know who is in the next room? A guy named Marshall Dillon."

Two 1982 students had the same name--Juan Rodriguez. They were also brothers. They had a 14-year old brother also named Juan Rodriguez. Three Juans in one family could be confusing. Their mom, however, had nicknames for them and each had a different middle name. Born in Caracas, Venezuela, Juan Carlos, the oldest (24), attended Coe College in Cedar Rapids, Iowa, and later worked in a Florida advertising agency before coming to CSCC. His brother, Juan Andres (20), attended Tennessee Military Institute in Sweetwater and Tennessee Tech before arriving at CSCC. Juan Carlos redesigned the college logo and masthead for the Employee Newsletter. He also designed a Coca-Cola logo and a World's Fair logo for the Southeastern Travel Agency.

In March 1982 John Bradley began writing a column titled, "The Inside Scoop," for the Employee Newsletter. In his first article he made fun of himself playing in a college charity basketball game against the Harlem Wizards. He indicated that one of his faculty teammates made an unkind remark about his legs. John said, "I looked at his and told him that his legs didn't exactly match those of Bruce Jenner. 'Yeah,' he said, 'but yours don't even match each other.'" In another article he noted that a self-study was being prepared for the college's reaccreditation renewal. The subtitle of the report was, "Implications for Institutional Improvement." An acronym for it would be IFII (pronounced "Iffey"). Bradley was concerned about spending so much time on an "iffey" project.

In other news Linda Kennett Scott of Cleveland was elected President of the CSCC Alumni Association. A nurse, she was an employee of the Hospital Pharmacies Company at Bradley Memorial Hospital. Other officers were: David Marr, Vice-President; Georgia Gann, Secretary; Lynn Marr, Treasurer; and Dot Langford, Member-at-Large. Warnie Finnell's theatrical group, "The CSCC Youth Players," performed in the college auditorium and in the 2nd Annual East Tennessee School Band and Orchestra Association Solo and Ensemble Festival. Approximately 400 music students representing 23 schools participated in the event. The coordinator of the festival was Tom Boles and the director was Ron Peace, the Cleveland High School Band Director. In other musical events CSCC student Sayoko Murakawa presented a piano solo, and later, a concert was conducted featuring soloists Jeanne Sawyer, David Creel, George Lewis, Laura Cochran and Ann Moore. The concert was directed by Tom Boles and the accompanist was Ray Calfee. In another musical event John Cantrell's Fashion Merchandising students performed a dance routine at the Cleveland Mall. The participants were Betsy Mullinax, Beth Moser, Michelle Hassen, Pam Ballew, Donna Davis, Sherry Roberts, Pam Walker, Evonne Wells and Brenda Williams. Others involved with the performance were Avis Wilkerson, Chalmer MeDermott, Lisa Elrod, Terrell Roberson and Bill Janis.

The college's annual events continued to attract support. The Allied Health Day, for example, had representatives from 20 hospitals and the fall Tennis Classic drew an amazing 243 entries. The annual High School Bowl Quiz contest had its largest representation in the history of the event. Sixteen teams competed and 1st Place was captured by Darlington Academy of Rome, Georgia, Bradley Central placed 2nd, Cleveland 3rd and Baylor 4th. The college's 2nd Annual Advanced Basic Computer Programming Contest was won by Bradley Central, and Cleveland High School placed first in the novice competition.

An important athletic event occurred in November 1982. Several former outstanding Lady Cougar basketball team members returned to campus to play in a scholarship fund drive game to honor the memory of Emily Penney Blake and her husband, Robert A. Blake. The Blakes were killed in an automobile accident. Emily had been captain of the first women's basketball team in 1974. She later played for two years at Western Kentucky. She taught for a short time in England, and afterwards, she coached at Sequatchie County High School. She had been hired to coach at the University of Arkansas shortly before the accident. The game was between the alumni and the current Lady Cougar basketball team. The alumni participants were Data Caldwell, Liz Hannah Turner, Zandra Morris, Tracy Walker, Cindy McMahan, Teresa Millsaps,

Sharon Armstrong Ray, Karen Armstrong Clark and Sharon Sliger Brown. Zandra Morris led the alumni scoring and Karen McConnell led the Lady Cougars in scoring. The college's current team won 57-53. More importantly, $1,444 was raised for the scholarship fund.

Another event (mentioned earlier) was a comedic basketball game played between representatives of the college and the Harlem Wizards. The college was represented by two former basketball players—Ricky Crutcher and Jimmy Webb--and other representatives were President Quentin Lane, John Bradley (as noted above), John Cantrell, Tom Losh, Ed Coates, Daivd Boatwright, Dr. L. E. Wooten, Dr. Charles Tollett and Dr. Spencer Culbreth. The Wizards, led by the former Harlem Globetrotter, Marques Haynes, were the obvious winners of the contest.

In athletics the Lady Cougar basketball team compiled a 21-5 record and played in the Region VII Tournament. The men's basketball team had a 15-10 record, and the baseball team won 25 and lost 14 and played in the TJCAA State Tournament. The Ladies' softball team had a 15-6 record and finished 2nd in the NJCAA Region VII Tournament. Two softball players, Jill Ross and Deidra Bates, were named to the NJCAA All-American Team. Ross and Bates, in addition to Lisa Partain, Carla Walker and Kelly Flora, were named to the Region VII All-Tournament Team. Ray Stephens was named to baseball's TJCAA Eastern Division Team, and Kim Bittle was named to the women's basketball TJCAA All-Conference Team. Stephens later played professional baseball.

Other students were also newsmakers. Michael Valcarcel was a 1st Place winner in the Tennessee Community College Art Council Competition Exhibition, and other awards were presented to Lawana Taylor, Tom Sain and Tim Wofford. The following were presented awards in the Cleveland Area Community Art Competition: John Holland, 1st Place; Denny Hill, 2nd Place; Billie R. Daniel, 3rd Place; and Mark Kissel, 4th Place. Honorable Mention was achieved by Sharm McDonald Keel, Gene Harrington, Diane Rankhorn, Katherine Tate, Eileen Adkins Card and Joyce O'Donnell. Valerie Waldrop placed 2nd in the Business Administration competition at the Phi Beta Lambda (PBL) Leadership Conference in Gatlinburg, and Bud Goza placed 3rd in the Data Processing II category. The college's PBL conducted a "Fuel Fund Drive" to collect donations for needy families to purchase fuel for the winter. Clayton Beaty of Beaty Hardware donated coal buckets for the charitable event, and the major participants were Stacey Dillingham, Pamela Brackett, Greg Clower, Tina Day, Carolyn Biggs, Angela Bates, Wayne Harris and the faculty sponsor, John Cantrell. In what was becoming a usual occurrence, the CSCC team won the International Future Secretaries Association (FSA) Scrapbook category at the Tennessee Division meeting for the Professional Secretaries International organization. The team was led by Sue Sampson, President; Kamy Rayburn, Vice-President; and Annette McCulley, Corresponding Secretary. Other team members were Angela Bain, Charlene Donahoo, Vicki Painter, Linda Bullins, Nanette Wray, Margaret Sorah and Joyce Jones. Another honor was achieved by Frank Smirkle.

He was one of five dental lab students to receive a scholarship from the American Foundation for Dental Health.

Several alumni were recognized in various issues of the Employee Newsletter. Sally Little, daughter of CSCC employee Sue Little, was employed with NASA in Huntsville, Alabama. Steve Holland, former editor of The Cherokee Signal, worked with UTK's Daily Beacon, was a reporter for the Chattanooga News/Free Press and served as a news editor for the LaFollette Press. Ron Galloway was teaching Biology at McMinn County High School, Mikel Caywood won a voice scholarship to Carson Newman, and Emily Cline was an accompanist for the UTK singers and was currently a choral music teacher at Alcoa High School. Other alumni devotees of music were: Vicky Stewart Edgings performed an honors concert at UTK and was currently a piano teacher and author of a piano methods course book; Joe Taylor performed with a vocal group, and he and his wife sang in gospel concerts; Keith Colloms presented his Senior year recital at Carson-Newman College; and Brenda Goodwill of Union University was on a concert tour.

The Employee Newsletter also recognized several non-traditional students for their achievements at the college. Courtney Bird, for example, was the mother of two sons and a college graduate who decided to attend Cleveland State. She was a teacher and administrator in education for twenty years. She taught at both the elementary and secondary school levels and was a former Principal. At the high scool level she taught everything from nutrition to oil painting, and she was a former Director of a School Commissary and Cannery. She received a two-year degree in Office Careers at Cleveland State and stated that she loved her time at the college. Joy Andies was the mother of six children, and when her oldest child turned sixteen, she enrolled in the Legal Assistant Program. She and her husband owned a carpet installation service. During her externship with the Southeast Tennessee Legal Services, her supervisor, Glenna Ramer, said that Mrs. Andies' contributions to the legal office had been extremely valuable. Kenneth Scoggins was a minister of two churches who attended Cleveland State. He suffered from a severe case of arthritis of the spine. In spite of this disability, he maintained an active schedule and graduated from CSCC. He enrolled at Tennessee Wesleyan and planned to attend Candler School of Theology at Emory University after receiving his four-year degree.

Several other students also were newsmakers in 1982. The Cheerleaders, coached by Norma Davis, were Melissa Humphries, Monique Stutes, Kelly Newman, Lisa Butcher, Loretta Presswood, Angel Thompson, Penny Pirkle, Jamie Rudder, Gail Crittenden and Karen Wallace. The Cherokee Signal staff was composed of the following: Karen Malik, Editor; Carolyn Green, Editorial Editor; Sandy Tinker, Photo Editor; Jennifer Jones, Business Manager; Polly Fowler, Typesetter; and David Suttles, Faculty Advisor. English Cartwright was the Homecoming Queen, and Jeff Miller succeeded Katie Bagwell as President of the SGA.

The commencement speaker, in June 1982, was Dr. Frederick Obear, the Chancellor of UTC. The Outstanding Faculty Award was presented to John Bradley, and the Outstanding Student Award was presented to Katie Bagwell (her brother, Mike, received the award in 1980).

– 1983 –

On the international scene there were chaotic events in the Middle East, the Far East and in Latin America. The war between Iran and Iraq continued and so did the Soviet-Afghan conflict. The Soviet Union shot down a South Korean passenger jet over the Sea of Japan, killing all 269 people on the flight. The plane had entered Soviet airspace on its way from Anchorage, Alaska to Seoul, South Korea. In Grenada, a small island in the Caribbean, a Marxist group overthrew the government and the prime minister was killed. Grenada's neighbors believed the event was staged by Cuba and was a subsequent threat to them. President Ronald Reagan dispatched American troops to the area, along with soldiers from six Caribbean nations, and they quickly regained control of the island. In September 63 people, including 17 Americans, were killed by a suicide bomber at the American Embassy in Beirut, Lebanon. Fighting had erupted in Lebanon when Israeli forces withdrew in early September. The Syrian-backed Druse, a group with beliefs similar to Islam, began to fight against the forces of a Christian militia and the Lebanese Army. In October a terrorist truck loaded with explosives crashed into an American Marine compound and killed 241 Marines and sailors. Later, another truck blew up a French barracks, killing 58 French soldiers. A third truck blew up an Israeli compound and killed 60 soldiers.

The major domestic events were: the first mobile phone was introduced by Motorola; President Reagan nominated Elizabeth Dole to be the Secretary of Transportation (the first woman to head a Cabinet Department in his administration); Dole was sworn in by the first woman to sit on the Supreme Court, Justice Sandra Day O'Connor; Soviet leader Yuri V. Andropov invited Samantha Smith to visit his country after receiving a letter from the Manchester, Maine, schoolgirl; four men were convicted for gang-raping a woman on a pool table in a Massachusetts tavern; the musical play "Annie" closed on Broadway after a run of 2,377 performances; the popular TV series "MASH" ended after eleven seasons on CBS; Country Music Television (CMT) made its debut with the video titled "It's Four in the Morning," performed by Faron Young; Hurricane Alicia hit the Texas coast and killed 21 people and caused over one billion dollars in damage; musician and singer Karen Carpenter died at the age of 32; playwright Tennessee Williams died at the age of 71; Sally Ride became the first American woman in space; Guion S. Bluford, Jr., the first black American in space, also completed his first space mission; Time magazine's "Man of the Year" was a computer; and many Americans became infatuated with a doll that, as the 1984 World Book noted, "came from a cabbage patch and cost a great deal of lettuce."

In popular culture the movie "Terms of Endearment" won the Academy Award for best picture; Robert Duvall ("Tender Mercies") won the best actor award; and Shirley MacLaine ("Terms of Endearment") won the best actress award. The Emmy Award for best comedy was presented to "Cheers" (NBC), and "Hill Street Blues" (NBC) won the award for best drama. The Grammy for best record was won by Michael Jackson ("Beat It"), and Michael Jackson's "Thriller" won the award for best album of the year; North Carolina State won the men's NCAA Division I Basketball Championship; the University of Southern California won the Ladies' NCAA Division I Basketball Championship; the Washington Redskins defeated the Miami Dolphins in the Super Bowl; and the Baltimore Orioles defeated the Philadelphia Phillies in the World Series.

A highlight of the year for the college was the announcement of another fund drive by the college's Foundation. Cleveland attorney, Mike Callaway, was appointed to lead the campaign. Callaway noted that the college had grown by over 1,000 students since 1976 (the date of the last big fund drive). He also said, "As a native of Bradley County, having lived here for forty-two years, I can say without hesitation that the greatest thing to happen to Cleveland was the establishment of Cleveland State Community College."

The Foundation officers that served in 1982 (as noted above) were re-elected to serve another one-year term. Among the new trustees and appointees to the board were; Sue Fair, President of the Cleveland Pilot Club; Tom Wheeler, President of the Cleveland Rotary Club; John Rossmaier, President of the Cleveland Kiwanis Club; Ed Battochio (Duracell); Herman Collins (Businessman); Harold Jernigan (Real Estate); Jay Leggett (M&M /retired); David Wagner (CSCC alumnus); Colonel James M. Stubbs CSCC/retired); William Franckhauser (Amtex Division of Ti-Caro); and Gene Miller, (Duncan Electric). The remaining members were George Carroll, Jimmy Cooke, Ernie DeShields, Bob Easterly, Jimmy Goddard, Beecher Hunter, Dr. Quentin Lane, Robert Larson, Roy Lillard, George Mathis, Scott Mayfield, James Morris, Carl Painter, Jr., Shelia Presswood, Phil Russell and Pledger Wattenbarger. The Steering Committee for the Foundation Endowment Drive was composed of Beecher Hunter, Dr. Lane, Phil Russell, Lucille Headrick, Jim Williams, Sam McReynolds, Ken Rayborn, Harold Almond, Sam Colbert, Dr. Mathis, Henry Barkley, Arch Fitzgerald, George Taylor, John Bradley and Mike Callaway, Chairman.

The comments of the 1983-84 student recipients of the Foundation Scholarships were enlightening. One said, "Thanks to your foresight and generosity, kids like me have the opportunity to attain life-long goals." Another said, "I plan to work hard and, hopefully, someday repay your kindness with a contribution to this wonderful organization." Another said, "I honestly can't begin to tell you how privileged I feel to have received this award. It is truly people like you that make the Cleveland area such a nice place."

In staff news Joan Haney, Coordinator for the college's Job Placement Center, was recognized for her achievements by <u>The Cherokee Signal</u> newspaper. In addition to her full-time job she also taught clogging at the college two nights a week. She developed a show team, named the "Orange Blossom Express," that performed at the World's Fair in Knoxville. The team won the 1983 Alabama State Clogging Team Championship. They also won several other competitions and appeared on the nationally televised program, "Dancing U. S. A." They were also awarded the title of Silver Dollar City Show Champions. In other staff news the college was saddened by the death of Ralph Casto, the Head of Campus Security. He was a 1976 graduate of the college and was employed at CSCC since 1975. He was killed in a car accident on Harrison Pike. His replacement was Walter Hackett. Hackett, who was employed by the college in 1977, worked with the Cleveland Police Department for over 8 years prior to that.

In other news the college was named as the administrative entity for the Job Training Partnership Act (JTPA). The JTPA was designed to be a partnership that included government, training institutions and industry. The intent was for government to supply the funds, training institutions to train individuals to enter the labor force and industry to supply the needed jobs. The state of Tennessee was divided into 14 districts, known as service delivery areas. Each service delivery area chose a Private Industry Council (PIC) and a 26-member board of Local Elected Officials (LEO). It was designed to provide economically disadvantaged people the training needed to hold jobs in the private sector. The budget for 1983 was approximately two million dollars.

The two councils (PIC and LEO) were comprised of business leaders and government officials in Bradley, Polk, McMinn, Monroe and Meigs counties. The director in 1983 was Rosemary Den Uyl, and the assistant director was Charles Priddy. Den Uyl was the former Director of the college's Cooperative Education and Business/ Industry Relations Department. She earned a B. S. degree in Business Management from Tennessee Wesleyan College and a M. S. degree from the UTK in Industrial Education. She had been a member of the Board of Directors of the Southern College Placement Association, past-president of the Tennessee College Placement Association and president of the Athens Industrial Personnel Association. She was also secretary-treasurer of Junior Achievement of Bradley and McMinn counties, chair of the Economic Education Committee of the Athens Chamber of Commerce, and she was affiliated with many other civic and educational organizations. Priddy completed a B. S. in Business Administration and Health and a M. S. degree in Education from MTSU. He also pursued graduate studies at UNC and New York University. He was a member of the National Rehabilitation Counseling Association, the Tennessee State Employees Association and numerous other organizations.

Another college organization, the Alumni Association, held elections for 1983-84. The new officers were: David Marr, President; Linda Scott, Vice-President; Georgia Gann, Treasurer; and Mitzi Jones, Member-at-Large. The college fall enrollment achieved a headcount of 3,663, and the FTE was 2,034. If non-credit students were added to the number, the total enrollment was 4,575. As of the fall of 1983, the American College Testing (ACT) competency exam was now required of all first-time college freshmen. Its purpose was to assist in placing students in classes that reflected their competencies. If weaknesses were revealed in specified areas, the affected students would be placed in developmental courses designed to prepare them for college-level courses. In addition the State Board of Regents mandated that students must take two courses in Algebra (or one course in Algebra coupled with one course in geometry), as pre-requisites for taking a college-level math course. This requirement became effective in the Winter Quarter of 1983-84.

Meanwhile, the college received acclaim in academics. The nursing graduates achieved a 100% passage rate, in both 1982 and 1983, on the State Board Licensure Exam. Twelve students of the Dental Laboratory Technician Program also achieved a 100% passage rate on the exam offered by the National Board of Certification of Dental Laboratory Technicians. The 1983 "Program for the Academically Talented" (formerly known as "The Youth Enrichment Program") was launched, and 75 "gifted" students from the Cleveland City School System were bused to and from the college on Fridays for special classes between 12:30 and 2:00 p. m. Five courses were taught for a ten-week period. Bob Taylor was the coordinator of the program and the courses and instructors were: Buford Guy, Astronomy and Physics; Thomas Acuff and Alex Nichols, Computers; Larry Speight, Physiology; Mason Sesler, Electricity/Electronics and Dr. Spencer Culbreth, Heroes and Villains.

The year 1983 was the occasion for another self-study. A team of ten members appointed by the Atlanta-based Southern Association for Colleges (SACs) visited the campus in November. The campus Chair of the Self-study Steering Committee was Dr. Jerome Taylor. The Chairs of the other committees were: James Allen, Physical Resources; Nancy Boyd, Educational Program; John Bradley, Faculty; Dr. Spencer Culbreth, Organization and Administration; Dr. Renate Hufft and Dr. Larry Longerbeam, Library co-Chairs; Ann McCoin, Purpose; Dr. Frank McKenzie, Implementation and Projections; Larry Speight, Student Development; Bob Taylor, Special Activities; and Dale Yates, Financial Resources. The toil of the committees was rewarded by the college's achievement of re-accreditation for another ten-year cycle.

The Dean of Academic Affairs in the early 1980s was Dr. Charles Tollett. He received his Bachelor's degree from Carson Newman, his Master of Science degree from the University of Mississippi, his Master of Arts from George Peabody College and his Doctorate in Education from UTK. A few other personnel were: Tom Losh was the Director of Admissions and Records; Dr. Rodney Fitzgerald was the Director of the Learning Skills Center; the bookstore managers (at various times) were Wanda Cartwright and Alice Selvidge; and the Supervisor of Maintenance, Buildings and Grounds was Bill Petit. Secretaries to the various academic areas were: Brenda

Elliott, Virginia Semak, Evonne Drown, Jennifer Lee, Janice Lowrance, Imogene Waddell, Johnie Benz, Karen Carty, Martha Lane, Sandra Moody, Jean Salter, June Parks, Joyce Casteel and Pam Ables. Those assigned to campus Maintenace were: David Hamilton, Fred Anderson, Paul Miller, Clarice Bonine, Levi Brown, Dorothy Cantrell, Paul Clowers, Matilda Evans, Marvin Green, Thomas Green, Henry Helton, Ida Hitson, Dexter Jenkins, Minnie Johnson, Lloyd McClane, Helen McCleary, Helen Piersaul, Wilburn Pritchett, N. W. Rayfield, Benton Shelton, Louvenia Thompson, Paul Underwood, Ricky Walker, Lillie Woods and Patsy Woods.

A major accomplishment in 1983 was the completion of a Fitness Trail behind the baseball field. Bob Taylor was the coordinator of the project, and other trail planners were Dr. Charles Tollett, Jim Cigliano and Al Fine. Construction started in the spring of 1982 and the State Department of Conservation loaned the tools for trail construction. Numerous groups and organizations assisted in the endeavor. Among these were CSCC students, faculty, staff and members of the Boy Scouts and Eagle Scouts. A grant from Wells Fargo was also helpful as well as sponsorships by Bradley County Memorial Hospital and Cleveland Community Hospital. When construction was completed, the scenic public trail extended for approximately one and three-fourths miles.

In other events two alumni medical doctors, Dr. Don Hamby and Dr. Robert Hartline, were guest speakers at the Alumni Association. Hamby was a 1974 graduate who later attended East Tennessee State University and UT at Memphis Medical School. He received his Doctorate in 1979. Hartline attended CSCC in 1967-68 and graduated from the UTK College of Dentistry in 1977. Twelve high schools competed in the annual Bowl Quiz that was sponsored by Phi Beta Kappa. Sandra Wright, assisted by Patricia Rutledge, coordinated the event, and David Suttles and Patricia Bishop also provided assistance in their roles as PBK sponsors. Four scholarships were awarded to students who excelled in the contest, and Cleveland High School won the event. Other participants were Bradley Central, Charleston, Polk, McMinn, Red Bank, Meigs, Copper Basin, Tellico Plains, Ootlewah and East Ridge High Schools. The college also hosted competitions for the Vocational Industrial Clubs of America Olympic Skills and for the Tennessee Office Education Clubs.

A major campus activity was the annual spring concert. A variety of music was presented in 1983. Johannes Sebastian Bach's "Magnificat" was performed by Ann Moore (soprano), Jeanne Sawyer (soprano) and David Creel (baritone). Tenor Randy Kincannon and Creel presented a duet ("Verily Thou Shalt Be in Paradise"); Sawyer and Tom Boles performed two Duets ("Wanting You" and "Desert Song"); and Ray Calfee, accompanist, played a Franz Liszt etude. Tunes from several Broadway musicals were presented as well as three Liebeslieder waltzes by Johannes Brahms. The choir members were: Veronica Berry, Victor Boykins, Leigh Ann Dills, Mike Gilland, Janelle Goodwill, James Jenkins, David Landrith, Felicia McCleary, Chalmer McDermott, Mollie Ann Miller, Tina Marie Skelton, Doris Smith, Karen Wallace, Gregory Wood, Sylvester Harris, James Kincannon,

Kim Moorhouse, Ritchie Stevenson, Tanya Wood, Kimberly Baxter, Michael Bible, Alan Boyd, David Creel, Jeffrey Crisp, Rene Fink, Tammy Grimes, Jennifer Johnson, Hoyt Martin, Ann Moore, Loretta Presswod, Jenna Wilhoit, Velma Hunter, Laura Cochran, Alice Higgins, Gary Lumbert and Regina Trotter.

Meanwhile, John Bradley continued to add levity to the campus in his column for the Employee Newsletter. He noted that once, while giving a speech in class, a student said that his major source for the speech was a book written by Hans Andersen, the Christian. Bradley explained that Christian was Andersen's middle name. The student replied, "Well, I wondered why that book didn't list anybody else's religion after their name." Bradley also gave three examples of insightful advice on restaurants by noting that: "if the cook carries a spatula in one hand and a flyswatter in the other, you are not in a good restaurant;" if there are nurses at the salad bar and an ambulance at the front door, you are not in a good restaurant;" and if the menu lists 'dog' as one of the entrees, you are not in a good restaurant."

In academic activities Dale Yates, Accounting Instructor, organized a free income tax service for the community. The assistance was provided by students in the Accounting 231 class taught by Yates. The students were required to pass an Internal Revenue Service exam prior to the activity. Nancy Boyd, Sherra Witt and Dr. Frank McKenzie attended the Tennessee Education Association annual conference in Nashville on September 23-24. Witt served as the liaison, Boyd as the presider and McKenzie as the host for one of the sessions. In another endeavor the Tennessee Committee for the Humanities (TCH) selected the college as a co-sponsor for Betty Duggan, a Humanities Scholar in Residence. CSCC provided office space for Duggan whose assignment, as part of a Tennessee Community Heritage Project, was to work with 18 area counties in developing cultural heritage projects and in applying for grants. She also served as a resource consultant for six pilot project communities: Charleston, Red Bank, Winchester, Manchester, Sweetwater and Clinton. Dr. Mary Barker, as a member of the TCH, was involved in Duggan's selection and Duggan was one of nine such scholars selected from across the state.

A few faculty members had publications in 1983. Dr. Jerome Taylor was one of three authors of a 7th Grade Social Studies Textbook, Panorama of Tennessee and a supplementary workbook. The other two authors were two State Department of Education personnel, Douglas Little and Tom Kelley. Their wives, Juanita Little, Jo Kelley and Sally Taylor assisted with the research, typing and proofreading. Dr. Spencer Culbreth, Head of the Education and Social Sciences Department, was the co-author of a new study guide published by Harcourt, Brace and Jovanovich in January, 1984. The guide accompanied a college-level American History textbook, The American Past: A Survey of U. S. History, written by Joseph Conlin, a professor at the University of California. Martha Lane, Secretary of the Social Sciences Department, typed the study guide manuscript and Culbreth's wife, Ann, assisted with the proofreading.

Harry Dean, associate professor of English, had three poems published. One poem, titled "Autumn Fantasy," was published in a Tennessee journal, another in a Montana publication, and a third in a California publication (Poetry Now). Dean was also the editor of the annual campus publication titled, Frontage Road. Community members, students, faculty and staff had an opportunity to submit poems and stories to the annual journal for publication.

Other faculty members were also in the news. Renate Hufft, Head of the Humanities Department, was selected for recognition at the "Celebration of Excellence" at UTK. The special event occurred every three years and was sponsored by the UTK Commission for women "to honor outstanding accomplishments of women, faculty, staff, students, alumnae and former faculty and staff members." The top 500 women scholars at UTK received awards, on November 10, 1983, in the auditorium of the Carolyn P. Brown Memorial University Center. Hufft also completed her coursework for her Doctorate. She came to the United States seventeen years ago from West Germany. She earned degrees from five universities, mastered three different languages and began teaching at Cleveland State in 1968.

In athletics the members of the Men's basketball team, coached by Charles Cogdill, were Jay Morgan, James Billingsley, Kevin Elston, Steve Kennedy, Curtis Russell, Bill Holt, Loring Rogers, Greg Green, Steve Bettis, Jon Miller, Monty Rowland, Robert Goldston, Mickey Shamblin, Michael Favors and Mike Wilson. The Lady Cougars Softball Team, coached by Hugh Walker, won the NJCAA Region 7 Women's Fastpitch Softball Tournament. Stephanie Layne pitched a one hit shutout, and Sandy Bryant had a home run, a single and three RBIs in a 10-0 victory over Columbia State. The Cougars later placed 7th in the National Tournament in Rockford, Illinois. The team compiled a 17-6 season record, and its members were Jay Pence, Rose Eakins, Norma Nelson, Cyndee Gentry, Stephanie Lay, Lisa Kyzer, Cindy Van Dyke, Delaine Sanders, Abby Armstrong, Rhonda Snow, Kelly Flora, Sandy Bryant and Debbie Fleenor. Angie Clayton was the Team Manager. Rhonda Snow was named to the NJCAA All-American First Team, and she led the Cougars in Home Runs, RBIs, and had a batting average of over .500. She also made only one error all season in her position as center fielder.

One of the outstanding baseball players for 1983 was Darryl Oliver. Oliver had a .370 batting average and stole 32 bases in 36 attempts. He also won a scholarship to the University of Mississippi and was later drafted by a professional team. Unfortunately, an injury cut short his career. Meanwhile, other former players also excelled. Greg Geren played for UTK and signed with the New York Mets; Ted Carson signed with the St. Louis Cardinals; Mike Jordan signed with the Houston Astros; and Larry Simcox (who played for the University of Mississippi) signed with the Houston Astros. Jordan was a two-time National Association of Intercollegiate Athletics (NAIA) All-American at Tennessee Wesleyan. He was the leading home run hitter in the entire NAIA his senior year and the most valuable player in the South Region of the NAIA.

Meanwhile, John Bradley continued to offer sage advice in his weekly column. For example, "It is not polite to snore during a faculty meeting; it is impolite to grovel during an evaluation conference with your supervisor; and it is impolite to ask your hostess for a knife to cut the gravy." He also recounted a few anecdotal remarks from student evaluations of professors. "The instructor works really hard to keep us awake; the instructor works really hard to keep himself awake; and the instructor needs a hair transplant."

In the student category, Viola Mason was one of the finalists in the 3rd annual student photo contest sponsored by <u>Photographer's Forum Magazine</u>. Her work was considered among the top 5% of the 19,000 entries. Several former CSCC Art students also made the news. Steve Rucker, Assistant Professor of Art at Loyola University in New Orleans, Louisiana, was featured in <u>Art News</u> magazine. His sculpture, "Firefly," was featured in an article called "Razzle-dazzle on the Levee" which described several artists of New Orleans. There was an article about his prints (created from slabs of clay) in <u>Ceramics Monthly</u>, two other articles in a New Orleans newspaper and yet another in the publication, <u>Art Papers</u>. His sculpture, "Air Dance,' was declared one of the best pieces of sculpture in the 1982 Craftmen's Guild Summer Program in Fulton, Mississippi. CSCC Art Professor Jere Chumley said, "His love of art and his contagious enthusiasm has catapulted him from Bradley Central High School and Cleveland State Community College to the vanguard of American art."

Jeff de Lude, another former CSCC student, also achieved success. His paintings were exhibited in Baltimore, Chicago, New York, Houston and other cities. He also won a poster design contest for the Houston Arts Festival. Other former art students were: Belinda Elrod, art teacher in Jackson, Tennessee; Bob Grayson, art director at Preston Company in Cleveland; Allen Rudd, commercial artist with Lehman Printing; Bob Young, a commercial free-lance artist in Knoxville; Jim Hodge, assistant gallery director at UTK; Rachel Green at Merle's Frame Shop in Cleveland; Anita Dotson Cain, Capitol Airways Printing in Smyrna, Tennessee; Kathy Bailey, teacher in Cleveland; Clay Grigsby, a potter in Cleveland; Will Rhodarmer, a muralist in Murfreesboro; and Michael Valcarcel, a free-lance artist in Cleveland.

An art student, Juan Rodriquez (mentioned earlier), did chirographic art and design on the walls of the college Library and the Admissions office. He also designed the new college emblem, lettering on menus for Jenkins Deli, brochures for Southeastern Travel Agency, logos for the Bradley County Education Association and a college catalog addendum cover. He later attended UTK, with plans to earn a degree in Advertising and become an advertising account executive in his native country of Venezuela.

Sadly, a former outstanding student, Dennis Grape, was killed in an auto accident in Perry, Georgia. Grape was an honor student in Criminal Justice at both CSCC and UTC. He graduated from the former in 1980 and the latter in 1982. A former cheerleader,

Renee Madden, graduated from MTSU and planned to enter the school of medicine in Santo Domingo. George Lewis, a current student and minister of music for Mount Olive Church of God, had written over 500 songs. One of them, "Home is Where the Heart Is," was number 11 on the national gospel hit list. He authored a musical comedy called "The Reverend is a Lady," and he also wrote children's music. A 71 year-old grandmother, Rosa Disspain, received her GED Diploma, and Yvette Grannie Jenkins, a Venezuelan and a CSCC Dental Lab graduate, was employed at Jenkins Dental Lab of Cleveland. Another student, Steve Morgan, received an International Studies Association Scholarship for summer study in Spain.

Several other students were also newsmakers in 1983. The Cheerleaders were Melissa Humphreys, Missy Flanigan, Selina Elrod, Linea Lawton, Sharon Killen, Kim Phillips, Kim Coffey and Stacey Brown. The advisor was Sherra Witt. Each year several students performed the tasks of student hostesses and hosts. Their duties were to assist the Student Personnel Office with campus functions and activities by serving as guides for individuals and groups and to support student events. In 1983 they were Donna Davis, Lisa Torbett, Kim Monroe, Kellye Harrison, Dawn Guthrie, Delaine Sanders, Debbie Fleenor, Barbie Davis, Barry Rowland, Anthony Gunn, Loring Rogers and Joe Miller. A new club, known as the Odd Parity Computer Club, was organized in 1983. Gail Randolph was the President, Allen Eldredge the Vice-President, Joe Hudgins the Treasurer and Stacey Dillingham the Secretary. The faculty advisor was Alex Nichols and the club was open to any student taking three hours of Data Processing.

The delegates to the 20th General Assembly of the Tennessee Intercollegiate State Legislature (TISL) were Robert Bradney, Denise Davis and Beth Scoggins. Also attending were Sam Richardson, Tony Pharr, Rhonda Mosley, Randy Mantooth and Lynette McDonald. The Cherokee Signal staff was composed of the following: Rene Fink, Editor; Tim Wofford, Editorial Editor; Dawn Guthrie, News Editor; Viola Mason, Photo Editor; Teresa Williams, Business Manager; Polly Fowler, Typesetter; and David Suttles, Faculty Advisor. The President of the Black Student Association was Michael Whaley, and the other officers were Previn Langham, Vanessa Sharpe, Donna Davis and Sylvester Harris.

The Homecoming Queen, Tammy Day, was also President of Phi Beta Lambda. A first for the college was having, at different times, two SGA Presidents in the same year— Jeff Miller and Bridgitt Poe. The commencement speaker was Dr. Arliss L. Roaden, President of Tennessee Tech University. The Faculty Merit Award was presented to Harry Dean, Associate Professor of English, and the Outstanding Graduate Award was presented to Harris S. Foss.

– 1984 –

The major international events of the year were: warfare between Iran and Iraq continued as well as the fighting between the Soviet Union and the rebels in Afghanistan; The Soviet Union and its satellite states boycotted the Summer Olympics in retaliation for the United States boycott in 1980; India's Prime Minister, Indira Gandhi, was assassinated by two of her Sikh bodyguards; the act was in retaliation for the Indian Army's assault on the Golden Temple in Amritsar, which Sikhs considered their holiest shrine; she was succeeded by her son, Rajiv; Great Britain's Prime Minister, Margaret Thatcher, narrowly escaped death by a bomb set off by the Provisional Irish Republican Army (five people were killed, including one member of Parliament); the Soviet leader, Yuri V. Andropov died and was succeeded by Konstantin U. Chernenko; Great Britain and China announced an agreement whereby Hong Kong would pass from British to Chinese control in 1997; on space shuttle <u>Challenger's</u> fourth mission, two American astronauts, Bruce McCandless and Robert L. Stewart, made the first untethered walk in space; Soviet astronaut Svetlana Savitskaya became the first woman to walk in space; American space shuttle astronaut Kathryn Sullivan became the first American woman to walk in space; thousands of people died after methyl isocyanate gas escaped from a pesticide plant operated by a Union Carbide subsidiary in Bhopal, India; and Italy and the Vatican signed an agreement declaring that Roman Catholicism was no longer the state religion of Italy.

The following were major domestic events in 1984: American Telephone and Telegraph was divested of its 22 Bell System companies under terms of an antitrust agreement, and seven regional companies took over local telephone service; recording star Marvin Gaye was shot to death by his father, Marvin Gay Sr.; the elder Gay (spelled differently than the son's name) pleaded guilty to voluntary manslaughter and received probation; a $180 million out-of-court settlement was announced in the Agent Orange class action suit of Vietnam veterans who charged they had been injured from exposure to the defoliant; US Representative Geraldine A. Ferraro of New York was the first woman to run for Vice-President on a major political party (Democrat) ticket; former Vice-President Walter F. Mondale won the Democratic nomination for President; Republican President Ronald Reagan was re-elected in an electoral vote count of 525-13; President Reagan signed a bill cutting federal transportation aid to states that maintained the alcoholic drinking age to under 21 years of age; Bernhard Goetz shot and wounded four allegedly menacing teenage boys on a New York City subway; he was later acquitted of major charges but was successfully sued; and Surgeon General C. Everett Koop declared there was "very solid" evidence linking cigarette smoke to lung disease in non-smokers.

In popular culture "Amadeus" won the best movie award; F. Murray Abraham ("Amadeus") won the Oscar Award for best actor; and Sally Field won the best actress award for "Places in the Heart." The Emmy Award for best drama was the "Dick Van Dyke Show" (CBS), and "Cheers" (NBC) won the award for the best comedy. The Grammy for the record of the year was won by Tina Turner for "What's Love Got to do With It," and the Grammy for album of the year was won by Lionel Richie for "Can't Slow Down." In sports the highlights were: the NCAA Division I Basketball Championship for men was won by Georgetown University; the winner of the ladies' tournament was the University of Southern California; the Los Angeles Raiders defeated the Washington Redskins in the Super Bowl; and Detroit defeated San Diego in the World Series.

In college news a record number of 139 students were recipients of an Endowment Scholarship. The Foundation Board was composed of 83 trustees in 1984. The officers for 1983-1984 were Dr. D. F. Adkisson, President; Eugene Callaway, Vice-president; Arch Fitzgerald, Treasurer; Dr. George L. Mathis, Secretary; and W. K. Fillauer and Dr. Quentin L. Lane were members-at-large. The Investment Committee members were Wayne Feehrer, (Chairman), Carl Painter, Harold Almond, Arch Fitzgerald and Dr. D. F. Adkisson (ex-officio). The Scholarship members were Dr. George L. Mathis (Chairman), Lucille Headrick, Arch Fitzgerald, Walter Presswood, James Cigliano, Dr. D. F. Adkisson (ex-officio); and Dr. L. Quentin Lane (ex-officio). Walter Presswood, Director of Community Relations and Development at Cleveland State, was the Foundation Coordinator, and Patricia Dausy provided secretarial support services for the Foundation. Henry M. Barkley, charter trustee and first treasurer of the Foundation, was honored for his service to the scholarship program. Although remaining as an active trustee, Barkley, owner of Quinn Supply Company, retired as the treasurer.

The Foundation's recent campaign goal of $200,000 was completed with a 38% increase above the goal. The first scholarship campaign, in the fall of 1976, raised $222,000, and the 1984 campaign netted $280,845. The chair of the campaign steering committee was Mike Callaway, and the coordinator was Walter Presswood. Presswood thanked several individuals and entities for their support during the campaign. Gratitude was extended to Beecher Hunter, editor of the Cleveland Daily Banner, the members of the Banner staff, Julius Parker and Barbara Rea of the Chattanooga News-Free Press, Randall Higgins of the Chattanooga Times, the Daily Post-Athenian, the Polk County News and radio stations WALV, WBAC and WCLE. Other individuals providing outstanding support were Harold Almond, Arch Fitzgerald, Ken Rayborn, Wayne Feehrer, Sam McReynolds, Bobby Taylor, Jim Williams, Beecher Hunter, Mayor Sam Colbert, David Marr, Ruth Hynes, Dr. George Mathis, Phil Russell, Henry Barkley, George Thorogood, Dr. L. Quentin Lane, John Bradley, Lucile Headrick, Roy Lillard, Dr. D. F. Adkisson and Chairman Mike Callaway. Those raising several scholarships were: Almond, 9; Presswood, 7; Callaway, 5; Williams, 5; Fitzgerald, 4; McReynolds, 4; and Rayborn, Taylor, Russell and Thorogood, 3 each.

In its fall meeting Dr. Adkisson gave tribute to the late Cletus Benton and Eugene Callaway, both Foundation trustees who died during the year. Benton assisted in raising $12,000 in the college's first fund drive, when he gave a car as a fund-raiser. Callaway, who never missed a meeting of the Executive Committee, served as Vice-President from the Foundation's inception. Two plaques were awarded at the fall meeting. Both were presented to Mike Callaway, son of Eugene. One was for his work in the recent campaign and the other in honor of his Dad's work for the Foundation. The new officers for 1984-1985 remained the same with the exception of Vice-President. Harold Almond replaced the deceased Eugene Callaway in that position. The trustees reappointed to three-year terms were Henry Barkley, W. K. Fillauer, Arch Fitzgerald, Dr. Wayne McCulley, Terry McGuire, Will McReynolds, Ken Rayborn, Walt Robinson, Henry F. Smith, Clarke Stamper, George R. Taylor, Bill Thomason and Lynn Turpin. The new three-year term appointees were Fred Zeller, Sam McReynolds, Claude Simpson, Wes Pritchard, Jim Sharp, Frances Taylor and Jim Clarke. Trustees appointed to one-year terms were: Debbie Arp, President of the Cleveland Pilot Club; Harlan White, President of the Cleveland Kiwanis Club; Sam Fair, President of the Cleveland Rotary Club; and Steve Stone, President of the Cleveland Civitan Club. As late as 1984 Cleveland State continued to have the largest endowment of any Tennessee Community College.

All but three of the community colleges experienced enrollment declines in the fall of 1984. The total headcount for Cleveland State was 3,895. The Western Interstate Commission for Higher Education had predicted a national college enrollment decline in a 1982 publication titled "High School Graduates: Projections for the Fifty States (1982-2000)." It predicted that high school graduates would decline between 1984 and 1987 to about 2.5 million. There were approximately 3.2 million graduates in 1977. Graduates would increase slightly to a peak in 1988-89, then fall to a new low of approximately 2.3 million in the period of 1990-94. This would be followed by an increase to about 2.6 million in 1999. These predicted fluctuations were the result of the nation's roller coaster age structure. In 1986 there would be 14% fewer high school graduates than in 1981; 10% fewer in 1988; 22% fewer in 1992; and 9% fewer in 1999.

Colleges responded to the enrollment crisis by expending more money on marketing and management techniques in their competition for students. Twenty-five percent of the nation's high school students did not graduate, and about 50% failed to graduate in the service area of Cleveland State. John Bradley made a humorous observation about the recent emphasis on competitive marketing by suggesting that the following courses be offered at low prices: Human Relations 261 could be a Valentine's Day Special for only $14.14; American History 201 could be a President's Day Sale for only $22.22; Speech 131 could be a Winter Clearance Sale for only $29.88; and Astronomy 172 could be a Moonlight Madness Special for only $39.95.

In 1984 a reorganization of the area of Academic Affairs was announced by President Lane and Dean Charles Tollett. Seven functional units were created and the members in charge were: James Cigliano, Assistant Dean of Student Services; Dr. Spencer Culbreth, Assistant Dean of Humanities and Social Sciences; Al Fine, Assistant Dean of Community Services and Continuing Education; Dr. Rodney Fitzgerald, Assistant Dean of Instructional Support; Dr. Frank McKenzie, Assistant Dean of Business and Economics; Dr. Irene Millsaps, Assistant Dean of Physical Sciences and Technologies; and Dr. Francis Williams, Assistant Dean of Health and Life Sciences.

An innovation in 1984 was the implementation of a new test, known as the ACT-COMP (College Outcomes Measure Project), which was required of all graduating sophomores enrolled in the transfer degree program. According to Dr. Rodney Fitzgerald, "The test is intended to measure skills better believed to be necessary for effective functioning in adult society." Another innovative program originated with the Education Committee of the Cleveland Bradley Chamber of Commerce. Known as the "Adopt-a School Program," area businesses and other entities were invited to assist city and county schools with tutors, educational materials, playground equipment or other similar assistance. Cleveland State adopted Taylor Elementary School, and the college remained an active participant in the program.

Praiseworthy academic news for the college was achieved with the announcement of the results of the State Board Licensure Exam for registered professional nursing in Tennessee. It revealed that CSCC had achieved another 100% passage rate. This was the third consecutive year that the Nursing graduates had achieved this distinction. Nursing instructor Glenna Lee noted that, "Each fall we admit 60 students from the 400 to 500 students who apply." Shelby Millsaps, the Director of Nursing Education, stated that, "Our graduates are very well thought of and 100 percent of those who take the test after graduation find jobs who want employment." Furthermore, Millsaps praised the 47 graduates of the class and the Nursing Faculty. The 1984 Faculty members were Vivian Armstrong, Joann Barber, Pat Crews, Elizabeth Eiswerth, Alleyna Ellis, Sheila Hales, Patricia Jenkins, Glenna Lee, Donna McCoin, Maryanne Markiewicz, Nancy Moore and Carolyn Morrow.

In a fall college faculty meeting Dr. Lane and Dr. Tollett announced good news for the entire faculty. A recent Board of Regents Instructional Evaluation process awarded the college 95 of 100 possible points. Other good news was the announcement that the Cooperative Education Program had concluded student-working agreements with twenty-seven different companies. According to Adrian Strother, the Coordinator of the program, "It allows the employer to identify, evaluate and develop a promising student for employment. It also reduces the hiring risk and turnover rate. The retention rate of co-op students is three to four times higher than blind hiring." The college's Astronomical Observatory continued to offer opportunities for both students and the community to increase their knowledge of astronomy. Buford Guy, Associate Professor of Physics and Astronomy, noted that CSCC "was the first college in the state of Tennessee to offer astronomy as a course." Guy also stated that, "The Barnard Society was helpful in shaping ideas and the approach and techniques for teaching at Cleveland State." Furthermore, according to Guy, "They were also responsible for aligning and calibrating the Cleveland State telescope." The original alignment and calibrating was done by the Barnard Society in 1974. The Oak Ridge Astronomical Society, however, completed the most recent procedure, which was repeated about every four or five years.

The official opening of the college's walking/jogging trail occurred in May 1984. Mayor T. Sam Colbert presented a proclamation to representatives from the college, Bradley County Memorial Hospital and Cleveland Community Hospital for their combined efforts in developing a community fitness resource. President Lane thanked Wells Fargo, also a trail sponsor, for providing design recommendations and other assistance. He also recognized Bob Taylor for his extensive efforts in the building of the trail. The USDA Forest Service also assisted in the endeavor. Comments were also made by Howard Kuhns of Bradley Memorial Hospital, Jim Whitlock of Cleveland Community Hospital and Eddie Cartwright, the representative of the Bradley County officials.

In other activities a scholarship was named for Warnie Finnell for her work on behalf of the Bradley West-Polk Chapter of the March of Dimes. Finnell, as noted earlier, was the Director of the college's Youth Players. She founded the local MOD-TAP (March of Dimes-Teens Against Polio) program in 1964, and her first year teenagers raised over $1,100. By 1974 the program was raising $11,000 a year, and the Bradley West – Polk TAP program was the top one in the nation. In 1984 Terry McGuire was both the chapter chairman for the MOD and the TAP Captain. Michelle McAllister was the TAP President. The completion of the Dennis Grape Memorial Scholarship Fund also occurred in May 1984. A twenty-mile Grape Bike-a-thon, chaired by Millie Sue Hawk, was the major event for the fund-raiser. The college's Program for the Academically Talented continued to function and 112 students from Cleveland City Schools enrolled in the courses in 1984.

The Tennessee College English Association (TCEA) met at CSCC in April 1984. The event was sponsored jointly by Cleveland State and Lee College. The officers of the organization were Dr. Sue Berry, President of David Lipscomb University, Dr. Carolyn Dirksen, Vice-President of Lee College (and the Progam Chair) and Dr. Allison Ensor, the Treasurer. Approximately 50 people attended the event. Cleveland State was represented by Associate Professor Harry Dean, Associate Professor Marilyn Fillers, Assistant Professor Cathalin Folks and part-time instructor Paul Putt. Dean chaired one of the panel discussions titled "Teaching the Nation's Newcomers: English as a Second Language in Tennessee." The college also hosted a Health Fair designed to reach a larger group of people than the annual local college activity. This event, a unique one for Bradley County, was sponsored primarily by Cleveland Community Hospital. Support was also provided by WRCB Channel 3 of Chattanooga, the Hospital Corporation of America and the Chattanooga-Hamilton County Health Department.

Meanwhile, John Bradley decided to have fun at the expense of teachers rather than students. A Master Teacher Exam had recently been administered by the State Board of Education for possible pay raises for outstanding teachers of Kindergarten through High School. Bradley jokingly wrote in his weekly column for the Employee Newsletter that one instructor failed when he believed "to germinate" meant to become a naturalized German citizen. Another failed when he wrote, "John Milton, who wrote Paradise Lost, later wrote Paradise Regained when his wife left him." Another thought a "polygon" was a pagan with many wives. Another answered that "bigotry" meant having two wives, and "trigonometry" meant having three wives. Still another believed the Red Sea and the Mediterranean Sea were connected by the Sewage Canal; that Arabia gave us the decimal system, which we still use when counting; that the moon is more important than the sun because it shines at night when we really need it; and that Samson is the most important figure in the Bible because he brought the house down.

Two plays were presented in 1984 with the proceeds going to the Dennis Grape Memorial Scholarship Fund Drive. One in March was entitled "Crimes of the Heart," and one in October was the "Zoo Story." In the former John Bradley was the Director and the cast included Connie Cox Gatlin, Suzanne Allen, Pat Meagher, Lois Wyche, Rick Melvin and Jim Nelson. The latter was a play with only two participants—John Bradley and Bill Gatlin.

In the spring the college was selected as one of the district locations for the Tennessee History Day Contest. The contest included students in grades 6 through 12 and was designed to encourage students to learn history by preparing projects, such as plays, historical papers, displays and models. The Cleveland State History Department (Delmus Ledford, Dr. Jerome Taylor and Dr. Spencer Culbreth) coordinated the event for the college's ten county district. The counties were: Blount; Bradley; Hamilton; Loudon; McMinn; Meigs; Monroe; Polk; Rhea and Roane. The 1st and 2nd place winners at the district level advanced to the state finals at MTSU, and the winner traveled to Washington D. C. for the finals of the National History Day Contest.

Other activities were: a new college ensemble was formed composed of David Creel, violin, Thomas Boles, piano and Betty Aldrich, cello; the ensemble, accompanied by the college choir (directed by Michael Lees and produced by Boles), was the main participant in the spring musical concert; the concert included songs by Boles, Jeanne Sawyer, Creel and Cathy Lowe; a series of seminars, on subjects such as Stress Management, were conducted by Dr. Rodney Fitzgerald for CSCC employees; John Egerton, author of Generations, was a guest speaker who stressed the importance of recording family histories; Jere Chumley won the "Best-of-Show Award," and student Richard E. Cox received "Honorable Mention" at the 1984 Athens Art League's Annual Exhibition; the winners of the annual PTK High School Bowl Quiz were Sweetwater High School, first place, Bradley Central High School, second place and Red Bank High School, third place; and David Marr, President, Linda Scott, Vice-President, and

Susan Campbell, Secretary, were re-elected (for the second consecutive year) as officers of the Alumni Association.

Numerous awards were presented at the 1984 Athletic Banquet. The guest speaker at the banquet was Joe Dean, Jr., Head Basketball Coach at Birmingham Southern. The Dr. Adkisson Athlete of the Year Award was presented to Rhonda Snow. She was named to the NJCAA All-American fast pitch softball first team for the second time (she planned to attend Southern Illinois in the fall). Another outstanding player, Kim Gentry, was also selected as a NJCAA All-American. The team finished the season with a 22-4 record and won 3rd place in the national tournament in Illinois. Two of the four losses were to four-year colleges. The Lady Cougars were defeated by Central Arizona, the team that won the championship. That team played 60 games during the season as opposed to Cleveland State's 26-game schedule. Jon Miller was named Most Valuable Player for the basketball team. He was also named to the first team of the 1984 NJCAA Men's All-American basketball team. He was the first men's basketball player from the college to achieve the honor. He averaged 25 points and eleven rebounds per game. He was also named to the All Eastern Division Team, the TJCAA All State Team, and he was co-player of the year for the All Region Team of two-year colleges in Tennessee, Kentucky and Mississippi.

Another NJCAA All-American in baseball was Doug Beard. He led the nation with 78 RBIs, was 2nd with 18 home runs and was 4th with a batting average of .525. The team had a great season, and Beard was also selected as the team's Most Valuable Player. With 12 games left, the team's record was 24-6, and pitchers Cordell Evans and Eric Shellnut had 5-1 records, and Brad Smith was 3-0 with three saves. Jennifer White won the George L. Mathis Scholastic Award, and the Cougar Club's Outstanding Member Award was presented to businessman Scott Ratterman. Scholarships to four-year colleges were awarded to Kelvin Elston (Birmingham Southern), Connie Horner (Coastal Carolina), Jose Pena (Austin Peay and Brian Metler (ETSU). Other athletes also received scholarships at a later date.

The coach of the Lady Cougar basketball team, Hugh Walker, won his 200th game during 1984. In ten seasons at Cleveland State, his teams won 205 games and lost less than 50. At that time, he was the 6th winningest junior college coach in the nation. His teams competed in two national tournaments and finished 4th and 7th. He was also a former coach of the year in the TJCAA. Dr. Lane noted that Walker had been the only basketball coach since the women's program started at Cleveland State. Lane also stated that Walker demonstrated fine "character and excellent principles of living and has taught the young women to be courteous, fair, friendly and competitive in the sports area as well as in life."

Charles Cogdill, the men's basketball coach, became both the new Lady Cougar basketball and softball coach. Morris Lyons was a standout player on the basketball team. He led the team to a divisional title and averaged 14 points per game. Jim Cigliano vacated the position of Athletic Director and devoted full time to his duties as Assistant Dean of Personnel Services. Steve Longley, former head baseball coach, became the Athletic Director and continued to teach classes in Physical Education. Dennis C. Helms, who had coaching experience in Iowa and Missouri, became the new men's basketball coach. He resigned, for personal reasons, shortly thereafter, and Dan Trotter became the 2nd men's basketball coach named in two months. Trotter compiled a 147-100 record at Martin Junior College and coached one All-American, five All-Regional, and fifteen All-Divisional players. He earned a Bachelor's degree from Columbus College in Georgia and a Master's degree from Georgia Southern College. Wayne Norfleet, as noted earlier, replaced Steve Longley as coach of the baseball team. The baseball team members for 1984 were Scott Erby, David Dinger, Brian Metler, Randall Key, Tony Ellis, Mark McGuill, Doug Beard, Jose Pena, David Shields, Monte Williams, Mike Bivins, Terry Sloan, Brian Scoggins, Tim Tuck, Bobby Hampton, Lester Hixson, Chris Cooper, Ernie Droke, Cordell Evans, Brian Moore, Tim Poteet, Eric Shellnut, Brad Smith and DeWayne Walters. The team finished third in the Division and compiled a 29-10 record.

Several faculty members and students excelled in extracurricular activities during 1984. Jere Chumley won 1st place in Drawing and 2nd place in Oil Painting at the Cleveland Creative Arts Guild Spring Festival. Three students also won awards: Ellen Reiser won 2nd place in Drawing; Mark Gregg won 3rd place in Drawing; and Margaret Richardson won 3rd place in Mixed Media. Faculty member Dale Yates (Associate Professor of Accounting) was elected as Director of the Tennessee Society of Accounting Educators (TSAE). Thirty-five Accounting Educators from twenty-one Tennessee colleges and universities attended the inaugural meeting of the organization at Tennessee Tech. Ann McCoin, Coordinator of the Legal Assistant Program, was elected to the Board of Directors of the American Association for Paralegal Educators at the 9th Annual Conference of Paralegal Program Directors and Educators. The conference was held in Lexington, Kentucky, and she was elected to a three-year term as a representative for public community and junior colleges. Shelby Millsaps, Head of Nursing, was elected as chairperson of the Deans and Directors for the Schools of Nursing Conference held in Nashville, and Dr. Charles Wheeler (Math and Science Department) was elected as the college's President of the Faculty Senate.

The Cherokee Signal wrote a feature on Associate Professor of Math, Joe Guest. Guest completed a Bachelor's degree in Education at Delta State College, received a Master's degree in Math from George Peabody College and completed post-graduate work at George Peabody and Auburn University. He taught at McNeese State University (in Lake Charles, Louisiana), UT Martin and Arkansas State University. He also taught high school in Pulaski, Tennessee. At CSCC he taught calculus, trigonometry and upper-level Algebra. He played an instrumental role in developing video tapes for math classes. He noted that the best job opportunities for math majors were in engineering and computer science.

Dr. Mary Barker, Director of Institutional Planning and Research, was one of four Tennesseans selected to attend a three-day training workshop for a national reading and discussion project. The event was sponsored by the American Library Association and funded by the National Endowment for the Humanities. Four-member teams, representing eighteen Eastern States, were invited to the Greenbriar Resort in White Sulphur Springs, West Virginia, to learn how to apply for grants for public libraries to conduct reading and discussion groups for out-of-school adults. Harry Dean, Associate Professor of English, was the featured speaker for the Virginia Community College Writer's Project (held in May 1984). Faculty members Nancy Boyd, Sherra Witt and Billie McCaffrey were the coordinators for the Annual Tennessee Office of Education Association Conference. Conducted at Cleveland State, two hundred students from 14 area schools participated in contests ranging from Accounting to Word Processing and to Job Interviewing.

In honor of the 1984 Summer Olympics, John Bradley wrote an article for the campus Employee Newsletter titled, "The Olympic Spirit." He made the following observations: if CSCC hosted the Olympics it could have a contest for jumping across Lake Ocoee; the state of Tennessee would win the competition for the most unusual theme song for a state prison system—"Free Again" (a reference to the numerous pardons granted by former Governor Ray Blanton as well as his release from prison); and that a female employee was so enthralled by the handsome male Swedish and Finnish athletes she was heard singing, "I got a liking for a Viking."

In other articles Bradley noted that religious scholars had made a startling discovery: the apostles traveled in a Honda. To prove their claim, the scholars quoted the Bible verse: "and the apostles were all in one Accord." In response to numerous student complaints about parking inconvenience at the college, Bradley wrote that Dr. Lane "has requested that the state architect design parking spaces within the classrooms, thus allowing students to drive right to their desks." Each semester students completed anonymous evaluations of their instructors. Bradley indicated that one student wondered if Bradley had been with Noah on the Ark and that Bradley's lectures gave him a headache. Bradley jokingly wrote, "That student will fail." Another student wrote that "I don't know whether to make you 10 years younger on account of your looks, or 10 years older on account of your intelligence." Bradley wrote, "That student will receive an A."

Several alumni were highlighted in the Employee Newsletter in 1984: alumnus Amanda Willoughby taught French part-time at the college and full-time at Cleveland High School; alumnus Jeffrey Johnson, son of Assistant Professor of Business, John Johnson, was accepted at the UT Medical School at Memphis; Denise Lunsford, a Photography and Art student, had her work published in the Best of College Photography Annual: 1984 (her work was one of the 6% selected from over 17,500 entries from more than 5,800 students); Cindy Hicks was working with the State Film Commission in Nashville; her sister, Donna Goins, was working in the Business Office at CSCC;

Rachel Green won the Best-of-Show award at the Advanced Painters Exhibition at MTSU; and James Richard Hodge, the first Art major to graduate from CSCC (in 1969), was the Assistant Director of the Art and Architecture Gallery at UTK. Hodge served as the judge for the Cleveland Community Art Competition of 1984, and 1st place was awarded to Elizabeth Harris of Cleveland, 2nd place was won by Stan Gilliam of Dalton, and 3rd place was awarded to Judy Mraz of Dalton.

Another highlight of the year was a piano recital performed by alumnus Sayoko Murakawa. A native of Nijagata, Japan, she was an EIL student at the age of 15. Her music teacher at CSCC was Tom Boles, and while attending college, she lived with the family of Dr. Charles Tollett. Tollett recounted a humorous story about Murakawa. After her return to Japan, she asked for the ingredients for pinto beans and cornbread. Tollett sent her cornmeal and a two-pound bag of dried pinto beans. Not realizing the beans would quadruple in size, she cooked the entire two-pound bag, and soon her kitchen was overflowing with beans.

Other student newsmakers were the members of the staff of The Cherokee Signal student newspaper. They were: Rene Fink, Editor; Dawn Guthrie, News Editor; Tim Wofford, Editorial Editor; Viola Mason, Photo Editor; Teresa Williams, Business Manager; Polly Fowler, Typesetter; and David Suttles, Faculty Advisor. Later, the staff members were: Dawn Guthrie, Editor; Sherry Lively and Lynette McDonald, News Editors; Viola Mason, Photo Editor; Ben Benton, Sports Editor; Teresa Williams, Business Manager; Polly Fowler, Typesetter; and David Suttles, Faculty Advisor. Also later, the Editor was James R. Milhouse, and the Photo Editor was Darrell Hoggatt. The members of the College Bowl Team were John Conner, Cynthia Poteet, Jeff Crisp, Keith Harper, Sam Richardson and Joe Conway. The faculty advisors were Pat Bishop and David Suttles. The members of PTK were: Loretta Jones, past-President; Teresa Williams, past-Secretary; Mark Odum, President; Lynda Knight, President; and Loring Rogers, Membership Chair. The faculty advisor was John Bradley.

A social outlet for many students was attending the "interactive" movie, the "Rocky Horror Picture Show." Lee Anne Allen, a student writing for The Cherokee Signal, listed the items one needed for the event. They were: rice for the opening scene; a squirt gun to create a wet atmosphere for the rain storm that occurs on the screen; a newspaper to protect one from the "rain;" a party noise maker to participate in Rocky's creation day; a roll of toilet paper to throw when the line "great Scott" is spoken; a piece of dry toast for when Dr. Frank proposes a toast; a deck of cards to be thrown when Dr. Frank sings the line "cards for sorrow, cards for pain;" and one must know how to dance the "time warp" in which the entire audience participated.

A couple of student newsmakers were Carla Jo Leamon and Steve Morgan. Leamon, a singer, made an album titled, "Country Girls Dream." She dedicated it to her Dad and brothers whose gospel-singing group had performed with the Oak Ridge Boys. In

1983 she won the title of "National Modern Miss." She was a finalist in the Miss Teen Pageant, and she won "Miss Photogenic" and "Miss Congeniality" at the contest. While a student at Cleveland State, she also performed several nights a week at the Holiday Inn in Oak Ridge. As noted earlier, Morgan was chosen by the International Studies Association to tour Spain. His Spanish instructor, Efrain Guillen, recommended him to the association and he was one of approximately 160 American students to be chosen. He spent a month living in the dormitories of the University of Madrid and he toured, among other sites, the Royal Palace, the Plaza Mayor and the Puerto del Sol. He also attended poetry readings, operas and concerts.

The 1983-84 officers for the SGA were: Robert Bradney, President; Denise Davis, Vice-President; Beth Scoggins, Secretary; and Randy Mantooth, Parliamentarian. Bryon Rickard served part of the time as Parliamentarian, and Scoggins served part of the time as both Secretary and Parliamentarian. The new officers for 1984-85 were Tony Pharr as President and Teresa Lougheed as Vice-President. The Homecoming Queen was Annette York, and the Commencement speaker was Dr. William H. Long, the Chief of Staff to Governor Lamar Alexander. The Outstanding Graduate Award was presented to Amy Lynn Oliver, and the Faculty Merit Award was awarded to Joe Guest.

– 1985 –

In 1985 international wars continued in Afghanistan, Kampuchea, Iran and Iraq. There were civil wars in Central America, the Philippines and several African nations. Violence was rampant in Lebanon, South Africa and Northern Ireland, and hijackings by Middle Eastern terrorists took heavy tolls of lives. The Soviet Union changed leaders three times between 1981 and 1985. Other major international events in 1985 were: world leaders gathered in New York to celebrate the 40th Anniversary of the United Nations; a debate in the British House of Lords was aired on television for the first time; Konstantin U. Chernenko, the leader of the Soviet Union, died and was replaced by Mikhail S. Gorbachev; the remains of the body of Dr. Josef Mengele, the notorious "Angel of Death" of the Nazi Holocaust, were exhumed in Brazil; an international "Live Aid" rock concert was broadcast via satellite to London, Philadelphia, Moscow and Sydney to raise money for Africa's starving people; a group of American pop stars recorded a song and video, for famine relief, titled "We Are the World;" this record, and a record by British pop stars, titled, "Do They Know It's Christmas," raised $45 million for aid; U. S. fighter jets forced an Egyptian plane carrying the hijackers of the Italian cruise ship Achille Lauro to land in Italy, and the gunmen were arrested; and President Ronald Reagan and Soviet leader Mikhail Gorbachev met for the first time in Geneva and agreed to work on a 50% reduction in nuclear weapons.

The major domestic events were: undersea explorers discovered the remains of the luxury liner, "Titanic;" Tennessee announced that the Saturn car would be built in Smyrna,

Tennessee; a new type of narcotic, known as "crack," made an appearance on the drug scene; the first internet domain name, "symbolics.com," was registered in Massachusetts; Jake Gam of Utah became the first sitting member of Congress to fly in space as the shuttle Discovery was launched; the legendary highway Route 66 passed into history as officials decertified the road; actor Rock Hudson died of AIDS at the age of 59 at his home in Beverly Hills, California; singer Rick Nelson, at the age of 45, died in a plane crash; eleven people were killed, and fire damaged two blocks of houses when Philadelphia police bombed a "rowhouse" occupied by members of the "Move" radical group; Coca-Cola announced that it would resume marketing soda made under its original "classic" formula; and General Electric bought RCA Corporation for $6.28 billion.

In popular culture "Out of Africa" won the award for best picture; William Hurt won the best actor award for "Kiss of the Spider Woman;" and Geraldine Page won the best actress award for "The Trip to Bountiful." The Emmy Award for best comedy was presented to "The Cosby Show" (NBC), and the Emmy for best drama was awarded to "Cagney and Lucy" (CBS). The musical group, USA for Africa, won the Grammy Award for record of the year for the song, "We Are the World," and Phil Collins won the Grammy Album of the year for "No Jacket Required." Winners in basketball were Old Dominion, for the NCAA Division I Women's Basketball Championship, and Villanova won the men's trophy. San Francisco defeated Miami in the Super Bowl, and Kansas City defeated St. Louis in the World Series.

Several students received good news in 1985. The College's Foundation provided a record amount of $75,000 to fund 131 full scholarships. Although he had retired as college President, Dr. Adkisson continued to serve as President of the Foundation until 1985. The Foundation Trustees honored his 15 years of service with a resolution naming him as a lifetime honorary member of the Foundation Executive Committee. Harold Almond was elected as the new President, and he served in that position until 1988. Other elected officers were; Arch Fitzgerald, Vice President; Mike Callaway, Treasurer; Dr. Mathis, Secretary; and W. K. Fillauer and Ray Coleman were named as members-at-large to the Executive Committee. The new trustees elected to three-year terms were: Donald Jarvis, manager of the Cleveland First Federal Savings and Loan; Sahira Sorrells, On-Job-Coordinator for the JTPA; Larry Henderson, engineer with Bowater Southern Paper Corporation; Nora McNeill, corporate secretary with Robinson Supply Company; Ray Coleman, interim President of Cleveland State; Dr. Mary Barker, Director of Institutional Research at Cleveland State; and Jim Cigliano, Assistant Dean of Student Services at Cleveland State.

The following trustees were given one-year appointments: Dr. Don Robinson, President of Cleveland Rotary Club; Reba Robbins, President of the Cleveland Pilot Club; Jim Workman, President of the Cleveland Kiwanis Club; and Beth Woodard, President of the Cleveland Civitan Club. Twenty-nine trustees were reappointed to three-year terms, and Carl Painter, President of Ducktown Banking Company, was reappointed to a four-year term on the Investment Committee. Investments, as of June 30, 1985, were $764,342.54. Interest earned in 1984 was $82,344.50, and contributions were $84,907.88.

Several interesting statistics were accumulated in 1985. A nation-wide Gallup Poll was conducted on the question of "How Important is a College Education?" The results were compared to 1978. In 1978 thirty-six percent believed it was "very important," and in 1985 the percentage increased to 64%. Sixteen percent believed it "not too important" in 1978 versus 7% in 1985. Another study revealed there were approximately 1,300 two-year colleges in the nation with about five million students. Of these students, 63% were part-time adults with and average age of thirty, and 53% were women. Over 40% of all students were enrolled in two-year colleges.

A Southern Regional Education Board (SREB) report (in 2015 the SREB had 16 member states) indicated that Cleveland State compared favorably with both SREB standards and Tennessee standards for the ratio of people served by the college per population. The SREB believed an acceptable rate of service was enrolling one out of 30 citizens, from the population age range of 15 to 24, and one out of 100 citizens from the population age range of 25 and above. In 1985 Cleveland State was serving one out of 17, for ages 15 to 24, and one out of 60, for ages 25 and above. Statewide, the average was one out of 32, for ages 15-24, and one out of 105, for ages 25 and above. According to one source, the college's total headcount enrollment for the fall of 1985 was 3,959 and the full-time equivalency (FTE) enrollment was 1,901. Another source indicated the headcount was 3,144 and the FTE was 1895.

Another 1985 nationwide government study indicated that one of every four college freshmen were enrolled in remedial math courses and one in six in remedial reading. Sixty-three percent of the colleges and universities surveyed reported that they had more students enrolled in remedial courses in 1984 than in 1978. A Tennessee State Board of Regents (TBR) report revealed that only 25% of students entering the state's universities and community colleges attained a degree within a five-year period. The high dropout rate was the result of the inability of students to fulfill the demands of college course requirements. In response to the problem the TBR (in 1985) made the American College Testing (ACT) exam a requirement for all students enrolling at the TBR's six universities, ten community colleges and four technical institutes. The exam would be used to assess the preparedness of students for college level coursework. The ACT exam did not apply to students 21 years of age or older, or for students of any age who were not enrolled in regular degree-credit programs.

The TBR also set aside specified funds to be used for rewarding the performances of its institutions that excelled in improving instruction. Prior to graduation, degree-seeking students were required to take a College Outcome Measures Program (COMP) exam to assess their readiness to function as an adult in society. The unique exam did not specifically address subject matter, such as reading, writing or arithmetic, but rather it asked questions involving problem-solving and thinking skills. "Performance funding" money was awarded, in accordance with a point system, to the colleges and universities that excelled on the COMP results. The TBR also decided, in its 1984 December meeting, to observe the Martin Luther King holiday beginning in January of 1985.

In the fall of 1985 Cleveland State and other Community Colleges began requiring entering freshmen to take placement tests if they scored below 16 on the ACT exam. The tests, known as the Academic Assessment Placement Program (AAPP), consisted of four subject areas: mathematics, reading comprehension, logical relationships and writing skills. Those who did not have satisfactory scores on the AAPP tests were required to take either remedial or developmental courses. Teaching the courses was challenging because students were often displeased that they were required to take them. The courses were whimsically referred to as "Rem-Devil" courses. In 1984 Tennessee high school students scored an average of 17.7 on the ACT exam. This placed Tennessee 21st of 28 states using the ACT. The other states used the Scholastic Aptitude Test (SAT). In other Tennessee statistical studies the following information was revealed: about 65% of high school students graduated in 1984 and almost 69% in 1982; in 1980, 20.6% of Tennessee children, aged 5-17, were living in poverty; the state's adult median education level was 12.2 years of schooling in 1980, and this ranked Tennessee 42nd in the nation; and the state's per capita income in 1984 was $9,549, and Tennessee was ranked 44th in the nation.

After spending fourteen years at CSCC, Dr. Quentin Lane decided he would retire on June 30, 1985. He had been President since July 1, 1978. A committee was formed to recommend an interim President. The members were: Sherra Witt, Chair; Ray Coleman and James Cigliano, Administrative co-Chairs; Walter Presswood, Alumni Chair: Tony Pharr and Amanda Lewis, Student Co-Chairs, Norma Davis and Tom Losh, Staff co-Chairs and Joe Dzikielewski, Faculty Chair. John Bradley was named Chair of a separate Retirement Committee which recommended that the Gym be named the L. Quentin Lane Gymnasium. It was approved by the SBR and became a reality on June 30, 1985. In addition CSCC employees gave tickets to Hawaii as a farewell gift to Dr. Lane and his wife.

Prior to the above recognitions, Bradley presented his comedic suggestions for Lane's retirement gift: help him pack; name a walkway for him and call it "Lane's Lane;" and have a bake sale and give the proceeds to him. Furthermore, Bradley wrote in his weekly column for the Employee Newsletter that a rumor indicated the college would no longer have a permanent President. Instead, there would be a President-of-the-Month Club. Each month the college would receive a brochure featuring the incoming President for the following month. The college could either accept or reject the selection by sending a refusal notice by the 20th day of each month. The college would be obligated, however, to accept at least four choices during each 12-month period.

Ray Coleman served as the interim President from July 1, 1985 to January 1, 1986. Arriving at CSCC in 1971, Coleman was, at various times, the Director of the Evening Division, the Director of Institutional Research and the Dean of Administrative Services. Prior to that, he had worked with the Chattanooga Public School System, in various teaching and administrative positions, since 1951. Meanwhile, Governor Lamar Alexander and the TBR Chancellor, Roy Nicks, appointed two key committees to assist with the selection of a new President. Alexander named an ad hoc TBR committee composed of the following: Ross N. Faires of Oneida, Chair; C. Scott Mayfield of Athens; and Dr. J. D. Johnson of Oak Ridge. An advisory committee named by Nicks, to assist with screening candidates, was composed of the following: Bob Sain, Manager of J. C. Penney; Harold Almond, President-elect of the college's Foundation; Tony Pharr, President of the SGA; Dr. Charles Wheeler, Faculty member; Alex Nichols, Faculty member; Ray Coleman, Interim President; and Evonne Drown, Staff member.

Chancellor Nicks also decided to meet with four other advisory groups concerning the selection of a new President. One group represented professional non-faculty and classified employee representatives. They were: Bill Clark, Ray Coleman, Rosemary Den Uyl, Josephine Pritchett, Lou Thompson, Dr. Charles Tollett and Gayle Wood. The second group was composed of community representatives. They were: Dr. D. F. Adkisson, Harold Almond, Arch Fitzgerald, William K. Fillauer, Mike Callaway, Dale Hughes (Principal of Bradley County High School and Vice-President of the Cleveland-Bradley Chamber of Commerce). The third group represented students. These were: Tony Pharr, SGA President; Teresa Lougheed, SGA Vice-President; Maria Parham, SGA Secretary; and Jim Millhouse, Editor of The Cherokee Signal. The fourth group represented the faculty and the members were: Dr. Charles Wheeler, President of the Faculty Senate; Dr. Larry Longerbeam; Vice-President of the Faulty Senate; Dr. Jerome Taylor, Secretary of the Faculty Senate; Alex Nichols, President of the CSCC Education Association (CSCCEA); Joe Guest, President-elect of the CSCCEA; Kathryn Johnson, Secretary-Treasurer of the CSCCEA; and Ann McCoin, the past-President of the CSCCEA.

Unfortunately, the college received a low score on performance for the year of 1984. The report was intended for internal management purposes and the scores fluctuated at all colleges from year to year. When a college scored a maximum of 100 points, it was awarded an increase of 5% of its total appropriation. Had the college achieved this number, it would have received $225,150. The modest score of 74, for that year, meant the supplement would drop to $166,611. Meanwhile, on November 8, 1985, the TBR named Dr. James W. Ford as the college's new President. Dyersburg State Community College also named a new President, Dr. Karen Bowyer. Both the appointments were blocked, however, because of a lawsuit against the state of Tennessee.

Both Ford and Bowyer were Caucasian. Therefore, attorneys for the plaintiffs argued that the TBR had failed to make adequate efforts to seek minority candidates. A federal court order, issued by United States District Judge Thomas A. Wiseman, imposed a temporary restraining order blocking the appointments. In addition the appointment of a new Director of the Tennessee Higher Education Commission was blocked, and the search for a new President for Tennessee State University was delayed until a determination was made if adequate searches for minority candidates had been conducted. In the meantime Ray Coleman continued to act as the college's interim President. State Attorney General Mike Cody, acting on behalf of the TBR, appealed the case and the blocks were eventually lifted. Dr. Ford assumed the Presidency on January 1, 1986.

Dr. James W. Ford, Jr. was Dean of Academic Affairs at Walters State Community College (since 1977). He received his Bachelor's degrees from South Florida, majoring in Physics and with minors in Math and Astronomy. He received his Doctorate at Vanderbilt University and majored in Physics with a minor in Math. He worked in the Vanderbilt Physics Department, was an Atomic Energy Commission Health Physics Fellow at Oak Ridge Associated University and worked at the NASA Electric Systems Branch in Cape Kennedy.

The Winter Quarter at the college was confusing because of the assaults of snow and ice on the campus and community. Classes had to be cancelled on various Mondays and Tuesdays and even one Wednesday. Thursday was the only day that escaped a cancellation due to inclement weather. Although the campus was still operating on a four-day week, Fridays became either Mondays or Tuesdays. As John Bradley noted in one of his articles for the Employee Newsletter, Monday, March 11, 1985 would be the most confusing day of the winter. He wrote, "From 8 a. m. until 5:59 p. m., that Monday will be a Wednesday. Then, at 6 p. m., as if by magic, that Monday, which had been a Wednesday, reverts to being a Monday again."

A variety of activities were presented by the college during the year. In March a two act suspenseful drama, "Night Watch," was performed for the campus and the community. The cast featured Pat Meagher, John Bradley, Suzanne Allen, Clyde Tidwell, Rick Melvin, Lois Wyche, Steve Gatlin and Perry Skates. The annual High School Bowl was held the next month, and Cleveland High School captured 1st Place honors. In November the CSCC Youth Players (ages 9 through 16) completed a video tape by the Media Department at the college. Titled, "Coming Home to Tennessee," the song was written by the Director of the group, Warnie Finnell. In an article for the Employee Newsletter, Finnell expressed thanks to the following employees: Pat Govan, Sam Neas, Dr. Charles Tollett, Dr. Rodney Fitzgerald, Walter Presswood, Al Fine, Joan Brown and Verna Moore. Later in the month the college conducted its first dinner-theater production. The performance was in the college's auditorium and it was preceded by a Spaghetti Dinner in the Community Services Building. The play, "Curious Savage," was directed by John Bradley and featured CSCC students Sandy Tinker, Todd Averett, Tracey Howard, Leonard Roll III and Jim Ludwig. Other cast members were Cheri Hancock, Dwayne Hall, Marianne Moisan, Gary Davis, Maurine Nichols and

Clyde Tidwell. Proceeds from the production were presented to the college's Cougar Club and to the Foundation Scholarship Fund.

The college's Alumni Association held elections for new officers in April. Outgoing President, David Marr, who had served two one-year terms, was replaced by Susan Campbell. Other officers were: Linda Scott, Vice-President; Janie Lawhon, Secretary; Carol Clark, Treasurer; and Wayne Harris, Member-at-Large. Alumnus Tedrick Elmendorfer made an unusual contribution to the college. He ran an advertisement for about a two-week period in three Chattanooga businesses that read, "At Cleveland State, we put YOU ahead." Elmendorfer was the Director of Operations for Pioneer Communications and stated that he wanted to show his appreciation to the college and his instructors for his education.

Other alumni in the news were Sally DeWitt Ealy, Jennifer Johnson, Sheila Freeman and Jerry Evans. Ealy, a Tennessee and American history teacher at Englewood Elementary School, received an Award of Appreciation for Outstanding Teachers of the Humanities by the Tennessee Humanities Council. Johnson, daughter of the college's Accounting Professor, John Johnson, became the first recipient of the Student Merit Scholarship given by the American Society for Personnel Administration. A senior at MTSU, she was selected from finalists at MTSU, Belmont and Tennessee State University. Freeman was working on her Master's at UTC and was employed with the Cleveland City Police Department. She received a Distinguished Service Award and was a finalist in the Jaycee Women's Outstanding Young Woman Award. Evans, also a CSCC graduate, received his Criminal Justice degree from UTC and was appointed as Chattanooga's new Fire Chief.

A long-time faculty member, Tom Boles, announced his retirement in 1985. Boles had been in charge of the Music Department at the college since his arrival in 1967. He played both the organ and the piano and was a baritone singer. Prior to his arrival at the college, he presented solo performances with the Knoxville Symphony, directed a chorus of 800 high school students at a Sullivan County Choral Festival and directed a girls' chorus of 350 at Science Hill High School. A graduate of ETSU, he had a Master's in Music from the University of Oklahoma, had taught at Morristown High School, been a Supervisor at Greeneville High School, and was the Head of the Music Department at three different locations: Bethel College, Science Hill High School and ETSU. Several of his students excelled in music. For example, Charles Layne won the Tennessee State Auditions competition sponsored by the Music Teachers National Association, and Joe Taylor toured with a group called "Regeneration." Taylor also performed at Epcot Center in Disney World.

In athletics the college men's basketball team achieved a record of 18 wins and 10 losses. The team members were: Joshua Bone, Norris Chesterfield, Lee Cigliano, Morris Lyons, Cassius Watkins, Hugh Cantrell, Brent Clarke, Chris Day, Archie Hughes,

Gary Rodgers, Kenny Stover, Keith Umberger, Leon Miller and Mike Wilson. Miller and Wilson were selected for both the All-Eastern Division and All-TJCAA teams. The coach was Dan Trotter, the manager was Gary Peavyhouse, and Dr. Herbert Cline, part-time instructor in Developmental Studies, served as a volunteer assistant coach. The team won the TJCAA Eastern Division title, finished second in the TJCAA tourney and played in the Region VII Tournament. Trotter was named TJCAA Eastern Division Coach of the Year. Coach Charlie Cogdill's Lady Cougar basketball team compiled a 17-7 record, and he was also named TJCAA Eastern Division Coach of the Year. Susan Stults was the leading scorer with a 14.3 average. She also averaged 8.8 rebounds per game and was named to the All-TJCAA team.

The 1985 Athletic Banquet was held in June and the following won Most Valuable Player Awards: Cordell Evans, baseball; Susan Stults, women's basketball; and Kim Gentry, softball. Susan Stults also received the Athlete of the Year Award. Earlier, she had been named 1985 Homecoming Queen. Janet Murray Ownby won the Scholastic Award and was named an Academic All-American by the NJCAA. Robert Kincaid, basketball timekeeper, received the Cougar Club Award for faithful and outstanding support of CSCC athletics. The guest speaker for the event was Roy Exum, Executive Sports Editor of the Chattanooga News-Free Press. The newspaper later changed its name to the Chattanooga Times Free Press (perhaps partially because E. B. White, in his book, The Elements of Style, noted that "news-free" means free of news).

A few staff members were also newsmakers in 1985. They were: Adeline Baskett was appointed Chair of a statewide task force on literacy for the Tennessee Library Association; Walter Presswood and Dr. David Watts attended a Council for Advancement and Support of Education (CASE) Conference in Williamsburg, Virginia; Dr. Mary Barker was named Chair of the Tennessee Committee for Humanities for 1985-86; and Maintenance personnel, Levi Brown and Arthur Foster, announced their retirement from the college. Personnel in the Departments of Student Services were: Jim Cigliano (Assistant Dean of Student Services), Norma Davis (Secretary),Tom Losh (Director of Student Information Services), Shelby Guliford, Lydia Norfleet, Bill Gatlin, Marty Allen, Gail Key, Alta Presswood, Ruth Miller, Doris Gettis, Ruth Bailey, Karen Lynn Gibson and Darlene Johnson. Personnel in the Departments of Student Development and Student Activities were: Karen Lee Gibson (Director of Student Development), Adrian Strother, Gayle Wood, Karen Tipps, Dot Cantrell, Robert Taylor (Director of Student Programs and Activities), Charles Cogdill, Wayne Norfleet, Sandi Armstrong and Daniel Trotter.

Other events in 1985 were as follows: the college was saddened by the news that James Robert Stephens, a member of the 1982 Cougar baseball team, died from injuries in an automobile accident; Lee Cigliano was named to the TBR Committee on Academic Policies and Programs; and, as noted above, Susan Stults was crowned Homecoming Queen during halftime of a basketball game in which she scored 18 points and grabbed 10 rebounds. The new SGA President was Amanda Lewis; and the new members of <u>The Cherokee Signal</u> staff were: Ginger Hinson, Editor; Connie Rudder and Tina Skelton, co-Sports Editors; Tracy Bacon, News Editor; Bernie Rubin and Michele Millhouse, Business Managers; Polly Fowler, Typesetter; Darrell Hoggatt, Photo Editor; and David Suttles, Faculty Advisor. The representatives to the Tennessee Intercollegiate State Legislature (TISL) were Amanda Lewis, Nancy Cartwright, Valerie Wheeler, Bill Hammons, Sharon Lougheed, Debbie Lougheed, Melissa Rogers, Ken Owens, Kinney Short and Pam Green.

The Commencement Speaker, in June 1985, was David Marr. He was a CSCC graduate in 1974 and received his Bachelor's and Master's degrees from Augusta Medical College. He served two terms as President of the college's Alumni Association and was Director of Nursing at Fentress County Hospital. The Outstanding Graduate Award was presented to Tony Pharr, and the Faculty Merit Award was received by Michael A. Dorset.

– 1986 –

The major international events of the year were: terrorism hit several countries and in one ten-day period terrorists staged five bomb attacks in Paris; in Sweden a gunman killed Prime Minister Olof Palme, and the crime has never been solved; President Ferdinand Marcos fled the Philippines after a fraudulent election, and Corazon Aquino, widow of an opposition leader who had been assassinated, replaced him; two American servicemen and a Turkish woman were killed in the bombing of a West Berlin disco club; the United States bombed military targets in Libya after evidence linked Libya to the disco bombing; Pope John Paul II visited a Jewish synagogue in the first recorded papal visit to a Jewish house of worship; at London's Heathrow Airport, a bomb was discovered in the bag of a pregnant Irish woman who had been tricked by her Jordanian fiancé into carrying it aboard an El Al jet heading to Israel; a nuclear reactor at the Soviet Union's Chernobyl power station ruptured and spread radioactive substances throughout Russia and the world; Britain's Prince Andrew married Sara Ferguson in London (the couple divorced ten years later); Haitian President Jean-Claude Duvalier fled to France and was replaced by a military-civilian council; Desmond Tutu became the first Black man to lead the Anglican Church in South Africa; and 22 million people visited Vancouver's "Expo 86 World Fair."

The major domestic events were: the nation officially observed Martin Luther King, Jr. Day for the first time on January 20th; a cyanide-tainted Tylenol tablet killed a woman in Peeksville, New York, and Johnson and Johnson announced it would no longer sell over-the-counter medications in capsule form; the U. S. space shuttle, "Challenger," exploded killing all six crew members and "Teacher in Space Project" participant, Christa McAuliffe; an estimated seven million Americans participated in

"Hands Across America" to raise money for the nation's hungry and homeless; in a four-day extravaganza in July, the U. S. celebrated the 100th birthday of the Statue of Liberty; a political scandal erupted when it was discovered that certain officials in President Reagan's administration were involved in secret arms dealings with Iran and that some of the money from the sales had been sent to the American-backed contra rebels seeking to overthrow Nicaragua's Marxist Government; Supreme Court Chief Justice Warren E. Burger retired and was replaced by Associate Justice William H. Rehnquist (Rehnquist's position was filled by Antonin Scalia); in an "insider trading" scandal, Ivan Boesky agreed to pay $100 million in fines for illicit profits and to plead guilty to an unspecified criminal charge; actor James Cagney died at the age of 86; actor Cary Grant died at the age of 82; and Robert Penn Warren was named America's first poet laureate by the Library of Congress.

In popular culture the academy award for best movie was awarded to "Platoon." Paul Newman received the best actor award for "The Color of Money," and Marlee Matlin was named best actress for "Children of a Lesser God." The Emmy Award for television's best comedy was presented to "Golden Girls" (NBC), and the Emmy for best drama was awarded to "Cagney and Lacey" (CBS). The Grammy Award for best record of the year was won by Steve Winwood for "Higher Love," and the Grammy for album of the year was won by Paul Simon for "Graceland." In athletics Texas won the NCAA Division I Women's Basketball Championship, and Louisville won the Men's Championship. The Chicago Bears defeated the New England Patriots in the Super Bowl, and the New York Mets defeated the Boston Red Sox in the World Series.

One of the earliest agenda items for 1986 was the four-day week. A committee was appointed by Dr. Ford to report on its pros and cons. The members were: Ray Coleman, Administration; Amanda Lewis, Student; Charles Wheeler, Faculty; Debbi Trotter, Classified Employee; and Gayle Wood, Professional non-Faculty. A few of the pros were: it benefited evening students because all administrative offices were open until night classes began at 6 p.m.; day class times were the same time for each of the four days; students could save money on gasoline expenses; and the college saved money on energy with a four-day week. The cons were: the library and other facilities were not open on Fridays; the belief that work production declined from 4:30 to 6:00 p.m.; college hours did not conform to other area business and industry work hours; and the number of classes students could take was somewhat limited by a four-day week. On June 1, 1986 the decision was made to return to a five-day week.

The college conducted alumni surveys on a regular basis to assess the effectiveness of its academic programs and to monitor the quality of its services. One of these instruments was the ACT Alumni Survey that asked students for their impressions of the college two years after their graduation. The 1986 survey was typical of most of the surveys. It included all 312 of the June 1984 graduates. Of those, 109 responded

(35%). A few of the responses were: 89% indicated CSCC was their first choice; 76% would choose CSCC again if they started college again; 64% declared they would select the same major; 86% indicated they selected their major for employment and salary purposes; 59% believed CSCC was about the same or better than other colleges, and 80% believed CSCC had improved the quality of their life. In the overall ratings, 33% were very satisfied, 54% satisfied, 7% neutral, 2% dissatisfied and 0% very dissatisfied.

A new construction project resulted in the creation of a weight training and wellness center facility in the gymnasium. The Dr. Scholl Foundation provided $5,000 in construction money and another $9,000 for equipment. A new management term was heard frequently in the 1980s, and thereafter, known as "Enrollment Management." It included activities associated with recruiting, enrolling and retaining students. Numerous committee meetings were conducted to formulate plans supporting the concepts.

The college received good news from THEC when it was announced that CSCC received a perfect score of 100 in Performance Funding. It was the highest score in the state of Tennessee, and it resulted in the college receiving an additional appropriation of $249,120 (which was 5% of the budget for the year). The major improvements were in COMP test scores of graduates and in the increased percentage of career students receiving employment in their area of study within ninety days of graduation. Equally good news was the record amount of $75,000 Foundation money that would be funded for 131 full scholarships to the college.

Another item of good news was the announcement by the TBR that the Nursing Department had been named a "Center of Excellence" and would receive $150,000 over the next three years. It was the first time this type of funding had been recommended for community colleges and technical institutes. The college would be required, however, to match the state's funding each year (with half of the designated amount of $50,000 per year) for the next three years. The money would enable the nursing department to acquire audiovisual materials, computers and various other types of equipment to enhance the program. The award was the result of the success of the nursing program at the college. Approximately 60 students were admitted each year, and about 50 graduated each year. Since 1969, 746 had graduated and approximately 99% of those graduating passed the National Council Licensure Exam. In July 1985, for example, 98% (43 of 44 students) of the nursing students passed the State Licensure Exam. Statewide, only 92% of those attempting the exam passed. Thirty-two schools of nursing and 1,544 students took the 1985 exam. In addition over 90% of CSCC nursing students had received jobs in a related field of employment during the last three years. The National League for Nursing Accreditation Team had just completed a reaccreditation visit to the college and had identified ten areas of strength and no areas of concern for the nursing program. The team concluded that the program was highly effective and had developed an excellent curriculum, possessed a competent faculty and maintained an excellent reputation.

Another event was the announcement of a Statewide School-College Collaborative for Educational Excellence. A luncheon was hosted by the college, on February 28, 1986, for area principals and superintendents to explain the goals and purposes of the collaborative. At the luncheon Dr. Ford described the upcoming change in requirements, which would begin in 1988-89, for admission to Tennessee's colleges and universities. He also noted that another purpose of the collaborative was to develop curricula that would make the transition from high school to college smoother for students.

According to the ACT profile of 1985 high school scores, Tennessee had an ACT composite score of 17.6 and a high school grade average of 2.9. The national averages for college-bound students were 18.6 and 2.9 respectively. One weakness of incoming students at CSCC was the lack of writing skills. In an effort to combat this deficiency a program known as "Writing Across the Curriculum" was initiated in 1986. Faculty members in all disciplines were encouraged to require students to practice writing in their courses. A faculty committee, with representation from Business, English, Math, History and Science areas, was formed to provide guidance and advice for the endeavor. The members were: Nancy Boyd, Chair; Harry Dean; Joe Guest; Dr. Frank McKenzie; Dr. Jerome Taylor; and Dr. Hugh Vroman.

In college activities Bill Gatlin began several one-man Davy Crockett performances in honor of the 200th anniversary of Crockett's birth. Gatlin, a CSCC transcript evaluator in the Office of Admissions and Records, appeared in numerous dramas and dinner theater productions. A few were "The Rainmaker," "One Flew Over the Cuckoo's Nest" and "Cat on a Hot Tin Roof." He made several appearances on the Nashville network and performed in numerous campus dramas. Ten high schools competed in the annual PTK Bowl Quiz, and Soddy Daisy won the 1st Place trophy. The college's Future Secretaries of America Club won two awards in state competition. The Club President was Loretta Mantooth and the faculty advisor was Sherra Witt.

A unique activity was the first "Wheelchair Tennis Clinic" which was conducted at the college tennis courts. Tony Cavett, the tennis professional at the Cleveland Country Club, originated the idea and led the instruction (he would later coach the CSCC tennis team). He was assisted by David Ingram, Robby Ray, Billy Tollett, Charles Tollett, Dale Yates and Kent Smith. The event was jointly sponsored by the Cleveland State Wellness Program and King Medical Equipment Company. Also present were Debbie Ingram, a physical therapist and Director of Rehabilitation for Erlanger Hospital, and Nancy Daffinson, an occupational therapist and employee of Erlanger. Tony's wife, Gena, handled registration, King Medical provided T-shirts, and Jenkins Deli Restaurant provided lunch for all the workers and participants. A "Wheelchair Basketball Game," organized by the college's Legal Assistant Association, also became a regular contest with the "Tennesse Wheelbillies" playing against Cleveland attorneys, who also played in wheelchairs.

Another unique campus event occurred early in the morning of April 5, 1986. Characterized as "Comet Fest '86," the astronomical gathering was jointly sponsored by the college and the Barnard Astronomical Society of Chattanooga. The coordinator of the event was Buford Guy, the college's Associate Professor of Physics and Astronomy. Approximately 2,000 area residents from Bradley, Polk, Hamilton and McMinn counties visited the campus from 3:00 a.m. to 6:30 a.m. to view Comet Halley. A telephone hotline was operated by the college and about 6,000 people contacted it during the twelve weeks of its operation. In addition, over 4,000 posters were distributed and hundreds of people signed the Comet Fest Guest Book and received a certificate commemorating the event. Memorabilia from the occasion was sealed in the college library archives and would be opened in 76 years—the next time Comet Halley appeared to earthlings.

Another major event in 1986 was a Martin Luther King, Jr. Commemoration Service. It was conducted at the St. James Cumberland Presbyterian Church and was sponsored by the CSCC Foundation's Martin Luther King Scholarship Committee, the Bradley County Ministerial Alliance and the Bradley County Chapter of the NAACP. Speakers at the event were: Drew Robinson, Cleveland Attorney; Gayle Wood, CSCC Counselor; Edward Robinson, Minister; Guilford Ron Hill, Minister; and Harvey Robinson, Minister. Music was provided by Greg Pitner, Marcus Dotson and the Church of God Sanctified Choir. Other program participants from the college were Cinda Adams, Bertha Goldston and Elaine Walker. It was announced that the Committee had reached its goal of endowing a scholarship to coincide with King's birthday. Committee members Adams and Goldston were instrumental in raising the funds. The scholarship would be awarded to a worthy student without regard to race, color or creed. Other committee members were co-chairs, Sahira Sorrells and Larry Henderson, Drew Robinson, Reverend James Bridgeman, Nena Howard, Walter Presswood, Helen Miller, Gayle Wood, Cathy Lowe, Dr. L. Quentin Lane and Sue Little.

A new cultural addition to the campus was the result of an initiative launched by Jere Chumley. It was a rotating outdoor sculpture exhibit that continued for the next eight years. During those years various sculpture exhibits were rotated from the CSCC campus to UTK, Walters State, Chattanooga State and Pellissippi State. Chumley traveled to numerous locations, sometimes at his own expense, to acquire sculptures. Several were part of the rotating exhibits while others were permanent donations to the campus.

Each year the Deans, Assistant Deans, Administrators, Faculty and other Supervisors, recognized relevant staff on Secretaries' Day by treating them to lunch, or by presenting them gifts, or by doing other favors for them. In 1986 someone suggested also implementing a "Bosses' Day." Accordingly, a luncheon for bosses was organized and emceed by the resident comedian, John Bradley. He asked, "How many Deans does it take to conduct a kidnapping?" The answer, according to Bradley, was ten. There should be one Dean to capture the subject and nine to write the ransom note. Bradley also asked the following: "If a Secretary and her boss jumped off the Empire State Building at the same time, which one would hit the ground last?" Bradley's response was that it would be the boss because he would need to stop and ask directions.

In one of his articles for the campus Employee Newsletter Bradley discussed the Academy Awards and jokingly suggested titles for CSCC movies. They were "Psycho IV," "The Wild Bunch Rides Again," "The Taming of the Crew," and "The Kiss of the Five-Day Week." In another article he commented on the "unknown student." He noted that during the last two weeks of a quarter he would invariably encounter a student at his office door asking, "What can I do to be saved?" Actually, the question was, "what can I do to pass the course?" Bradley answered the student's question with another question, "Who are you?" The usual response was that the student had not had time to attend class. Bradley wrote (jokingly) that he frequently told the student there was nothing he could do to be saved, and therefore he must be "cast into the world of the utterly failed."

In other news the college was saddened by the death of Betty Bull. An indefatigable worker, she had developed a reading program for the college, taught classes designed for teacher recertification in English and Elementary Education, developed a Medical Vocabulary course and had worked closely with the Etowah School System. Her good friend and Associate Professor of English, Marilyn Fillers, said that Betty "was completely dedicated to her profession." Funds were raised for a scholarship in her name within a short period of time.

Other faculty and staff were in the news. Elizabeth Eiswerth, Associate Professor of Nursing, attended a Southern Regional Educational Board (SREB) meeting at the University of Alabama in Birmingham. The workshop was sponsored by the SREB and the Division of Nursing of the U.S. Department of Health and Human Services. Eiswerth was one of 95 Nursing Faculty who attended the workshop on computer technology. Another faculty member, Jere Chumley, was chosen from a field of 125 state artists as one of the "Ten in Tennessee" to participate in the "Homecoming '86" touring art exhibition sponsored by the National Endowment for the Arts. Staff member Janice Matthews was elected 1986 Woman of the Year by the local Heritage Chapter of the American Business Women's Association. She served as a research technician for the college's Institutional Planning and Research Office and had served in several positions for the Heritage Chapter as President, Recording Secretary, Corresponding Secretary and Vice-President. Janice Lawhorn, Secretary for Dr. Frank McKenzie (the Assistant Dean of the Division of Business and Economics) was named as the 1968 Secretary of the Year by the Cherokee Chapter of Professional Secretaries International.

The college welcomed Steve Huskins as the new Grounds Supervisor. Huskins had a Bachelor's degree in Agriculture from UTK. Dr. David Watts was assigned as the new Supervisor of the Evening School, and Al Fine was assigned the duties of supervising off-campus classes. As noted earlier Watts taught Biology and had a Bachelor's degree from Tennessee Tech, a Master's degree from UTK and a Doctorate from Oklahoma State University. His wife, Judy, was an Associate Professor of Biology at the college. Fine, in addition to his new assignment, was also serving as the Assistant Dean of Community Services and Continuing Education. He received a Bachelor's and a Master's degree from Tennessee Tech and had previously been a Counselor and a Supervisor of the Evening Division at Cleveland State.

Important staff members for the college were Security personnel. In 1986-87 these were Walter Hackett, Robert Pierce, David Powell, John Welch and Mitchell Cox. Examples of other staff members were: Susan Gray, Executive Secretary to President James Ford; Evonne Drown, Secretary to the President; Ray Coleman, Assistant to the President (and Secretary, Sandra Moody); Dr. Charles Tollett, Dean of the College (and Mitzi Hooper, Secretary); James Morris, Business Manager (and Brenda Ledford, Secretary); and Alice Selvidge, Bookstore Manager (and Assistants Mary Holder and Melba Long).

An athletic event in March attracted about 4,000 visitors to the campus. It was the Region 3, Class AA, High School Basketball Tournament. Charles Cogdill was the Tournament Director, and the event was covered by both the WRCB and WTVC television stations in Chattanooga, four area radio stations and Cleveland and Chattanooga newspapers. The college hosted numerous High School Basketball Championships on an annual basis for many years.

The Cougar Club established two Foundation scholarships in 1986. One created the Scott Ratterman Memorial Scholarship and the other completed the Darlene Longley Memorial Scholarship. Ratterman, who died in an automobile accident, was an officer of First American Bank, and Longley, who died of cancer, was a kindergarten teacher and wife of the college's baseball coach, Steve Longley. Mark Smith, Vice-President of the Cougar Club, and Jim Cigliano, Assistant Dean of Student Services and Athletic Director, presented the donations to Harold Almond, the CSCC Foundation President.

In other sports news Jim Cigliano was selected as the Director of Region VII of the NJCAA. He served a two-year term on the Board that governed the athletic programs of 25 two-year colleges in Kentucky, Alabama and Tennessee. The responsibilities of the Director and the Board were numerous. Among other things, the Director planned regional tournaments, determined player eligibility, selected locations and dates of tournaments, determined the teams that played, selected officials, determined financial policies, notified the national office of possible violations of rules and imposed penalties and sanctions if violations were discovered.

The Athletic Banquet was held in May 1986. Morris Lyons was voted the D. F. Adkisson Athlete of the Year and was named the Most Valuable Basketball Player. Lee

Cigliano was presented with the George L. Mathis Scholastic Award. Approximately 250 people attended, and the guest speaker was Mack McCarthy, the Head Men's Basketball Coach at UTC. Roy Exum, Executive Sports Editor of the <u>Chattanooga News-Free Press</u>, was the emcee. David Daniel was named the Most Valuable Baseball Player, and Gina Warwick was named the Most Valuable Basketball Player for the Lady Cougars. In other athletic news Charles Cogdill resigned to accept the position of Boys' Basketball Coach at Lenoir City High School. During his nine years at CSCC, he served two of those years as an assistant men's coach, five years as Men's Head Coach and two years as Women's Coach.

Several students were also newsmakers. Tammy Rapp received a full scholarship to study and work in Germany as part of the U. S. Congress/ West German Bundestag Youth Exchange Program. Sponsored by the Carl Duisberg Society, she was one of 60 students in the US selected to spend a year studying at a German University. She was assisted by Dr. Renate Basham, the college's Professor of Languages. Three students received honorable mention in the 7th Annual State Community College Art competition. They were Margaret Richardson, Wayne Harris and Richard Cox. Other students who excelled in art exhibitions were: Annette Lawson, Cheryl Barker and Judy Fox Nelms. The Homecoming Queen was Sherrie Duggan and the SGA President was Bill Hammons.

The 1986 Commencement Speaker was Thomas J. Garland, Chancellor of the State University and Community College System. He served in the Senate for 21 years and was the Senate Minority Leader for 17 of those years. He was also a former Chair of the Board of Trustees of Tusculum College. The Outstanding Graduate Award was presented to Lee Cigliano, and the Faculty Merit Award was presented to John Cantrell.

– 1987 –

In international news the major events were: British millionaire Richard Branson and Per Linstrand became the first hot air balloon travelers to cross the Atlantic; Klaus Barbie, the former Gestapo chief known as the "butcher of Lyon," was convicted by a French court of crimes against humanity and sentenced to life in prison (he died in 1991); Rudolf Hess, the last member of Adolf Hitler's inner circle, died by suicide at Spandau Prison at the age of 93; fighting erupted in Mecca between Saudi Arabian police and Iranian religious pilgrims; Soviet officials were embarrassed by an unauthorized landing of a private plane by a West German pilot in Moscow's Red Square (the pilot, Mathias Rust, was freed the following year); and the Soviet Union's Mikhail S. Gorbachev adopted a policy of "glasnost" (openness).

In domestic news the major events were: the 200th Anniversary of the United States Constitution; Philadelphia, the birthplace of the Constitution, conducted a huge party to celebrate the occasion highlighted by a six-hour parade on September 17, 1987; the imbroglio over the U. S. diverting money from arms sales to Iran (in apparent violation of US law) to support contra rebels fighting Nicaragua's Marxist government continued to be debated; Congressional hearings on the Iran-Contra affair indicated the major players were Lieutenant Colonel Oliver North and his boss on President Reagan's National Security Council, Rear Admiral John M. Poindexter; Jim and Tammy Baker resigned leadership of the "Praise the Lord" (PTL) Ministry (a $200 million television and theme park religious empire) after Jim Bakker admitted having an affair with church secretary Jessica Hahn (subsequent revelations of accounting fraud led to his imprisonment); thirty years after it was expelled, the Teamsters Union was welcomed back into the AFL-CIO (however, the Teamsters separated from the AFL-CIO in 2005); President Reagan produced the nation's first trillion-dollar budget; the Federal Drug Administration approved the first drug (AZT) shown to be effective in the fight against AIDS; an Iraqi missile killed 37 sailors on the USS Stark in the Persian Gulf (Iraq called it an accident); President Reagan and Soviet leader Gorbachev signed a pact to dismantle all 1,752 US and 859 Soviet missiles with a 300 to 3,400 mile range; U. S. stocks lost nearly one-fourth of their value on Black Monday (October 19, 1987); Supreme Court Justice Lewis F. Powell retired; the Federal Communications Commission repealed its "fairness doctrine" which was a policy that since 1949 required television and radio broadcasters to air opposing sides of controversial issues; comedian-actor Jackie Gleason died in Fort Lauderdale, Florida, at the age of 71; Academy-Award winning actor Lee Marvin died in Tuscon, Arizona, at the age of 63; Henry Ford II, chairman of Ford Motor Company, died in Detroit, Michigan, at the age of 70; Pianist Liberace died in Palm Springs, California, at age 67; artist Andy Warhol died in New York City at age 58; comedian Danny Kaye died in Los Angeles, California, at age 74; actress Rita Hayworth died in New York City at age 68; and Maria von Trapp, whose life story was the inspiration for the musical, the "Sound of Music," died in Morrissville, Vermont, at age 82.

In popular culture the Academy Award winning movie was "The Last Emperor," the best actor was awarded to Michael Douglas for "Wall Street," and the best actress award was won by Cher for "Moonstruck." The Emmy for television's best comedy was "Golden Girls" (NBC), and the Emmy for best drama was "L. A. Law" (NBC). The Grammy for record of the year was presented to Paul Simon for "Graceland," and the album of the year was awarded to U2 for "The Joshua Tree." In athletics UTK won the Women's NCAA Division I Basketball Championship, and Indiana won the Men's Championship. The National Football League players declared a 24-day strike over the issue of "free agency," and the owners hired replacement players. The dispute was settled before the Super Bowl, which resulted in a victory for the New York Giants over the Denver Broncos. The Minnesota Twins defeated the St. Louis Cardinals in the World Series.

A huge celebration of National Community College Month occurred in February 1987. The annual recognition was established in February 1986 by President Ronald Reagan and Congress. A highlight of the event was a lecture by John W. Gardner, former Secretary of Health, Education and Welfare. His speech was the cornerstone of the 2nd annual Harry S. Truman Lecture series which recognized the important role Truman and the 1947 Truman Commission on Higher Education played in establishing the community college educational system. By 1987, 1,220 community, technical and junior colleges had been established in the nation, and they enrolled the majority of all first-time college students in the US.

In April CSCC became the first community college in Tennessee to reach a one million dollar scholarship endowment fund. Both the Chancellor of the State Board of Regents, Tom Garland, and the Board Chairman, William Farris, praised the college trustees for their "exemplary private sector support" for a community college and its students. The college's President, Dr. James W. Ford, thanked Harold Almond (President of the Foundation), Mike Callaway (Chairman of the Scholarship Endowment Drive), Arch Fitzgerald, Dr. George Mathis, Henry Barkley, Dr. D. F. Adkisson, Sam McReynolds, the late Eugene Callaway, Walter Presswood and Dr. L. Quentin Lane for the significant efforts they expended on raising funds for the endowment.

The college had many other significant accomplishments during the year. Among these were: minority student enrollment increased by 32%; a computer-aided design (CAD) lab was designed for architectural technology students; tennis and golf teams were restored in athletics; the Foundation provided $100,000 to fund 145 scholarships; teleconferencing became a new technology at the college; a "JOBS 2000"marketing campaign, designed to enhance future employment opportunities, was launched for the five-county service area; and a plethora of new equipment purchases were made. Among these were a desktop publishing system, weight room equipment, an autoclave-sterilizing device for microbiology, microcomputers and mannequins for the Nursing program, the addition of eight new ports in the computer center, the building of a firing range for the Law Enforcement program and new scoreboards for the gymnasium.

An outstanding achievement for the college was a perfect performance score (100 points) from THEC. This earned the college additional state funding of $244,987 (equaling 5% of its current operating budget). It was the second consecutive year that the college earned a high mark. Several factors were considered in the performance evaluation such as: (1) the results of a pre-graduation exam that tested the students' knowledge in their major area of study (as well as their general academic performance); (2) alumni and graduating students' attitudes toward the quality of education they received; and (3) the results of a job placement survey. The currently enrolled students rated the quality of instruction as "excellent" in classroom instruction, and the college exceeded the national score in five of six categories related to instruction. Three college programs (Legal Assistant, Medical Laboratory Technician and Nursing) were accredited by national accrediting agencies. All three received perfect scores. The college also attained perfect scores in program evaluation, general education, job placement and instructional improvement.

A campus committee was formed to develop a ten-year, one million dollar campus master landscaping plan. The committee was composed of representatives from students, faculty and staff members. The plan was designed to install flowerbeds, strolling gardens, promenades between buildings, water gardens and an outdoor amphitheater. In addition the plan recommended the construction of a water fountain and sign near the main entrance, the removal of trees for increased visibility from Interstate Highway 75 and landscaping improvements at the intersection of Norman Chapel Road and Adkisson Drive. The plan also proposed the construction of a new theater entrance, an art gallery, an information booth and pedestrian shelters.

A major academic achievement for the campus was THEC's approval of $53,000 funding for a Nursing Lab and multimedia center. The 1986 results of the National Licensure Examination (NCLEX) for registered nurses were announced, and CSCC achieved a 98% pass rate. Since 1981 nursing students had achieved pass rates of more than 97% and pass rates of 100% in 1983 and 1984. Shelby Millsaps, Director of Nursing, said, "Our continued success on the NCLEX tells us that we have one of the best nursing programs in the nation. This is due not only to the academic expertise of our faculty, but to the personal interest and attention they give to each nursing student."

The college humorist, John Bradley, continued to provide entertainment to the campus with his articles in the Employee Newsletter. Writing about the Academy Awards he noted that, instead of "Platoon" CSCC would soon offer its own film titled "Spittoon." The latter would be about a campus struggle over smoking and non-smoking areas on the campus. The college's three competitors for the movie, "Children of a Lesser God," would be "Teachers of a Lesser Salary," "The Absence of Money" and "The Color of Money." The Art Department would produce a rival to "Blue Velvet" titled, "Purple Matador on Black Velvet," and the college's rival to "A Room with a View" would be "A Loon with a Pew."

In other activities Mitzi Hooper received her Certified Professional Secretary (CPS) rating on her initial attempt. At that time only 10% of secretaries passed the exam on their first attempt. Hooper began work as a staff member of the college in 1970 and graduated from the college in 1974. She held numerous positions while at CSCC— secretary for both Dr. Adkisson, and later, Dr. Lane, secretary in the Business Office, secretary for the Community Relations Office and secretary for Dean Charles Tollett.

Shelby Millsaps attended a meeting for the Board of Review for the Council of Associate Degree Programs for the National League of Nursing in New York City. Committee members were selected from all over the nation, and she was one of very few chosen from the South. Harry Dean was one of the platform speakers during the Vietnam Veterans' Memorial Exhibit held in Athens, Tennessee, on Labor Day. One of the other speakers was General William Westmoreland. Dean read a poem that he wrote for the occasion titled, "The Vietnam Dead." Ann McCoin attended the American Association for Paralegal Educators in Baltimore, Maryland. In 1987 Legal Assistant was the fastest growing professional program in the United States. The JTPA continued to assist with job training for area residents. The personnel in the Cleveland State office were: Rosemary Den Uyl (Director), Mona Rose, Carla Adams, Sandra Brakebill, Dan Aultman (who became Director in 1988), Cathy Boettner, Warren Brewster, John Dixon, Susie Fisher, James Peck and Sahira Sorrells. Shirley Phillips and Mary Alice Ogle were located in Madisonville, and Emily Guinn, Jane Chastain, Raymond Latham, Nancy Odonex and Beverly Walker were in Athens.

The first Martin Luther King, Jr. college banquet was held on January 17 in the George L. Mathis Student Center. Dr. Robert S. Wood, the General Secretary of the Second Cumberland Presbyterian Church, in Huntsville, Alabama, was the guest speaker. A native of Bradley County, he received his Bachelor's degree from Bethel College, his Master of Divinity from Memphis Theological Seminary and his Doctor of Ministry from Vanderbilt Divinity School.

Another native of Bradley County, Henry Trewhitt, also spoke at the campus. Trewhitt was the Deputy Managing Editor of the US News and World Report. He was also a former diplomatic correspondent for the Baltimore Sun and Newsweek magazine. His speech was about his specialty, foreign affairs. A play was performed in the Community Services Building titled, "Taken in Marriage." The cast included Tricia Frey, Sandy Tinker, Connie Gatlin, Suzanne Allen and Pat Meagher. The annual High School Bowl contest consisted of thirteen teams. After 156 separate matches, the winner was Bradley Central High School. The event was sponsored by PTK and the faculty advisor was Dr. Hugh Vroman. In a similar event students from eighteen area high schools participated in the college's District E-4 "Competitive Events for the Tennessee Office Education Clubs (TOEC)." The faculty organizers of this event were Sherra Witt and Nancy Boyd. Two alumni received honors during the year. Margaret S. Richardson (a 1986 graduate) was named UTC's Outstanding Senior in Fine Arts, and Larry Wallace (a 1973 graduate) was appointed Head of the Tennessee Highway Patrol by Commissioner Robert Lawson.

A Humanities Symposium was conducted in the spring on the subject of "The Humanities: Avenues for Coping with Economic Change." Sponsored by the Department of Humanities and Social Sciences, the three main speakers were: (as noted earlier) Henry Trewhitt of the US News and World Report magazine; Ricki Rhodarmer Tigert of the Board of Governors of the Federal Reserve System (the daughter of Sue Martel, one of the college's Psychology instructors) and William J. Harbison, Justice of the Tennessee State Supreme Court. An Art/Photo Exhibit was also conducted in conjunction with the symposium. Wayne Harris won First Place in the competition, which was organized by Jere Chumley.

Another 1987 college spring event was a Cleveland Business and Industry Forum. The keynote speaker was Chris Whittle, Chairman of Whittle Communications in Knoxville. Whittle, a native of Etowah, was a former publisher of Esquire magazine and played a major role in the renovation and development plans of downtown Knoxville. Whittle spoke on the "Role of the Entrepreneur in Economic and Community Development." The event was co-sponsored by the Cleveland/Bradley Chamber of Commerce, Cleveland State and Cleveland Associated Industries. Representatives from these organizations were Ed Battocchio, Plant Manager of Duracell, Jim Williams, President of First American Bank and Dr. Frank McKenzie and Dr. Mary Barker of Cleveland State.

In college athletics the Men's Basketball Coach, Dan Trotter, announced his resignation to accept a new coaching position at Carrollton High School in Georgia. His teams were 18-10 in 1984-85, 18-8 in 1985-86 and 22-7 in 1986-87. The new coach was Roby Phillips, a 1969 graduate of Cleveland High School and a 1971 graduate of Cleveland State. Phillips received his Bachelor's and Master's degrees from MTSU. He was a former Coach at Volunteer State Community College and an Associate Coach with Joe Dean at Birmingham Southern University. Tennis and Golf returned to the college's intercollegiate athletic program in 1987. Bob Taylor was named Tennis Coach, and he continued to teach Physical Education. Eddie Sherlin became the Golf Coach, and he continued to coach the Lady Cougars basketball team.

Meanwhile John Bradley, in one of his comical columns for the Employee Newsletter, noted that a student, in a speech about the elderly, said, "One of the major causes of old age is living too long." Another student submitted a paper titled, "My Analysis of Edgar Allan Poe's Poem, the Rave." Another student combined the names of two books when he announced that his speech was about George Orwell's novel, "The Animal Farm in 1984." Bradley made fun of a speaker at a conference in Nashville who supposedly said she was there "to dialogue about the use of psychometrics and psychometricians in the development of endemic holistic evaluative monitoring systems." In another article he suggested names of new courses for the college. Nursing could offer "The Joys of Hypochondria" and "Creative Suffering and Whining." Physical Education could teach "Basic Dribbling" and "The Repair and Maintenance of Your Coaching Staff." Psychology could teach "Overcoming Happiness" and "Exorcism for Relaxation." Criminal Justice could offer "Criminal Behavior for Educators" and "Redecorating Your Cell." Industrial Technology could teach "Electrifying Your Bathtub," Humanities could teach "You and Your Thesaurus," and History could offer a course entitled, "Famous Morons in Government."

Among many students excelling outside the classroom were the staff members of The Cherokee Signal. They were: Michael Kubba; Editor; Gary Peavyhouse, News Editor; Robby Brown, Sports Editor; Dewey Esquinance, Photo Editor; Jennifer Bige, Advertising; Bernie Rubin, Business Editor; Dean Merritt and Mark Byars, Illustrators; Jim Sells and Mike Kubba, Editorial Editors; Polly Fowler, Typesetter; and David Suttles was the Faculty Advisor. Other student newsmakers were Laura Hughes, Homecoming Queen, and Jan Hester was the new SGA President (the Faculty Advisor for the SGA was Dr. Jerome Taylor). Lisa Guy, student President of the college's chapter of the Future Secretaries of America (FSA), and Angela Goodner attended the International FSA Conference in San Juan, Puerto Rico, (the Faculty Advisor for the FSA was Sherra Witt). The student hosts for 1987 were: Lisa Guy, Melissa Guthrie, Shelia O'Kelley, Carol Colvard, Tina Skelton, Joseph Kottor, Jan Hester, Paula Ott, Melissa Queen, Kelly Key, Edie Elkins and David Goodwill.

During the year awards for twenty years of service to the college were presented to five of the original employees. They were: Jere Chumley, Associate Professor of Art; Jim Cigliano, Assistant Dean of Student Services; Joe Guest, Associate Professor of Math; Sally Phillips, Supervisor of the Language Lab; and Norma Davis, Secretary of Student Services. In addition awards for ten years of service were presented to faculty members Elizabeth Eiswerth (Nursing) and Sherra Witt (Office Careers). Staff members receiving Ten-Year Awards were: Carole Belk, Business Office; Martha Lane, Secretary of Humanities and Social Sciences; Curtis McNeely, Computer Center; Janice Lawrence, Library; Mary Breen, Library; Karen Gibson, Student Development; and Walter Hackett, Security.

The 1987 Commencement Speaker was S. B. "Skeet" Rymer, the Chairman and CEO of Magic Chef. At that time Magic Chef was the fourth largest manufacturer of home appliances in America and was Cleveland's largest employer. The Outstanding Graduate Award was presented to Lisa Guy, and the Distinguished Faculty Member Award was presented to Larry Speight (Biology). A new award, the Distinguished Staff Member Award, was presented to Norma Davis (Student Services).

– 1988 –

The major events in international affairs were: a US Navy Frigate struck an Iranian underwater mine in the Persian Gulf that injured 10 crew members, and in retaliation, the US destroyed two Iranian oil platforms and damaged or sunk six Iranian ships; Soviet troops began to pull out of Afghanistan (eight years after entering the country); Vietnam began pulling troops out of Kampuchea (Cambodia); the USS Vincennes accidentally shot down an Iranian jetliner over the Persian Gulf, killing all 290 people aboard; King Hussein of Jordan renounced claims to the West Bank and the Gaza Strip (which Jordan lost to Israel in 1967); Iran and Iraq started peace talks; the Palestinian Liberation

Organization (PLO) renounced terrorism and recognized Israel's right to exist; the US and the Soviet Union signed an Intermediate-Range Nuclear Forces Treaty and began destroying a few missiles; the Soviet Union's leader, Mikhail Gorbachev, announced a policy of "glasnost" (openness in the flow of information) and "perestroika" (economic restructuring); a bomb blew up a Pan Am World Airways jet over Lockerbie, Scotland, killing all 259 people on board and eleven more on the ground; and Benazir Bhutto became Prime Minister of Pakistan (the first woman elected to head a Muslim nation).

The major events in domestic affairs were: the Supreme Court ruled that the first Amendment rights of free speech and free press do not protect school newspapers, plays and other school activities from censorship; Anthony M. Kennedy was sworn in as an Associate Justice of the Supreme Court; Surgeon General C. Everett Koop declared cigarettes addictive; a federal judge sentenced Terry Nichols to life in prison for his role in the Oklahoma City bombing; Congress passed a law apologizing to Japanese-Americans interned in World War II and provided $20,000 tax-free payments to those interned; George Bush defeated Michael S. Dukakis in the Presidential election; and the Air Force unveiled the Stealth Bomber.

In popular culture the Academy Award for best movie was awarded to "Rain Man." The best actor award was presented to Dustin Hoffman ("Rain Man"), and the best actress was awarded to Jodie Foster ("The Accused"). The Emmy for the best television comedy was won by "The Wonder Years" (ABC), and the best drama was "Thirtysomething" (ABC). The Grammy Award for best record was won by Bobby McFerrin for "Don't Worry, Be Happy," and the Grammy Award for album of the year was presented to George Michael for "Faith." In athletics the NCAA Division I Women's basketball champion was Louisiana Tech, and the men's champion was Kansas. The Washington Redskins defeated the Denver Broncos in the Super Bowl, and Los Angeles defeated Oakland in the World Series.

For the second consecutive year the college received a perfect score in the statewide performance funding evaluations. The criteria for the appraisal were: program accreditations; testing and placement in career programs; results of general education testing for transfer-oriented students; surveys of currently enrolled students and alumni; and quality of planning efforts. In another measure of effectiveness the College Outcomes Measure Program (COMP) exam was taken by all Associate of Arts and Associate of Science graduates, and the results exceeded the national average. Another evaluation procedure, the Student Instructional Report (SIR), indicated that the quality of instruction at Cleveland State exceeded the national averages in five of the six factors in SIR evaluations and equaled the national averages in the sixth factor.

The 1988 Alumni Satisfaction Survey also yielded a favorable report for the college. The survey was mailed to approximately 300 of the 1985-86 graduates and 135 responded. The results were: 94% were satisfied or very satisfied with the college at the time they graduated; after two years, 91% were still satisfied; 85% indicated they would attend Cleveland State if they could start college again; 85% indicated they were employed; the overwhelming majority believed the college had contributed to their skills and adaptability; and 90% rated the faculty as either good or excellent. The survey, as well as other Alumni Surveys through the years, indicated that the major reasons students chose Cleveland State were: location; cost; opportunity to work and attend college; course offerings; academic reputation; availability of financial aid; and the advice of their parents.

The Job Training Partnership Act (JTPA) office received the news that it would continue to be the grant recipient and administrative entity for Service District Area 5 for the next two years. Perry Storey, Director of the JTPA program, stated, "I personally appreciate the time and energy PIC-LEO officials have put in the planning process over the last 30 days. Our common goal is to help local employers meet their job needs. I believe this two-year plan reinforces that volunteer effort." Among the goals in the plan were efforts to help dislocated workers, mature workers and long-term welfare recipients find jobs.

The college Foundation elected Arch Fitzgerald as its third President for a two-year term. He succeeded Harold Almond, who served from 1985-1988. Other officers elected were: Mike Callaway, Vice-President; Dr. George Mathis, Secretary; Fred Zeller, Treasurer; W. K. Fillauer, Member-at-large; and Dr. James W. Ford, Member-at-large. Dr. D. F. Adkisson served as a lifetime member of the executive committee. A special committee was formed to assist in establishing a Foundation scholarship to honor Mark Dausy, the deceased son of Edward and Pat Dausy. Pat worked in the Office of Community Relations and Development at the college. The scholarship was initiated by the Wesley Memorial Scout Troop Number 44 of which Mark was a member. The committee members were: Dana McClanahan, Counselor at Bradley Junior High School; Mike Samples, Assistant Scout Master; Reverend Jack Edwards, Pastor of Wesley Memorial United Methodist Church; B. R. Blair, troop committee member; Buford Guy, CSCC faculty member; and Paul Ramsey, Assistant Principal of Bradley Junior High School. Other committee members were Doris Donohoo, Bill Bates and Dr. Paul Smith.

In academics the college completed the conversion from a quarter to a semester system. Several new programs were also instituted. Students pursuing an Associate Degree in the Human Services Specialist Program could elect to take a major course of study in either Gerontology, Substance Abuse or Mental Health. Upon completion of the degree students could become counselors, technicians or assistants in these areas. They would also be prepared for jobs in nursing homes, substance abuse centers, senior citizen centers and hospitals. In addition new Certificate Programs were offered in Substance Abuse Counseling, Quality and Productivity in Business and in Banking and in Accounting. Generally, degree programs required about 65 or 66 semester hours of coursework, and certificate programs required 24 or more hours of coursework. A degree option in Management and a Health Care Management option, under the Business and Management Degree, were also added to the curriculum.

A grant, funded by the Division of Nursing of the US Department of Health and Human Services, was implemented to strengthen nursing faculty skills in using computers. Over 5,000 nurse educators in the fifteen-member (later 16 members) Southern Regional Education Board (SREB) states benefited from the two-year program. Unfortunately, the nearest workshop for CSCC students was at the University of Alabama at Birmingham. In other news Dr. Mary Barker became the new Dean of Academic Affairs, and Dan Aultman was the new Dean of Administrative Services. Dr. David Watts became the new Director of Institutional Research and Planning. Watts would be responsible for strategic planning, scheduling of facilities and performance funding.

The college lost a dedicated employee when Ray Coleman announced his retirement after 37 years of service to public education in Tennessee. He served as a classroom teacher, principal, coach, administrator, supervisor and interim President at CSCC. He came to Cleveland State in 1971 as Director of the Evening Division and Continuing Education. He was later Head of Institutional Research, Assistant to the President, Head of Personnel and Community Relations and Development and interim President from July of 1985 through December of 1985.

Dr. L. E. Wooten, Professor of Sociology, participated in the annual national meeting of the Academy of Criminal Justice Sciences in San Francisco. Wooten chaired a panel discussion on "Decision Making in the Juvenile System," and he delivered a paper on "Cultural Perspectives on Juvenile Justice." The Academy was a national organization comprised of professionals in criminology whose purpose was to foster education and research in criminal justice in higher education. Dr. and Mrs. T. P. Mathai, and sons George and Paul, were recipients of the annual W. M. and Ruth Hale Master 4-H Family Recognition Program Award. The award recognized 4-H families on the county, district and state levels that had shown leadership ability and exceptional participation in 4-H club work.

Roy G. Lillard, Cleveland State faculty emeritus, was named Bradley County Historian. He was the author of Bradley County and later, editor of The History of Bradley County. He was presented a certificate of merit by the Tennessee Historical Commission, and Tennessee Governor Ned McWherter named Lillard to the State Historical Records Advisory Board. Lillard also served as Chair of the Bradley County Commission of Public Records and was also Polk County Historian. Donna McCoin, a former Nursing Instructor, and Pat Jenkins, a current Assistant Professor of Nursing, wrote an article for the February 1988 issue of the Journal of Nursing Education. The article was titled, "Methods of Assignment for Preplanning Activities (Advance Student Preparation) for Clinical Experience."

The college was saddened by the death of Ann Morelock, a former teacher of Literature and English Composition at the college. Only 43 years old, she died following a long bout with cancer. She also taught Technical Writing and sponsored the Experiment in International Living program at the college. Jere Chumley exhibited several of his art works at the Chipola Junior College in Marianna, Florida. It was the grand opening of Chipola's new art gallery. Another instructor and former coach, Steve Longley, was married in February 1988, to Angela D. Gentry.

John Bradley, in one of his humorous articles for the Employee Newsletter, offered his annual suggestions for movie titles. Instead of "The Last Emperor," he proposed "The Last Whimperer." Readers could select a "cry-baby" in the current news as the subject of the movie. Instead of "Empire of the Sun," he suggested "Empire of the Moron," and readers could select any politician, with whom they disagreed, as the movie's subject. Instead of "Fatal Attraction," he suggested "Faded Attraction." Instead of "Broadcast News," he suggested "Broadcast Feuds," and readers could select any of the Presidential debates for the subject of the movie.

In the spring of 1988 the college conducted a Sports Festival. The events included a tennis tournament, a 5-kilometer road race, and a karate tournament. Scott and Ruth Ann Shamblin (the college's part-time karate instructors) were the directors of the karate tournament, and Roby Phillips (the Head Men's Basketball Coach) directed the 5-kilometer race. The tennis tournament committee was chaired by Bob Taylor and the other members were Nancy Casson, Sylvia Coates, Ken Newton, Dale Yates and Dr. Spencer Culbreth. In other sports news Melissa Parker won the award for the state's most valuable women's basketball player.

An ACT profile study of approximately 400 CSCC students, who enrolled in the fall of 1988, revealed that their composite score on the ACT exam was 15.3, and their high school grade average was 2.8. The national average composite score was 19.0, and the high school grade average was 2.9. Of those listed in the CSCC profile, 46% were 25 years or older, 64% attended part-time, 58% were women and 40% received some form of financial aid. A total of 195 students withdrew from the college in the fall of 1988. This was 7% of the total student population enrolled in credit classes. It was a typical figure for the college throughout its history. The reasons given for withdrawal were also typical. Of those responding, 58 cited work conflict, 23 cited personal reasons, 20 cited illness, 15 cited moving reasons and 7 cited financial reasons.

There were several student newsmakers in 1988. Students in the college's Collegiate Secretaries International (CSI) received one of three Achievement Awards for outstanding participation in CSI activities in 1987-88. The chapter members were: Lisa Miles, President; Kristie Brown, Vice-President; Vickie Still, Treasurer; Meg Deford, Corresponding Secretary; Charlotte Bird, Historian; Anita Stubbs, the chapter's Professional Secretaries International President; Janie Lawhorn, the chapter's Professional Secretaries International Advisor; Tammy Martin, member; Kitty Green, member; and Helen Doffe, member. The faculty advisors were Nancy Boyd and Sherra Witt. In addition to the Achievement Awards the chapter also received the Tennessee Division Scrapbook Award. The club was named CSCC's outstanding student organization for 1987-1988. Students producing The Cherokee Signal were: Angie Taylor, Editor; Lora Bullard and Christine Hicks, News Editors; and Eddie Johnson,

Photographer. The newspaper's faculty advisor was David Suttles. The Homecoming Queen was Tina Casada.

In other activities the Tennessee Office Education Clubs held their annual competition at CSCC. The event attracted hundreds of area High School students each year. The faculty coordinators were Dr. Frank McKenzie, Nancy Boyd and Sherra Witt. Sahira Sorrells, a staff member of the JTPA office, also assisted with the 1988 event. The 2nd annual MLK Jr. Scholarship Fund was also held at the college. The co-chairs of the event were Sahira Sorrels and Larry Henderson. The guest speaker was Dr. Henry Bradford, Dean of Music at Alabama A & M University. A play titled, "Divorce, Southern Style," was held at the college in March. Directed by John Bradley, the cast included Lois Wyche, Sandy Tinker, Karla Shrewsbury, Jim Ludwig, David Boatwright, Rick Melvin and Leita Crawley. In October a two-person play, "The Owl and the Pussycat," featured John Bradley and Sandy Tinker.

The commencement speaker was Dr. Sandra Packard, Provost of the University of Tennessee at Chattanooga. The Distinguished Graduate Award was presented to Jan Hester, the Distinguished Faculty Award was awarded to Dr. Renate Basham, and the Distinguished Staff Member Award was presented to Alta Presswood.

– 1989 –

The major events in international affairs were: the collapse of the "iron curtain" and the beginning of democratic reforms in Hungary, Poland, East Germany, Bulgaria, Czechoslovakia and Rumania; Emperor Hirohito of Japan died; Soviet troops completed their withdrawal from Afghanistan; the oil tanker Exxon Valdez ran aground on a reef in Alaska's Prince William Sound and leaked approximately 11 million gallons of crude oil into the Pacific Ocean; over one million Chinese teachers, students and workers marched through Beijing demanding greater democracy; Iran's Supreme Leader, Ayatollah Ruhollah Khomeini, died; actor and director Laurence Olivier died in England at the age of 82; deposed Philippine President, Ferdinand E. Marcos, died in exile in Hawaii at the age of 72; Communist East Germany opened its border with Czechoslovakia, and tens of thousands of refugees fled to the West; East Germany tore down the Berlin Wall, and its borders were opened to allow citizens to travel freely to the West; and the Communist Rumanian President, Nicolae Ceaucescu, and his wife, Elena, were executed during a popular uprising.

The major domestic events were: serial killer Theodore Bundy was executed in Florida; former heavyweight boxing champion Joe Louis died in Las Vegas, Nevada, at the age of 66; former White House aide Oliver North was found guilty of three criminal charges related to the Iran-Contra scandal—obstructing a congressional inquiry, destroying documents and accepting an illegal gratuity (his conviction was thrown out on appeal in 1991 because of his immunized testimony); Army General Colin Powell became the first black Chairman of the Joint Chiefs of Staff; President George H. W. Bush ordered 1,900 troops to Panama to protect Americans there due to election violence; Hurricane Hugo swept through the Caribbean and the Carolinas killing at least 86 people and causing $7 billion in damage in the Carolinas alone; a jury in Charlotte, North Carolina, convicted televangelist Jim Bakker of fraud and conspiracy (he was later sentenced to 25 to 45 years in prison and fined $500,000); actress Bette Davis died in France at the age of 81; an earthquake, just before a World Series game, struck the San Francisco Bay area and caused 63 deaths; Douglas Wilder won the Virginia gubernatorial election and became the first elected black governor in American history; and U. S. troops invaded Panama and overthrew Manuel Noriega, who was wanted on drug charges.

In popular culture the Academy Award for best picture was "Driving Miss Daisy." The award for best actor was presented to Daniel Day-Lewis ("My Left Foot"), and Jessica Tandy won the best actress award for "Driving Miss Daisy." The Grammy for best record of the year was presented to Bette Midler ("Wind Beneath My Wings"), and Bonnie Rait won the Grammy for album of the year ("Nick of Time"). The Emmy for best TV comedy was won by "Cheers" (NBC), and "L. A. Law" won the Emmy for best drama. The Lady Volunteers of Tennessee won the NCAA Division I Basketball Championship, and Michigan won the Men's title. The San Francisco 49ers defeated the Cincinnati Bengals in the Super Bowl, and Oakland defeated San Francisco in the World Series.

Memphis State University prepared another economic impact study based upon the 1987-88 fiscal year. It indicated that CSCC pumped over $48.6 million into the local economy that fiscal year. The counties affected by it were Bradley, McMinn, Meigs, Monroe and Polk. Of this total, $27 million was directly attributed to money spent by the faculty, staff, students and campus visitors.

The college's Foundation Board of Trustees announced that it had awarded over $95,000 in scholarships to 169 students during the 1988-89 fiscal year. The board also decided to raise the amount of money necessary to endow a scholarship to $10,000. In other Foundation news the entire slate of officers from 1988 (as noted above) was re-elected for another term. Those members reappointed to three-year terms were E. A. Battochio, Bernice Calfee, George Carroll, Jimmy Cooke, Bob Easterly, Dr. James Ford, Jimmy Goddard, Bob Harrill, Fred Hayes, Corky Hoover, Beecher Hunter, Harold Jernigan, Robert Larson, Jay Leggett, Roy Lillard, Dr. George Mathis, C. Scott Mayfield, Gene Miller, James Morris, Carl Painter, Lou Patten, Sheila Presswood, Lloyd Rogers, J. D. Silver, Gary Smith, Col. James Stubbs, David Wagner and Pledger Wattenbarger. Those new members appointed to thee-year terms were Eric Beard, Donald Coltrane, Wayne Cooke, James Dixon, Robert Hamilton, Elizabeth Harting, Alan Jones, Verna Moore, Jeff Morelock, Mickey Norsworthy, Tom Wheeler and Joe V. Williams. A new fund raising campaign was launched to increase the scholarship endowment to $2.5 million. The "Quarter Century Campaign" was scheduled to culminate in 1991-92, the 25th anniversary of the college. Fred Zeller, the retired CEO of Hardwick Stove Company, chaired the campaign, and he was assisted by a 26–member steering committee.

The Tennessee Board of Regents (TBR) announced that, because of low enrollments, 77 academic programs would be eliminated. Fortunately, only five one-year certificate programs were affected at CSCC. College President Dr. Ford noted that eradicating them would have little impact on the college because "students in these areas of study preferred to go for degrees and not certificates." In another enrollment-related development, the Tennessee General Assembly passed legislation that permitted Georgia students in Walker, Whitfield, Catossa, Murray and Fanin Counties to attend CSCC at in-state tuition rates. These counties were granted waivers because they shared a border with Tennessee. The number of waivers, however, could not exceed 3% of the college's full-time enrollment. The fall headcount enrollment for the college was 3,450 and the full-time equivalency (FTE) number was 1,860. The latter figure represented the total credit hours being taken by all students, divided by 15 (a full-time load), and was the basis of funding from the state. The FTE represented a 3.4% increase from the previous year. Minority enrollment increased by 5.5% over 1988.

Beginning in the fall of 1989 all state college and university students were required to complete the ACT exam for admission. Those scoring below 16 were required to take placement tests to determine if they needed remedial work. All degree-seeking students under the age of 21 were required to take the ACT exam. At CSCC, those with a composite score below 19 were required to take a placement test. In addition the TBR decreed that first-year students attending college should have completed, in high school, four years of Math, including Algebra II and Geometry, as well as an advanced Math course. Students should complete, in high school, four years of English, two years of Science (including at least one with a lab experience), US History (and one other Social Studies class), two years of one foreign language and one year of visual or performing arts. Students must meet these basic requirements before enrolling in a state university. Although community colleges retained an "open door" policy, under-prepared students were required to take either remedial or developmental courses before taking college-level courses.

During the year another academic innovation was established by the college. Known as the "Early Alert System," it used classroom attendance information to determine when a student demonstrated a problem with absenteeism. The college's "Retention Center" used a computerized program to identify students needing assistance with their classes. The center also provided help with advisement, orientation, tutoring and testing. Susan Webb-Curtis, the college's retention specialist, stated that the system would "catch a student before it is too late." Later, an academic progress report and a "buddy system" were implemented. The latter, coordinated by Jeff Ryans, monitored the attendance and the academic progress of minority students. Further assistance was provided by seminars on Resume Writing and Interviewing Skills. A few of the guest speakers at the seminars were: Ray Beckler, Eaton Corporation; Marcie Jones, Scholl's Corporation; and Jim Graham, JTPA.

A major accomplishment in 1989 was a course transfer agreement with UTC. Known as a "Two-Plus-Two" agreement, it was signed by Dr. James Ford and Dr. Frederick Obear, the UTC Chancellor. The agreement provided a clear outline of requirements that made transferring from CSCC to UTC easier. To obtain a four- year degree at UTC, for example, transfer students must take their last 60 semester hours at UTC. Another CSCC campus innovation, which was a health benefit, was the prohibition of smoking in certain areas on the campus. Designated lounges, equipped with air control devices, and outside locations were the only smoking areas.

The college engaged in a plethora of activities in 1989. A community-wide event was referred to as the "Ninety Day Meltdown and Shape-up Program." Sac County, Iowa, held the title of "the healthiest county in the nation." The Cleveland/Bradley Chamber of Commerce challenged the county to a meltdown. A total of 21 local teams participated and each contestant agreed to donate a canned good to the United Services Food Bank for each pound lost. Victory was based upon the percentage of a weight lost by the group rather than individual losses. The college's team was named "Super Seven and Two Cleveland State Team." The CSCC members were: Sherry Arthur, John Cassidy, Norma Davis, Harry Dean, Bertha Goldston, Jean Hall, Helen Mizell, Polly Fowler and Mary Wilson. Although Sac County won the contest, the health of all the participants improved.

A major spring event was the Arts Festival conducted by the Division of Humanities and Social Sciences. The event was launched by the annual course, "Great Decisions." A brief booklet was produced each year by the American Foreign Policy Association on important foreign policy issues facing the nation. It attracted a broad spectrum of class participants from college students to college graduates residing in the community. Faculty members presented a brief lecture and moderated discussions on each of the topics. The topics and faculty moderators for 1989 were: "Ethics in International Relations," Dr. Spencer Culbreth; "Latin American Debt," Dale Yates; "The Persian Gulf," Dr. Spencer Culbreth; "Arms Agreements," Dr. Jerome Taylor; "China," Delmus Ledford; "Farmers, Food and the Global Market," Judy Watts; "The Horn of Africa," Harry Dean; and "The International Drug Market," Dr. L. E. Wooten.

The Festival also featured two movies—"The Haunting" and "The Manchurian Candidate." A guest speaker, Dr. Jack Turner, associate professor of Political Science at MTSU, lectured on "A Kinder and Gentler Soviet Union?" Associate Professor Jere Chumley led a couple of walking tours of the college's campus sculpture exhibits and coordinated the eighth annual Cleveland Area Community Art Competition and Exhibit. The sculpture exhibit began in 1986 (as noted earlier) and Chumley, with assistance from the college's maintenance department, traveled throughout the state and acquired, on loan, works by artists. The festival concluded with a musical performance by Diana Notaro, Mike Rorex and Howard Peterson. Their performance featured classical, jazz, folk, romantic and Broadway music. Notaro taught Voice at the college and also at Lee College and Covenant College. Rorex was a minister of music at Wesley Memorial Methodist Church, and Peterson was an adjunct teacher of music and math at CSCC, Tomlinson College and UTC.

In July 1989 over 400 youths from the CSCC service area attended the JTPA Summer Youth Program. The guest speaker was James R. White, Tennessee's Commissioner of Labor. Workshops were conducted on the military, financial aid, office careers, nursing, accounting, computer information, desktop publishing and curriculum offerings at the Athens Vocational-Technical School. Presentations were also made by; Mike Seago, M&M/Mars; Pat Mahery, Bowater Southern Paper Corporation; Shirley McDonald, Volunteer Electric; Lance Lucci, TRW Koyo; Scott Slater, WCI Athens Range Plant; and Ralph Willig, Allied-Signal Bendix Corporation. In another JTPA activity, members of the private industry council (PIC) and local elected officials (LEOs) toured training programs operating in the 5th District. The "VIP Tour" members were: Dr. James Ford, CSCC President; Emily Guinn, JTPA training supervisor; Donna Hubbard, Bradley County Executive; Gereldeene Lewis, PIC chairperson; and Perry Storey, JTPA Director. Later, Storey and Guinn teamed with the UTC Center for Community Career Education and presented a weeklong series of workshops. Thirty-nine students from CSCC's service area were selected to attend. The workshops dealt with a variety of subjects from "Financial Aid Plans for College" to "Communication Skills."

Other on-campus activities were: a presentation of a telecommunications program, via satellite, on the contributions of blacks to America; a college day program with about 25 colleges represented; a health fair sponsored by the college, Bradley Memorial Hospital and the Cleveland/Bradley Chamber of Commerce; the 3rd Annual Business and Industry Forum, with Carl Johnson, the Commissioner of the Tennessee Department of Economic and Community Development, as the keynote speaker; a performance by the Air Force Rock Band; a field trip, led by Dr. Renate Basham, to a performance of "Nutcracker" at Chattanooga's Tivoli Theater; and a college golf tournament coordinated by Bob Taylor (Co-Chair), Rusty Melvin (Co-Chair), Dr. L. E. Wooten (committee member) and Ken Newton (committee member). In October former professional football player Eugene "Mercury" Morris spoke on campus about his sad experiences with drugs. The program was emceed by WRCB-TV news anchor, Cindy Sexton. It was held in the Coleman Auditorium and was sponsored by CSCC and the Bradley County Chapter of the Governor's Alliance for a Drug Free Tennessee. Special musical entertainment was provided by Bradley High School's singing group, Ranstrassy, and by Lisa Robertson, Miss Tennessee of 1989.

In personnel news Dr. Matt Reiser retired after 19 years of service to the college. He was a former professor of Photography, the Director of Career Education and an Assistant Dean. Others receiving honors or attending conferences were: Dr. Irene Miillsaps, Assistant Dean of Math and Natural Sciences, attended the Matrix Theory for Applications Conference at the University of Wyoming; Mike Dorset, Associate Professor of Biology, attended the National Workshop for Anatomy and Physiology in Reno, Nevada; Dr. Joe Semak was elected President of the Faculty Senate; Jere Chumley, Associate Professor of Art, was elected as a committee member for the Governor's School for the Arts; John Bradley was named Dean of the Faculty of the Collaborative Academy at a meeting at Tennessee Tech; Dr. T. P. Mathai completed a Chemistry textbook; Ann McCoin was appointed to the Board of Directors of the American Association for Paralegal Education; and Dr. Frank McKenzie, Assistant Dean of Business and Technologies, was elected President-elect of the Tennessee Business Education Association.

Shelby Millsaps, Assistant Dean of Health and Public Service Technologies, announced that 32 of 33 nursing graduates passed the National Council Licensure Exam. This 97% graduation rate exceeded the national average rate by 7%. Millsaps was also elected to serve a three-year term on the NLN Board of Review, and she was appointed Vice-Chair of the Executive Committee for the Southern Council for Collegiate Education. John Bradley, Associate Professor of English and Speech, was selected to serve as a moderator for the 1990 Key West Literary Seminar. He moderated a panel discussion on "Money and Ethics: The Moral Dilemma." Bradley was also appointed by the Tennessee State Board of Education to serve on the Speech and Theater Subcommittee of the Licensure Committee. Jere Chumley opened an exhibition of his work in oils and mixed media at Lincoln Memorial University's Giles Art Gallery. Nancy Boyd was appointed an honored nominee in the National Professor of the Year Program that was sponsored by the Council for the Advancement and Support of Education. Walter Presswood, Director of Institutional Advancement, was named the 1989 Cleveland Kiwanian of the Year.

In athletics CSCC was featured in the Juco Review, the official magazine of the NJCAA. The article noted that the college's basketball, golf and tennis teams excelled by achieving participation in national tournament playoffs. The Men's basketball team won the NJCAA Region VII by defeating the number one ranked Kentucky team (Sullivan College), 91-77. The team, coached by Roby Phillips, compiled a 22-13 record. It was the first Men's basketball regional championship in the history of the college, and Coach Phillips was named Region VII Coach of the Year. The tennis and golf teams also won the Region VII championship. The tennis team tied for 12th place in the National Tournament held at Tyler, Texas. The tennis team members were C. T. Hardison, Clee Parks, Kevin Baker, Chris Leggett, David Boatwright, Chad Cocks and Franklin Elrod. The coach was Robert Taylor.

In other athletic news Jim Cigliano, Dean of Student Affairs, was appointed to the six-member executive committee of the NJCAA and was also re-elected as Director of the NJCAA Region VII. A new Women's basketball coach, Rusty Melvin, was appointed in the summer of 1989. Melvin, from Gallatin, Tennessee, coached at Hiwassee College in Madisonville from 1986-1988. He compiled a 41-18 record, and his team won the TJCAA state championship in 1987 (with a 12-0 conference record). He was also named TJCAA Coach of the Year in 1987. He had only three CSCC returning players from last year—Kristie Green, Tina Lawson and Julie Ingram. Cleveland State lost to graduation the state's most valuable player, Melissa Parker. Joining the three returnees were Tammy Starr, Kristie Pratt, Debbie Woods, Diane Bradley, Kim McCary, Kristy Curtis, Shelby Ferguson, Michelle Ralston and Rachel Ivey (Lori McGowan was the team manager).

Several students covered the news for The Cherokee Signal. The editor was Carol Malone and the staff members were Lora Bullard, Patrick Dixon, Christine Hicks, Christy Pruett, Tammie Bancroft, Michele Drabicki, Rick Erwin, Mike Harper, Stephanie Hill, Suzy Silvers, Margaret Smarekar, Eddie Johnson, Teresa Lovejoy and Teresa Maskew. Student cheerleaders were Cheree Burgess (co-captain), Crissy Elrod (co-captain), Stacey Cross, Janet Davis, Carmen Driggers, Dawn McIlwain, Mollie Majors, Beth Noble, Jennifer Phillips, Bethany Smith, Ginni Lively (mascot) and Mary Stevens (mascot). The SGA President was Stephanie McCorkle, the Vice-President was Glynis Varlack, the Secretary was Julie Odom, and the Parliamentarian was Clee Parks. The Homecoming Queen was Missy Brewer. The President of the Student Nurses Association was Virginia Aultman, the Vice-President was Rhonda Gregg, the Secretary was Sonya England, and the Treasurer was Faye Geren. The President of the United Student Association was Sylvester Harris, the Vice-President was Lori McCowan, the Secretary was Tiffany Cody, the Treasurer was Yolanda Patterson, and the Parliamentarian was Faye Johnson. Jeff Ryans served as the advisor. The President of the Student Hosts was Paula Sudderth. Sudderth also served on the Board of Regents Committee on Vocational-Technical Education.

The May 1989 Commencement address was delivered by Dwight Henry, a former student at Cleveland State. While attending CSCC, from 1971 to 1973, Henry served as SGA President and was the Business Manager of The Cherokee Signal. He graduated from Tennessee Tech University, where he also served as President of the SGA and was the first student member of the Tennesee Board of Regents. Henry, a native of Athens, Tennessee, was the State Representative for District 42. He was the assistant floor leader, and he served on the Education Committee and the Government Operations Committee of the Tennessee House of Representatives. He was previously the mayor of Cookeville and was the youngest person ever to hold that position. During the graduation ceremony, Nancy Boyd, Associate Professor of Office Careers, received the Distinguished Faculty Member Award, Curtis McNeely (computer programmer) received the Distinguished Staff Member Award, and Angela Taylor received the Distinguished Graduate Award.

Dr. David F. Adkisson
1967 – 1978

Dr. L. Quentin Lane
1978 – 1985

Dr. James W. Ford
1986 – 1993

Dr. Owen Cargol
1993 – 1996

Dr. Carl Hite
1996 – 2014

Dr. William Seymour
2014 – present

CSCC First Site

Original Administration Building

Current Administration Building

Campus Overhead View

Founding Trustees (1972 Meeting)
*Seated from left: Harry Dethero, Kenneth H. Brown, Dr. Wayne McCulley, Pearson Mayfield, George Thorogood, Pledger Wattenbarger, Lloyd Callaway Jr., John Besse;
Standing from left: Roy G. Lillard, Clarence E. Gregg, Harold Almond, Eugene Callaway, Will McReynolds, George Castings, Frank Manly, Clarke Stamper, Henry Barkley, W. K. Fillauer, Dr. George Mathis, Jim Morris and Dr. D.F. Adkisson.*

Humanities Building

Gymnasium

Astronomical Observatory

THE NINETIES

– 1990 –

In international affairs the major events were: Nelson Mandela, the South African activist, was freed from jail after 27 years in captivity; Namibia, after 75 years of South African rule, became an independent nation; the ousted Panamanian dictator, Manuel Antonio Noriega, surrendered to US authorities; Iraq invaded Kuwait, and the United States launched Operation Desert Shield by sending troops to protect Saudi Arabia and liberate Kuwait; the United States and the Soviet Union agreed to end production of chemical weapons and to destroy their stockpile of most of these weapons; British Prime Minister Margaret Thatcher, after losing leadership of the Conservative Party, announced her resignation; Lech Walesa became President of Poland; the removal of the Berlin Wall began, and the reunification of East and West Germany was completed; the Leaning Tower of Pisa was closed because of safety concerns (it was reopened in 2001); Mikhail Gorbachev was awarded the Nobel Peace Prize for easing Cold War tensions (and for internal reforms made in Russia); and British and French workers met after digging an underwater tunnel across the English Channel.

In domestic affairs the major developments were: the average cost of a new house was $123,000; the average income per year was $28,960; the average monthly rent was $465; the cost of a gallon of gasoline was approximately $1.34; the minimum wage was $3.80 per hour; General Motors introduced the Saturn car; one of the largest and well-preserved skeletons of a Tyrannosaurus Rex was found in South Dakota; an Alaskan jury convicted Exxon Valdez skipper, Joseph J. Hazelwood, of misdemeanor negligence in connection with the 1989 oil spill (he was sentenced to $50,000 in restitution and ordered to spend 1,000 hours cleaning oily beaches); the nation entered a major economic recession; John M. Poindexter, the former national security advisor, was convicted on multiple felony counts for his involvement in the Iran-Contra affair; the space shuttle Discovery launched the Hubble Space Telescope into orbit; William Brennan resigned from the Supreme Court, and his replacement was David Souter; the Americans with Disabilities Act was passed, which outlawed discrimination against disabled people in employment, government services, transportation and access to public facilities; a new Clean Air Act was passed that focused on urban pollution and cancer-causing emissions from industrial sources; and President George H. W. Bush presented the Congressional Gold Medal to the widow of Olympic legend Jesse Owens.

In popular culture the Academy Award for best picture was won by "Dances with Wolves." The best actor was Jeremy Irons for "Reversal of Fortune," and the best actress was Kathy Bates for "Misery." The Grammy for the record of the year was presented to Phil Collins ("Another Day in Paradise"), and the best album prize went to Quincy Jones ("Back on the Block"). The Emmy for best comedy was won by "Murphy Brown" (CBS), and the best drama was "L. A. Law" (NBC). There was a growing enthusiasm for animated movie entertainment in the late 1980s and early 1990s. A few of the hits were "The Simpsons," "Fantasia," "Who Framed Roger Rabbit," "The Land Before Time," and "The Little Mermaid." The winner of the NCAA Division I Women's Basketball Championship was Stanford, and the Men's winner was the University of Nevada at Las Vegas. The San Francisco 49ers defeated the Denver Broncos in the Super Bowl, and Cincinnati defeated Oakland in the World Series.

A statewide higher education program, known as "Tennessee Challenge 2000," was developed in 1990. The Tennessee Higher Education Commission (THEC) was directed by the state General Assembly to work with the Tennessee Board of Regents and the UTK Board of Trustees to develop long-term quantifiable goals for higher education. Arliss Roaden, the Executive Director of THEC, stated that, "As we move from a manufacturing-industrial society to a service-information society, the tangible and intangible benefits of having a good education will steadily increase." Six goals were eventually established which laid the framework for developing quality instructional programs (with assessments) designed to prepare students for the future.

The campus enrollment for the fall of 1990 was 3,313 students. Although a statewide effort was announced to reduce expenditures (due to another decline in state revenues), approval was received for the erection of an entrance sign to the campus which would make the campus more visible to Interstate 75. The $98,000 sign was completed by the end of the 1991 spring semester.

A major college event in 1990 was the addition of a state-certified training site for law enforcement officers. The official approval by the Tennessee Police Officers Standards Training Commission (POST) was announced in a news conference jointly by the Tennessee Public Safety Commissioner Robert Lawson and Dr. James Ford. Bradley County Sheriff Dan Gilley, a member of the Post Commission, played an instrumental role in acquiring the site for the college, as well as Lawson, who was also from Bradley County. Walters State Community College had an academy that served a portion of northeastern Tennessee, and Dr. Ford, a former employee of that college, contended that Cleveland State would be a convenient location for serving southeastern Tennessee. The commissioner's action enabled law enforcement officers to receive the same intensive eight-week training at Cleveland State as at Walters State and at Donelson Training Academy in Nashville. The college was one of ten academies in the state, and the philosophy of the Academy was to provide educated police officers to the community by emphasizing principles of community policing, modern police concepts and the importance of community service. The first official training officer was Lieutenant David Loftis of the Soddy Daisy Police Department, and oversight of the program was assigned to Dr. Spencer Culbreth, the Assistant Dean of Humanities and Social Sciences.

The training of a law enforcement officer involved more than learning how to shoot a weapon, drive a patrol car and make arrests. It included the development of skills and knowledge in emergency medical training, professional and ethical conduct, human relations, administration, interpersonal communications, knowledge of drugs, physical training, firearms training, tactical driving, finger printing, white collar crime, detecting child abuse and competence in academic studies. Academic studies included basic law, constitutional law, civil and criminal liability, writing skills, nutrition and health, psychology of human behavior and written communications. Approximately 70 subjects and skills were taught to the students. Students included both males and females, and applicants had to be 18 years of age, possess a high school or GED diploma and be employable as a law enforcement officer. Candidates also had to undergo a background check, a psychological and physical evaluation and numerous other screening measures. The first class of 19 students graduated in November 1990.

The college also announced the creation of an interactive videodisc computer lab designed to provide academic assistance to all students. The purpose was to teach college students basic skills, provide additional reference material for certain classes and provide career and academic guidance. A free tutorial service was also adopted for all remedial and developmental classes. Rodney Dennison, Head of the Tutorial Service, and advisor Pam Sheats, directed the program. Ten tutors were available to assist students. A program was also designed to assist athletes in improving their performance in the classroom. Known as "EDGE," the program monitored the academic progress of athletes to ensure they graduated (and/or transferred to a four-year college) in a reasonable length of time. A "no pass, no play" policy was also implemented.

A new academic concentration in Small Business Management was adopted in the fall of 1990. The Assistant Dean of Business and Technology, Dr. Frank McKenzie, noted that 97% of all Tennessee businesses had fewer than 100 employees. He said that, "these small businesses provide over two-thirds of all new jobs, but these same businesses experience an inordinately high failure rate during their first three years of operation." Furthermore, McKenzie declared that the two leading causes of these failures were insufficient capitalization and "the lack of business management knowledge and skills." The new course offerings were designed to improve this situation.

The Nursing Program received another distinction when all 47 of the nursing graduates passed the National Council Licensure examination. The Assistant Dean of Health and Public Service, Shelby Millsaps, noted that, "The 100 percent passing rate on the exam reflects the hard work among our students and the faculty's commitment toward quality education." Dr. Mary Barker, Dean of Academic Affairs, declared that, "We have a faculty that stays updated on any new developments in the profession. Their expertise and dedication inspires students to do their best." In another academically oriented endeavor, the college participated in a project which resulted in a $5,000 Tennessee Humanities Council Grant. Dr. Renate Basham, Associate Professor Harry Dean and Dr. Spencer Culbreth met with representatives of Chattanooga State and UTC and completed the grant forms for a series of five lectures on the subject of "How Do We Communicate? Language in the Chattanooga Community." The first lecture, in the Coleman Auditorium, was presented by Dr. Gurney Norman, Associate Professor of English at the University of Kentucky. He delivered a reading/lecture on "Appalachian Language in Fact and Fiction."

Other activities were: the Chattanooga Bach Choir, under the direction of Dr. James Greasby, presented a concert in Coleman Auditorium (the event was arranged and coordinated by the college's instructor of Music, Will Benson); Reverend Sharon G. Austin, Associate Pastor of Ebeneezer Baptist Church of Atlanta, was the guest speaker at the annual MLK banquet; John Bradley hosted a community film series; Jere Chumley organized the annual Community Art Competition and Exhibit, as well as a walking campus sculpture tour; and Fred Wood, Will Benson and Gilbert Schmitt participated in a music recital. The last three events were part of the annual Spring Arts Festival.

Several other faculty members were newsmakers in 1990. Dr. Jerome Taylor completed work on a Middle School History textbook. He was also co-author of three other history books—A Panorama of Tennessee I and II and Civics: The United States and Tennessee. He was President-elect of the Chattanooga Historical Association, a member of the Board of Directors of the Chattanooga Chapter of the American Civil Liberties Union and the recipient of the most votes in a field of five candidates to fill the seats on the three-member Ridgeside City Commission. Taylor was also named to the Board of Governors for the Tennessee Presidents Center which published the papers of the three American Presidents from Tennessee—Andrew Jackson, James K. Polk and Andrew Johnson. Shelby Millsaps, the Assistant Dean of Health and Technologies, was appointed to serve on the National League for Nursing Committee on Accreditation. Dr. T. P. Mathai, Professor of Chemistry, was selected to participate in a National Science Foundation workshop which was sponsored by Georgia State University and the Georgia Institute of Technology. The workshop's major topic was the use of nuclear magnetic resonance for the detection and identification of organic molecules in undergraduate teaching. Dr. Mary Barker, Dr. Renate Basham and Dr. Spencer Culbreth attended a TBR Conference at the Vanderbilt Plaza on "Integrating the Study of Women into the Curriculum."

In other faculty and staff news Barry McCaskill, Associate Professor of Industrial Technology, was appointed to the Vocational-Technical Education Task Force of the Tennessee Collaborative for Education Excellence. Jere Chumley, Associate Professor of Art, received the Juror's Choice Award in the Huntsville Museum of Art Exhibit. The award, which included a $2,000 prize, was for his oil painting titled "Totems." His work was chosen from 1,650 objects entered by 550 artists. The new faculty officers for the campus faculty senate were Ann McCoin (President), Mike Dorset (Vice-President) and Cathalin Folks, (Secretary). Dr. Irene Millsaps, Assistant Dean of Math and Science, announced her retirement. She was one of the original faculty members in 1967 and served as a Math Instructor prior to becoming an Assistant Dean. She previously worked at the University of Montevallo, Auburn University, North Georgia College, Copperhill High School and UTK. Bill Gatlin, Admissions Evaluator, performed in the UTK Clarence Brown Theater's production of Romulus Linney's "Heathen Valley." Don Geren was hired as the Director of the Small Business Center, and Walter Presswood and Joe Brandenburg attended an Atlanta district conference of the Council for the Advancement and Support of Education.

In athletics there were also (like the Women's team) only three returning players for the Men's team (and no returning starters). The three returnees were Dedric Bradley, Hank Kirkland and Ray Marshall. The other players were Kendall Andrews, Terance Fleming, Randy Brady, Todd Walker, Steve Simpson, Kenny Mee, Derrick Smartt, Derrick Anders, Randall Coleman, Alanda Kinamore, Kerry Scott, Rafael Young and Duane Chattam. The coach was Roby Phillips. The golf team, coached by Rusty Melvin, participated in a ten-college match at Lake Arrowhead, Georgia. Only four-year colleges finished ahead of CSCC. The team defeated, among others, Lee College and Belmont College. The team members were Treye Prichard, Alan Dillard, Paul Cooper, John Hickman, Andy Williams, Jason Chambers, Jason Wade and Tony Bales. Treye Prichard was named to the All-Tournament Team and was one of the top ten medalists. A highlight of the tennis team's season (coached by Bob Taylor) was their match with the lower seeds of UTK's number two nationally ranked team. Although CSCC lost 6-2, they played well. Clee Parks, CSCC's number five seed, defeated the number 10 UTK player, and Marty McGinnis, CSCC's number five seed, defeated UTK's number 13 seed. Other players, in addition to Parks and McGinnis, were Chip Day, Trent Giles, Dargin Johnson, Claudio Silberberg, Shannon Brown Craig Jordan, Louie Royal, Hobert Brabson, Brent Boatwright, Mike O'Brian, and Daniel Porter. The baseball team, coached by Steve Longley and Assistant Coach, Rusty Melvin, was composed of Robert Rumfelt, Shane Ricketts, Rod Walker, Brad Butler, Mark Roy, Scott Shell, John Smith, Merle Brown, Treye Calfee, Harold Douglas, Scott Keith, Brad Weir, Bart Brannon, Brent Clift, Steve Coffman, Barry Marshall, John Kimberlin, Jeff Crane, Jeff Stafford, Greg Reeves, Matt Flory and David Siatkowski.

In other athletic news the annual community-wide Fall Tennis Classic was held in September with over 200 entries. The committee chair was Bob Taylor and the committee members were Dale Yates, Dr. Spencer Culbreth, Nancy Casson, Ken Newton and Sylvia Coates. The college's Athletic Council's Executive Committee members were: Mark Smith of Smith Management, Chair; Steve Ratterman of Cornutt, McIntire and Ratterman, Vice-Chairman; Sherry Miller, a college staff member, Secretary-Treasurer; Dr. James Ford, the CSCC President, member; Jim Cigliano, the CSCC Athletic Director, member; Ken Newton, CSSC faculty, member; Tom Losh, CSCC staff, member; Nancy Casson, community member; and Henry Payne, community member.

Many students were active in extra-curricular affairs. The Cherokee Staff members were: Carol Malone, Editor; Teresa Lovejoy, News Editor; Stephanie Hill, Advertising Manager; and Theresa Maskew, Sports Editor. The faculty advisor was David Suttles.

The SGA President was Stephanie McCorkle. McCorkle was also the second student from Cleveland State to serve as a regent on the TBR. The first was Dwight Henry who graduated from Cleveland State in 1974. The student regent one-year term position alternated between community colleges (12) and universities (6) within the TBR system. The Homecoming Queen was Suzanne Carson, a Sophomore Nursing student.

In Foundation news W. K. Fillauer was elected as President to a two-year term. The spring 1990 commencement address was delivered by L. H. "Cotton" Ivy, the Tennessee Commissioner of Agriculture. The Outstanding Faculty Member Award was presented to Dr. Joe Semak; Mitzi Ownby received the Outstanding Staff Member Award; and Stephanie McCorkle received the Outstanding Graduate Award.

– 1991 –

The major international events of the year were: on February 27, President Bush announced that Kuwait was liberated and the Iraqi army was defeated; Edith Cresson was appointed by French President, Francois Mitterand, as France's first female prime minister; the republics of Croatia and Slovenia declared their independence from Yugoslavia, and a Balkan War began; Boris Yeltsin became the first elected President of the Russian Republic; a communist coup in the USSR failed, and the non-Russian Republics began declaring their independence; eleven of the twelve former Soviet Republics proclaimed the birth of the Commonwealth of Independent States and the death of the Union of Soviet Socialist Republics; the Soviet Union recognized the independence of the Baltic states of Lithuania, Latvia and Estonia; the city of Leningrad was given approval to restore the city's pre-revolutionary name of St. Petersburg; the UN Security Council chose Boutros Boutros-Ghali of Egypt to be Secretary-General; radicals in Lebanon released American and British hostages, including Alann Steen, Terry Anderson and Terry Waite (all had been held captive for several years); Lech Walesa was elected as President of Poland; Pan American World Airways ceased operating; Winnie Mandela, the wife of Nelson Mandela, was sentenced to six years in prison for her role in the kidnapping of four youths; and Bush and Gorbachev reached an agreement for a Strategic Arms Reduction Treaty (START) regarding long-range nuclear weapons.

In domestic affairs the major developments were: the average cost of a new house was $120,000; the average income per year was $29,430; the average monthly rent was $495; the cost of a gallon of gas was approximately $1.12; Rodney King, a motorist, was severely beaten (after a high-speed chase) by Los Angeles police officers; William Kennedy Smith, the nephew of Senator Edward Kennedy, was accused of rape but was later acquitted; Supreme Court Justice Thurgood Marshall retired; despite sexual harassment allegations by Anita Hill, the Senate narrowly confirmed (52-48) Clarence

Thomas appointment as a Supreme Court Justice; children's author, Dr. Seuss (Theodor Seuss Geisel), died at the age of 87; Richard Speck, who murdered eight student nurses in 1966, died in prison; the Dow Jones Industrial Average closed above 3,000 for the first time; Jeffrey Dahmer was arrested after the remains of eleven men and boys were found in his apartment; the automobile airbag was invented; the web browser was introduced; the 911 Emergency Number was tested in several cities; professional boxer Mike Tyson was arrested and charged with rape; and Eastern Airlines ceased operations after flying two years under bankruptcy protection.

In popular culture "The Silence of the Lambs" won the Academy Award for the best movie; Kevin Spacey was named the best actor for "American Beauty;" and Hilary Swank was named the best actress for "Boys Don't Cry." The television Emmy Award for the best comedy was presented to "Cheers" (NBC), and the best drama award was won by "L. A. Law" (NBC). The Grammy Award for both record of the year and album of the year was Natalie Cole's "Unforgettable." In sports the University of Tennessee won the NCAA Women's Division Championship, and Duke won the men's title. The New York Giants won the Super Bowl, and the Minnesota Twins won the World Series.

The college's year began with the establishment of five-year goals. The major goals were: increase enrollments, expand off-campus course offerings, improve graduation rates, increase partnerships with businesses, increase the amount of grant awards, expand the Small Business Development Center and add modern equipment to the Police Academy. The Foundation office announced that it had issued receipt number 10,000 which represented gifts since 1976. The receipts indicated the Foundation had over $1.5 million in assets, and total donations had averaged $100,000 annually for the last fifteen years. The Foundation, as of 1991, provided approximately 140 students with full scholarships each year.

James Morris, Dean of Financial Affairs, resigned and accepted a similar position at Chattanooga State Technical Community College. Morris had several accomplishments while at the college. These were: a former chair of the TBR Business Affairs Sub-council; President and Chair of the Board of Directors of the North Bradley Utility District; former Vice-President and Loan Officer of the Cleveland-Bradley County Federal Teachers' Credit Union; trustee of the Cleveland State Foundation; former President and member of the Cleveland Rotary Club; former Elder in the Cleveland Christian Church and the Tasso Christian Church; a consultant to the Southern Association of Colleges and Schools; and a member of various sub-committees of the THEC and the TBR.

As was customary the college engaged in a profusion of activities in 1991. For example, a variety of video presentations were shown during Black History Month, and the keynote speaker for the 5th Annual MLK celebration was Dr. Otis L. Floyd, Jr., the Chancellor of the TBR. A tax education workshop for small business owners was taught by the Small Business Development Center and the Office of Community Services. The Student Development Office sponsored several seminars on "Succeeding in College." In the spring of 1991 the college hosted the students and advisors of the

Southeast Tennessee Vocational Industrial Clubs of America (VICA). Eighteen high schools were represented, and 282 students and advisors attended. Faculty members Barry McCaskill and Carol Gavagan coordinated all of the activities for the event.

Another event was a HOSA conference which attracted 315 students and 23 advisors and chaperones to the campus. Thirteen high schools sent representatives, and the college's Nursing faculty and students were commended for their work by one of the advisors, Edward C. Mann of the UTK Department of Technological and Adult Education. A month-long series of activities were also conducted as part of the Spring Arts Festival. Coordinated by the Division of Humanities and Social Sciences, the events were: a film festival featuring "All the King's Men," "Cabaret," "All the President's Men," "A Dry, White Season," and "Crimes and Misdemeanors;" a Berlin Wall Photographic Exhibit; a drama production by the Cleveland Creative Arts Guild; a walking sculpture tour and a sculpture creation by Steve Rucker (a CSCC graduate); the 10th Annual Cleveland Area Community Art Competition; and musical performances by the Jim Wilson Quartet and by the college's instructors--Will Benson (clarinet), Lisa Schmitt (piano), and Cheryl Gilbert (voice). The major coordinators of the event were Martha Lane, Harry Dean, Jere Chumley, Will Benson, John Bradley, Dr. Renate Basham and Dr. Spencer Culbreth.

The college's Phi Theta Kappa organization sponsored the annual High School Bowl, and twenty faculty members served as moderators. They were Patricia Bishop, John Bradley, Will Benson, Pat Jenkins, Dr. Larry Longerbeam, Dr. Jerome Taylor, Dr. Spencer Culbreth, Jerry Davis, Marilyn Fillers, Cathalin Folks, Scott Joines, Charles Laws, Judy Watts, David Suttles, Hugh Vroman, Dr. L. E. Wooten, Sue Martel, Paul Ketron, Delmus Ledford and Kathryn Johnson. Another annual event, sponsored by the college and Bradley Memorial Hospital, was the annual Health Fair that offered cholesterol testing, glucose screenings, eye and ear diagnostic screenings and cardio-vascular tests. Other activities included the annual Tennis Tournament, a speech by Senator Al Gore and a benefit for military families. The latter, which included several CSCC employees, featured the Knights of Columbus Players and the Bradley High School singing group, "Ranstrassy." It was videotaped by the WTVC television station and was sent to area servicemen in the Persian Gulf.

John Bradley, the college's "paragon of punditry," wrote, in the Employee Newsletter, his suggestions of new titles for several movies. The college's offering for "Dances with Wolves" should be "Rassles with Wranglers"—a movie about a CSCC secretary that won a Mud "Rassling" Championship. The movie's theme song should be "You're the Grease of Love in my Pan of Life." The college's competitor for "The Hunt for Red October" should be "The Hunt for College Textbooks," and the offering for "Driving Miss Daisy" should be "CSCC is Driving Me Crazy."

In athletics the college baseball team had another successful year. Coached by Steve Longley, the team won both the State and Region VII championships and was ranked 4th in the nation in the final season poll. The team members were Brad Butler, David

Siatkowski, Chris Lefoy, Jeff Hostetler, Mark Roy, Steve Coffman, Shane Ricketts, Chris Bevil, Scott Shell, Willie Diaz, Shane Robertson, Darrell Baggett, Trey Calfee, Brad Weir, Chris Jerles, Brandon Gash, Bryan Morgan and Todd Addison. Siatkowski was named as an All-American by the National Junior College Athletic Association (NJCAA).

The tennis and golf teams also excelled. The tennis team won the State and Region VII championships for the second straight year, and interim coach David Boatwright was named the TJCAA Coach of the Year. The team consisted of Dargin Johnson, Chip Day, Claudio Silberberg, Mike O'Brien, Jeff Underwood, Hobert Brabson, Trent Giles, Clee Parks and Daniel Porter. Tony Cavett, the head tennis professional at the Cleveland Country Club (and a 1974 graduate of CSCC), was named the new tennis coach for the 1991-92 season. The golf team won 2nd place in the Region VII tournament, and Jack Williams made the All-Tournament Team. Other players, in addition to Williams, were Allen Dillard, Andy Williams, Dustin Jones and Paul Cooper. The coach was Rusty Melvin, and Chris Byrd and Jeff Curtis were the consulting professionals.

The college also served as the host for the Kiwanis-Ronald McDonald House Holiday Basketball Tournament. Over $5,000 was raised for the House which provided facilities for families with sick children in the hospital in Chattanooga. Both Henry F. Smith, Chairman of the Board of Directors of the House, and Charles B. Burns, Jr., Attorney and President of Kiwanis, wrote thank you letters praising the work of the following on behalf of the event: Norma Davis, Rusty Melvin, Tom Losh, Sherra Witt, Tony Fox, Joyce Fox, Cele Curtis, Sandra Smith, Sarah Elrod, Sherry Miller, Roby Phillips and Dean Jim Cigliano.

A sad event in early 1991 was the death of Roy G. Lillard. As noted previously, he was the former Head of the Social Sciences and Business Division, an advisor to both the SGA and the Baptist Student Union and a founding Trustee of the CSCC Foundation. He authored local histories of both Bradley and Polk counties and was active in numerous state and local historical organizations. The Tennessee Historical Records Advisory Board passed a resolution recognizing his achievements.

Jim Allen, Associate Professor of Architectural Drafting, resigned after twenty-three years of service to the college. He developed the Architectural Drafting program in 1973 and was responsible for the preliminary drawings of the Career Education Building. He also served as Golf Coach from 1974-1977, and his teams won three straight Region VII Championship titles. He was named the TJCAA golf coach of the year in 1975, 1976 and 1977. His wife, Marty, worked in the college's Admissions and Records Office. In other news Jere Chumley won the Juror's Choice Award at the 2nd Red Clay Survey, and he exhibited at the Huntsville Museum of Art. Dean Jim Cigliano was appointed Chair of the National Tennis Committee for the NJCAA.

In student news Copper Kiser was the SGA President for 1990-1991. The other SGA officers were: Angela McClure, Vice-President; Shannon Badwell, Secretary; and Mike

O'Brien, Parliamentarian. Angela McClure was elected SGA President for 1991-92 and re-elected as President for 1992-93. The staff members for The Cherokee Signal were: Tammie Bancroft, Editor; David Jones, News Editor; Joel Prince, Sports Editor; Terri Ballinger, Advertising and Circulation Manager; and Jamie Kruse, computer operator. Tammee Rumba was named the 1991 Homecoming Queen, and Michael Holsomback won 1st Place in the 10th Annual Cleveland Area Community Art Competition.

The commencement speaker was Fred Zeller, the former President of Hardwick Stove Company and the Chair of the "Quarter Century Campaign" for the college Foundation. The Distinguished Faculty Member Award was presented to Dr. T. P. Mathai, the Distinguished Graduate Award winner was Leslie Smith, and the Distinguished Staff Member Award was presented to Steve Huskins. Leslie Smith, in a letter to the college, expressed her appreciation for the help and support she had received during her two years at the college. She wrote, "I have thoroughly enjoyed the faculty, students and administration at CSCC. I feel very proud to have graduated from such a fine school." Another graduate, Ginny Schild, wrote, "Everyone at CSCC made me feel right at home from the very beginning and showed concern and compassion for me as a student and as a person."

– 1992 –

The year's major international events were: President George H. W. Bush and President Boris Yeltsin met at Camp David and formally declared an end to the Cold War; European Community members signed the Maastricht Treaty which founded the European Union; Yitzhak Rabin became Prime Minister in Israel; former West German Chancellor, Willy Brandt, died; the United States and the United Nations intervened in Somalia in an attempt to end famine and a civil war; Bosnia-Herzegovina declared its independence, and a three-year civil war followed between Muslims, Serbs and Croats; McDonalds opened its first restaurant in Beijing, China; Euro Disneyland opened in France (and a few French bemoaned the invasion of American pop culture); President H. W. Bush recognized the independence of Croatia, Slovenia and Bosnia-Herzegovina; Islamic forces overthrew the Communist Government in Kabul, Afghanistan; Prince Charles and Princess Diana legally separated; former Panamanian leader Manuel Noriega was convicted in Miami of eight drug and racketeering charges; in a peaceful separation, Czechoslovakia dissolved and became the Slovak Republic and the Czech State; the North American Free Trade Agreement was signed between the United States, Canada and Mexico; and South Africans voted to end apartheid and create a power-sharing multi-racial government.

In domestic affairs the major events were: the average cost of a new house was $122,5000; the average per year income was $30,030; the cost of a gallon of gas was

$1.05; serial killer Jeffrey Dahmer was sentenced to life in prison; mob boss John Gotti was sentenced to life in prison for murder and racketeering; comedian Sam Kinison was killed in a car accident; five days of rioting erupted in Los Angeles after white police officers were acquitted of using excessive force for beating black motorist Rodney King (a later trial convicted two of the officers for violating King's civil rights): the space shuttle Endeavour completed its first flight; actor Robert Reed of television's "The Brady Bunch" died; orchestra leader Lawrence Welk died; Johnny Carson, of television's "Tonight Show," retired after almost 30 years of broadcasting; the Mall of America opened in Bloomington, Minnesota; in the first of three Presidential debates, President George H. W. Bush, Arkansas Governor Bill Clinton and businessman Ross Perot debated in St. Louis; Bill Clinton won the Presidential election over George H. W. Bush; actor Anthony Perkins died; Carol Moseley-Braun defeated Illinois Senator Alan Dixon in the primary election (she later won the general election and became the first black woman in the U. S. Senate); both R. H. Macy Company and Trans World Airlines filed for bankruptcy; and the 27th Amendment was adopted which prohibited any law that increased or decreased the salary of members of Congress from taking effect until the start of the next set of terms of office for Representatives.

In popular culture the Academy Award for best picture was won by the movie titled, "Unforgiven." Al Pacino was awarded best actor for "Scent of a Woman," and the best actress was Emma Thompson for "Howard's End." The TV Emmy for best comedy was awarded to "Murphy Brown" (CBS), and the best drama was "Northern Exposure" (CBS). The Grammy for best record was awarded to Eric Clapton for "Tears in Heaven," and the album of the year was Eric Clapton's "Unplugged." In sports Stanford won the NCAA Division I Women's Basketball Championship, and Duke won the men's championship. The Washington Redskins defeated the Buffalo Bills in the Super Bowl, and Toronto defeated Atlanta in the World Series.

In college-related events the Tennessee Higher Education Commission approved a new technical program for the two-year colleges. The new program enabled students to earn degrees in the Associate of Applied Science in General Technology at CSCC. This program complemented the 1992 High School diploma approach (which was later changed) that allowed students to pursue careers in technical/industrial skills or other fields of endeavor. Those high school students going into the workforce completed additional shop and vocational/industrial courses, whereas students headed for college completed college prep courses.

Dr. Frank McKenzie, the college's Assistant Dean of Business and Technologies, noted that the Tennessee Board of Regents encouraged articulation between the state's two-year higher education colleges and the Area Vocational/Technical Schools. McKenzie declared that, "a student can be awarded up to 28 credit hours of electives for prior learning, which can form the major area in their A. A. S. degree." A student would also be able to take college level coursework in general education and complete a two-year occupational degree from CSCC, in either a Business Technology Concentration or an Industrial Technology Concentration.

Another new program was referred to as "Students on Track." The Jobs Training Partnership Act (JTPA) Office, the Student Services and the Financial Aid Departments were involved in this college drop-out prevention project that was coordinated by Marsha Goolesby. About 25 to 30 percent of the students were receiving welfare. Most were returning students, laid off workers and/or divorced, single moms. The "Students on Track" Program won the Governor's Award for Outstanding Educational Programs and was funded by JTPA and TBR grant money.

Another endeavor was designed to acquaint welfare recipients with programs available to them. Referred to as "Survival Skills of Women," it was a joint effort of UTC and the JTPA. Perry Storey, CSCC's JTPA Director, said the goal was to remove women from welfare rolls and onto tax rolls. He also noted that 410 people had been placed in jobs in 1991.

A unique event for CSCC was the creation of a time capsule in recognition of the college's 25th Anniversary. The President of the SGA, Angela McClure, organized the material for the capsule, and President James Ford directed the maintenance department to devise a durable PVC pipe capable of preserving the items. Several campus clubs also assisted in the endeavor. The capsule will be opened during the college's 50th Anniversary celebration, in 2017.

Much of the fall was characterized by campus controversy. State Senator Lou Patten and State Representative Steve Bivens of Cleveland noted that campus morale was exceptionally low because of several issues. Dr. Otis Floyd, Chancellor of the Board of Regents, led an investigation of the dispute and directed Dr. Ford to submit a management plan to the TBR. On Friday, September 11, the faculty met and submitted a vote of "no confidence" in President Ford to the TBR. Faculty dissension centered on the issue of micro-management. By the spring of 1993 Dr. Ford had vacated the office and the quest for a new President began.

Meanwhile, the search for a new men's basketball coach ended, and A. J. Kilby was selected. Kilby attended Ferrum Junior College and later, Virginia Commonwealth University, on a basketball scholarship. He graduated from Lincoln Memorial University in 1976 with a Bachelor's Degree in Health and Physical Education. He was an assistant coach at LMU for three years and a Head Coach for five years. He was also an assistant coach for two years at Georgia Southern University. His first team compiled an 11-17 record. He was able to recruit the college's first seven-footer, Jimmy Costner, for the 1992-93 season.

The 1991-92 Lady Cougar basketball team, coached by Rusty Melvin, compiled a 17-7 record. Carla Northcutt was named to the TJCAA All-State Team, the TJCAA All-Eastern Division Team and the NJCAA All-Region VII Team. Tonya Scott was named to the All-Eastern Division Team and the All-Region VII Team. Scott was also the second leading rebounder in the nation (averaging 15 rebounds a game), and she ranked seventh in field goal percentage (60%). Danita Duncan was also named to the

All-Eastern Division Team. The tennis team, coached by Tony Cavett, placed second in Region VII. The leading players were Claudio Silberberg, Scott Moreland and Chris Culberson. The baseball team, coached by Steve Longley, compiled a 39-13 record with a final ranking of 18th in the nation. The team won the State and Region Championships and was the runner-up in the NJCAA District Tournament held in Spartanburg, South Carolina. Christopher Wood was named to the All-Eastern Division Team, was the Most Valuable Player of the State Eastern Division, was selected to the All-NJCAA Region VII Team and was named as an NJCAA All-American. He led the team in batting average (.493), RBIs (47) and doubles (19). Ryan Coe led the team in home runs (15) and was also named to the All-Eastern Division Team, the All-Region Team and received NJCAA All-American honors. Other standouts were Kevin Johnson, Shane Roberson, Bubba Trammell (a pre-season NJCAA All-American who was later drafted by the Baltimore Orioles), Darrell Bagget, Bryan Morgan, Richie Conway, Jason Carruth and Jimmy Erwin.

Mike Callaway began a two-year term as the new President of the College Foundation. The cheerleaders for the year were Sara Dailey, Lisa Johnston, Tina Mix, Copper Kiser, Vonda Blair, Judy Renfro, Ericka Billingsley, Patrick Turner and Will Moss. The SGA President for both 1991-1992 and 1992-1993 (as noted above) was Angela McClure, and the Vice-President was Marta Morrison. The Homecoming Queen was Karen Craig. The Commencement Speaker was the Southern Humorist, Jerry Clower. The Outstanding Faculty Member Award was presented to Barry McCaskill, the Outstanding Staff Member Award was awarded to Bill Clark, and the Outstanding Student Award was presented to Kenny Longley.

– 1993 –

In international affairs the major events were: the UN Security Council unanimously approved the establishment of an international war crimes tribunal to punish those responsible for atrocities in the former country of Yugoslavia; Queen Elizabeth announced that Buckingham Palace would be open to tourists to help pay for damage caused by a fire at Windsor Castle; the United States and the Soviet Union signed a treaty reducing nuclear warheads by 3,500 each; Kim Campbell was elected as Canada's first female prime minister; Israel and the Palestinian Liberation Organization's leaders, Yitzhak Rabin and Yasser Arafat, signed an agreement whereby the PLO recognized Israel's right to exist, and Israel recognized the PLO as the representative of the Palestinian people; and the war in Bosnia-Herzegovina continued.

In domestic affairs the major events were: the average cost of a new house was $113,200; the average income per year was $31,230; the cost of a gallon of gasoline was $1.16; the Martin Luther King, Jr. holiday was observed for the first time in all

50 states; retired Supreme Court Justice Thurgood Marshall died; Tennis Hall of Fame member, Arthur Ashe, died; an explosion in the World Trade Center killed six people and injured over 1,000; Janet Reno became the first female Attorney General; four agents of the Federal Bureau of Alcohol, Tobacco and Firearms Agency, and six members of the heavily armed Branch Dravidian religious cult were killed in a gun battle in Waco, Texas; the 51 day siege of the Branch Dravidian cult compound ended when cult members started a fire that killed their leader, David Koresh, and approximately 80 other people; singer Marian Anderson died; the Family and Medical Leave Act, that required businesses with 50 or more employees to grant up to twelve weeks of unpaid leave for medical emergencies (or to care for a new child) became a law; President Clinton announced that the United States had launched missiles against Iraqi targets because there was "compelling evidence" that Iraq had plotted to assassinate former President George H. W. Bush; Secretary of Defense, Les Aspin, removed restrictions on aerial combat roles for women in the armed forces; a huge flood inundated approximately 15 million acres in nine Midwestern states, leaving about 50 dead and $15 billion in damages; "don't ask, don't tell, don't pursue" became official policy for homosexuals in the military; Ruth Bader Ginsburg became the second woman to serve on the Supreme Court; and the Brady Bill, a major gun control measure named after Sarah Brady and former Reagan press secretary James Brady, became a law.

In popular culture "Schindler's List" won the award for best picture, Tom Hanks won best actor for "Philadelphia," and Holly Hunter won best actress for "The Piano." The Emmy for best comedy was awarded to "Seinfeld" (NBC), and the best drama award was won by "Picket Fences" (CBS). Approximately 93 million TV viewers watched the final episode of "Cheers." The Grammy Award for best record was presented to Whitney Houston for "I Will Always Love You," and the album of the year was won by Whitney Houston for "The Bodyguard." In sports Texas Tech won the NCAA Division I Women's Basketball Championship, and North Carolina won the Men's Championship. The Dallas Cowboys defeated the Buffalo Bills in the Super Bowl, and Toronto defeated Philadelphia in the World Series.

Campus affairs centered on the quest for a new college President. Chancellor Otis Floyd announced the appointment of an advisory committee to assist in the endeavor. The faculty members were Dr. T. P. Mathai, Sherra Witt, Kenneth (Tom) Williams, Dr. Renate Basham and Maryanne Markiewicz. Others were: Susan Webb-Curtis, staff member; Sandra Brown, student representative; Diego McCoy, SGA President; Mitchell Walker, Minister of St. James Cumberland Presbyterian Church; Mike Callaway, President of the College Foundation; George Johnson, President of Franco Corporation; and Tom Wheeler, General Manager of Cleveland Utilities. Beginning July 1, 1993, Dr. Peter Consacro, the TBR Associate Vice-Chancellor for Academic Affairs, served as the interim President. Later in the year, the college, and the entire community served by the college, was saddened by the death of CSCC's first President, Dr. David F. Adkisson.

In August 1993 it was decided that the new President would be Dr. Owen Cargol. Cargol had degrees from Oregon State University, Louisiana State University and Penn State. He held faculty and administrative positions at North Idaho College, LSU, Highline College and Penn State.

The year 1993 was the occasion for another re-accreditation visit from the Southern Association of Colleges and Universities (SACs). The college's self-study director was Buford Guy, and the visiting committee was chaired by Dr. J. Bryan Brooks of Davidson County Community College in Davidson, North Carolina. The careful preparation for the visit was rewarded when SACs conferred re-accreditation to the college in 1994. Meanwhile, Melinda Hillman was named the new Executive Director of the Foundation. She succeeded Walter Presswood, who had been the Director since 1977.

The college received a letter of appreciation from Phil Campbell, President of the Etowah Area Chamber of Commerce. The college's Small Business Development Office assisted the Etowah Chamber in hosting a business event for their area. In a letter to the college, Campbell praised Don Geren, head of the college's office, as well as Rosemary Den Uyl, head of the college's Department of Institutional Advancement, for their contributions to the event. Another letter of appreciation was received from Dr. Edward C. Mann, Associate Professor of UTK. He commended Barry McCaskill and the Technologies Faculty for their outstanding work in conducting the Southeast Tennessee Vocational Industrial Clubs of America (VICA) Competitive Events.

The college's Office of Career Planning and Placement conducted a weeklong series of activities on the theme of Career Exploration. The Coordinator of the Department was Susan Webb-Curtis. She had a Bachelor's in Psychology from East Tennessee State University and a Master's in Counseling from Stetson University in Florida. In addition to Webb-Curtis, those assisting with the endeavor were Jim Cigliano, Norma Davis, Marsha Goolesby, Brenda Myers, Tom Losh, Michael Stokes, Lynn Boettler, Luis Vazquez, Jodi Johnson, Marcia Owens, Ann McCoin, Donna Martens, Bill Clark, Sandy Tinker, Steve Roper, Steve Huskins (and the Maintenance staff), and Walter Hackett (and the Security staff).

Although a huge snowstorm of over 20 inches blanketed the area in the spring, the college was able to sponsor several campus events. One of these was a presentation of the play, "Love Letters," performed by Maurine Nichols and John Bradley. A "Dress for Success Seminar" was also conducted in the spring, and the following staff and faculty organized the event: Brenda Myers, Susan Webb-Curtis, Geraldine Parks, Norma Davis, Sandy Tinker, Ann McCoin, Linda Everett, Mel Parkman, David Suttles, Larry Burns and Marsha Goolesby. The High School Academic Bowl was won by McMinn High School. Organizers and moderators were: Patricia Bishop, Cindy Golledge-Franz, Harry Dean, Mel Parkman, Dot Stern, Jerry Davis, Patricia Bishop, Marilyn Fillers, Rosemary Dworak, Dr. Larry Longerbeam, Lynn Boettler, David Suttles, Sandy Tinker, Dr. Neil Greenwood, Mike Dorset, John Squires, Melinda Hillman, Dr. Joe Semak, Dr.

Renate Basham, Dr. James Ford, Mike Callaway, Verna Moore, Mason Sesler, Dr. Hugh Vroman and Norma Davis.

Numerous staff and faculty members attended conferences and/or received recognitions throughout the year. These were: Ann McCoin (Legal Assistant instructor) was elected President-Elect for the National Board of Directors of the American Association for Paralegal Education; Eric Jiang (Computer Science instructor) was the co-author of a research paper, titled "Parallel Algorithms for Solving Bended Toeplitz Linear Systems," that appeared in the Journal of Neural, Parallel and Scientific Computations; Karen Wyrick, Beverly Laws (Remedial/Developmental instructors) and Charles Laws (Math instructor) attended the "Equity 2000 Agenda for Higher Education Mathematics Institute" in Nashville; Laws and Helen Darcey (Math instructor) attended a workshop at MTSU on "Math, Precalculus and Calculus with a Focus on Technology Integration;" Paul Ketron (Math instructor) completed a National Science Foundation seminar at UTK on the subject of computers and graphing calculators in teaching calculus; Dr. Neil Greenwood (History instructor) attended the 1993 Conference of Tennessee Historians at the University of the South in Sewanee, Tennessee; and Efrain Guillen (Spanish and Sociology instructor) attended the Tennessee Foreign Language Teaching Association's 26th Annual Conference in Nashville.

Others who attended meetings or made news were: Jerry Davis (Criminal Justice instructor) attended the annual Criminal Justice convention in Charleston, South Carolina; Bill Clark (Media Center Office) attended a "Toaster" Training Seminar in Nashville; Shirley Nettles (Remedial/Developmental instructor) attended an Interactive Math Seminar at Morehouse College in Atlanta; Cynthia Golledge-Franz (Remedial/Developmental instructor) and Lynn Boettler (Student Development Office) attended a National Conference on Student Retention in New Orleans; Remedial/Developmental instructors, Pat Jenkins, Millie Sieber, Cindy Golledge-Franz and Lynn Boettler, attended a Nashville Tech College workshop on "Working with Students with Learning Disabilities;" Dr. Michael Stokes (Student Development) was a co-presenter at the annual conference of the Southern Association for College Student Affairs in Greenville, South Carolina; Daryl Schaefer was hired as the Tech/Prep Consortia Coordinator; and John Squires (Remedial Developmental instructor) was awarded the Outstanding Graduate Student Academic Achievement Award from the UTK Department of Mathematics.

The Phi Theta Kappa Student Club won several top honors at the regional convention in Knoxville. CSCC won first place for the Most Improved Chapter Award, second place for the Service Hallmark Award, third place for the Leadership Hallmark Award and third place for the Outstanding Chapter Award. The college's chapter also increased its international standing to the One Star Level. The college's chapter student President, Marta Morrison, the President-elect, Michael Orick, and faculty advisors Cindy Golledge-Franz and Harry Dean were invited to attend the international convention in Dallas, Texas. Other student newsmakers in 1993-1994 were Diego McCoy (SGA President) and Ivey Leverett (Homecoming Queen).

The big news in athletics was the retirement of baseball coach, Steve Longley. After completing his 14th year of coaching baseball, he decided to hang up his cleats. His final team gave him an impressive season record of forty wins and only eleven losses. He was honored at the annual season-ending Athletic Banquet and praised for his success as a coach. He departed baseball with a coaching record of 440 wins and only 179 losses. The tennis team, coached by Tony Cavett, placed second in the Regional Tournament. Scott Moreland and Chris Cunnygham were regional winners and participated in the National Tournament in Corpus Christi, Texas. Moreland, Cunnygham and Shannon Brown were named to the All-TJCAA team. Athletic Director, and Dean of Student Affairs, Jim Cigliano, announced that women's fast-pitch softball would return as a campus sport in 1994.

The Commencement Speaker was Charles E. Smith, Commissioner of Education for Tennessee. Awards were presented to Judy Watts (Outstanding Faculty Member), Dovie Buckner (Outstanding Staff Member) and Angela McClure (Outstanding Student).

– 1994 –

The major international events for the year were: Israeli Prime Minister Yitzhak Rabin and PLO leader Yasser Arafat signed an agreement that granted Palestinians self-rule in the Gaza Strip and Jericho; Nelson Mandela became South Africa's first black president; the thirty-one mile channel tunnel (called 'the Chunnel") opened between England and France; the presidents of Rwanda and Burundi were killed in a mysterious plane crash, and the civil war between Hutus and Tutsis increased in intensity; France celebrated the 50th Anniversary of the World War II Allied landings; the North American Free Trade Agreement (NAFTA) of the United States, Canada and Mexico became operational; Jordan and Israel signed a peace treaty ending the state of war that had existed between them since 1948; The Irish Republican Army announced a "complete cessation of military operations;" the United Nations Peace Keeping Force withdrew from Somalia; tensions began over inspection of nuclear plants in North Korea; 40,000 Russian troops invaded Chechnya to prevent a secessionist rebellion; the world's first satellite digital television service was launched; and Netscape Navigator was released and quickly became the market leader for browsing the web.

The major events in domestic affairs were: the average cost of a new home was $119,050; the average income per year was $37,070; the cost of a gallon of gasoline was $1.09; the average cost of a new car was $12,350; figure skater Nancy Kerrigan was attacked by four men, including the ex-husband of her rival, Tonya Harding; the men who attacked Kerrigan were sentenced to prison and Tonya Harding was fined $100,000, sentenced to 500 hours of community service, forced to resign from the Figure Skating Association and was given three years of probation; the first genetically modified tomatoes were created and genetically modified foods were approved; O. J. Simpson was charged with murder and led police on a nationally-televised 90 minute chase on an interstate highway before surrendering; former first lady Jacqueline Kennedy Onassis died; Republicans won a majority in both houses during the mid-term elections, and Newt Gingrich became the first GOP Speaker of the House in four decades; President Clinton lifted the 19-year ban on trade with Vietnam; Byron De La Beckwith was convicted of the 1963 murder of civil rights leader Medgar Evers; the last American soldiers left Germany after an occupation that began in 1945; CIA officer Aldrich Ames and his wife were charged with spying; the Whitewater hearings began; tornadoes struck the southeastern states; and an earthquake hit Los Angeles.

In popular culture "Forrest Gump" won the best movie award, and Tom Hanks received the best actor award for the same movie. The best actress award was presented to Jessica Lange for "Blue Sky." "Frasier" (NBC) won the Emmy for best comedy, and "Picket Fences" (CBS) was recognized as the best drama. The Grammy for best record was awarded to Sheryl Crow for "All I Wanna Do," and the album of the year was Tony Bennett's "MTV Unplugged." In athletics Wayne Gretzky broke Gordie Howe's National Hockey League career record with his 802nd goal. The University of North Carolina won the NCAA Division I Women's Basketball Championship, and Arkansas won the Men's Championship. The Dallas Cowboys defeated the Buffalo Bills in the Super Bowl, and a professional baseball player's strike led to the cancellation of several games (as well as the World Series).

In college news the Athens Area Vocational-Technical School was converted to the Tennessee State Technology Center, and additional funding was provided to upgrade both the physical and technological facilities. Formal reaccreditation was presented to CSCC at the SACS convention in San Antonio, Texas. Buford Guy, Self-Study Director, and John Bradley, Self-Study Editor, represented the college at the centennial convention. Approximately $110,000 was expended for the Institutional Self-Study and this amount was irrespective of the personnel costs for the numerous committee meetings, surveys and other duties related to the event. In other college news, smoking, and the use of tobacco products, was prohibited from use indoors in all campus buildings. Tobacco was also outlawed in college-owned vehicles. Smoking was prohibited within ten feet of all doors, windows and air intake appliances associated with the college.

A major event in 1994 was the inauguration of the Dual Enrollment program. The program was designed to permit junior and senior high school students to receive high school and college credit simultaneously. The program was partially funded by local school boards, and eligibility was based on student ACT scores and grade point averages. In some instances high school instructors were also CSCC adjunct faculty, and this situation enabled students to work on their degree while attending classes on their high school campus. Fifty-six students enrolled in Dual Enrollment during the fall of 1994.

In the spring the college conducted another "Career Exploration Week' with a profusion of workshops on subjects such as careers in technology, careers in banking, resume writing, interviewing techniques, job search strategies and dressing for success. The event concluded with a mock trial by the Legal Assistant students. The first annual Tennessee Valley 5 kilometer road race was conducted to raise money for the college Foundation. Approximately sixty runners participated, and over $1,500 was raised for the Foundation. The following college personnel assisted with the race: Melinda Hillman, Chair, Lynn Boettler, Dr. Owen Cargol, Andrea Dake, Rosemary Dworak, Rubi Porter, Kaye Zerk and Tom Losh (and his family). Sponsors were: Benton Baking Company, Bishop Baking Company, Cleveland Bank and Trust, Grey Epperson's Ford-Mercury, Hardee's, Johnston Coca-Cola, McDonald's, Manufacturer's Soap and Chemical Corporation and Maytag Cleveland Cooking Products.

The spring was also the occasion for the annual college Arts Festival. The major events were: a lecture/slide presentation and art exhibit by Art Professor David LeDoux of MTSU; a community art exhibition; guided walking tours of the campus sculpture exhibit led by Jere Chumley; lectures by history student Robert Thompson and by former history professor Rebecca Mobbs; and a musical performance by the "Society for the Preservation of Music by African-American Composers."

In other activities McMinn County High School won the college's 1994 Academic High School Bowl for the second year in a row. The annual College for Youth Program was conducted in the summer. Designed for six to fourteen year old youth, it was held for two one-week sessions and was taught primarily by CSCC faculty and coordinated by Rubi Porter. Among the numerous course choices were Chinese culture, computers, French, golf, karate, pet care, photography, Spanish, Science, tennis and drama. A unique event, conducted later in the year, was a baby-sitting clinic for baby sitters aged twelve through sixteen. Participants were introduced to games and activities to amuse youngsters.

As of 1994 the faculty members in charge of academic affairs were: Dr. Frank McKenzie, Dean of Applied Science and Technology; Dr. Charles Wheeler, Dean of Mathematics and Natural Sciences; and Dr. Spencer Culbreth, Dean of Humanities and Social Sciences. The Department Heads were: Nancy Boyd, Business; Shelby Millsaps, Health/Science; Barry McCaskill, Technology; Helen Darcey, Mathematics; Dr. T. P. Mathai, Natural Science; Dr. Larry Longerbeam, Humanities; and Dr. Jerome Taylor, Social Sciences. A college retiree, Josephine Pritchett, died in Griffin, Georgia. She had been Head of the Office Careers Department from 1967-1976.

A lagniappe of humor was restored to the campus Employeee Newsletter when John Bradley renewed his column titled "The Inside Scoop." Bradley suggested CSCC movie titles to compete for the Oscar nominations. Instead of "Six Degrees of Separation," he suggested that the college produce "Ten Feet of Separation." It would be a film about a campus Security Guard measuring the distance between a smoker and a building's entrance. Instead of "The Fugitive" (a film about an innocent man on the run), he suggested that the Nursing Department produce a film entitled "The Purgative." It would also be a story of a man on the run, but for completely different reasons. Bradley suggested that the campus smoker's lobby should counter the movie "Sleepless in Seattle" with "Smokeless in Cleveland." The Psychology Department's answer for the movie "Fearless" should be "Mindless."

The faculty and staff continued to be active in 1994. Ann McCoin was elected President of the American Association for Paralegal Education. Dr. Neil Greenwood (History) was a guest speaker at the Sertoma Club. His topic was "Recreation and the Civil War Soldier." Later, coaches Rusty Melvin and L. J. Kilby were also speakers at the same club. They talked about the ladies' and men's basketball teams and the competition in the upcoming season. Efrain Guillen (Spanish) was a guest speaker at both Stuart and Blythe Avenue schools. His lectures were on the topic of life in Mexico. Dr. Jerome Taylor (History) and Dr. Larry Longerbeam (English) taught dual enrollment courses at Meigs County High School during the year. Don Geren (Small Business Center) was a guest speaker for Business classes at Tennessee Wesleyan, Tellico High School and at CSCC off-campus classes in McMinn County.

In athletics the college conducted a community-wide golf tournament in the summer, and proceeds were used to benefit the college's athletic programs. Mike Policastro became the new baseball coach. While coaching at Tennessee Wesleyan, his 1993 team compiled a 35-9 record and won the Tennessee-Virginia Athletic Conference. He had four CSCC sophomores returning: Steve Hailey, pitcher; Jonathan McCluhan, catcher; Regan Harris, infielder; and Scott Marshall, infielder. Incoming freshmen were: J. W. Holt, pitcher; Travis McClanahan, pitcher; Dustin McPherson, pitcher; Clay Green, center fielder and Jason Clabo, shortstop. Policastro's first CSCC team qualified for both the TJCAA and Region VII Tournaments.

In other news The Cherokee Signal experimented with a one-page publication and (for a short period of time) changed its name to The Signal. The editor was Amy Carpenter. Dinah Fleming was the SGA President, and Kimberley Reed was the Homecoming Queen. The CSCC Foundation President was Mike Callaway.

The speaker for the June Commencement was Clifford H. (Bo) Henry, Jr., a Regent of the TBR. In his career he taught in the Blount County School System, worked at the Johns Hopkins University Applied Physics Laboratory, was Vice-President of First American Bank in Maryville and served in the Tennessee House of Representatives from 1974-1982. He was the House's Assistant Minority Leader and a member of the House Ways and Means Committee. The Distinguished Staff Award was presented to Leona Watson, the Distinguished Graduate Award was awarded to Donna Flattery, and the recipient of the Distinguished Faculty Award was Buford Guy.

– 1995 –

The major international events were: warfare in the former country of Yugoslavia dominated the news; as noted earlier, Croatia, Slovenia, Macedonia and Bosnia-Herzegovina had declared their independence, and only Serbia and Montenegro remained as the Republic of Yugoslavia; bitter fighting occurred in the former Yugoslavia, and the Serbs were accused of "ethnic cleansing" of the Muslim population; NATO began a series of successful bombing campaigns against Serbian artillery positions; a peace accord was signed in Dayton, Ohio in 1995, and NATO troops occupied the Kosovo region as peacekeepers; the United States pulled troops out of Somalia; radical members of a religious cult in Japan released Sarin nerve gas on five Tokyo subway cars, killing 12 people and injuring over 5,000; the United States imposed economic sanctions against Iran; the United Kingdom's oldest investment banking firm, Barings Bank, collapsed after a securities broker lost $1.4 billion by speculating on the Tokyo Stock Exchange; in New York City, 170 countries agreed to extend the Nuclear Nonproliferation Treaty indefinitely; the World Trade Organization replaced the General Agreement on Tariffs and Trade as a major regulator of international trade; Israeli Prime Minister Yitzhak Rabin was assassinated by a right-wing Israeli gunman; a Quebec referendum to become independent from Canada was narrowly defeated; and in an unique event the U. S. space shuttle Atlantis docked with the Russian Mir space station.

In domestic affairs the major events were: the average cost of a new home was $113,150; the average income per year was $35,900; the average price of a gallon of gas was $1.09; President Clinton authorized a $20 billion loan to Mexico to help it avert a financial collapse; a truck bomb, planted by Timothy McVeigh, exploded at an Oklahoma City federal office building and killed 168 people; the U. S. announced it was reestablishing relations with Vietnam; O. J. Simpson was found not guilty of the murders of his former wife and a friend of hers; ten Muslim terrorists were found guilty in a failed plot to blow up the United Nations headquarters; Dow Jones closed above 5,000 for the first time; the federal mandated speed limit of 55 mph, imposed during the 1973 Middle East oil crisis, was repealed; a partial government shutdown, due to political differences, occurred from November 14 to November 20; thousands of black men participated in a "Million Man March" and rally in Washington, D. C.; five Americans were among seven killed in the bombing of a U. S. military post in Riyadh, Saudi Arabia; Steve Fossett became the first person to complete a solo flight across the Pacific Ocean in a hot air balloon; JavaScript was introduced; Windows 95 was released; Ebay online auction and shopping website was launched; and the Violent Crime Control and Law Enforcement Act was passed to make parents aware of the presence of convicted sex offenders in their neighborhood.

In popular culture "Braveheart" won the Academy Award for best picture. Nicolas Cage won best actor for "Leaving Las Vegas," and Susan Sarandon won best actress for

"Dead Man Walking." The Emmy Award for TV's best comedy was won by "Frasier," and "NYPD Blue" won the best drama award (ABC). The Grammy for best record was awarded to Seal for "Kiss From a Rose," and the album of the year was won by Alanis Morissette for "Jagged Little Pill." In athletics Major League baseball players ended a 232-day strike; Connecticut University won the NCAA Division I Women's Basketball Championship, and UCLA won the Men's Championship. The San Francisco 49ers defeated the San Diego Chargers in the Super Bowl, and Atlanta defeated Cleveland in the World Series.

The college had a record number of students (3,673) enroll for the fall of 1995. The previous record of 3,663 had existed since 1983. The new Foundation officers were Sam McReynolds (President), Grey Epperson (Vice-President), Nora McNeill (Secretary) and Don Lorton (Treasurer). Newly elected trustees were Sherry Brown, Walter Presswood and Paul Willson. The efforts of the college's first community leaders were given recognition with the dedication of a "Founders Room" in the Student Center. The college received a $2,700 Geier Grant for a professional development activity. The grant, written primarily by Rubi Porter, was for additional training for instructors of students with writing problems.

A joint University of Illinois at Chicago and Penn State University research project, headed by Professor Ernest Pascarella of the University of Illinois at Chicago, concluded that attending a two-year college, for the first two years of college, was more cost-effective than attending a four-year school. The average annual tuition for a year of community college was, in 1995, approximately $1,392 ($994 at CSCC) which was substantially lower than tuition at virtually all four-year schools. In Warren, Michigan, another study found that students, who transferred from Macomb Community College to four-year universities in the area, consistently achieved higher grades than those who started at the four-year schools as freshmen. A third research project focused on community college transfers to Arizona's state universities. It concluded that the more courses students completed at the community college level the better they performed when they attended a four-year school.

The college received good news from the results of the annual evaluation by the Tennessee Higher Education Commission (THEC). CSCC scored 92 out of a possible 100 points. The state average score was 89. Rankings were based on factors such as student and alumni satisfaction, general and subject area knowledge of graduates, peer reviews and accreditation programs. The college was also awarded two other grants—one from the THEC and one from the TBR. The former grant, coordinated by Shirley Nettles, was for the purpose of promoting participation of minority students in pre-professional programs. The latter grant, coordinated by Sherry Allen and Efrain Guillen, was for the enhancement of coordination between high schools and colleges in foreign languages.

The Joint Training Partnership Act program (JTPA) was awarded $15,000 in Job Opportunity and Basic Skills (JOBS) funds and $22,000 in discretionary funds from the Economic Dislocated Workers Program. The former program was coordinated by Regina Turpin and the latter by Sue Hamilton. One of the JTPA initiatives was to develop on-line information systems in all of the region's Workforce Development Centers. The JTPA Students on Track Program at CSCC reported that 41 students participated in the program in 1995, and approximately 13% of the college's graduating class were program participants. The program served students in the following categories: adult/ non-traditional learners, single parents, dislocated workers, minorities, AFDC Aid to Families with Dependent Children recipients, individuals with disabilities and other groups. The participants received financial assistance, counseling, advisement, tutorial assistance, job placement assistance and other services. The Training Coordinator, Marsha Goolesby, noted that the average GPA of the JTPA academic award recipients was 3.6, and the overall GPA of all JTPA participants was 3.0.

Opportunities were available at the college for students desiring part-time or full-time employment. One avenue was the college's Cooperative Education Program. Courses were designed to integrate classroom theory with practical work experience. It required specific periods of classroom attendance with specific periods of employment. Courses such as Job Search Skills, Succeeding on the Job, and Workforce Development were combined with minimum hours of work in a job. The college enrolled 103 students in the 1995 fall Co-op Program, and they worked with 53 employers throughout the college's service area. The program's Director, Al Fine, noted that students earned $178,050 on Co-op jobs in the year 1994. The college's Job Placement Office also assisted students in finding employment while attending the college and/or after graduation. Over 200 jobs were posted by approximately 100 different employers during the first month of the fall semester of 1995. In 1994 students earned in excess of $500,000 on jobs they secured through the Placement Office.

The college received good news in 1995 when the National Association of Industrial Technology (NAIT) granted accreditation to the Industrial Technology program. The visiting team was obviously highly pleased with the college's report because the meeting lasted only five minutes. The comment was made that this speedy approval could have been a first in the history of NAIT hearings. NAIT was founded in 1967, the same year that CSCC opened its doors, and its purpose was to improve the curricula for schools of higher education. Barry McCaskill, Associate Professor of Technology and Department Chair, noted that the college had a 95% placement rating in programs such as construction technology, drafting and design, electro-mechanical, electronics and industrial management. Dr. Frank McKenzie, the Dean of Applied Science and Technology, stated that technology programs were growing because business and industry leaders needed to retrain their workers to operate new equipment. McKenzie added that there was a growing demand for skilled employees with a team approach philosophy and that wages for career-technical jobs were attracting employees.

Another technology-related enterprise was the Fundamentals in Technology (FIT) Block program. The 15-credit-hour program could be completed in one semester.

It provided entry-level skills in a variety of areas such as electronics, mechanical principles, computer usage, blueprint reading, industrial calculations, fluid power systems and industrial safety. An emphasis was placed on communication skills and problem solving techniques.

Other college initiatives were programs in Medical Office Assistant (MOA) and Solar Energy. A new course in Parenting was also added that often became a court-mandated course in judicial cases involving divorce or involving parenting skills. The MOA program enabled students to become medical assistants. As faculty member Nancy Boyd noted, "The duties of a medical assistant cover the full spectrum of activities in a doctor's office. They assist doctors in patient examinations and lab testing as well as perform administrative functions." The Solar Energy program eventually expanded into a Construction Technology Concentration that included, among others, courses in Renewable Energy, PV Panel Installation, Energy Efficient Residential Elements, Energy Star Residential Ratings and Ground Sourced HVAC.

The college's programs in Social Work and Human Services also expanded in the 1990s. Enrollments in courses such as Social Welfare, Substance Abuse, Aging in America and Elder Care, The Family Experience, Crisis and Mental Health and Social Welfare Policy and Programs grew in popularity. Ed Hale, Coordinator of the Human Services Specialist Program, noted that many students combined these, and other courses, with work in the college's Cooperative Education Program.

Meanwhile, efforts to assist students in mastering course material continued. Susan Webb-Curtis, Director of Student Relations, working with the college's computer programmer, Curtis McNeely, upgraded the "Early Alert Student Tracking System." Webb-Curtis noted that the system was designed to "reach out and communicate with students." Faculty members received special computer-generated rosters of students in their classes. The faculty members marked them in accordance with attendance and/ or an academic problem. The Office of Student Relations compiled a report that was submitted to relevant administrators, directors, coordinators and the faculty advisors of students. A personal letter, in a sealed envelope, was sent by the Office of Student Relations to the individual students, and they were advised that a problem had been noticed and they were directed to specific offices for assistance.

A noteworthy academic effort was the adoption of a new computer program known as ASTROLINK. It provided students with information about astronomy and provided access to major observatories such as Mount Wilson, Pike's Peak and Arricebo. Students could also connect with the Hubble space-based observatory and view and download computer images. Associate Professor Buford Guy organized the enterprise and it was also made available to students and teachers in the local school systems. Professor Guy also attended a week-long National Science Foundation Workshop at the Harvard Smithsonian Center for Astrophysics. He was one of 36 participants chosen for the workshop. The workshop featured training in the latest imaging and software techniques used in Astrophysics.

The college engaged in a profusion of activities throughout the year. Black History Month (February) began with a celebration of Dr. Martin L. King, Jr. in the Ray Coleman Community Services Auditorium. Members of the college and community presented songs, dances and dramatic readings, and the featured speaker was Reverend Harold Middlebrook of Knoxville. Later in the month, the college's Speech and Theater Department, the Multicultural Council and the Cultural and Educational Enrichment Committee presented the play, "Raisin in the Sun." Directed by John Bradley, the cast included Jackie Westfield, Will Benson, Velda Glass, Adrian Westfield, Deanda Ware, Randy Moore, Caesar Thomas, Willie Glass, C. J. Scoggins, Rayceen Johnson and Mary Thompson.

In January and February, a collection of photographic works by Chattanooga State Art Professor, Denise Frank, was exhibited in the Administration Building. Another play, "A Midsummer Night's Dream," performed by the National Shakespeare Company, was sponsored by the college's Cultural and Education Enrichment Committee, the Student Activities Department and Phi Theta Kappa. The spring High School Bowl Quiz event was contested by eleven teams, and the winner was McMinn Central High School. Bradley Central was second, and Cleveland placed third. Several students, faculty and staff participated in the year's American Heart Walk. The event was highly successful as approximately $44,000 was raised for the charity. The chair of the event was Norma Davis, and other college participants were Debra and Will Capobianco, Tanya Hall, Becky Didona, Garry Belk, Wendy Russell, Kelly Haynes, Harry Perkins, Dr. David Watts, Sharon Ziegler, Alisha Ziegler, Pat Bishop, Sandy Tinker, Tiffani McCaskill, Cathy Smith, Melissa Patrone, Dr. Spencer Culbreth, Heather Wilson, Harry Dean, Larry Burns, Dr. Rodney Fitzgerald, Sherra Witt, Wes Harden and Sherry Tunks.

An important activity for students having problems with Math was introduced in 1995. A tutoring service was offered to students by the Math faculty. Those faculty participating were Dr. Charles Wheeler, Helen Darcey, Shirley Nettles, Paul Ketron, Beverly Laws, David Guardiani and Samuel Ofori. An opportunity for foreign travel was offered to students in May 1995. Sharee Allen, language instructor, offered an International Studies class that included a trip to Europe. Students visited such places as the Eiffel Tower, the Louvre, Les Invalides, Napoleon's Arc de Triomphe, Catalonia, Madrid, Barcelona, Toulouse, Versailles and Chateaux along the Loire River. Later in the year two award-winning poets presented poetry readings in the Humanities Building. Organized by Associate Professor Harry Dean, the poets were Bradley Paul of Iowa and Regina Wilkins of Michigan. Paul was an Iowa Arts Fellow, a recipient of a Bread Loaf Writer's Conference scholarship and a William E. Brock Scholar at UTC. Wilkins was the recipient of the Chattanooga Artists and Writers' Guild Scholarship and a Randall Jarrell Poetry Fellow at the University of North Carolina at Greensboro. Another literary activity was a reading and writer's workshop presented by Tamara Baxter. Baxter was a member of the Appalachian Writer's Association and the author of Appalachian fictional works.

Several art-related events organized by Associate Professor of Art, Jere Chumley, occurred throughout the year. Howard Hull, Professor of Art Education at UTK, and a classmate of Chumley, exhibited his art at the college in March, 1995. Hull completed a Bachelor's and Master's degree from MTSU and an Education Specialist degree from George Peabody College of Vanderbilt University. He and Chumley were MTSU's first two graduates in art. Anita Dotson, a CSCC 1979 graduate, who also received a Bachelor's degree in Fine Arts from MTSU, exhibited her artistic creations in the campus Administration Building. CSCC art student, David Smith, also exhibited his works during the year. The 14th annual Cleveland Area Community Art Competition, which was renamed the Tennessee Valley Art Competition (TVAC), had 76 entries by 35 artists. The juror for TVAC was Joe Helseth, Professor of Art at Chattanooga State. First place was awarded to Joyce Simpson of Athens for her drawing titled, "Young Love."

In other cultural activities CSCC professors Millie Sieber and Katharine Trewhitt were active participants in the numerous events sponsored each year by the Cleveland Storytelling Guild. In addition to Sieber and Trewhitt, frequent contributors from the community at storytelling events were Nancy Brewer, Maurine Nichols (whose husband, Alex, was a CSCC Computer Science instructor), Debbie Parrish, Sylvia Idom and Linda Stuckey. Other college-sponsored events were: Psychology professors, Sue Martel and Pat Bishop, arranged a lecture by Dr. Glenn Geralds, a clinical psychologist, on the subject of "Parenting in the 90s;" Jack Malone, a local educator and seasonal ranger at Chickamauga National Military Park, presented a lecture on Civil War Soldiers; and an Adult College Fair was conducted for prospective non-traditional college students.

In college athletics Kyle Turnham became the new men's basketball coach. He replaced L. J. Kilby who resigned to accept another position. Turnham was Chattanooga State's coach for five years and was an assistant coach at Brewton-Parker College (in Georgia) and at MTSU. John Squires, who was also a Math Professor, became the softball coach. The baseball team ended the 1994-95 season with a 28-18 record. Jeff Bramlett led the team with a .359 batting average, Mike Moore led in RBI's, with 41, and Clay Greene led both the team and the state with an amazing 43 stolen bases. Coach Mike Policastro praised the sophomores for their outstanding play during the past two years. They were: Clay Greene, center fielder; Jason Clabo, also left fielder; Justin Carpenter, second baseman; Johnie Allison, catcher; Casey McDonald, right fielder; and pitchers Travis McClanahan, Chad McDowell and Phil Marshall.

Coach Rusty Melvin's Lady Cougar Basketball team had an outstanding player in Melinda Godfrey. She was named to the TJCAA All-Eastern Division Team, the All-State Team, the All-Region Team, and she received All-American Honorable Mention. Godfrey was 7th in scoring among all junior college players in the nation. As a sophomore, she averaged 22 points and 11 rebounds per game. She had 66 assists, 51 steals, and 24 blocked shots. She also scored the most points in a game (42), most free throws in a career (303), and her 74% free throw average was also a record.

In student activities the college's Phi Theta Kappa (PTK) Chapter (the International Honor Society for two-year colleges) achieved recognition as a Five-Star Program (for the second consecutive year) at the regional conference in Maryville, Tennessee. Receiving a Five-Star award was the highest award attainable for PTK chapters. The chapter also received a first place Service Award, a third place Regional Outstanding Chapter Award, a second place Best Yearbook Award and a second place Scholarship award. Professor Patricia Bishop, PTK faculty advisor, stated, "We are very pleased at being recognized as an outstanding chapter." CSCC President, Dr. Owen Cargol, noted that, "these students have excelled in their efforts to make this a remarkable program." A few of the outstanding students of PTK were Dinah Fleming, Tanya Hall, Angie Wilcox and Rebecca Didona. In addition to Patricia Bishop, other faculty and staff advising PTK were Larry Burns and David Suttles. Didona received a prestigious honor by being elected as the Editor of PTK's Regional Employeee Newsletter. Another PTK member, Vickie Jones, was named to the National Dean's List for 1994-95. This honor made her eligible to compete for a $1,000 scholarship. Only one-half of one percent of the nation's college students received this award. A few examples of the college's PTK annual activities were: a campus wide yard sale; the Healthy Choice American Heart Walk; a trip (with 70 students) to the Little Theater of Chattanooga to see Tennessee William's play, "Cat on a Hot Tin Roof;" a "star gazing" activity from the college's observatory; adoption of an overseas armed forces troop; and an annual food drive.

There were several other student newsmakers during the year. Jill Rybak, President of the college's Collegiate Secretaries International (CSI), won first place in proofreading at the CSI conference in Memphis. Those attending the conference, in addition to Rybak, were: Sherry Carpenter, Treasurer; Heather Wilson, Historian; Eva LeCea, Past-President; and Sherra Witt, Faculty Advisor. Claudine Joyner, President of the college's Circle K Club, a member of PTK and a member of the college's Writers' Club, received a $19,080 scholarship to study Neuroscience at the University of Rochester. She also attended summer internships at Vanderbilt University and NASA. Chanda Atchley, a Broadcasting major, was hired to host 90-second spots on cable TV's Channel 53 during the daily children's show. The cheerleaders for 1995 were Kelly Brown (Captain), Holly Patterson (Vice-Captain), Natalie Benton, Heather Brunner, Lesley Burger, Nikki Carroll, Stacey Dorsey, Stacy Johnson and Julie Snellgrove. In addition a pep squad was added for the first time, and it included Crystal Corrao (Co-Captain), Rhonda Monger (Co-Captain), Tina Carson, Heidi Lenker and Tamie Wilson. The mascot was Paige Duck.

The President of the Student Senate (formerly referred to as the SGA President) was Tanya Hall. The Homecoming Queen was Kelly Hunt, and the Editor of The Signal student newspaper was Rebecca Didona. The staff members were Shelley Cornell, Marcy Eibel, Kimberly Jenkins, Fiana Logan, Rachel McCullough, Anne Newman, Jennifer Owens, Jarrod Smith and Tonya Watson. David Suttles was the faculty advisor, and Sandy Tinker was the publication technician.

The Commencement speaker for the spring graduation ceremony was Ricki Tigert Helfer. She was the daughter of CSCC faculty member, Sue Martel. Helfer received her J. D. with honors from the University of Chicago Law School and was Chair of the Federal Deposit Insurance Corporation (FDIC). She had been the chief international lawyer for the Federal Reserve Board, a clerk for the U. S. Court of Appeals Judge (John M. Wisdom), chair of the American Bar Association's International Banking and Finance Committee, a member of the American Law Institute, a member of the Council on Foreign Relations and a member of the Visiting Committee of the University of Chicago Law School. She also had degrees from the Universities of Vanderbilt and North Carolina.

During the graduation ceremony, awards were presented to the following: Dinah Fleming was the Outstanding Student, Al La Fleur was the Outstanding Staff member, and Patricia Bishop was the Outstanding Faculty Member.

– 1996 –

The year's major international events were: the United Nations adopted a Comprehensive Nuclear Test Ban Treaty that prohibited testing nuclear explosions above or below ground; Kofi Annan was elected as the UN's seventh Secretary-General; Taliban forces captured Kabul and declared the Islamic State of Afghanistan; the United Kingdom's Prince Charles and Princess Diana were divorced; the Mad Cow disease hit Great Britain; Israel launched air strikes on Hezbollah targets in Beirut; gunmen killed 17 Greek tourists in Cairo; IBM's "Deep Blue" computer defeated Chess Champion Gary Kasparov; Dolly the sheep became the first mammal to be successfully cloned; a bomb exploded at Khobar Towers military complex near Dhahran, Saudi Arabia, killing 19 American service personnel; and the world's largest container ship (at that time), the Regina Maersk, began operation.

The major events in domestic affairs were: the average income per year was $36,300; the average cost of a new house was $118,200; the cost of a gallon of gasoline was $1.22; the minimum hourly wage was $4.75; thirty black churches in Mississippi were burned in an 18 month period; the Summer Olympics was held in Atlanta; a bomb exploded in Centennial Park, Atlanta, killing one person and injuring over 100 others (an anti-government extremist, Eric Rudolph, later pleaded guilty to the bombing); the Mars Pathfinder rocket began its launch to Mars and arrived in July 1997; and President Bill Clinton was elected to a second term.

In popular culture the Academy Award for best picture was won by "The English Patient." Geoffrey Rush won best actor for "Shine," and Frances McDormand won best actress for "Fargo." The Emmy Award for best comedy was awarded to "Frasier" (NBC), and "ER" (NBC) won the Emmy for best drama. The Grammy Award for the record of the year was won by Eric Clapton for "Tears in Heaven," and the album of the year was Celine Dion's "Falling Into You." In sports UTK won the NCAA Division I Women's Basketball Championship, and Kentucky won the men's title. The Dallas Cowboys defeated the Pittsburgh Steelers in the Super Bowl, and the New York Yankees defeated the Atlanta Braves in the World Series.

In campus news President Owen Cargol announced his resignation. He accepted a new position as President of the University of Maine at Augusta. A search committee for a new President was formed and was composed of Dr. Renate Basham (Vice-President of Academics), Harry Dean (faculty) Will Benson (faculty) Dr. Michael Stokes (Vice-President of Student affairs), Carole Belk (staff) and Bill Clark (staff). Students on the committee were Brook Adams and Tanya Hall.

Dr. Cargol's resignation was effective on August 1, 1996, and in December Dr. Carl Hite was named the new President by the TBR Chancellor, Dr. Charles E. Smith. Hite received his Master's and his Doctorate at the University of Florida in Higher Education and Administration, and he received his Bachelor's from Florida State University. He had recently been the Vice-President/Provost at Hillsborough Community College in Florida. Hite said that, "I found the community to be warm and friendly...I just felt there were so many pluses that I am so glad and thankful to get this position."

The college Foundation, under the leadership of its new President, Ron Braam, continued to excel in fund raising. It raised $14,000 in 1995, and the Foundation announced that it had provided scholarships to 2,200 CSCC students since 1976. A recent graduate declared that, "I would never have been able to earn my degree without the financial support of a Foundation scholarship. Now, I hope to give back to my community even more than the Foundation has given me."

In other good news the audit team from the state comptroller's office completed a "no-findings" financial and compliance audit of the college's financial records. Hugh Robinson, the college Director of Budget and Accounting, said, "We have had four no-finding audits out of the last five at Cleveland State. This shows how hard the different college offices work together in making sure the business aspects of Cleveland State are handled properly and efficiently." State auditors conducted audits at colleges and universities every two years. They were on the CSCC campus for 12 weeks reviewing accounting and financial records for all aspects of the college including JTPA and the Tennessee Technology Center at Athens (which was administered by the college). All of the audits resulted in "no-findings."

In academic matters the college implemented an honors program in the fall of 1996. The program was intended to be an addition to the normal requirements for a degree. Students applying for admission to the program required a high school grade point average (GPA) of 3.5 or higher, an ACT score of at least 24 or a SAT score of 940 or higher. Currently enrolled students were required to have completed a minimum of 12 semester hours and a GPA of 3.25 or greater. The purpose of the Honors Program was to offer a more in-depth study of the content of a course and place more emphasis on critical thinking. Program completers received a Seal of Honors Achievement on their diploma or an Award of Honors Recognition. The organizer of the program was Assistant Professor Patricia Bishop who was also in charge of a Faculty Honors Review Committee.

Another unique event for the college was the introduction of its first internet course. Associate Professors Pam Brune and Dale Yates embraced the new technology with their team-taught course in Business Applications on Microcomputers. Brune noted that, "Students will be able to log on, download the assignments, put the assignment on diskette and mail the work back to us." Yates added that, "This is a whole new arena for instruction. We must anticipate problems that could occur with the assignments and have helpful hints available online in order to help students." Dr. Ken Adcock, Business Management Professor, taught another internet course, Supervisory Management, in the spring of 1997.

Several other new courses were added to the college's curricula in 1996. They were: Workplace Communication Skills; Print Reading for the Construction Industry; Standard Building Codes; Mechanical Projects; Issues in Health Care; Storytelling as Communication; Whitewater Rafting; and Oral Interpretation. The college's Curriculum and Academic Standards Committee also approved two new Certificate Programs. One was a Business and Management Technical Certificate (with emphases in Computer Business Applications), Hospitality Management, Quality Management, Retailing and Supervisory Management. A second certificate was in CAD (Computer Assisted Design) Technology, with emphases in Architectural Technology, Construction Technology and Mechanical Technology. A summary of the fall "Early Alert" program revealed that 112 students received a letter indicating that their classroom attendance was unsatisfactory, 543 received a letter indicating their academic progress was unsatisfactory and 272 received a letter indicating they needed improvement in both attendance and academic progress.

A plethora of non-credit courses was also offered by the college every year. Some examples of those offered in 1996 were: Introduction to Microsoft Excel for Windows; Introduction to Microsoft Word; Introduction to Windows; Introduction to Powerpoint; Calligraphy; Drawing; Watercolor; Floral Courses; Woodworking; Cooking; Landscaping; Furniture Refinishing; Guitar; Spanish; Yoga; Dance; Business and Careers; Gun Safety; Photography; and Gymnastics.

An exciting element was added to the college with the amazing success of the newly formed Debate/Forensics Team. Coached by Speech Professor, Dr. Sally Snider, the teams performed exceedingly well during the 1990s and in the following years. As noted earlier, four-year colleges usually brought more than one team to the debates, and Cleveland State teams generally competed against their peers. In the fall of 1996 the team competed at MTSU in the "Cosmic Country Breakdown Revival Forensics Tournament." They won four debates and placed first in Individual Events. The team included Robert Birdwell, Natalie Benton, John Miller, Diane Sykes, Chris Caldwell, Bryan Gaston, Lacey Kramer, Melissa Yates, Jodi Mullinax and Brian Bechtel. The MTSU hosted tournament was composed of national champions and top debaters and speakers from universities and colleges across the eastern United States. CSCC was one of five community colleges competing against four-year universities in the "Individual Events" category. CSCC was the only community college participating in the "Debates" category. Several universities competed, among these were the Universities of Vanderbilt, Alabama, Florida, Clemson, Western Kentucky and Arkansas State (as noted earlier, four-year schools usually entered several teams in debates and CSCC usually competed against their peers). The Cleveland State team won four debates and placed 1st in "Individual Events." The debate team of Lacey Kramer and Chris Caldwell defeated teams from Hillsdale College and Southeast Louisiana University. Kramer won top speaker points in both debates. The John Miller and Bryan Gaston team won against Harding College and Southeast Louisiana University. Miller earned top speaker points against Harding, and Gaston won top speaker points against Southeast Louisiana. In the Individual Events, Robert Birdwell won two 1st Place rankings in Extemporaneous Speaking, and Diane Sykes won a 1st Place ranking in Poetry Interpretation.

Later, the team traveled to Rome, Georgia, to compete in two tournaments hosted by Berry College. The team won 2nd Place among two-year colleges at the Mountain Magic Forensics Individual Events Tournament. Diane Sykes earned ten points with a first place finish in a dramatic interpretation round. She placed second overall in the same category. Lacey Kramer also placed first in an impromptu speaking round and sixth overall in informative speaking. John Miller ranked first in an impromptu speaking round. In Berry College's Mountains Individual Events Tournament, Diane Sykes and Brian Bechtel each ranked first in impromptu speaking rounds. The team also appeared in a CSCC debate in the Student Center. Chris Caldwell assumed the role of the Public Broadcasting System's Jim Lehrer and served as the moderator. Brian Bechtel assumed the role of President Clinton, and John Miller assumed the role of Senator Dole. The mock debate was a part of "Voice Your Mind" week which also involved speeches by state representatives and other activities.

The Debate Team excelled in two other tournaments—one hosted by Carson Newman College and one by Walters State Community College. In these tournaments, the team of Robert Birdwell, Natalie Benton, John Miller, Diane Sykes and Lacey Kramer won First Place in the Two-Year College Sweepstakes in Jefferson City and Second Place in the Sweepstakes in Morristown. In these events Natalie Benton ranked first in a Prose Interpretation and a Dramatic Interpretation round, and Diane Sykes ranked first in a Poetry Interpretation Round. Benton placed sixth overall in Dramatic Interpretation and second place overall in Poetry Interpretation.

In his article for the campus <u>Employee Newsletter</u>, John Bradley proposed a way to earn money for a summer job. He suggested opening a combined car wash/beauty salon/taxidermy shop with the slogan, "we buff 'em, fluff 'em and stuff 'em. He also suggested an approach for making money from the 1996 Olympics that would be featuring water events on the Ocoee River. He suggested that several college personnel rent a barn or dilapidated house near the Ocoee, dress like the Beverly Hillbillies, find a couple of old dogs and banjos, sit on a porch and hang a sign reading, "Have Your Picture Made With a Hillbilly--$10."

Another campus event turned a hoax into a reality. Angela Sackett, a bookstore employee, sent a picture and a brief biography of Johnny Brogdon (Maintenance Department) to Cosmopolitan magazine. The result was a feature in the magazine on Brogdon, who was also a raconteur, a talented, local nightclub singer and a guitarist. The popular Brogdon became a campus sensation. Another maintenance employee with a sense of humor was Paul Miller. One Saturday a co-worker stopped his car near Miller's house to say hello. Miller was working in his vegetable garden with a can of his favorite beverage beside him. His co-worker said, "Paul, what are you doing?" Miller replied, while pointing to the can, "Trying to get these things to grow."

Meanwhile college personnel participated in an abundance of activities. Rosemary Dworak (adjunct faculty) and Melinda Hillman (staff member) attended the lengthy titled International American Marketing Association's Seventh Symposium for the Marketing of Higher Education. They presented a paper at the conference. CSCC was the only community college in the nation asked to present at the conference. The Multicultural and the Cultural and Educational Enrichment Committees sponsored a banquet in celebration of Black History Month. Reverend C. H. Charlton, Pastor of Friendship Baptist Church in Johnson City, was the guest speaker. Proceeds were contributed to the college's Emergency Loan Fund for students who needed emergency assistance for tuition, fees and/or books. The organizers of the event were Will Benson, Bertha Goldston and Rubi Porter.

The Psychology Department sponsored a seminar on violence with Bradley County Sheriff, Dan Gilley, as the guest speaker. The event was organized by Associate Professor Sue Martel. Other events were: Mick Gray-Barnes, a CSCC graduate with a Bachelor's degree from MTSU and a Master's from UTK, presented an art exhibit at the college; Rochelle Mears, Minority Counselor, organized a reception for minority students; the 3rd Annual Tennessee Valley 5 Kilometer Road Race was held, and the benefits were given to the Foundation; Assistant Professor Millie Sieber organized a Storytelling Festival that featured Michael Parent, a three-time featured storyteller at the National Storytelling Festival; and Jim Frank (English faculty), with the assistance of Rochelle Mears (Student Services) organized an International Student Club. Mears noted there were four different student minority groups at CSCC—African-American, Asian, East Indian and Latino-Hispanic. The club was open to any student and its purpose was to raise funds for an international trip. The first two international students to join the club were Ivette M. Soto of Puerto Rico and Rikke Nielson of Denmark.

In other events the 100 Black Men of Bradley County organization and representatives from CSCC conducted a workshop on "How to Join the Winners in America." The workshop treated subjects such as discipline, respect and progress in the workplace. The guest speaker was author T. R. Gunn, and city officials, police officers, school teachers and school administrators led workshop sessions. The annual Tennessee Valley Art Competition, the Campus Health Fair, and a seminar on Parenting Skills were other important events. The organizer of the art exhbit was Jere Chumley, and the juror was Joni Lovell of Signal Mountain. First Place was awarded to Mark Shoup, 2nd Place to Janet McNutt and 3rd Place to Freddie Brewer. Cleveland State's Rubi Porter, Bradley Memorial Hospital, and Radio Station WCLE organized the Health Fair. Dewayne Belew, Director of Marketing and Public Relations at the hospital, wrote the following to Rubi Porter: "My compliments to you and the entire staff at Cleveland State for once again doing a super job of orchestrating the logistics of the annual Community Health Fair." The Parenting Skills Seminar was also a success, and Joey Martel-James, Director of Head Start, played an instrumental role in organizing the event.

Other campus occurrences were: CSCC graduate, Margaret Richardson, presented an art exhibit; the Student Development office sponsored a Social Fitness Week; and Jodi Johnson and Sherry Miller were named as the new advisors of the Student Hosts. Another CSCC graduate, Will Rhodarmer (son of Associate Psychology Professor, Sue Martel), displayed his artwork and performed with his blues band, the Mojo Men, in the Student Center. Pat Bishop organized a performance of "Twelfth Night" by the National Shakespeare Company, and Sue Martel arranged a Psychology Department Noon Seminar Series featuring a speech by Dr. Deborah R. DiStefano on "Women in Medicine and New Techniques in Opthalmology." There was also a "Telebration" (storytelling) event featuring B. J. Abraham, a storyteller who had performed at the National Storytelling Conference, the Atlanta Storytelling Festival and the Norwegian Cultural Olympiad.

In other faculty news Pam Brune, Instructor of Computer and Information Systems, was nominated for the National Business Education Association Post-Secondary Teacher of the Year Award. Brune served as chairperson of the organization's membership committee and the annual conference registration committee. She received her Master's degree from UTK and she began teaching at CSCC in 1994. Sadly, the college lost a long-time professor of Computer Science, Alex Nichols. He died in late 1996. His wife Maurine, continued to perform in several plays and story-telling events at the college. Sam Burnette, the air conditioning and heating mechanic for maintenance, also died. Several faculty and staff members resigned or retired in 1996. They were: Warren Brewster, JTPA); Dr. Ozane Adams, Physical Education; Dr. Cynthia Golledge, Humanities; Ed Hale, Social Sciences; John Johnson, Applied Science and Technologies; Kyle Turnham, Student Services and Basketball Coach; Shirley Nettles, Math; Adeline Collins, Head Librarian; Helen Piersaul, Maintenance; and Louie Vazquez, Student Development and Testing.

In other activities John Bradley directed and performed in a play titled, "Daddy's Dyin'! Who's Got the Will?" Other cast members were Sandy Tinker, Nanci Williams,

Suzanne Allen, Lisa Martin-Witt, Pat Meagher, Chuck Lynn and David Boatwright. The Art Student League hosted the First Student Competition Exhibition in April. The juror was Lee Ann Mitchell of Watkinsville, Georgia. She was a professional artist with a Master's degree from UTK. The annual Drug and Alcohol Awareness Day, and the Octoberfest Celebration (which featured games and food), were also held during the year.

In athletics Lee Cigliano, a graduate of CSCC and recipient of the college's Outstanding Graduate Award (in 1986) became the new basketball coach. Cigliano, the son of the Vice-President of Student Affairs, Jim Cigliano, completed his four-year degree at Belmont University and his Master's at Cumberland College. Later, in 2006, he completed his Doctorate at East Tennessee State University. Lee Cigliano played basketball at CSCC for two years and at Belmont College for two years. He served as Head Coach at Donelson Christian Academy, Head Coach at Madisonville High School, Assistant Coach at Notre Dame High School, Assistant Coach at Western Carolina University and Assistant Coach at Cumberland College. Coach Cigliano said, "I like the competition at this level, I enjoy the recruiting aspect, and I like the Cleveland State environment." He replaced Coach Kyle Turnham who resigned to accept a coaching position at Riverdale High School in Murfreesboro.

Coach Turnham's basketball team was 13-14 during the 1995-96 season and the players were C. C. Ivery, Jason Brooks, Josh Gardner, Butch Ownby, Chris Baumgartner, Eric Council, Micah Howard, Adam Mobley, DaShaun Coreton, Norance Berry and Jonathan Cantrell (son of Associate Professor of Management and Business, John Cantrell). The coach of the Lady Cougars was Rusty Melvin, and the team members were Denise Murray, Ashley Billings, Quran NaLory, Robin Smith, Karen Peel, Kellie Lend, Melissa Denton, Whitney Robinson, Amanda McLaughlin, Emily McNabb, Allison Ferrell and Melissa Webb. The baseball coach, Mike Policastro, was named the TJCCAA Coach of the Year. He was also named as the new Athletic Director, and he continued to coach baseball. Jim Cigliano, the former Athletic Director, who held the position since 1975, remained as the Vice-President of Student Affairs.

Student newsmakers in 1996 were: Kylee B. Miller, the daughter of Sherry Miller (Student Services), was awarded the Otis Floyd Scholarship (named for the former Head of the TBR); Kim Fort, a former CSCC student, was awarded the Jim Bilbo Excellence in Teaching Award at Lee College; the President of the Student Senate was Brooke Andrews; Natalie Benton was Homecoming Queen; Tonya Watson was the Editor of The Signal and the staff members were Aaron Robinson (Assistant Editor), Paul Griffith, Amy Nunley, Donna Smith and Jeremy Belk. David Suttles was the faculty advisor and Sandy Tinker the publication technician.

An article in the <u>Cleveland Daily Banner</u>, in April, 2007, featured a "Personality Profile" of Ashley Cranfield-Cummings, a 1995-96 CSCC student. She was a member of PTK and was a Dean's List student. By 2007 she was a special agent/forensic scientist with the Tennessee Bureau of Investigation at the Regional Crime Lab in Knoxville. After her two years at CSCC, Cranfield-Cummings received her four-year degree from Tennessee Wesleyan with a major in Biology. She indicated that her classes at CSCC gave her "a solid education and understanding in Chemistry and Biology classes." Furthermore, she noted that, "the classes were smaller than at large universities, the professors actually know you by name…and you don't feel lost in a class of 200 or more."

The Graduation speaker for the 1996 Commencement was Dr. Jane Walters, the State Commissioner of Education. She was the first woman to hold the position since the position was created in 1923. She was formerly the Principal of Craigmont Junior and Senior High School in Memphis. The Outstanding Faculty Member Award was presented to Ed Rowlee; the Outstanding Staff Member was Shirley McDaniel; and the Outstanding Student was Tanya Hall.

In another college activity, Junior and Senior Class students from Cleveland and Charleston high school participated in a two-day "Economics in Action" conference. Sponsored by the Cleveland/Bradley Chamber of Commerce and Junior Achievement (JA) the event was organized by John Cantrell, Management Instructor, and Carolyn McDole of JA. The students toured several local businesses and industries and attended lectures at the college.

There continued to be a large number of campus clubs available for students. A few of the clubs and their faculty/staff sponsors were the: Student Government Association, Jerome Taylor; Office Education Association, Sherra Witt and Nancy Boyd; Phi Theta Kappa, John Bradley; Student Nurses Association, Alleyna Ellis; Fellowship of Christian Athletes, Tom Losh and Bob Taylor; <u>The Signal</u> newspaper, David Suttles; Future Secretaries Association, Nancy Boyd; Baptist Student Union, Galen McBride; Phi Beta Lambda, John Cantrell; Paralegal Club, Ann McCoin; Black Student Association, Gayle Wood; Cheerleaders, Norma Davis; United Methodist Student Association, Patricia Bishop; Christian Student Center, Joe Guest; and Circle K Club, T. P. Mathai.

Meanwhile, John Bradley continued to provide amusement through his weekly columns in the <u>Employee Newsletter</u>. According to Bradley, one student "announced she was very upset about the 'inflammation' on the economy." He also noted that a new sports car was named the Mafia because there was a hood under the hood. Someone suggested that a father purchase his kids an encyclopedia. He said, "No, let them walk to school just like I did."

– 1997 –

In international affairs the major occurrences were: Hong Kong was returned to Chinese rule from British rule; approximately 70 people, mostly foreign tourists, were killed by Islamic extremists in Egypt's Valley of the Kings; Princess Diana was killed in a car crash in Paris; 150 countries were represented at a global warming conference in Kyoto, Japan; Tony Blair became Prime Minister of the United Kingdom; Mother Teresa died in India; Scotland voted to create its own Parliament after 290 years of union with England's Parliament; stock markets around the world crashed because of a global economic scare; Wales voted in favor of devolution and the formation of a National Assembly; the first book in the award winning Harry Potter series by J. K. Rowling was published; Hong Kong killed 1.25 million chickens to stop the spread of a potentially deadly influenza strain known as Avian flu; the comet Hale-Bopp had its closest approach to earth; and Tara Lipinski, at age 14 years and 10 months, became the youngest ladies' world figure skating champion during world finals in Lausanne, Switzerland.

In domestic affairs the major events were: the average cost of a new house was $124,000; the average income per year was $37,006; the cost of a gallon of gasoline was $1.22; the minimum wage was raised to $5.15; Madeleine Albright became the first female Secretary of State in United States history; former CIA official Harold Nicholson pleaded guilty to spying for Russia; 39 members of the Heaven's Gate religious cult committed suicide in California; Timothy McVeigh was convicted of conspiracy and murder in the 1995 Oklahoma City bombing (Terry Nichols was convicted on related charges); two Islamic militants were convicted for playing key roles in the 1993 bombing of the World Trade Center; Microsoft became the world's most valuable company valued at $261 billion dollars; the Dow Jones Industrial Average closed above 7,000 for the first time; Woolworths closed its remaining discount stores after more than 100 years of trading; a jury panel found O. J. Simpson guilty in a civil trial; the Mars Pathfinder landed on the surface of Mars; WorldCom and MCI Communications announced the largest merger in history; and Microsoft bought a minority stake in Apple Computers for $150 million.

In popular culture the Academy Award for best picture was won by "Titanic." Jack Nicolson won best actor for "As Good As It Gets," and Helen Hunt won best actress for the same movie. Television's Emmy Award for best comedy was won by "Frasier" (NBC), and the best drama was won by "Law and Order" (NBC). The Grammy Award for best record of the year was Shawn Colvin's "Sunny Came Home." The best album of the year was Bob Dylan's "Time Out of Mind." In athletics Mike Tyson was suspended from boxing for biting the ear of Evander Holyfield. Tiger Woods, at 21 years old, became the youngest golfer in history to win the Masters' Tournament. The University of Tennessee at Knoxville won the NCAA Division I Women's Basketball

Championship, and Arizona won the Men's Championship. Green Bay defeated New England in the Super Bowl, and Florida defeated Cleveland in the World Series.

In campus news a college in Great Britain, known as Cleveland Redcar, contacted CSCC and proposed the formulation of a student/faculty exchange program. In September officials from the British college visited Cleveland and discussed a collaborative agreement. Principal Lynne Howe and her husband, Dennis, toured CSCC and met with Dr. Hite and other campus officials. Redcar, located in northwest England, offered vocational training as well as transfer degree programs. An agreement was reached, and both faculty and student exchanges occurred frequently for several years.

During the year, a marketing survey of 175 CSCC graduates revealed the following statistics: 38% were 17-24 years old, and 27% were 30-39 years old; 41% were from Bradley County, and 26% were from Monroe County; 43% received an Associate of Applied Science degree, and 29% received a Certificate; 32% enrolled for the purpose of a career change; 27% were recent High School graduates; location and cost were the primary factors in choosing CSCC; 50% of those surveyed had a relative who attended CSCC; and 97% indicated they would recommend attending CSCC to any prospective student.

The Tennessee Board of Regents (TBR), in an effort to strengthen performance funding requirements, developed another academic accountability measure. Known as a General Transfer Academic Review (GTAR), it was completed by the college in 1997. Beginning in 1995 faculty and administrators in the college transfer programs reviewed the transferability of all courses and all course syllabi. The Co-Chairs of the committee were Associate Professors Patricia Bishop and Buford Guy. One of the TBR requirements was for an out of state evaluator to assess the completion of the GTAR. Dr. Nancy Womack, Dean of the College Transfer Division at Isothermal Community College, in Spindale, North Carolina, was invited by Dr. Spencer Culbreth, the CSCC Dean of Humanities and Social Sciences, to serve as the evaluator. Dr. Womack submitted a glowing report and concluded that CSCC's transfer program was "outstanding."

Another accountability measure for performance funding was TBR's requirement that all colleges adopt the ACT COMP test as a means for assessing graduating students' skills. COMP was an acronym for the College Outcome Measures Program. The college's Director of Student Development, Dr. Michael Stokes, noted that the American College Testing COMP exam was different from the ACT assessment that many students completed prior to enrolling in college. COMP was designed to test a student's skills and knowledge in six areas: communicating, solving problems, clarifying values, functioning within social institutions, using science and technology and using the arts. Instead of testing a student's recall of facts, the COMP exam measured a student's ability to apply "acquired" knowledge to situations. In the 1990s CSCC students generally performed above the average of students in the 450 two-year colleges nationwide that used the COMP test.

Another achievement for the college was a second and third place award from the National Council for Marketing and Public Relations District II Medallion Awards presentations. District II included community colleges in Alabama, Washington D. C., Florida, Georgia, Mississippi, North Carolina, Pennsylvania, South Carolina, Tennessee, Virginia and West Virginia. CSCC won the Silver Medallion of Merit Award for its "Cleveland State of Mind" billboard and the Bronze Medallion of Merit Award for its "Go Forward, So No One Can Hold You Back" billboard.

The Dual Enrollment program continued its steady growth. As noted before, fifty-six students enrolled in the first year of the program (in 1994). In the fall of 1997, 108 high school students enrolled. The breakdown for each high school was as follows: 49 from Bradley County; 36 from Cleveland; 20 from Meigs County; one from McMinn County and two home-schooled students. The college also joined with Chattanooga State, Pellissippi State and Roane State in forming a Tennessee On-line Community College Consortium (TOCCC). The colleges worked together in delivering on-line educational and training services. In addition (as noted above), CSCC beamed off-campus courses to Vonore (and later Athens, Copperhill and Decatur) through televised distance learning technology. Students could hear and see instructors as well as have two-way communication between the sites.

Lynne Craver was named as the new Director of the Library, and she and her staff initiated several changes during the year. A new web-based database, known as the Health Reference Center Academic, enabled students to search for information in health care and medicine. Students could retrieve and download text from periodicals, pamphlets and reference books. Students studying numerous other subjects could do likewise by utilizing the SIRS Researcher. Westlaw software provided Legal Assistant students access to legal documents and court cases. The card catalog system was replaced by the electronic Online Public Access Catalog (OPAC). Access to OPAC was available through terminals in the library, through "dial access" in remote areas and via the Library web page (which was created by Alan Goslen, the Public Service Librarian). Numerous personal computers were added to the library's computer lab as well as throughout the library. The library also stored the videos needed by students enrolled in video courses, and the library served as a federal depository for the Congressional District and collected thousands of documents from the Federal Government.

Craver was the college's Public Service Librarian for four years before being named the Director. Prior to her arrival at CSCC, she had been the Director of Preston Medical Library at the UTK Medical Center in Knoxville. She was also Director of the UTK Hospital's Consumer Health Information Center. Other CSCC library staff members, in addition to Craver and Goslen, were Deon Sprague, Sam Neas, Suzanne Ratcliff, Ann Draper and Sandra Hixson.

In those early days of computer usage, when the equipment was scarce and expensive, the college responded to the growing demand for access to it through the creation of an Instructional Computer Technology Center. Located on the second floor of the administration building, the center was supervised by Al LaFleur, the Director of College Computing. Other staff members were Garry Belk, the Director of Multimedia, Charles Reidel, Barbie Wood-Fisher, Bob Parker and Lynne Smith. In addition to conducting labs and workshops for staff and faculty, the center provided Windows 95, Word for Windows and Excel and Powerpoint software for students to use on the lab's computers (there were only 15 available initially). The center also enabled students to acquire a free e-mail account and scanners to record pictures for use in papers or other materials they might be producing.

There was a profusion of activities throughout 1997. Dr. Neil Greenwood and John Bradley judged a Martin Luther King, Jr. essay contest for students. The top five winners were Jacqueline Zacher 1st, Glenn Williams 2nd, Joshua Bishop 3rd, Kara West 4th and Marsha Smith 5th. Dr. Tonea Harris Stewart, an actress, performed a "One Woman Show of Poetry and Song" in observance of the MLK holiday. Stewart performed in television shows such as "In the Heat of the Night," "Matlock," "Beulah Land," "Just Around the Corner," "Leave of Absence," and "Caroline and Minstrel Man." She also acted in several films including "A Time to Kill," "Invasion of the Body Snatchers III," "Living Large" and "Mississippi Burning." There were also a series of campus events recognizing "Celebrate Our World Week." These were sponsored by the Student Development and Testing Center and the Cultural and Educational Enrichment Committee (CEEC). A "Reading Nook" of donated books, magazines and newspapers was started by Associate Professors Jean Crockett and Millie Sieber. Cleveland's Mayor, Tom Rowland, declared February 10-14 as "CSCC Financial Aid Awareness Week." The event featured a series of lectures and seminars to assist students in learning how to apply for financial aid. Campus staff and faculty members, Heather Sealy, Rubi Porter, Wilma Ownby and Sherra Witt, organized an American Cancer Society Relay for Life walk. Seventy-three people participated and raised approximately $1,500 for the society.

Associate Professor of Psychology, Sue Martel, organized a series of speakers as a weekly event throughout the year. Chattanooga's WRCB-TV newscaster, Tonya Gipson, presented a seminar on "Women in News and Television;" Nancy Allen, the County Executive of Rutherford County, Tennessee, lectured on the subject of "Women in Politics;" and Cleveland's Dr. Brenda A. Snowman lectured on "PMS: Its Psychological and Physiological Effects." Other speakers planned for the fall were Dr. Robert Cantonese ("Memory and Learning"); Dr. Ronald Free ("Pain Control"); Cleveland State's Dr. Ed Hale ("Alcohol and Drug Effects"); and Dr. Sarath Gangavarapu ("Bipolar Depression").

In other activities Associate Professor Millie Sieber organized an Ocoee Story "Fest" featuring Janice Harrington. Roschelle Mears, of the Student Development Office, worked with the Boy's and Girl's Clubs of Cleveland and the 100 Black Men of Bradley County Organization in sponsoring a workshop on "Avoiding the School Daze." The workshop provided information on how to choose a college, how to apply to one and how to request financial aid. Mears also organized a Native American Cultural and Educational Festival that featured discussions on tribal, social and family life as well as numerous dances by Native American performers. The college also presented another play for the campus and the community. The play, "Sylvia," was directed by John Bradley and the cast included Sandy Tinker, Maurine Nichols, John Bradley, Jeff Langston, Suzanne Allen and David Boatwright. Two National Shakespeare Company performances were sponsored by the college's Educational Enrichment Committee, the Student Services Department, Phi Theta Kappa and the Arts Build Communities Program. One was "Much Ado About Nothing," and the other was "Richard III." Another performance, organized by Associate Professor John Cantrell, was Roy Roman's trumpet concert sponsored by the Enrichment Committee and the college's chapter of the Fellowship of Christian Athletes. Roman had performed at three Presidential inaugural balls and at an event for England's Queen Elizabeth.

The year 1997 was characterized by a multitude of art exhibits. Associate Professor Jere Chumley devoted many hours to organizing the events. During the year he received acclaim for one of his own exhibits. It was for his oil painting, "Hale-Bopp at Avallon,"which appeared in the "Artstravaganza" exhibit at the Waterhouse Pavilion located in Chattanooga's Miller Plaza. The exhibit was arranged by the Association for Visual Artists and the Hunter Museum of American Art. In addition he coordinated numerous exhibits on campus throughout the year. Two graduating art students, Tyson Hayes and Chris Hamby, displayed their work in the lobby of the Administration Building. Hayes planned to attend UTC and become an art illustrator. Hamby planned to attend UTK and become a graphic design major. There was also an exhibit featuring the works of Joe Helseth and another exhibit featuring the works of Freddie Brewer. An important event was the 2nd Annual Students' Art Competition. First Place was awarded to Jason Carusillo, 2nd Place to Sara Goforth and 3rd Place to Liz Conner. The judge was Ken Page, a Chattanooga State Art Professor. Chumley also organized the 1997 Tennessee Valley Art Competition Exhibit (TVAC). Forty-seven artists entered 112 works in the exhibit. Chumley stated that, "This is one of the largest and best TVAC exhibits that we've had." First Place was awarded to Ethel Carroll of Athens, 2nd Place to Joni Sharp of Signal Mountain and 3rd Place to Mark Shoup of Chattanooga. The Juror for the event was Mark Wood. In another exhibit, brothers Bryan Textor and Glen Textor, of Benton, Tennessee, exhibited a collection of their works in Raku, clay and paintings. Co-owners of the Textor Handicraft Studio in Benton, Bryan earned a degree in Fine Arts from Ball State University, and Glen completed the same degree at Indiana University-Northwest. David LeDoux, a retired MTSU Art Professor, also exhibited at the college. LeDoux had exhibited in New York, Texas, Alabama, North Carolina and other states. Another studio owner, Billie Nipper, also exhibited at the college. Nipper, a Cleveland native, owned a studio in town, served as arts chairman of the Cleveland Creative Guild and won numerous awards for her art. President Ronald Reagan owned her print, titled "Something Special," and she painted a portrait of actress Zsa Zsa Gabor and her horse, Silver Fox. She was well known for her Tennessee countryside paintings and her portraits of Tennessee Walking Horses.

A major event for the college was the hosting of a workshop for Science teachers from eleven Olin Corporations (from July 14 through July 18, 1997). The college's Foundation and the Department of Continuing Education worked with Olin in planning the workshop. The eleven Olin locations nominated two Science teachers (one from grades 5-6 and one from grades 7-8) to attend the event. The 22 teachers received hands-on training related to the Science Education for Public Understanding Program. The participants also received chemical kits and training which they could share with their students and fellow teachers.

Several faculty and staff were newsmakers in 1997. Ron Hammontree, The Director of the Tellico Education Consortium, left the position to become the Director of the Tennessee Reservoir Development Agency (TRDA). Hammontree continued to work closely with the college at its Vonore off-campus site (which was located at the TRDA). Hammontree had valuable experience with the Department of Labor. As Director of the Knoxville International Energy Exposition he played an instrumental role in recruiting and employing over 19,000 people during the six-month long Knoxville World's Fair in 1981-1982. Afterwards, he became President of Southern Cinemas and World Sound. He sold those businesses in 1987 and became the Assistant Commissioner of the Tennessee Department of Labor from 1987 to 1989. From 1989 to 1992 he was the Deputy Commissioner of the Tennessee Department of Labor, and he was the Director of the Tellico Education Consortium from 1992 to 1997. He also served, for a brief period, as Interim Director of the Job Training Partnership Act program (JTPA). Hammontree played an instrumental role in recruiting students for Cleveland State in the areas of Vonore and Monroe County. After Hammontree's departure Dr. Rodney Fitzgerald assumed the position of interim director of JTPA while the search for a permanent one continued. Meanwhile, Dr. Frank McKenzie, Dean of Business and Technology, was appointed as the interim director of the Vonore Workforce Development Center. Later, Pam Price became the Director of the college's off-campus center at Vonore's Tellico Education Consortium (and Michelle Jenkins served as the Secretary). Sue Hamilton was a valuable employee at the location who assisted dislocated workers in Monroe County through the various job programs of the Comprehensive Employment and Training Act (CETA), the JTPA and Workforce Investment Act (WIA).

In other activities Dr. Frank McKenzie, Pam Brune, Sherra Witt, Sylvia Taylor and Nancy Boyd attended the Tennessee Business Education Conference in Nashville. Later, McKenzie and Daryl Schaefer presented a series of roundtable discussions on "the Community/Career Investment Scholarship" at the National Tech Prep Network Conference in Nashville. Mark Wilson, Debbie Callahan and Wanda Huffman (Student Development and Testing) attended the annual meeting for Tennessee GED Examiners in Gatlinburg. Ann McCoin (Coordinator of the Legal Assistant Program) was a speaker at the Eastern District of the US Attorneys' Office Retreat held at Fairfield Glade. College participants in the Bradley County American Heart Walk raised $1,631 for the organization. Approximately 1,000 residents participated in the Walk, and about $82,500 was raised for the organization. Efrain Guillen, the Spanish and Sociology instructor, presented a paper on "Understanding the Roots of Modern Mexican Culture through the History of the Encounter" at the South Carolina Foreign Language Teachers' Association held at Myrtle Beach, South Carolina. Millie Sieber assisted in organizing a "Tellabration" event that featured Charles Maynard, a storyteller from Signal Mountain. Local "tellers" were Nancy Brewer, Bob Burr, Peggy Jones and Maurine Nichols. A unique occurrence at the event was the participation of a student, Jim Cofer, of Bradley High School. Jim Frank, an English faculty member, organized a Writer's Workshop featuring Judson Mitcham. Mitcham was Chair of the Psychology Department at Fort Valley State University and adjunct professor of Creative Writing at Emory University. He published his first novel, The Sweet Everlasting, in 1996. David Boatwright, Computer Science Faculty member, attended a National Science Foundation workshop on "Instructional Computing: Current Issues and Solutions," held in Venice, Florida.

Once again John Bradley provided levity with his comments in the Cleveland State "Update" publication. While searching on the internet, he found examples of ways to maintain a healthy level of insanity in the workplace. Among these were: develop an unnatural fear of staples; when people ask you to do something, ask them if they want fries with that; drape mosquito netting from the ceiling around your desk; discover where your boss shops and buy exactly the same outfits—always wear them one day after your boss wears them; put your garbage can on your desk and label it "In Box;" put decaffeinated coffee in the coffee maker for three weeks and then switch to espresso; and send an e-mail message to every employee reading "free pizza and free donuts in the break room." When people complain to you, rub your stomach and say, "You gotta be faster than that."

An athletic highlight of the year was the donation of a new $12,000 scoreboard for the baseball field by Johnston Coca-Cola Company. The men's basketball coach, Lee Cigliano, initiated a new academic support system for his players. Players were required to attend study hall twice a week in the Student Development Center. Players spent 1.5 hours each visit and received tutoring assistance from personnel in the Student Development Office. Team members were Shey Spears, Travis Glover, Matt Collins, Blake Fellows, Casey Holder, Brian Massengill, Jacob McClary, Tim Bayne, Dewey Roberts, Ricky Patrick, DaJuan Hodge, Demetrius Morgan, Terrell Cox, Nate Davis, Jesse Cole, Jr. and team trainer, Candice Dixson. Daniel Lumpkin was hired as the new women's basketball coach. Lumpkin earned a Bachelor's and a Master's degree in English from Austin Peay State University and was a Graduate Assistant Coach for their basketball team. He later was the Softball Coach and Assistant Basketball Coach at Martin Methodist College from 1994-1997. His 1997 Lady Cougar team members were Amanda Akins, Sara Colbaugh, Julie Dockery, Michelle Shields, LaShanda Smartt, Kim Horton, Florida Wynn, Crystal Ward, Amber Wilson, Amy Bowan, Jenni Carter, Kari Collins and Krisy Steelman.

The college's Debate/Forensics team earned top honors at the Tennessee Intercollegiate Forensics Association Tournament at Trevecca College in Nashville.

Coached by Dr. Sally Snider (Speech faculty), the nine-member team received the Best Two-Year College Trophy and won second place, behind Carson Newman College, in the overall ranking. Diane Sykes was the CSCC point leader. She garnered 33 of the team's 104 points. She reached the final rounds in Impromptu Speaking and in Persuasive Speaking and Duo Interpretation. Team member Robert Birdwell became the Tennessee Extemporaneous Speaking Champion. CSCC's Chris Caldwell and Lacey Kramer won the Debate Championship, and CSCC's Greg Cain and Johnna Hampton captured second place. Wes Montgomery in Persuasive Speaking, Brian Bechtel in Impromptu and Informative Speaking and Will Dale in Duo Interpretation also scored points for the team. In a debate at CSCC, the team placed third among eight teams from area colleges. Will Dale and Wes Montgomery placed third overall in the debate contest. Among the several judges in the tournament were college faculty members Jean Crockett, Harry Dean, John Bradley, Dr. Spencer Culbreth and Dr. Larry Longerbeam.

A large debate competition, the Scott Pejaver Debate Tournament, was held at MTSU in September 1997. Cleveland State was the only two-year college represented at the tournament of 26 colleges and universities from 14 southeastern states. CSCC's Cross Examination Debate team of Bryan Gaston and Johnna Hampton defeated teams from Southeast Louisiana, Tennessee Tech, Vanderbilt and MTSU in preliminary rounds and eliminated other Vanderbilt teams in the "Octafinals" and Quarterfinals. They lost to Appalachian State, the winner of the championship. Gaston placed 8th in speaker points among 64 debaters in a 32-team field (as noted above, four-year colleges usually entered more than one team and CSCC usually competed against peer teams). CSCC's team of Chris Caldwell and Lacey Kramer defeated teams from Vanderbilt, Alabama, Cumberland and Webster in preliminary rounds before losing the "Octafinal" round to Harding. Kramer ranked 10th in speaker points, and the team of Jane Petit and Josh Couch also earned points by winning a preliminary round.

In another debate tournament at MTSU, CSCC competed against two other community colleges and 17 four-year colleges and universities. In this tournament, with the lengthy title of the "Cosmic Country Breakdown Individual Events and Parliamentary Debate Tournament," Diane Sykes and Brian Bechtel were finalists in Program (Poetry/Prose) Interpretation and Critical Analysis and Extemporaneous Speaking. Sykes placed fifth in Program Interpretation and 6th in Rhetorical Critical Analysis. Betchel ranked 6th in Extemporaneous Speaking. Bechtel and his partner, Dwayne Jeffries, defeated Meridian College in Parliamentary Debate. In December the debate team advanced to the championship round in the Crimson Classic Debate Tournament in Tuscaloosa, Alabama. Teams representing 14 four-year colleges and universities, and one community college (CSCC), met at the University of Alabama for the debate. Bryan Gaston and Johnna Hampton led the CSCC team by defeating teams from the University of Alabama, Vanderbilt, Southeast Louisiana, Webster and MTSU in preliminary rounds. In "out-rounds," Gaston and Hampton defeated Miami University in quarterfinals and a MTSU team in semifinals before losing the championship round to another MTSU team. In other debates Chris Caldwell and Lacey Kramer defeated teams from Florida, Alabama and Vanderbilt before losing rounds to MTSU and Southeast Louisiana. Jane Petit and Josh Couch defeated two Alabama teams and lost to MTSU and Southeast Louisiana. At one point during 1997, the college's debate team was ranked 10th nationally (among two-year colleges) by the Cross Examination Debate Association.

The year 1997 was also a successful one for the college's Phi Theta Kappa (PTK) Chapter. The Chapter, led by faculty advisor Patricia Bishop, and assisted by David Suttles and Larry Burns, won 21 awards at the Regional Conference. Ten of the 16 Tennessee chapters were represented at the regional conference held at CSCC. The college's PTK Chapter won a 5-Star program, which was the highest chapter award attainable. It also won Outstanding Tennessee Chapter, first place; Scholarship Hallmark, first place; Service Hallmark, first place; Fellowship Hallmark, first place; and Leadership Hallmark, second place. The Hallmark categories were judged by a panel of three judges from Mississippi. Judges from Tennessee Wesleyan College awarded the chapter several Literary Awards. Kathy Torres won first place for her short story, and Daniel Corn won third place. Torres also won first place in the poetry category, and Linda McAlister won third place. Matthew Stallard won third place in the essay category. In the Members' Choice Art Award category, Rebecca Didona won second place, James York won third place, and Margaret Killebrew won fourth place. The chapter also won third place for its yearbook and three scholarships to the Honors Institute in Bellingham, Washington. Lacey Kramer was elected as Tennessee's Regional Vice-President, and Matthew Amick was elected as the Tennessee Regional Newsletter Editor. Patricia Bishop was named the region's Outstanding Advisor.

The chapter received other prestigious awards at the International Convention in Dallas, Texas. One of these was the Distinguished Chapter Award. This was awarded to only the top 25 chapters out of approximately 1,200. CSCC's chapter was ranked 13th in the top 25. Out of 1,200 or more chapters, CSCC ranked 7th in Service Hallmark and 10th in Fellowship Hallmark. Cleveland State student Joshua Bishop, the son of Patricia Bishop, was one of only 25 members to receive a Distinguished Chapter Member Award. He was competing against approximately 60,000 members for this award. Rebecca Didona was named Distinguished Regional Officer, and only five members out of 150 competitors nationwide received this award.

Several other students were also campus newsmakers in 1997. Jane Petit was the college's student representative to the TBR. She was President of the CSCC Collegiate Secretaries International and a recipient of a scholarship awarded by the Club. She also served as Secretary of the Student Senate, was a Traffic Appeals Court member, a Student Host and a member of PTK, Circle K and the Debate Team. Leslie Wilson, a CSCC graduate, became the first graduate majoring in the Medical Office Assistant Program to become board certified. Wilson earned her Certified Medical Assistant credential by passing the 1997 American Association of Medical Assistants' Certification Exam.

She was employed in Dr. Gregory Terpstra's office in Cleveland. Student Cheerleaders in 1997-98 were Liza O'Conner (Captain), Kristin Dodd (Co-Captain), Lesley Burger, Shanalda Belcher, Sally Wall, Daniel Gonzalez, Donna Ward, Ruth Barroso, Michele Cormier, Logan Buchanan and Leighann Tubb. The Student Senate President was Greg Cain, the Homecoming Queen was Anita Brock, and the members of The Signal student newspaper staff were: Johnna Hampton, Editor; Holli Dykes, Assistant Editor; Pam Winder, Design; Brad Hughes, Sports; Dwayne Jeffries, Editorial Cartoon; and Tamika Hickey, Christy Carver and Jane Petitt, staff members. The faculty advisor was Associate Professor of English, Gayle Garner.

In other student-related news, the Black Student Association changed its name to the Minority Student Association. Roschelle Mears, advisor to the group, said the name change was an effort to adopt a more cosmopolitan perspective by including all ethnic minorities at the college. Several student organizations competed in a chili cook-off and pumpkin-carving contest. There was also a "fake" sumo-wrestling contest, and the Society of Creative Anachronism demonstrated what it was like to live in Medieval times. Anita Brock was named Homecoming Queen, and Jonathan Cantrell was named Homecoming King. Special student awards were given to Norma Davis (the Service to Students Award) and to Jim Frank (an Outstanding Instructor Award).

The Commencement speaker was Dr. Fred Obear, Chancellor of UTC. His Bachelor's degree was from the University of Massachusetts at Lowell, and his Doctorate in Chemistry was from the University of New Hampshire. The Distinguished Graduate Award was presented to Joshua Bishop. Dr. Sally Snider was awarded the Distinguished Faculty Member Award, and Andy Semak was named the Distinguished Staff Member.

– 1998 –

The major events in international affairs were: the world's largest airport opened in Hong Kong; terrorist bombing attacks at two American Embassies in Nairobi and Dar es Salaam killed 250 people; the United States launched cruise missile strikes against al-Queda training camps in Afghanistan; the Belfast agreement was signed between the Irish and British governments for the purpose of ending terrorism in Northern Ireland and mainland Britain; a tsunami killed approximately 1,500 people in Papua New Guinea; in China the Yangtze River broke through the main bank and killed over 12,000 people; in Indonesia protests over mismanagement led to the resignation of President Suharto after 32 years of authoritarian rule; the Japanese economy entered a recession due to the collapse of land and property prices; the Soviet Union's banking system suffered a meltdown when the ruble lost 70% of its value; Europeans adopted a single currency, the Euro; Israel celebrated the 50[th]Anniversary of its founding; the world's largest suspension bridge (1.234 miles long) was completed in Japan; India and Pakistan tested nuclear weapons; Pol Pot, the notorious leader of the Khmer Rouge, died at age 73 (and evaded prosecution for the deaths of two million Cambodians); and 19 European nations agreed to forbid human cloning.

The major events in domestic affairs were: the average cost of a new house was $129,300; the average income per year was $38,100; the cost of a gallon of gas was $1.15; President Bill Clinton denied he had "sexual relations" with former White House intern Monica Lewinsky (but later admitted it); the federal government announced the first budget surplus in 30 years; forest fires in Florida forced over 120,000 people to flee their homes; President Clinton was impeached by the House of Representatives for perjury and obstruction of justice (he was later acquitted by the Senate); a "Master Settlement Agreement" was signed between tobacco companies and most states and territories (the amount was $206 billion over 25 years—the largest civil settlement in American history--to cover public health costs related to smoking); Exxon and Mobil merged to create the world's largest petroleum company; the search engine Google was founded; a bomb exploded at an abortion clinic in Birmingham, Alabama, killing a guard (and critically wounding a nurse), and the bomber, Eric Rudolph, was later captured (in 2003) and given a life sentence in prison; Theodore Kaczjnski pleaded guilty to being the "Unabomber" and was sentenced to life in prison without parole; John Glenn, at age 77, roared back into space aboard the Discovery shuttle; country music singer Tammy Wynette died at age 55; and singer-actor Frank Sinatra died at age 82.

In popular culture a concert at the Soccer World Cup in France, by the three tenors, Jose Carreras, Placido Domingo and Luciano Pavarotti, was seen by a live audience of 100,000 and by another 3 billion around the world. The television sitcom, "Seinfeld," aired its final episode after nine years on NBC. The Academy Award for best picture was won by "Shakespeare in Love." The best actor award was won by Roberto Benigni for "Life is Beautiful," and the best actress award was presented to Gwyneth Paltrow for "Shakespeare in Love." The Emmy award for best television comedy was won by "Frasier" (NBC), and the best drama was "The Practice" (ABC). The Grammy Award for record of the year was Celene Dion's "My Heart Will Go On," and the album of the year was Lauryn Hill's "The Miseducation of Lauryn Hill." In sports UTK won the women's NCAA Division I Women's Basketball Championship, and Kentucky University won the men's championship. Denver defeated Green Bay in the Super Bowl, and New York defeated San Diego in the World Series.

A noteworthy development for the college was the signing of an agreement with officials from Great Britain's Redcar and Cleveland College located in Redcar, England. The agreement established goals for faculty and student exchanges, curriculum offerings, business and community relations and guest lectures via distance learning and the internet. The CSCC Technology Department started a pilot program with Redcar in computer-aided design (CAD) and computerized numerical control (CNC). Students had the opportunity to earn either a certificate, a degree or a European City and Guilds certificate. The latter was an international certification that measured a student's level of competency. Both colleges had similar courses in construction technology, drafting and design, office systems, computer information systems, electronics, computer-aided manufacturing, health care, journalism and communications. The most active participants from Cleveland State in the endeavor were: Carol Gavagan, Business and Technology Instructor; Bob Lance, Technology Faculty; Barry McCaskill, Technology Department Chair; and Dr. Frank McKenzie, Dean of Applied Science and Technology. Several staff and faculty from Redcar visited the campus April 6-9. They were: Lynn Howe, Principal; Alan Old, Vice-Principal; Jeanette Judge, Assistant Principal of Students and Quality Assurance; Denise McFarlane, Assistant Principal of Resources; Tim Kinneavy, faculty; Gary Winn, faculty; and Ian Whisker, faculty.

In other developments the college partnered with a TV station (eventually known as WTNB) that began airing Bradley County news on July 1, 1998. The station was housed in the campus Media Center and the partnership gave students the opportunity to learn how to operate cameras, produce programs and report the news. David Suttles, Journalism and Communications faculty member, was named the station's News Director. The co-anchors of WTNB were professional broadcasters Linda Edwards-Boston and Jesse Hamby. The Sports Director was Jeff Chardos, and news reporters were Mary Ann Jones and Lyndsay Thurston. Hamby was a graduate of CSCC and he was also the station manager. He received a degree in Broadcasting from UTK, and he had worked with a small TV station in Dalton, Georgia. In September the college initiated a program titled "Cleveland State Focus." The moderator for the series was President Carl Hite. It was a 30-minute program on community services, community issues and community economic growth. The first program aired on September 21, 1998, and the topic was "Focus on Education." Dr. Hite's guests were Dr. Rick Denning, Director of Cleveland City Schools, and David Holloway, Superintendent of Bradley County Schools.

In other occurrences the college began work on a Tennessee Quality Award, and Susan Webb-Curtis was named Chair of the Committee. Other committee members were Dr. Frank McKenzie and Business faculty member, Dr. Ken Adcock. In academic matters the TBR approved the college's new "Concentration" in Occupational Therapy Assistant. Dr. Dan Bernardot, an expert on nutrition, made a speech at the college. Bernardot was a sports nutritionist for the gold medal-winning United States Gymnastics Team during the 1996 Olympics. The college's Public Relations Department was awarded the Gold Paragon Award for "The Best Successful Recruitment Marketing Program." The award was presented by the National Council for Marketing and Public Relations at the annual national conference in Charleston, South Carolina.

A major development at the college was a gift of $250,000 from the Tennessee Valley Authority for an expansion of the Cleveland/Bradley Business Development Center (CBBDC). The total funding for the project was $867,500. Renovations were made to the Technology Building, and approximately 25 spaces, ranging from 100 square feet to 4,000 square feet, were created to provide space for start-up businesses. Personnel from the college's Small Business Development Center assisted business owners in developing their business. The entrepreneurs were required to submit a business plan and an application for the space. Don Geren, the Center's Director, said, "We project the CBBDC will have annual sales of about $10 million and will create approximately 50 jobs."

Astronomical studies received a boost in the summer of 1998 when the observatory telescope was shipped back to Celestron International for a complete overhaul. Associate Professor of Physics, Buford Guy, noted that the telescope's mirrors needed cleaning after 25 years of use. The Observatory had been a gift in 1975 from the Thomas Carter Lupton Foundation of Chattanooga. Computers, LAN fiber optics and CCD imaging hardware and software for high-resolution telescopic image and photometer lab work had been installed in 1995. By September the telescope was operational again.

In off-campus news CSCC was named the college of first choice for the Tellico Education Consortium. If a business needed a course that the college could not provide, Roane State or Pellissippi State had an opportunity to deliver the course. A new campus addition was the creation of the Office of Campus Recreation, Programs and Services. Its purpose was to sponsor intramural events, organize outdoor adventures, encourage fitness and wellness activities and offer a variety of special events. Three Assistant Coordinators directed the office. They were: Jason Sewell, student activities and intramural sports; Heather Sealy, campus recreation and fitness; and Kristy Kelly, wellness. Norma Davis, Secretary, was responsible for clerical support and program planning.

An important incentive for attending college was apparent from a 1998 study by two economists, Dr. Victor Ukpolo and Dr. Thomas Dernburg. They studied the impact higher education had on Tennessee's economy. For every dollar a student invested in a two-year associate degree, the student could expect $5.84 in return. The return would be $5.43 for a Bachelor's degree and $5.20 for an advanced degree. A two-year graduate could expect to earn $127,144 more than what a graduate with only a high school degree could earn in a lifetime. With a four-year degree the lifetime earnings would be $280,607 more than a high school graduate, and with an advanced degree, the lifetime earnings would be $417,873 more than someone with only a high school diploma.

Several college groups were active in community service projects during the year. For example, October 24, 1998 was the 8th Annual "Make a Difference Day." The event was created in 1992 by USA Weekend magazine, in partnership with the Points of Light Foundation. The purpose of the event was for citizens to spend a day helping others. In 1998 the college's Student in Free Enterprise (SIFE) organization joined forces with United Way of Cleveland and several local merchants in a food and clothing drive. The SIFE team helped disseminate free Coca Colas and hot dogs to everyone who donated food and/or clothing items for the project. The PTK Chapter hosted an AIDS Week event by assembling a quilt in memory of former student John Killebrew.

The quilt was presented to the Southeast Tennessee Regional Names Quilt Office. PTK members also participated in the "Cleveland Reads" project in support of President Clinton's "America Reads Challenge." Other PTK projects were: tutoring court ordered juveniles; tutoring in elementary schools; participating in the college bookstore's once monthly "Story Time" event; and assisting with public service commercials and book drives. In another event several college employees hosted high school students as part of the "Education Edge Job Shadowing Day."

There were numerous other activities during the year. They were: Photographer Greg Evans, a health physicist at Watts Bar Nuclear Plant, exhibited his works in the Administration Building; author Carl Ellis was the speaker for Race Awareness and Cultural Education Week (he wrote Beyond Liberation, Free at Last and Malcolm: The Man Behind the X); Roschelle Mears organized the 3rd Annual Cultural Cuisine Food Festival; later in the year, Mears organized an event named "The Cultural College: Multicultural Festival '98;" Mary Peterson, a language pathologist, was featured at a "Tellabration;" the Ocoee Writers featured Mike Magnuson at a creative writing workshop; Jere Chumley was one of 19 artists selected for a one-person art exhibit at the Tennessee Arts Commission Gallery in Nashville; the college Drama Department and the Ocoee Players presented three performances of "On Golden Pond;" the annual Health Fair was conducted in the gym; Jere Chumley recruited Mark Wood, Assistant Professor of Art at Chattanooga State, for a photography exhibit; Millie Sieber secured the services of Betty Ann Wylie of Atlanta to lead a workshop on "Tools and Tips for Storytellers" for the "Ocoee Story Fest '98;" the National Shakespeare Company made their 5th appearance at the college and performed "The Taming of the Shrew" and "Othello;" on separate occasions, Mark Shoup, a Chattanooga artist, and Michael Holsomback, Art instructor at Chattanooga State, exhibited their art works at the college; and Maurine Nichols, of the Cleveland Storytelling Guild, chaired a story-telling event in the college's Foundation Room that featured Mary Peterson (a Speech/Language pathologist from Kentucky) and seven local storytellers—Nichols, Millie Sieber, Debbie Parrish, Sylvia Idom, Sean Crews, Bob Burr and Jerry Bancroft.

A multitude of speakers appeared throughout the year at the Psychology Luncheon Series. Organized by Associate Psychology Professor Sue Martel, the speakers were: Jill McGregor, a certified Acupuncture Specialist, lectured on "Introduction to Oriental Medicine;" Glenna Ramer, a Chattanooga Attorney, lectured on "Women in Law;" Timothy Hooker, part-time English instructor at CSCC and Chattanooga State, spoke on "The Historical Contribution of Women;" Dan Gilley, Sheriff of Bradley County, lectured on the "Psychological Profile of Gangs;" and Dr. Steven McFadyer-Ketchum, Research Associate and Lecturer in the Department of Psychology and Human Development at Vanderbilt University, lectured on the topic, "Parents are the Key."

During the 1990s televisions were placed in the classrooms by the campus media center. Professors could call the center and request that a specific educational video tape, relative to their subject matter, be shown to the class. Television monitors were also placed in selected campus building hallways for viewing of a campus calendar of events. The College TV Network (CTN), the nation's largest provider of entertainment and information for colleges, was televised from TV monitors in the student center and the gym lobby. CTN provided news, music, videos, sports cartoons, and short film features designed for college students.

A new campus organization, the CSCC Civitan Club, was formed to provide leadership skills for students. The advisor was History Professor Dr. Neil Greenwood. The club featured activities to enable members to network with community leaders and provide services for the community. A host of other student clubs continued to provide important experiences for students. A few of the clubs and their faculty/staff advisors were: Art Student League, Jere Chumley; Baptist Student Union, Efrain Guillen; Cheerleaders, Nancy Kafsky; Collegiate Secretaries International, Nancy Boyd and Sherra Witt; Creative Writers' Club, Harry Dean and Jim Frank; Delta Epsilon Chi, Pam Brune and Dr. Ken Adcock; Environmental Club, Gayle Garner; Human Services Student Organization, Larry Deyton; Minority Student Association, Roschelle Mears; Legal Assistant Association, Ann McCoin; Outdoor Recreation Club, Jim Frank and Nancy Kafsky; PTK, Patricia Bishop, Gayle Garner, David Suttles and Larry Burns; Parents as Students, Bishop, Garner and Suttles; The Cherokee Signal, Gayle Garner and Steve Gillon; Student Hosts, Jason Sewell; Student Nurses' Association, Janice Gilmore and Glenna Lee; Student Tennessee Education Association, Dr. Frank McKenzie; and Students in Free Enterprise, Steve Gillon.

Another innovation was the creation of a college preparation, retention and enrichment program for minority high school students. Roschelle Mears organized the two-week summer event especially for 1998 high school minority graduates in the college's service area. From 8:30 a. m. until 12:30 p. m., Mondays through Thursdays, students attended "Learnshops" that included the following subjects: Enhancing Writing and English Skills, Computer Connections, Making it in Math, Career Challenges, Careers in Law Enforcement, Business and Management, Finding $ for School, Personal Responsibility and Science and Engineering.

In his humorous article for the Cleveland State "Update," John Bradley offered only one recommendation for a college film version to compete for an Academy Award. Instead of "Titanic," he suggested the college make a film and name it "Minuscule." It would be a film about the state's recent lack of a pay raise for college personnel. As Bradley noted, "CSCC's film earned nothing. In fact, our raise was nothing!"

A humorous development occurred involving Associate Professor of Management and Business, John Cantrell. While helping his son work on a job, Cantrell remembered he had to make a phone call to cancel an appointment. The job was in the parking lot of an apartment complex. Cell phones were non-existent in those days; therefore, Cantrell knocked on the door of one of the apartments, and a half-dressed male student of his answered the door. Cantrell recognized him as being a student who had cut his class numerous times. The flabbergasted student thought Cantrell was there to admonish him for missing classes. He immediately began to make excuses for his negligence, and Cantrell told him that his attendance needed to improve, and by the way, could he borrow his phone.

In another incident Associate Professor of Computer and Information Technology, Dale Yates, had a student who frequently fell asleep at his desk during class. At the end of one class, Yates held his finger to his lips and asked the class to quietly tiptoe out of the classroom and let the student sleep. The student did not awaken until a different class, with a different professor, started several minutes later. The embarrassed student immediately grabbed his books and fled from the classroom. He remained awake in Yates's class thereafter.

Several faculty and staff received recognitions or publicity during the year. These were: Marcia Owens was elected President of the Tennessee Educational Association of Veteran Program Administrators; Dr. Samuel Ofori attended a Developmental Mathematics workshop in Atlanta; Sherra Witt was awarded Advisor of the Year at the Collegiate Secretaries International Conference; Lynne Craver was elected Chair-Elect of the TBR Library Directors; Will Benson was the first faculty representative from CSCC elected to Chair the TBR Faculty Sub-Council; and Dr. Rodney Fitzgerald received the Cleveland-Bradley Chamber of Commerce's 1998 Robert W. Varnell, Jr. Leadership Award. Sadly, the college lost an outstanding faculty member when Lisa Rose died. She taught Computer Science and Business courses and was a highly regarded member of the college community.

The college was well represented in athletics in 1998. John Squires served as both an instructor in Math and as the softball coach for the Lady Cougars. He was assisted by Coach Dane Blanchard. The team members were: Wendy Meadows, Lori Smith, Kylie Hill, Mandy Moore, Ranahan Chastain, Emily Burns, Monica Lewis, Jennifer Mitchell, Airebis Baron, Amy Griswold, Cayci Johnson, Ann Brockett, Mandi Ramey, Haley Carroll, Kathey Payne and Laura Cline. The baseball coach was Mike Policastro, and his assistant was Jason Sewell. The players were: Logan Brummit, Matt Baber, Cliff Morgan, Brandon Maynard, Donnie Long, Mark Beckler, Mike Seebode, Jared Thate, Robert Cox, Heath Pullium, Andre Spurgeon, Blake Pierce, Kevin Pearson, Brandon Potts, Shane Newberry, Mark Hunter, Brent Fair, Nathan Davis, Travis Adams, Henley Hayes, Cory Sharpe, Chad Rogers, Andy Lawson and Drew White.

The Lady Cougars' basketball team was coached by Dan Lumpkin. The team members were: Amber Wilson, Jenny Carter, Amanda Akins, Sarah Colbaugh, Cassi Kile, Julie Thornton, Erica Johnson, Tonya Cummings, Kasey Woodlee, Brittany Morrison, Kim Jenkins, Sam Schulz, Melissa Patterson, Kristi Seivers, Amy Morris, Pam Stevens and Buffy Moore. Amber Wilson was selected for the TJCCAA All-Eastern Division Team for the 1997-98 season. The men's basketball team, coached by Lee Cigliano, won the 1997-98 Eastern Division Championship. The team members were: Frank Walker, Logan Johnson, Tim Bayne, Matt Collins, Star Armstrong, Jacob McClary, Gabe Johnson, Nate Davis, Jason Davis, Jesse Cole, Terrell Cox, Adam Case,

Jard Shoemake, Demetrius Morgan and Nat Phillips. The Cheerleaders were Ruth Barrosso, Tiffany Mull, Jennifer Rose, Tracy Jennings, Vanessa Vernon, Sarah Hood, Julie Ingle, Carri Wicker and Amanda Lakey. Angie Chastain was the mascot.

The spring college debate team, coached by Dr. Sally Snider, had another outstanding year. At one time during the year, the team was ranked the number one community college team in the nation by the Cross Examination Debate Association. Bryan Gaston won the top speaker award in a debate at Morehouse College in Atlanta. He earned 166 points by outscoring 36 Cross Examination Debaters from 15 colleges and universities. Chris Caldwell finished fifth and was only six points behind Gaston. The team of Gaston, Caldwell, Johnna Hampton and Jane Petitt was number one in team speaker points and outscored teams from Alabama, Appalachian State, Clemson, Cumberland, Emory, Florida State, Middle Tennessee State, Southeast Missouri, Tennessee Tech, Georgia, Missouri, South Carolina and Vanderbilt. In Debate rounds, Gaston and Caldwell lost in the quarterfinals to a Vanderbilt team that lost the final round to MTSU.

In another debate at the Tennessee Intercollegiate Forensics Association Debate Tournament, the team won the Tennessee championship in Cross Examination Debate. Hampton and Pettit compiled a 4-0 record and defeated Tennessee Tech in the championship. Hampton was awarded the Second Place Individual Speaker trophy, and Pettit earned 10th Place. Later, the team competed against 20 colleges and universities from 10 different states at the Southeast and the Southeast Central Cross Examination Debate Tournament. Bryan Gaston and Johnna Hampton were among the final eight in the quarterfinals. They lost in that round to the eventual tournament champions from Vanderbilt. Chris Caldwell and Jane Petitt tied for 7th place in speaker points.

The 1998 fall semester debate team was also successful. The members were Kesha Webb, Tameka Phillips, Deanna Wilson, Garth Best and team researcher and peer coach, Jennifer McDaniel. CSCC was the only community college at the Governor's Classic Debate Tournament at Austin Peay State University. The team of Webb and Best finished 3rd on one of the debate topics and, in the process, defeated teams from Tennessee Tech, Cumberland College, Alabama and Austin Peay. They reached the quarterfinals before losing. Phillips and Wilson defeated teams from Southern Illinois, Austin Peay, Tennessee Tech and Vanderbilt before losing the semifinal round to the champions from Cumberland College.

In another humorous campus episode, Associate Professor of Biology, Larry Speight, had a student who was always late for his class. The student, named Johnny, would stumble into the class late and often disrupted the flow of the lecture/discussion. Speight would ignore the situation and continue to teach. This was the time period of the popular television "Tonight" show featuring Johnny Carson. One day, the student arrived late again, and Speight used the familiar introduction of Carson's sidekick, Ed McMahon, and shouted, "And here's Johnny." The class erupted in laughter and the embarrassed Johnny was never late again.

The college's Omega Omicron Phi Theta Kappa Chapter won several awards at both the PTK Regional Conference and the International Conference. The student officers for 1998-1999 were: Rebecca Bishop (daughter of Associate Professor of Psychology, Pat Bishop), President; Melanie Behling, Vice-President; Matthew Rasmussen, Secretary; and Rachel Dyson, Archivist. The advisors were Pat Bishop, David Suttles, Larry Burns and Gayle Garner. At the Regional Conference, the chapter received the First Place Most Distinguished Chapter Award. The chapter also won the First Place Scholarship Hallmark Award, Second Place Leadership Hallmark Award, Second Place Fellowship Hallmark Award, Second Place Outstanding Yearbook, First Place Service Hallmark Award and was named a 5-Star Program (which is the highest chapter award attainable). In other awards Melanie Behling received the first place Visual Arts Award; Rachel Dyson won second place; and Jennifer Barnes and Rebecca Didona tied for third place. Other awards were: CSCC Chapter Advisor Patricia Bishop was awarded Second Place Most Distinguished Advisor; Rebecca Didona was elected as Regional Newsletter Coordinator; the chapter received the Special Horizon Award; Rebecca Bishop and Matt Rasmussen won scholarships to attend the PTK Officer's Academy in Nashville; and the chapter was awarded one scholarship to the International Honors Institute in Williamsburg, Virginia.

The college's PTK also won several awards at the International Conference in Nashville. Out of a total of about 1,200 chapters, the chapter was the fourth runner-up for the International Most Distinguished Chapter Award. The chapter also received the Fifth Place Distinguished Service Hallmark Award, 17th Place Fellowship Hallmark Award, the 5-Star Level Programming Award and the Beta Alpha Continued Excellence Award. Individual awards were presented to: Matthew Amick, the Distinguished Chapter Officer Award; Rebecca Didona, the George O. Bierkoe Distinguished Member Award; Larry Burns, the Alumni Hall of Honor Award; and Chapter Advisor Patricia Bishop, the Horizon Award. Cleveland State's Lacey Kramer was runner-up in the 1998-1999 International PTK Presidential race. Dr. Carl Hite stated that the chapter's "achievements are unparalleled....It is an achievement in which PTK, Cleveland State and the community can be proud." Hite also praised the students and advisors "who have worked so hard to earn this prestigious recognition."

The PTK continued to be heavily involved in campus and community affairs. The members, for example, were active in the "Adopt-A-Spot" program. Four times a year PTK students walked beside Norman Chapel Road collecting trash and carrying it to a recycle center. They were also involved in the annual "Household Waste Day" at the Bradley County landfill. This was a one-day collection event of household waste such as antifreeze, paint, insecticides and other toxic waste products. They also continued to participate in the quilt panel program that honored Tennesseans who died from AIDs.

Two PTK students, Matthew Amick and Amy Renner, were nominated for the "All USA Academic Team." Both Amick and Renner were on the "All-Tennessee Team." The team was sponsored by the USA Today newspaper, the American Association of Community Colleges and the PTK International Honor Society. The program recognized scholarly achievements of students enrolled in community, technical and junior colleges. The CSCC PTK also nominated Renner for the Distinguished Chapter President International Award and Amick for the Distinguished Chapter Officer International Award. Renner received a PTK transfer scholarship to UTK, and Amick received one to UTC.

Students in Free Enterprise (SIFE) members were also active in 1998. They joined with Junior Achievement volunteers in lecturing to K-12 students on understanding the Free Enterprise system. Their presentations included a discussion of the key economic and workforce issues that students would encounter in adult life. The Cherokee Signal (the word "Cherokee" had been re-adopted for the paper) staff members in the Spring of 1998 were: Holli Dykes, Editor; Dwayne Jeffries, Cartoonist; and Staff Members Al Swilling, Beth O'Grady, Ivette Soto, Eve Van Hook, Ann Luxmore, Shelly Wilbanks and Tamika Hickey. The faculty advisor was Associate Professor of English, Gayle Garner. The Homecoming Queen and also President of the Student Senate was Solmaz Zarrineh.

The Commencement speaker was Steve Holland. A former CSCC student (1974-76), he graduated with a Bachelor of Science degree from UTK. He was one of four White House correspondents for the Reuters News Service in the 1990s. A journalism major, he was a former editor of The Cherokee Signal.

Award recipients at the spring 1998 Commencement were: Sherra Witt, Distinguished Faculty Award; Don Geren, Distinguished Staff Award; Johnna Hampton, Distinguished Graduate Award; and Walter Presswood received the first Distinguished Alumnus Award. Certificates and degrees were awarded to 455 students. During the ceremony Ron Braam, the CSCC Foundation President, announced that, "In its history, the Foundation has awarded $1.4 million dollars in scholarships to 2,700 students." Braam was succeeded by Gray Epperson as the new Foundation President, and Beirne Beaty succeeded Melinda Hillman as the new Foundation Executive Director. Hillman had served from 1993 to 1998, and Beaty was the director from 1998 to 2011.

– 1999 –

The major international events were: the world's population exceeded six billion; fighting renewed between Pakistan and India over Kashmir; Abdurraham Wahid was elected President of Indonesia in the country's first fully democratic election; NATO launched airstrikes against Yugoslavia's Serbian fighters; the European Union banned beef imports from the United States ostensibly because of the widespread use of growth hormones; the Euro currency was introduced in eleven countries; Bertrand Piccard and Brian Jones circumnavigated the world in a hot air balloon without stopping; Helen Clark became the first elected female Prime Minister in New Zealand; the International

Criminal Tribunal indicted Slobodan Milosevic and four others for war crimes and crimes against humanity committed in Kosovo; Jordan's King Hussein died of cancer at the age of 63 and his son, Abdullah, succeeded him; Boris Yeltsin resigned as President of Russia and was later replaced by Vladimir Putin; Queen Elizabeth presided over the first Scottish Parliament meeting in 300 years; millennium celebrations started early in several countries (although many believed it should not be celebrated until 2000 or 2001); and countries began to test for a possible Y2K problem and the millennium bug that had the potential of disabling computers and causing world-wide business, government and infrastructure failures.

The major domestic affairs were: Ford Motor Company bought Volvo; the Senate voted to acquit President Clinton of perjury and obstruction of justice; an F5 tornado hit Oklahoma City, killing 36 people; Hurricane Floyd, a category 4 storm with 140 mph winds, killed 56 people in North Carolina; two students shot and killed 12 of their fellow students and one teacher at Columbine High School in Colorado (before taking their own lives); Jack Kervorkian was sentenced for the second-degree murder (assisted suicide) of Thomas Youk; the West Nile virus made its first appearance in the U. S.; Mattel's Barbie Doll celebrated its 40th birthday; the Liberty Bell space capsule was recovered in Florida during an expedition sponsored by television's Discovery Channel; and John F. Kennedy Jr., his wife, Carolyn, and her sister, Lauren Bessette, died when their plane (piloted by Kennedy) plunged into the Atlantic Ocean near Martha's Vineyard, Massachusetts.

In popular culture "American Beauty" won the Academy Award for best movie; Kevin Spacey won the Oscar for best actor (for the same movie); and Hillary Swank won the best actress award for "Boys Don't Cry." The Emmy Award for television's best comedy was won by "Ally McBeal" (FOX), and the Emmy for best drama was won by "The Practice" (ABC). The Grammy for best record of the year was won by Santana for "Smooth," and the best album was awarded to Santana for "Supernatural." In athletics the U. S. women's soccer team won the Women's World Cup Championship; Purdue defeated Duke in the NCAA Division I Women's Basketball Championship; Connecticut defeated Duke in the Men's Basketball Championship; Denver defeated Atlanta in the Super Bowl; and the New York Yankees defeated Atlanta in the World Series.

In campus news the Small Business Development Center celebrated its 10th Anniversary. Don Geren, Center Director and Counselor, noted that the Center averaged about 200 clients each year. Geren, and Counselor Rick Platz, provided personal counseling to small business owners in Bradley, Meigs, McMinn, Monroe and Polk Counties. All counseling was free and confidential and included such issues as licensing requirements, state and federal taxes, business formation and financing. The Center also sponsored numerous seminars on these topics and on marketing and the use of the Internet. It provided an "Incubator" for new businesses and it offered low rental costs, access to the Incubator's counseling support services and the use of equipment such as computers, copiers and fax machines. The funding was provided by grants from the Federal Economic Development Administration, the Tennessee Valley Authority and both the City of Cleveland and Bradley County Governments. The current Director of the Incubator, Hurley Buff, noted that the Incubator (known as the Cleveland/Bradley Business Incubator or CBBI) had a great reputation—"We have . . . gotten calls from Hilton Head, SC, Florida, Alabama . . . to see how we do it." In 2012 the CBBI expanded to include the new Innovation Center, located on the north end of the campus, which has specialized in hosting new businesses in alternative energy, conservation, recycling, efficiency and other related technologies.

In faculty news the campus was saddened by the deaths of Buford Guy (Physics and Astronomy) and Kathryn Johnson (Biology). The campus also lost several faculty and staff to retirement. Retirees were: Pat Crews, Nursing; Elizabeth Eiswerth, Nursing; Janice Gilmore, Nursing; Millie Sieber, Humanities; Larry Pritchett, Maintenance; John Bradley, Humanities; and Sally Phillips, Humanities. Jere Chumley was selected to feature his artwork at the Inaugural Art Exhibition at the Renaissance Center in Dickson, Tennessee. Out of 234 art entries, his oil on canvas painting, titled "Chromospheric Landscape," was one of 40 selected for the event. Nancy Boyd, Associate Professor of Office Administration, received the Woman of Achievement Award for 1999 from the Cleveland Business and Professional Women's Organization.

In the spring of 1999 several students from Redcar, England, visited the campus to complete their training in Robotics. They attended classes in the Applied Science and Technology Department and were taught by Instructor Bob Lance. They resided in the homes of various staff, faculty and community members. Representatives from a college in Germany (Heinrich Schickardt Shule) also visited the campus to discuss the possibility of an exchange program.

As usual, there were numerous activities throughout the year. The Ocoee Players and CSCC presented the Play, "The Trip to Bountiful," in the A. Ray Coleman Auditorium. The play was directed by John Bradley, and the cast included Virginia Orr, Lisa Schmitt, Mac Crox, Barak Womak, Sandy Tinker-Boatwright, Greg Dangerfield and Ed Callais. Dan Keding, a storyteller and singer of ballads, performed at the annual Ocoee Story Fest in the same facility. He also conducted a workshop titled, "Tips for Tellers." Another performance in the auditorium was by the Chattanooga-based Jericho Brass Band. Later in the year, New York's National Shakespeare Company returned for its 6th appearance. The eight-actor cast conducted a matinee and an evening performance of both "Romeo and Juliet" and "A Midsummer Night's Dream." Separate campus art exhibits, in the Adkisson Administration Building, featured Brian Robinson, an Adjunct Art Instructor at UTC, and Deborah Baker, a Chattanooga artist. Gerald Charles Dickens, Great-Great-Grandson of the famous British writer, Charles Dickens, presented "A Christmas Carol" at the Coleman Auditorium in late November 1999. The event was sponsored by CSCC and the Friends of the Cleveland Public Library.

The Psychology Noon Speaker Series had several lecturers during the years. Organized by Associate Professor of Psychology, Sue Martel, one of the speakers was

Dr. Elwood Dunn, Professor of Political Science at the University of the South. He spoke on the "Challenges of a Changing Africa." Another was Attorney Drew Robinson, who spoke on "Sexual Harassment," and another was Ann Culbreth, Principal of E. L. Ross Elementary School, who spoke on "Women in Education."

In November the National Storytelling Association, which originated in Jonesboro, Tennessee, featured several local storytellers at the college. They were: Jerry Bancroft, veternarian; Penny Champion, builder; Seane Crews, graphic arts designer and dulcimer artist; Bob Burr, counselor, Maurine Nichols, actress and teacher; Jesse Buttram, teacher; Deborah Holland, teacher; Sylvia Idom, teacher; and Millie Sieber, CSCC assistant professor. Sieber, the organizer of the event, also taught an elective course titled "Storytelling as Communication."

In business-related activities Olin Corporation continued its recently adopted program of annually hiring 16 Co-Operative Education students. The students worked as field technicians in the Information Technology Systems area. Terry Leonard, Manager of Information Technology at Olin, stated that it was a win-win situation because, "Students receive hands-on training with cutting edge technology while Olin is able to employ students that are well-trained." In other computer news two students in Dr. Ken Adcock's Programming in C++ class presented papers at the fall conference of the Mid-Southeast Association for Computing Machinery Conference held in Gatlinburg. Dr. Adcock noted that the Association was formed in 1959 and the fall Gatlinburg meeting was considered by many as one of the most prestigious chapter meetings in the nation. Cynthia Davis presented a paper on "Ethical Issues in Software Piracy," and James Rose won 3rd Place in one of the four speech categories with his paper on "The Use of Artificial Intelligence in Computer Games."

The college's Associate Professor of Health and Physical Education, Nancy Kafsky, assisted by English faculty member, Jim Frank, scheduled numerous activities for the college's Student Outdoor Recreation Club. Among these were a monthly hike on the college's Hiking Trail, a white water rafting trip on the Ocoee River, the 3rd annual cookout and hike at Benton Falls, the 2nd annual horseback ride, a joint camping excursion and hayride and a mountain biking trip. The Environmental Awareness Club, advised by English faculty member Gayle Garner, raised enough money through T-shirt sales to save and protect over two acres of rainforest in Sierra Nevada de Santa Marta, Colombia. The Brazilian Amazon Rainforest was 1999's priority for the Nature Conservancy and Earth Foundation.

The college's Debate Team continued to receive accolades. Kesha Webb was selected as a Cross-Examination Debate Association (CEDA) Academic All-American Debate Scholar. She was one of 30 students nationwide to receive the award. Tameka Phillips was named to the All-American Debate Squad of CEDA. Phillips was one of 30 debaters selected from top-rated squads in the nation. She earned her spot by winning the Top Speaker Award in the Southeast/Southeast Central Region by a margin of over 100 points. CSCC ended the 1998-1999 season with a CEDA first place ranking regionally and a seventh place ranking nationally among two-year colleges. CSCC also ranked third nationally among two-year colleges in the National Debate Topic Association.

The Tennessee Mathematics Association for Two-Year colleges sponsored a new statewide Math competition in 1999. Cleveland State placed two students in the top ten at the event. Stephen Hatchett tied for ninth in the Developmental Algebra category, and Scott Smith tied for sixth in the Calculus category.

The college's Phi Theta Kappa Chapter had another active year. Several members worked with the Bradley County Juvenile Court to provide tutoring in Math, Reading, English and other subjects for juveniles who needed academic assistance. The CSCC PTK students received guidance in the endeavor from Lisa Wiley, a Bradley County Juvenile Court official, and Judge Van Deacon. The PTK also provided assistance to Cleveland's Blythe Avenue School by serving as classroom tutors, by providing books for all of the 250 children at the school and by presenting the students with gifts of "Beanie Babies" and other treats. The chapter's student President, Rebecca Bishop, remarked that, "Our goal is to improve reading skills and help the children discover the joy of reading." The PTK also hosted the Tennessee Regional Honors Institute. The Honors study topic was "The New Millennium: Past as Prologue." Representatives from PTK chapters at Walters State, Pellissippi State, Northeast State, Chattanooga State, Nashville State Tech and Hiwassee College attended the event. An original comical script was written by DeAnna Wilson, chapter co-President, and Marisa Poplin, chapter Secretary, for the occasion. The play was titled "What, That's Not the End?" The cast included Wilson, Poplin, Michael Cochran, Rob Thurman, Ruth Ann Elwinger, Charlie Howard and Raymond Taylor.

CSCC's 1999 PTK Chapter continued its tradition of receiving prestigious awards at conventions. The Chapter received an International Distinguished Chapter Award at the international convention in California in April 1999. It also received a first place for the Most Distinguished Scholarship Hallmark Award and third place for the Distinguished Service Hallmark Award and the Five-Star Programming Award. The Chapter won the Beta Alpha Continued Excellence Award for the second year in a row. Rebecca Bishop received a Distinguished Chapter President Award, and Melanie Behling received a Distinguished Chapter Officer Award. Rebecca Bishop also placed first runner-up for the position of Southern Vice-President of PTK.

In athletics Coach Dan Lumpkin's Lady Cougar Basketball players were: Angie Ivey, Britney Goble, Brittany Morrison, Sarah Colbaugh, Julie Thornton, Ashley Martin, Tonya Cummings, Kasey Woodlee, Buffy Moore, Mandy Chenkus, Melissa Patterson, Kim Jenkins, Sam Schultz, Cassi Kile, Erica Johnson and Joy Smith. Cassi Kile and Julie Thornton were selected for the 1998-99 All-Eastern Division Team. The 1998-99 men's team, coached by Lee Cigliano, compiled a 17-9 record.

The Editor of <u>The Cherokee Signal</u>, in 1998-99, was Deborah Rhodes and the staff members were: James Rose, Ivette Soto, Carol Smith, Elizabeth Abernathy, Ed Cormell, Rebecca Bishop, Nathan Debusque, Daniel James, Al Swilling, Carolyn Taylor, Eva Van Hook, Janelle Musick and Stacey White. The faculty advisor was Gayle Garner and the SIFE students were the Business Managers for the paper. The college's student representative to the Tennessee Board of Regents was Amanda Parsons. The Student Senate President was Justin Key and the Homecoming Queen was Sheena Moss. In a special student vote the students gave recognition to: Bruce Franks, Outstanding Service to Students Award; Dawn Gregory, Outstanding Senator Award Recipient; and Steve Longley, Outstanding Instructor Award.

The Commencement speaker was Roger K. Crouch. He was a native of Jamestown, Tennessee, and a graduate of Polk County High School. He was a payload specialist aboard the space shuttle Columbia in April 1997 and in July 1997. He earned a Bachelor's degree from Tennessee Tech and a Master's and Doctorate in Physics from Virginia Tech. The awards presented at the graduation ceremony were: Nancy Boyd, Outstanding Faculty Member Award; Bertha Goldston, Outstanding Staff Member Award; and David Barnes, Outstanding Graduate Award.

THE EARLY TWENTY-FIRST CENTURY

– 2000 - 2016 –

– 2000 –

The major events in international affairs were: the European Union's Euro fell to a record low against the dollar; a Concorde Air France Flight crashed just after takeoff from Paris and killed all 109 aboard and five on the ground; Pope John Paul II visited Israel and prayed for forgiveness of the sins of those involved in the Holocaust; the Summer Olympics event was held in Sydney, Australia; the concerns over Y2K passed without the serious, widespread computer failures that had been predicted; the world's largest Ferris Wheel ("The London Eye") opened; according to NASA, the hole in the Ozone layer over Antarctica increased from .62 square miles to 17 square miles in only 12 months; the European Airbus Consortium announced plans to build the world's largest passenger plane (to accommodate 656 passengers); a destructive computer virus, "I Love You," was spread by e-mail and shut down computers in many parts of the world; and scientists from Great Britain and The United States announced jointly that they had determined the structure of the human genome.

The major events in domestic affairs were: the average cost of a new house was $134,150; the average income per year was $40,343; the cost of a gallon of gasoline was $1.26; the average monthly rent was $675; the state of Vermont passed a bill legalizing civil unions for same-sex couples; the Microsoft co-founder and creator of the modern personal computer, Bill Gates, left his position as CEO to spend more time with charitable work; seventeen U. S. sailors were killed, and the USS Cole was badly damaged by two suicide bombers in Aden, Yemen; control of the Panama Canal was handed over to Panama after 75 years of United States control; after an international custody dispute, six-year old refugee Elian Gonzalez was returned to his father in Cuba; the Food and Drug Administration announced approval of a pill that induced abortions; and George W. Bush became President-elect when Vice-President Al Gore conceded the election (after the Supreme Court, in a 5-4 party-line vote, reversed a state court decision for recounts in Florida's contested election).

In popular culture "Gladiator" won the Academy Award for best movie; Russell Crowe was named best actor for his performance in "Gladiator;" and Julia Roberts won best actress for her role in "Erin Brockovich." The Emmy for best television comedy was won by "Will & Grace" (NBC), and the best drama was awarded to "The West

Wing" (NBC). The Grammy for best record was presented to U2 for "Beautiful Day," and the Grammy for best album was won by Steely Dan for "Two Against Nature." Tiger Woods became the youngest player, at the age of 24, to win all four of golf's major tournaments. The University of Connecticut defeated UTK to win the NCAA Division I Women's Basketball Championship, and Michigan State defeated Florida to win the Men's Championship. The St. Louis Rams defeated the Tennessee Titans in the Super Bowl, and the New York Yankees defeated the New York Mets in the World Series.

The year 2000 featured visits to the campus from the college's counterparts in Europe. Students and faculty from both Redcar and Cleveland College, in Great Britain, and from Heinrich Schickhardt Schule, in Freudenstadt, Germany, arrived on campus in February. The students were housed in the homes of various faculty, staff and community members. Three days of their visit overlapped with each other and this provided opportunities for cultural exchanges among the British, German and American students.

The Redcar students were on campus from February 18 through February 27, and they received training in robotics and toured several sites such as M&M Mars and Olin Chemical Corporation. They made an overnight camping trip to Big South Fork Recreational Area, watched a soccer match at the Mouse Creek facility in Cleveland and attended a party with CSCC students and the German students. The party featured the Dexter Thomas Band and was sponsored by the college's PTK Chapter.

The German students were on campus from February 24 through March 5, and they studied environmental issues and business-related subjects. The college's SIFE students served as their guides. They visited the Electric Vehicle Information Center, the Tennessee Aquarium, Santek Environmental, the Bradley County Landfill, Hamilton County Recycling, Duracell and the Forest Service. They also made a short trip to the Smokey Mountains. CSCC students were invited to visit Germany in the near future to study the environment with German students from Heinrich Schickhardt Schule.

Six CSCC students traveled to Redcar and Cleveland College during the summer of 2000. They were: Aimee Ables, Allen Baeumel, Sara Goforth, Nicholas Hawkins, Bianca Hudson and Kristie Westfield. They were accompanied by faculty members Richard Stevens, Ed Rowlee and Denise King. The students studied environmental issues and robotics, and they also explored several sites related to environmental issues: North Yorkshire Moors, National Park, Cleveland Potash Mine, Farne Island Bird Sanctuary, Seal Sands, Marsden Bay Coastal Walk, Darwin House, the British Museum and the Natural History Museum.

During the year the college began to stress the importance of volunteering for community projects. Referred to as "service learning," several Co-Operative Education students participated in the endeavor. A summary indicated that: 40 students volunteered 16,156 hours in Bradley County; 19 students donated 4,333 hours in McMinn County;

two students donated 358 hours in Meigs County; 15 students donated 15 hours in Polk County; and 12 students donated 2,372 hours in Monroe County. A few of the organizations receiving assistance from CSCC students were: United Way, American Red Cross, Special Olympics, Adopt-A-Spot, Big Brothers and Sisters, MS Walk, Diabetes Walkathon, Toys for Tots, Meals on Wheels and Children's Miracle Network.

Both Olin and Arch Chemical Companies were important hosts for the college's Co-Operative Education Program. Students Mark Swanson, Derrick Malone, Richie Glover, Katina Roy, Kendra Ellis and Michael Manis were program employees at Olin. Dr. Carl Hite gave an Award of Appreciation to Phyllis Harris, Manager of the Olin Clor Alkali Products Information Technology Systems, for her assistance with the program. Students Cindy Burgess, Phil Clark, Jerry Pendergrass and Jason Sharpe Lee worked with Arch Chemical Corporation. Rick McCormick, Information Technology Manager of Arch, said, "These students will receive better consideration from future employers because of this Co-Op experience."

A college "Fact Book," prepared by Dr. David Watts, the Director of Institutional Research and Assessment, indicated that the total number of graduates in all academic programs, from 1969 to 2001, was 9,702. The headcount enrollment for the fall of 2000 was 3,056. Of these, 1,641 were from Bradley County, 569 from McMinn, 278 from Monroe, 190 from Polk, 140 from Hamilton, 79 from Meigs and the remainder from other locations. The study also revealed that in 2000 the four public universities that received the most transfers from CSCC were UTC (253), Tennessee Tech (39), MTSU (29) and UTK (14). Of the 3,056 students, 1,290 were males and 1,766 were females. Another interesting statistic indicated the job placement percentage of "eligible graduates." Eligible graduates were those who majored in career-technical fields, did not join the military following graduation and did not continue college enrollments for additional degrees. In 1990-91, 93% were placed, and in 2000-2001, 91.43% were placed.

In personnel matters the college was saddened by the deaths of Dr. George Mathis, the former Dean of Student Affairs, and William K. Fillauer, a former Foundation President and Trustee. There were three new arrivals for staff positions at the college. Dr. Charles Hurley was the new Vice-President of Finance and Administration. He earned a Bachelor's degree from UTK in Business, a Master's from UT Nashville in Business Administration and a Doctorate in Education from East Tennessee State University. Midge Burnette was the new Director of Admissions and Records. She had a Bachelor's degree in Elementary Education and a Master's in Educational/Psychology and Counseling from UTK. Mary Evelyn Lynn was the new Director of the Library. She graduated from UTK with a Bachelor's degree in Zoology, and she received a Master's degree in Library Science from Louisiana State University. Hurley had been the Vice-President of Business Affairs at Northeast State Technical Community College, Burnette had admissions experience at the University of Arkansas at Fayetteville (and at UTK) and Lynn had library experience at Carson Newman College, East Tennessee Baptist Hospital, Knox County Public Library and New Orleans Public Library.

Several faculty and staff attended conferences and/or received recognition in 2000. Dr. Carl Hite (President), Dr. Renate Basham (Vice-President of Academics), Carole Gavagan (Business and Technology Faculty) and Denise King (Biology Faculty) made presentations at the Global Education Seminar in Nashville. They were accompanied by Bill Clark (Media Center Specialist) and Bruce Franks (English Faculty). In February staff members Deborah McLachlan, Andy Semak and Mark Wilson attended the American College Testing (ACT) Asset Workshop at the TBR office in Nashville. In March Dr. Ken Adcock, Associate Professor of Business Management, and Pamela Brune, Associate Professor of Computer and Information Systems, received a Distance Education Award from the TBR. Adcock taught six individual web courses, and Brune taught four courses. Gail Greenwood was named Cleveland's 2000 Administrative Professional of the Year by the local chapter of the International Association of Administrative Professionals. Katherine Smith, Remedial and Developmental Writing and English instructor, was awarded a fellowship by the Virginia Center for the Creative Arts. One of Smith's poems, "Belleville," was published in "Poetry," a prestigious Chicago-based journal. She also had an essay, "The Artist as Single Mother," published in a University of Georgia Press publication.

Several other activities in 2000 were: the college hosted the TSSAA District 5AA Basketball Tourney; Chris Ramsey, the President of the Board of Directors of the Boys' Club of Chattanooga, delivered a speech on "Leadership and Career Development;" the Workforce Development program of JTPA received a $54,000 award for exceeding performance standards in their employment and training services; and the National Shakespeare Company performed "Hamlet" and "Twelfth Night." Two storytellers, Mary Hamilton of Frankfort, Kentucky, and Charles Maynard of Seymour, Tennessee, presented stories and workshops at the college and in six area schools from March 22 to March 24, 2000.

Art Exhibitions, organized by Jere Chumley, Associate Professor of Art, were in the forefront of college activities in 2000. The first Alumni Art Exhibition was on display throughout much of the year in the Adkisson Administration Building. Nineteen alumni participated in the event. One of these was Jim Hodge, the college's first declared Art Major (in 1967). Other exhibitors were: Tom Sain, David Smith, Jack Cain, Tim Butler, Cynthia Morrison, Ellen Epperson Ralls, Will Rhodarmer (son of Psychology Professor, Sue Martel), Bob Rothwell, Anita Dotson, Mick Gray Barnes, Margaret Richardson, Avery McNeese, Elder Gary Jones, Calvin Walton, Clay Grigsby, Mary Ann Thompson Copes, Steve Rucker and Michael Valcarcel. In addition the 5th Annual Art Students' League Exhibit was displayed in several campus buildings.

The Nineteenth Annual Tennessee Valley Art Competition was held in April in the college library. The event was organized by Chumley and sponsored by the Art Department and the Cultural and Educational Enrichment Committee. The competition was juried and judged by artist Mary B. Lynch of Lookout Mountain, Georgia. First place was awarded to Bob Short of Sewanee, second place to Freddie W. Brewer of

Dayton and third place to Lorri Y. Kelly of Chattanooga. Later in the year, David Le Doux, Professor Emeritus of MTSU, exhibited at the college. He began teaching at MTSU in 1956, and he previously exhibited in 14 state galleries from New York to Oklahoma.

The college's "Update" provided levity for the faculty and staff with a series of fictitious newspaper headlines that were as follows: "Something Went Wrong in Jet Crash, Expert Says;" "Police Begin Campaign to Run Down Jaywalkers;" "Drunk Gets Nine Months in Violin Case;" "British Left Waffles on Falkland Islands;" "Teacher Strikes Idle Kids;" and "Squad Helps Dog Bite Victim." Another column explained the difficulties involved in learning English. Examples were: "We polish the Polish furniture;" "A farm can produce produce;" "The dump was so full it had to refuse refuse;" "The soldier decided to desert in the desert;" "The present is a good time to present the present;" "At the Army base, a bass was painted on the head of a bass drum;" and "The dove dove into the bushes."

Two faculty and one staff member retired during the year. One of those, Sally Phillips, had been at the college for 32 years. She was one of the original employees in 1967. A graduate of Nashville Business College, she also played basketball for the school. She once played on a team that competed against a Russian team in Madison Square Garden. She also played a game in Washington, D.C., that featured Robert Kennedy assisting with the opening ball toss. She participated in the 1963 Pan American Games in Sao Paulo, Brazil, and her team won the gold medal in basketball. Phillips began her 1967 employment at CSCC as Secretary for McKamy Hall, the college's first Business Manager. She later became the Language Lab Assistant and held that position for 25 years. She supervised several technological upgrades in the lab. One extensive improvement was made possible by a generous gift of $50,000 from Foundation member Sam McReynolds and his wife, Ann. It enabled Phillips to upgrade software for foreign language students and other students requiring assistance in reading and writing skills. The college honored the McReynolds family by naming the Language Arts Lab for them.

A second retiree was Mildred Sieber. Sieber was active in teaching Developmental courses, Reading courses, and Storytelling courses. She was also a regular participant in the local storytelling organization. She worked with staff member Deborah McLachlan in creating the Emerging Scholars Program that recognized students who successfully passed remedial and developmental courses (before taking college level courses). Sieber also worked with Joy Yates, Director of Instruction for the Bradley County Schools (and wife of faculty member Dale Yates), in developing a community service learning course in reading.

Another retiree was John Bradley. Bradley, like Phillips, was an original employee of the college. He graduated from MTSU and Ohio University with a Bachelor's and a Master's degree. He taught English Composition and Public Speaking courses and was responsible for performing and directing numerous dramatic productions at the college.

He was a past-president of the Ocoee Players and of the Tennessee Theater Association. He also served for three years as the Dean of the Tennessee Collaborative Leadership Academy, a weeklong summer workshop for teachers at Tennessee Tech University. His wit and sense of humor, as evident in his articles for the campus Employee Newsletter, provided the faculty and staff laughter on many occasions.

The college continued to provide community service, leadership and academically competitive opportunities for students. A new club, started by Dr. Ken Adcock, Business Management Professor, and Cynthia Davis, Computer Programming student, was affiliated with the Association of Computer Machinery. Davis served as Chair of the club; Beverly Newman was Vice-Chair; and J. Keith Haney was Secretary-Treasurer. The Tennessee Mathematics Association for Two-Year colleges sponsored a statewide Math competition. Two CSCC students placed in the contest. Scott Pigg tied for 6th place in the Calculus category and Steve Gorenz placed 6th in the Pre-Calculus category. Achievement certificates and a gift certificate to O'Charley's Restaurant were presented to the top five students from each division in the contest. The top five in Intermediate Algebra were: Seth Moses, John Upchurch, Jamie Nelson, Johanna Belcher and Kelli Williams. The top five in Pre-Calculus were: Steven Gorentz, Allen Baeumel, Marisa Poplin, Derek Dicks and Bonny Swallows. The top five in Calculus were: Scott Pigg, Dustin Lane, Pinal Patel, Sean Mikel and Jonathon Talley.

The college's Students in Free Enterprise (SIFE) Club was named the Regional Champion (in the two-year division) at the Regional Competition and Job Fair in Atlanta. The college's student team, one of the smallest at the event, captured First Runner-Up and Rookie Team of the Year in their League. The team also won awards for its Five Points Area Marketing Presentation, its Make a Difference Day Activities and its Cleveland Boys and Girls Club Computer Lab Educational and Maintenance Projects. Major contributors to the club's portfolio of free enterprise education projects were: DeAnna Wilson, Team President; Cynthia Davis, Boys and Girls Club Project Manager; Amanda Parsons, TBR Student Representative; Art Clem, Web Master; and Jonathan Withrow, Small Business Development Center Web Page Designer. The student leader for the Boys and Girls Club project was Cynthia Davis. She and other SIFE members worked with the Boys and Girls Club in the installation of "Naturally Speaking" software on the new 19 computers at the club. In another project student leader Art Clem worked with Rick Platz in the Small Business Development Center to develop a website dedicated to providing information on how to start a new small business.

Steve Gillon, Business faculty member and the SIFE club's faculty advisor, was awarded the Sam M. Walton Free Enterprise Fellow Award at the event. Community leaders who assisted the club were Mayor Tom Rowland, Main Street Cleveland Executive Director Angela McClure, United Way Vice-President Doug Eberhart, Boys and Girls Club Director Jeff Nichols, Small Business Development Center Specialist Rick Platz and Junior Achievement Coordinator Gina Akins. A new course that had a special appeal for SIFE students was also launched by the college. It was Business 1280, Comparative Cultures/International Studies. The course included a trip to Freudenstadt, Germany, to syudy at the Heinrich Schickardt Shule. The course emphasized the business aspects of conservationism and environmentalism.

The college's Debate Team and the Environmental Club remained active during the year. Faculty Advisor, Dr. Sally Snider, noted that DeAnna Wilson, the Debate Team Captain, won second place, and team member Joyce Chord won fourth place in the Tennessee Intercollegiate Forensics Association State Tournament in Knoxville. The Environmental Club scheduled several projects for the year. Among these were: cleaning up the campus, assisting the PTK Club in cleaning the roadside of Norman Chapel Road, maintaining the campus walking trail, assisting the Bradley County Nursing Home in maintaining its grounds and selling T-shirts to raise funds for saving rainforests in Brazil. The club's President in 2000 was Pam Hughes, and the faculty advisor was Gayle Garner.

Phi Theta Kappa also had another good year. The college chapter's faculty advisor, Patricia Bishop, was appointed Interim Coordinator for the 15 chapters in the Tennessee Region. Bishop had served as an advisor for the college's chapter since 1993, and she won the Most Distinguished Advisor Award at the 1999 Tennessee Regional Convention. The college's chapter won 19 awards and an Honors Institute Scholarship at the 2000 PTK Regional Conference. The chapter also won the First Place Most Distinguished Chapter Award for the fifth consecutive year. The student president of the regional conference for 1999-2000 was Cleveland State's Marisa Poplin.

The college's chapter won several awards at the 2000 Regional Conference held at Chattanooga State. These were: First Place Leadership Hallmark Award; First Place Fellowship Hallmark Award; First Place Service Hallmark Award; First Place Scholarship Hallmark Award; and the chapter was named a 5-Star Program, which is the highest attainable chapter award. Several chapter members also won awards. Marisa Poplin and Robert W. Thurman captured second and third place in poetry. Cynthia Davis received honorable mention in poetry. Thurman won second place in short story competition, and Michael Cochran received honorable mention. Lynne Smith received second place in Visual Arts, and advisor Larry Burns received the Horizon Award. Brenda Taylor received the third place America Reads Challenge/Individual Award, and honorable mention was presented to Michael Cochran, Nancy Finnell, Marisa Poplin, Matthew Rasmussen and Ramon Taylor. Taylor received the Most Distinguished Chapter Member Award, and Rasmussen was elected as regional Newsletter Coordinator. The chapter received second place for Outstanding Yearbook, first place for the American Reads Chapter Award, and the chapter was awarded one scholarship to the International Honors Institute.

Several Cleveland State PTK students attended the organization's 82nd International Convention in Orlando, Florida. They were: Dei Elrod, Ramon Taylor, David Martella, Marisa Poplin, Matt Rasmussen, Earlene Baxter and Nancy Finnell. Also in attendance were advisors Patricia Bishop and Larry Burns, as well as three alumni: Rebecca Didona, Rebecca Bishop and Kyle Elrod. Out of approximately 1,200 chapters in the United States, Canada, Germany, Japan and Guam, CSCC was the 18th ranked Distinguished International Chapter. The college's chapter was the only one in Tennessee to be named a distinguished chapter or to rank in the top 100 chapters.

The college's chapter also accumulated several other awards. These were: second place as a Most Distinguished Chapter in Scholarship Hallmark Award, second place in the Distinguished Fellowship Hallmark Award, a Journey Challenge Award and a Five Star Level of Programming Award. Matthew Rasmussen received a Distinguished Chapter President Award, Patricia Bishop received a Robert Giles Distinguished Advisor Award, Larry Burns received a Horizon Award, and Dr. Carl Hite received the Shirley B. Gordon Award of Distinction. The chapter also received the Beta Alpha Continued Excellence Award for the third consecutive year. Cleveland State's Nancy Finnell was one of 10 students nationally to receive a $1,000 Guistwhite scholarship by the PTK International Honor society. She was the only student from Tennessee to receive the award. Dr. Hite praised the chapter by noting that, "We are very proud of our students and the awards they have won. The students have worked extremely hard to obtain these honors."

An important event during the year was an Honors Institute hosted by the college's PTK. Approximately 50 members, advisors and guests (representing six regional PTK chapters) studied and discussed the topic of "In the Midst of Water: Origin or Destiny of Life." Dr. Carl Hite, in his capacity as the host college President and the PTK Tennessee Regional Presidential Ambassador, welcomed participants for the one-day (September 23, 2000) event. Four Cleveland State faculty members played key roles in the seminar. Jean Crockett (English) presented a provocative discussion on water and its place in literature throughout history. Will Benson (Music) led a discussion of water imagery in music. Rich Stevens (Biology) lectured on the indispensability and fragility of water as a precious resource. Denice King (Biology) led a discussion on the biological composition of water and its properties and guided the group to the Biology lab to view microorganisms present in water. Several participants extended their visit and toured Cleveland's waste treatment facility, visited the Chattanooga Aquarium, toured the Lost Sea in Sweetwater and/or made a rafting trip down the Ocoee River.

Several faculty and staff members were responsible for the development of a new performing choir. These were: Nancy Montgomery (Ocupational Therapy faculty), Harry Dean (English faculty), Will Benson (Music faculty), Amy Fowler (Business faculty) and Cheryl Gilbert (Music faculty and Director of the choir). Approximately 20 to 30 faculty and staff participated in the choir and they performed at the college and at other locales such as the Bradley Nursing Home, the Elks Lodge (for a Sertoma Club meeting) and the Museum Center at Five Points.

In athletics the baseball team enjoyed a successful season. Late in the season ten players were hitting over .300, and the team batting average was .323. Among the leaders in batting average were Phillip Russell and Jim Higgins. Brad Steele and Ryan Haun were leading home run hitters; Brad Steele, Dusty Hammett and Ryan Haun excelled in runs batted in; and Jeremy Hannah led in stolen bases. An outstanding pitcher for the team was Jason Davis. Davis became the third "Cougar" under Coach Mike Policastro to sign a professional baseball contract. Davis signed with the Cleveland Indians, and in previous years Jeff Bramlett signed with the Los Angeles Dodgers and Clay Greene with the New York Giants. Davis and his teammates finished third in the region tournament, and Davis finished his CSCC career with a 15-6 record and nine saves in 41 appearances. He compiled a career earned run average of 2.49 and had 159 strikeouts in his two years at Cleveland State. He pitched in professional baseball with the Cleveland Indians (and later with the Pittsburgh Pirates).

The leading hitters for the Lady Cougars' softball team were Tiffany and Julie Thornton. Late in the season they were hitting over .500. Angie Ivery was hitting over .400 and Erica Johnson over .300. Samantha Martin was the primary pitcher for the team. Coach Dan Lumpkin's Lady Cougar 1999-2000 basketball team was ranked among the top 25 teams in the NJCAA. Cassi Kile was on the All-Conference Team, and Julie Thornton was the Most Valuable Player of the 1999-2000 TJCCAA All-Star game.

Four CSCC students completed the City and Guilds certification. It was a required certification for employment in most technical fields in the European market. A high level of competency in "Autocad," for example, was one of the requirements for completion of the certificate. The students were Shena Pitts, Dennis Sprinkle, Marvin Trew and Damien Ledford. Bob Carrick, from Redcar and Cleveland College, England, was the certifying instructor. Another student newsmaker was Cynthia Davis. She graduated with two degrees—an Associate of Science in Engineering and an Associate of Applied Science in Computer Information Systems. She was a Student Government Senator, President of the Computing Machinery Club, a Student Host, a SIFE Project Leader and a member of PTK and the Environmental Club.

Other outstanding students were Nancy Finnell and Marisa Poplin. They were recipients of the All Tennessee Academic Team Award. Sheryl Musgrove served as the Student Senate President in 2000, and Anita Key was the Homecoming Queen. The fall Managing Editor of The Cherokee Signal was Samantha Quinn and the spring Editor was Daniel F. James. The staff members were: Ed Cormell, Geoffrey Freeman, Christina Cosme, Sheryl Musgrove, Joy Swafford and Marcie Webb, Jon Franks, Jeff Helton and Sara Goforth. The faculty advisor was Gayle Garner.

The commencement speaker for 2000 was CSCC's John Bradley. Recognition was given at commencement to three college retirees: Dr. T. P. Mathai (Chemistry faculty), Sue Martel (Psychology faculty) and Don Geren (Head of the Small Business Incubator). Award recipients at graduation were: Cynthia Davis, the Distinguished Graduate Award; Rebecca Locke (Science Department Lab Assistant), the Distinguished Staff Award; and Glenna Lee (Nursing faculty), the Distinguished Faculty Award.

– 2001 - 2016 –

The number and frequency of shocking international and national developments in the last few years has been staggering. A multitude of political and social issues such as global warming, terrorist attacks, trade issues, health-care reform, government shutdowns, immigration issues, same-sex marriages, alternative life-styles and seemingly endless warfare in the Mideast filled the headlines in newspapers and dominated other sources of news.

A few of the major events were: on September 11, 2001 two hijacked commercial airliners struck the World Trade Center's two towers in New York City, a third hijacked plane destroyed a portion of the Pentagon and a fourth crashed in a field in Pennsylvania (approximately 3,000 people were killed in the terrorist attacks); the Department of Homeland Security was created; the U. S. invaded Afghanistan; the Euro became the currency of the European Union; Queen Elizabeth celebrated her golden jubilee, and ten years later, her Diamond Jubilee; the US-led offensive against Iraq began; Saddam Hussein was captured by US forces and later executed by the new Iraqi government; in 2004 President Bush was re-elected; Condoleezza Rice became the first black woman Secretary of State; Barack Obama, the first black President in US history, served two terms; in 2007 the US housing bubble collapsed, and in 2008 a number of high profile financial institutions reported huge losses caused by a financial and economic collapse that led to a worldwide recession; a CIA-led squadron of US Navy SEALs killed the Al-Queda leader, Osama bin Laden; and numerous terrorist attacks occurred throughout the world and in America. By 2016 the cost of a new house in the U. S. was approximately $290,000; the average cost of a gallon of gasoline had dropped from about $4.00 in 2013 to about $2.00 in 2016; the average income per year was approximately $50,000; and the minimum wage in 2015 was $7.25.

In popular culture a few of the award winning movies were "Gladiator," "A Beautiful Mind," "Million Dollar Baby," "The Departed," "Slumdog Millionaire," "The King's Speech" and "Spotlight." A few of the award winning television shows were "Everybody Loves Raymond," "30 Rock," "Modern Family," "The West Wing," "The Sopranos," "Mad Men" and "Homeland." In popular music a few of the musicians were Madonna, Bon Jovi, U2, Faith Hill, Shania Twain, Keith Urban, Blake Shelton, Carrie Underwood, Whitney Houston, Michael Jackson, Prince, Celine Dion and Taylor Swift.

The college continued to sponsor an assortment of annual unique activities during the years of 2001-16. Examples of these were: the first annual Starship Career Fair began in 2002 with approximately 1,000 eighth graders in attendance and with representatives from sixty-five area business and industries present; the first annual Latin Night Celebration (organized by Associate Professor Alejandra Hoffer) was conducted; in 2004 the first annual "Dr. Seuss Day" (organized by Suzanne Wood and the Childhood Education Faculty and Students) was held in the campus library (in 2008 approximately

1,300 students attended a celebration of Dr. Seuss's 50th birthday); in 2008 the first annual Multicultural Fair was conducted; in 2009 the first annual Environmental Awareness Celebration occurred; Health Fairs, organized by the Nursing Department, were an annual event since the first years of the college's existence; an annual "College is for Me" program was initiated to give elementary students a campus tour and create a desire for them to attend college after high school (the program developed when Linda Whitmire, a former counselor with Waterville Elementary School, requested a campus tour for her students); in 2013 CSCC and Cleveland Associated Industries conducted the first annual "Make It Happen" Event designed to introduce students to the world of manufacturing (a few of the industry participants were Cormetech, Olin, Lonza, Mars Chocolate North America, Eaton Electrical, Cleveland Tubing and Mueller Company); in 2012 both the Merck Foundation and the college's Foundation sponsored a series of lectures known as the "Bridging Cultures Program;" the first annual Science, Technology, Engineering and Math (STEM) Camp for Middle School students was held; in 2015 the first annual Peak Performance Business Excellence Symposium was presented jointly by CSCC and Lee University; and in 2016 the first annual "Burgers and Badges" Luncheon was held to support the college's First Responder programs (the event was sponsored by Alvin Word, Coca Cola, Tasteful Gatherings and the CSCC Wildlife Society).

The college's commitment to spreading knowledge of the environment was evident when it received several annual recognitions as a "Tree Campus USA" from the Arbor Day Foundation. Level 1 Arboretum status, for example, was attained by identifying over 30 species of trees on the campus and assigning placards of scientific names to them. By 2014 the college had met the five standards of the Arbor Day foundation—maintaining a tree advisory committee, a campus tree-care plan, dedicated annual expenditures for the campus tree program, an Arbor Day observance and a student service-learning project. Tree Campus USA was a national program created in 2008 to honor colleges and universities for effective campus forest management and for engaging staff and students in conservation. Toyota's Foundation launched the program and provided financial support for it.

In 2014 the college's efforts to assist veterans in such endeavors as education, jobs and franchising earned it the distinction of being a "Tennessee VETS Campus" and recognition by G. I. Jobs magazine as a "Military Friendly School." The college's support of good health was manifest in 2009 when the entire campus became "smoke-free." In addition a "Quality Enhancement Plan" (QEP), as a requirement of every college's re-accreditation procedure, was submitted to the Southern Association of Colleges and Schools. The plan was titled "Student Involvement: A Key to Learning." The college collected an assortment of "best teaching practices" to be shared by the faculty in their constant endeavor to enhance student academic achievement. The college was also selected by the American Association of Community Colleges to be part of the "Pathways Project" to help students succeed.

A major innovation that drew national attention was a redesign of the mathematics curriculum. Associate Professor John Squires played an instrumental role in procuring a grant for that purpose, and other Math faculty, such as Associate Professor Karen Wyrick, assisted in arranging the curriculum into "bite-sized" modules to expedite student learning. The new approach to math instruction earned the college the prestigious Bellwether Award in 2009. The Bellwether Awards were established to recognize outstanding programs at the forefront of innovation throughout the United States and Canada. President Barack Obama mentioned Cleveland State in a speech at the University of Texas at Austin in 2010 when he said, "There are community colleges like Tennessee's Cleveland State that are redesigning remedial math courses and boosting not only student achievement but also graduation rates."

In 2014 Cleveland State and Chattanooga State won the Futures Assembly Legacy Award for their joint "Do the Math" program. At both colleges Developmental Math student success rates increased significantly, and "Do the Math" was replicated at numerous colleges and high schools in Tennessee and around the nation. A grant provided funds for redesigning the fourth-year high school math bridge course for students with an ACT score of 19 or below at the end of their junior year. Courses were developed that involved a one-hour class meeting and two hours of additional lab work each week (instead of the usual three-hour class meeting format).

Although Squires later accepted a faculty position at Chattanooga State, he and Wyrick continued to work together on the project. Wyrick, a National Center for Academic Transformation Redesign Scholar and Math Department Chair, worked to improve Math success rates with colleges around the nation. She also worked with local high schools to incorporate the course redesign in their dual enrollment classes. In 2012 the Miller Family Math Endowment Fund was created to support students in their Math studies, and in 2013 the college's Math Lab was named for the Miller Family (Fred A. Miller, President of Miller Furniture Company, and Nancy Painter Miller, Drew Miller and Debra Miller). As John Squires noted, "The positive impact the program has made on students has been great to see." The program was featured in an article in <u>The Chronicle of Higher Education</u> publication titled, "Introducing a Remedial Program that Actually Works." It was also mentioned in blogs and articles from several national organizations.

In 2001 a score of 93 on the Performance Funding Evaluation of Instruction Report earned the college an award of $415,769. A few years later an economic impact study indicated the college's annual average contribution to its five-county service area (over the past five years) was $36.9 million. The college "Fact Book," prepared by Dr. David Watts, the Director of Institutional Research and Assessment, indicated that the total number of graduates in all academic programs from 1969 to 2001 was 9,702.

The college continued to offer other new programs and courses. An Advance Program, directed by Dr. Steve Warren, the Director of the Business and Industry Institute, was developed as a scheduling alternative for working adults. It was an accelerated course of study for students that were 21 years of age (or older), had at least three years of work experience and were recommended by the employer for the program. Later the program was directed by Dan Wallen. Wallen had vast experience in management with foreign corporations and was later on a team of businessmen and political leaders that played a role in convincing Germany's Wacker Chemicals to locate a new plant in Bradley County. Wallen had previously worked with Don Geren and Rick Platz (Directors) in the Small Business Development Center (SBDC). Later Directors of the SBDC were Brenda Sheehy and David Hudson, and Hurley Buff (as noted earlier) was the Executive Director of the Business Incubator.

Other innovative developments were: a course in Commercial Truck Driving (taught jointly with Chattanooga State Technical Community College); an Aquaponics Teaching Lab was located in the newly constructed Cleveland/Bradley Innovation Center; the lab, (directed by Associate Professor of Biology, Robert Brewer) combined fish and plant recirculating systems; an Occupational Therapy Assistant Program was adopted (under the coordination of Nancy Montgomery); and annual disaster simulations were conducted, led by nursing, medical assistant, emergency medical technician/paramedic and social work instructors and students.

Meanwhile, the college's "Campus Kitchen" manager, James Payne, decided to "go green" by purchasing biodegradable items, buying produce from local vendors, providing healthy snack options in vending machines and by installing bottle-fed water fountains; a high tech "Studio Connect" space for students was located in the library (in honor of Bill Stark, a former CSCC employee in the Information Technology Department); a Child Development Associate Degree Program was launched under the coordination of Associate Professor Suzanne Wood; and new courses were offered in Rock Climbing, Rappelling and Canoeing.

In 2013 the college formed a partnership, and provided a location, for the "Caring Place's Sac Pac Program;" a free community computer repair and maintenance service, using skilled student interns, continued under the leadership of Professors Dr. Megen Saez and Bob Uhl; and the college's History Department, led by the efforts of Associate Professors Bryan Reed and Dr. Neil Greenwood, worked with Volunteer Voices (a part of the Tennessee Electronic Library) to photo-digitize the history of the college's service area by establishing a website known as the Southeast Tennessee Digital Archive (SETDA). Participants in the digitization project were representatives from all of the college's five county service area Historical Societies, Libraries and Museums.

In other developments the TBR established a Regents Online Degree Program (RODP) enabling students to obtain a college degree via the web. All state colleges and universities participated in the program. Cleveland State developed a new online course, organized by Dr. Ann Cunningham, Associate Professor of Computer and Information Systems, titled "Introduction to Health and Technology." The course blended information technology with healthcare information. An evening nursing program was added to the existing daytime program, and a significant monetary contribution to the program was made by CSCC Foundation Trustee, John Sheehan. The TBR also held extensive training for its member colleges in a new administrative-related information technology program known as "Banner" (college staff members devoted numerous hours to mastering the new program). The college also added a mandatory Freshmen Success Course to assist students with their educational, career and life objectives. In 2011 the college initiated a Freshmen Connection Day to assist first-time students and their family in such things as becoming acquainted with the campus, purchasing books, finalizing college expenditures and academic expectations.

An unusual organization, La Societe des Quarante Hommes Et Huit Chevaux (often referred to as the "Forty and Eight"), provided annual scholarships for two Nursing students. This independent fraternal organization of veterans acquired its name from the French railroad boxcars that transported men and horses to the front lines during World War I. Stencils on the side of the cars read "40 or 8." This meant that the boxcar capacities were for either 40 men or 8 horses. The Society was organized in 1920 as the honor society of American Legionnaires.

In 2012 the college's Law Enforcement Training Academy (started in 1990) received a highly successful academic audit by the TBR's Academic Affairs Office. The result was zero recommendations, four commendations and three affirmations. Dr. Jerry Faulkner, the Vice-President for Academic Affairs, noted that, "The fact that the LET program received a report with no recommendations is directly attributed to the hard work of our faculty in that program." The Directors of the Academy, since its inception in 1990, were David Loftis, Gerald Duerr, Warren Moberg, Craig Hamilton and Dwight Williams (the current Director, assisted by Jarrett Crawford, the Assistant Director). All of the Directors were experienced in Law Enforcement. Loftis worked with the Soddy Daisy Police Department; Duerr majored in Criminal Justice at Citadel College; Moberg retired from a long career with the FBI; Hamilton was an officer with the Bradley County Sheriff's Department; Williams was a Deputy Sheriff and Training Officer for the Loudon County Sheriff's Department; and Crawford was employed with the Miami, Florida, Police Department.

The Academy usually operated with approximately 20 instructors and from 25 to 35 students. The training was increased from eight to twelve weeks, and as noted earlier, it included both academics and physical training. Williams and Crawford, in addition to their administrative duties, also served as instructors (as did the previous administrators). Williams concentrated on patrol and defensive tactics and Crawford on criminal investigations and crime scenes. Jerry Johnson, with the Bradley County Emergency Management Agency, and Richard Taylor, retiree from the Tennessee Emergency Management Agency, taught in every academy since 1990. Sonny Hayes, of the Bradley County Emergency Medical Service, taught in all but one of the academies.

Admission to the Academy required a comprehensive background check. When students completed the training, their certificates were dispatched for approval to the

Tennessee Peace Officers Standards Commission. Job placement of graduates has been successful. A typical year, for example, was 2011 when 85 graduated out of 97. This yielded an 88% graduation rate and an 83% job placement rate. Although the majority of students have been males, Williams noted that three female students (in one of the 2012 Academies) were exceptional. They were Michaela Flowers, Mehye Scott and Krystan McClure.

A unique Tennessee program, known as "TnAchieves" (Tennessee Achieves) was created by Tennessee businessman Randy Boyd (he was also the Tennessee Commissioner of Economic and Community Development). The program's mission was to provide "last-dollar" community and technical college scholarships that connected students with volunteer mentors (and required students to complete a minimum of eight hours of community service each semester). From 2008-2014 the program supported over 10,000 students with more than $15.5 million privately raised for "last-dollar" student scholarships. Sixty-five percent of the scholarship recipients were first generation college attendees, and seventy percent came from families that earned less than $50,000 annually (94 percent of the graduates reported they completed their post-secondary education debt-free).

On the local level the Allan Jones Foundation provided $839,500 for 657 students to attend Cleveland State. The "Allan Jones College of Knowledge" scholarship was the first major endorsement of "TnAchieves," and it enabled any graduating public high school senior at Bradley Central, Cleveland High or Walker Valley High to attend CSCC at no cost. CSCC President, Dr. Bill Seymour, stated that "the Jones scholarship gave vital help to students who otherwise would have struggled to pay for a college education." In 2015 Jones received the Excellence in Philanthropy Award from the TBR and was awarded an honorary degree from Cleveland State (the first and only such degree the college has ever awarded).

A statewide innovative program was an outgrowth of "TnAchieves." Known as "Tennessee Promise," it was inaugurated by Governor Bill Haslam in 2014. It was both a scholarship and mentoring program designed to increase the number of students that attend college in Tennessee. It enabled Tennessee students to attend a community or technical college tuition free. It provided money to cover tuition and fees not covered by the Pell Grant, the HOPE Scholarship or state student assistance funds. It also provided a mentor volunteer for the student and required eight hours of community service per semester. On August 24, 2015 Governor Haslam visited the CSCC campus to welcome the first class of students that received Tennessee Promise funding. Approximately 60,000 high school seniors applied for Tennessee Promise for the fall of 2016. In addition the Tennessee Board of Regents and the University of Tennessee systems developed the Tennessee Transfer Pathway Guarantee. If a student followed the program for the first two years of college, the student was guaranteed admission, as a member of the Junior Class, to all public universities in the state. For many years prior to the Pathway Guarantee, Cleveland State developed numerous similar agreements with both public and private universities throughout the state (such as UTC, UTK, Tennessee Tech, Tennessee Wesleyan, Lee University and many others).

Sadly, a college landmark, the astronomical observatory, had to be razed. Its equipment was outmoded, and as the city of Cleveland grew, lights became a major distraction for effective viewing of the stars. A few years prior to its demise a humorous incident occurred that involved Jim Cigliano, the Dean of Student Affairs, and Tom Losh, the Director of Admissions. They were chatting one day in Cigliano's office when a student rushed in and said that the observatory was on fire. Cigliano and Losh grabbed a fire extinguisher and ran to the edifice. Smoke was billowing from the observatory, and they rushed in and began spraying the inside. They soon discovered, however, that there was no fire. The smoke was caused by an anti-insect decanter placed there by the maintenance department. Although fighting fire was not in their job description, their efforts were laudatory.

Grants have been an integral part of the college's success through the years. One of these was $150,000 provided by Wacker Industry to assist with an addition to the Technology Building (the $1.2 million addition was completed in 2012). A ribbon cutting ceremony for the addition was held in September 2012 and those attending were: John Morgan, TBR Chancellor; Dr. Carl Hite, CSCC President; Konrad Bachhuber, Vice-President and Site Manager at Wacker; Gary Davis, Bradley County Mayor; Tom Rowland, Cleveland City Mayor; Mike Bell, Tennessee State Senator; and Kevin Brooks, Tennessee State Representative. A new Technology program was instituted in connection with the construction project. It was designed by Allan Gentry, Department Chair, and Associate Professors Charles Barkley, John Hannah, Charlie Womac and David Laman. Gentry praised J & J Construction for their expertise and speed in building the addition.

Examples of other important grants were: $861,840 from the Community Based Job Training Initiative which assisted with the Energy Efficient Residential Construction Program; in 2014 NASA awarded $499,689 to the Tennessee Community College Space Grant Consortium ($45,000 of that amount was earmarked for CSCC students enrolled in Science, Technology, Engineering and Math-related degree and certificate programs); the Appalachian Regional Commission provided the college with a matching grant of $100,000 for Innovation Training in Workforce Readiness Programs; a Perkins Reserve Grant of $34,000 was awarded to the college to prepare students for jobs in career and technical education and for funding a part-time Career Services Coordinator; and $50,000 was provided by the Denso North American Foundation to fund capital investments for competency-based Denso Manufacturing Training.

Grants were becoming a major source of income during the 2001-2016 years. Examples of others were: the Tennessee Early Childhood Training alliance gave a grant to enhance the children's section of the college library with child-size furniture and equipment (Suzanne Wood, Coordinator and Associate Professor of Early Childhood Education, Mary Evelyn Lynn, Director of Library Services, and Janet

Caruth, Acquisition and Reference Librarian, worked closely to develop the area in the library); the college received $102,000, from Title One of the Carl D. Perkins Career and Technical Education Act (to purchase equipment, such as an ambulance, for the Paramedic and EMT programs); in 2013 the college received $200,000 from the Governor's Competitive Grant for Workforce Development; in 2016 a grant of one million dollars was presented to both CSCC and the Tennessee College of Applied Technology in Athens to meet workforce needs for the area; the college was awarded a $90,700 Institutional Outcome Improvement Fund grant from the Tennessee Higher Education Commission (CSCC was one of only six institutions receiving the grant); an anonymous donor enabled the college to purchase $300,000 worth of new technology equipment; and a $959,267 Labor Education Alignment Program (LEAP) grant was awarded to CSCC and Pellissippi State Community College (which was evenly divided between the two colleges). The college's Grants Specialist during much of the 2001-2016 period was Michelle Anderson.

A significant portion of the LEAP grant was used to purchase equipment (primarily electrical mechanical materials) for the college's new Monroe County facility in Vonore. The college operated an off-campus site in Vonore for many years. The location was later moved to Madisonville and then back to Vonore. Ron Hammontree (as noted previously) was the Director of the Tellico Reservoir Development Agency (TRDA), and the TRDA donated the new Vonore facility to the college. In the early years (as noted previously) Pam Price was the Director in Vonore and Michelle Jenkins the Secretary. Since 2006 the Director of both the off-campus sites in Vonore and Athens has been Patricia Weaver. Weaver received her Bachelor's degree from UTK and her Master's degree from Tusculum College (and she completed coursework for her Doctorate at East Tennessee State University). A few of the other former Directors in Athens were Mary Lou Williams, Emily Guinn, Merv Weerasakeera, Susan Webb-Curtis, Ennis Taylor, Charles Woodard, and Janie Evans. The 2016 enrollment at Athens was approximately 480 students. Through the years Hammontree has been a dedicated supporter of the college in the Vonore-Madisonville area, and Paul Wilson (President of Citizens National Bank) has provided similar support in the Athens area.

In December 2011 a campus ribbon-cutting ceremony was held to open the newly constructed Cleveland-Bradley Innovation Center. Those present were: Phillip S. McMullan, Program Manager of Economic Investments and Economic Development with the TVA; David Collett, Area Director of the United States Department of Agriculture for Rural Development; Dr. Carl Hite, CSCC President; Gary Davis, Mayor of Bradley County; Tom Rowland, Mayor of Cleveland; Jeff Morelock, Chairman of the Board of the Cleveland-Bradley Incubator; Gary Farlow, President and CEO of the Cleveland-Bradley Chamber of Commerce; Daphne L. Kirksey, District Director for U. S. Representative Chuck Fleischman; and Hurley Buff, Executive Director of the Business Incubator. The Innovation Center housed tenants with "green" businesses that used environmentally sound practices (such as the aforementioned Aquaponics Teaching Lab).

Both the Cleveland-Bradley Business Incubator and the Tennessee Business Development Center assisted business owners from offices located on CSCC property. Both helped in different ways. The Incubator began operations in 2000 to make office and manufacturing space available for new businesses to rent. The rental fees were set at prices compatible with their smaller budgets until they could "graduate" and move elsewhere. The Small Business Development Center helped businesses with the details of establishing a business through workshops, private consultations and other services. The workshops included everything from tax preparations to government contracting, and the consultations addressed everything from business plans to investments. The Center was funded by the US Small Business Administration and was one of 14 centers (20 if merely offices are counted) statewide. From 2010 to 2016 the Center assisted over 1,400 businesses, and a major result was the creation of 930 jobs. In recent years the Executive Director of the Incubator has been Hurley Buff, and the Director of the Center has been David Hudson.

In other news the college received a national award on four different occasions by being named to the US President's Higher Education Honor Roll (in 2010, 2013, 2014 and 2015). In each of these years the college was one of approximately 36 community colleges nationwide to receive the recognition. The recognitions were primarily for the college's support of volunteering, service learning and civic engagement. Associate Professor Susan Webb-Curtis (the Director of Cooperative Education, the Director of Service Learning, and later, the Dean of the Business and Technology Division) played an instrumental role in increasing student volunteering for community projects. The college's leadership role in this endeavor was manifest by Cleveland State's hosting of a 2012 Service Learning Conference for eight Tennessee Community colleges. Later, Webb-Curtis was assisted by Sherry Holloway, the Coordinator of Service Learning. The program also acquired additional help when it received approval to hire Kourtney Yonge for an "AmeriCorps VISTA" (Volunteers in Service to America) position.

In 2013 Webb-Curtis received a prestigious award from the League for Innovation in Community Colleges (a consortium of over 750 community colleges and universities worldwide). The award, known as the John and Suanne Roueche Award, was for Webb-Curtis's outstanding contribution to teaching, leadership and learning. College President, Dr. Hite said, "Susan Webb-Curtis is one of a kind that every campus needs to have." Dr. Denise King, Vice-President for Academic Affairs, noted that Webb-Curtis "exuded energy, displayed creativity and was an outstanding instructor."

The US President's Higher Education Honor Roll began in 2006, and it annually highlighted colleges and universities that played a significant role in solving community problems and that inculcated students with a desire to become involved in civic affairs. A similar community program was VISTA. It was founded in 1965 as a national service program to fight poverty, and it currently has about 6,500 members who serve in approximately 1,200 projects across the country. A highlight of the service-learning project was the beginning of annual "Make a Difference Now Volunteer Expos" in

2010. The "Expos" allowed students, faculty and community members to interact with community agencies on an informal basis. Because of the success of the college's program, the service-learning staff members were invited to make a presentation at the Gulf South Summit for Service-Learning in Louisville in 2013 and at Auburn University in 2014. They also made presentations at the 2013 Points of Light National Conference for Volunteering and Service in Washington, D. C., and at the 2014 Points of Light Conference in Atlanta.

The college also received the 2013 Platinum Partner of the Year Award, along with the college's BEST partner, Taylor Elementary School. The award was for exceeding their basic partnership agreement with excellence. As noted previously, BEST (Business and Education Serving Together) was an ongoing Chamber of Commerce program that encouraged interaction between businesses and local schools. The college also won three awards from the Chattanooga Advertising Federation and eighteen awards from the National Council for Marketing and Public Relations. Tony Bartolo, the college's Director of Marketing and Public Information, said, "I am extremely proud of my staff in the Marketing Department." He praised Jeff Reep, Senior Designer; Holly Vincent, Public Information Coordinator; John Dezember, Web Developer; Yolanda Gibson, Marketing Assistant; and Donna Benton, Graphic Designer and Publications Coordinator.

In 2013 the college changed the "Campus Security" Department to "Campus Police." The alteration, which required the permission of the Tennessee P.O.S.T. Commission, was to enhance campus safety. Those assisting with the process were Mike Hodges, Chief of Campus Police, Dr. Tommy Wright, Vice-President of Finance and Administration, and local Law Enforcement Officers, David Bishop and Wes Snyder. The college also used grant money, from the aforementioned Appalachian Regional Commission to develop an innovative project at the Athens Center for students seeking certificates in Process Controls Fundamentals, Electrical Maintenance and Mechanical Maintenance. Susan Webb-Curtis, the newly appointed Dean of Business and Technology, noted that, "The classes are in accelerated format, and some are online." Tim Wilson, Technology Instructor and Department Chair, stated that, "These programs are ideal for the person who is employed full-time, but is lacking certain skill sets." The aforementioned grant from NASA was used to assist with the college's robotic program and for hiring a "completion coach" for the college's Engineering Technology students. Additional funds were allocated to increase student enrollment (both male and female) in Engineering Technology. Marcia O'Connor, Director of Institutional Research and Effectiveness, noted that while 61 percent of the state's total enrollment was female, only 12 percent of them enroll in Engineering Technology programs.

Examples of other activities were: Jason Holcomb, EMT Instructor, and Alejandra Hoffer, Associate Professor of Spanish, led students on a trip to Honduras to assist Dr. Ronald Coleman (of "Doctors Without Borders") to provide free medical services to citizens of impoverished Honduran communities; Instructors Margaret Horten and Sandy Whetmore organized Early Childhood Education students in a project to develop

Math and Science kits for pre-K through 3rd grade teachers at Taylor Elementary School; Robert Brewer (Associate Professor of Biology) partnered with the U. S. Department of Agriculture Forestry Service and the Tennessee Wildlife Resources Agency for students to volunteer in the Cherokee National Forest (students surveyed trout populations and treated infested hemlock forests); Sonya Franklin, Associate Professor of Nursing, partnered with the staff of Rhea County Volunteers in Medicine for sophomore nursing students to assist with a regional free medical clinic; Dr. Megen Saez (Associate Professor of Computer and Information Systems and Business Department Chair), was honored with the Gary C. Filan Excellence in Leadership Award through the Chair Academy; and an extensive renovation (which included a new entrance, lobby and classrooms) was made to the auditorium, and it was renamed the George R. Johnson Cultural Heritage Center in memory of George Johnson (whose Foundation provided the funds for the project).

In other campus occurrences, Jana Pankey, Associate Professor of Human Services/ Social Work, recruited students to conduct a "Free Store" to provide clothing, furniture, household items, toys and books for over 50 deserving families; Dr. Michael J. Copps, one of the nation's five members of the Federal Communication Commission (and roommate of this author while attending graduate school at the University of North Carolina) made a presentation about the role of the FCC; Nancy Thomas, Associate Professor and Nursing Evening Coordinator, and Maureen Baksh-Griffin, Assistant Professor of Nursing, developed a service-learning program for students that entailed assisting a diverse population at such activities and locales as free clinics, health fairs, senior homes, emergency centers, medical centers, and home-health-care facilities (students invested about 3,100 hours and served over 1,200 people in the endeavors); in 2015 the local Tennessee Career Center moved from downtown Cleveland back to the campus; Bob Uhl, Associate Professor of Computer Information Technology, Dr. Megen Saez, Assistant Professor of Computer Information Systems, and Kara Headrick, Assistant Professor of Accounting, sponsored a campus Computer Repair Shop to provide free services to the college's five county service area (students invested about 1,200 hours and provided free service to 338 computers).

A few other developments were: a June 2016 Tennessee state law allowed faculty and staff, with valid permits, to carry guns with them on campus; a welding lab was completed in 2016; approximately 70 students received training to become certified facilitators in preventing sexual abuse of children (the training was offered through a partnership with "The Hope Center," the 10th Judicial District Children's Advocacy Center and a grant from Athens Federal Bank); Associate Professor of History, Bryan Reed, identified important Civil War sites in Bradley County, researched African-American local history and served as President of the Bradley County Historical and Genealogy Society; and Kelly Ormsby, Associate Professor of English/Learning Support, led a team of students, teachers and community personnel in developing a "Literacy Garden" (where books and writing were connected to nature) at Taylor Elementary School.

A humorous incident that was an example of the occasional disconnection between generations, occurred in one of Dr. L. E. Wooten's Sociology classes. Wooten had been stressing the importance of reading the textbook assignments before attending class. A female student, who had apparently not been paying attention, asked Wooten a question and he politely replied that she could find the answer in the text. The student held up her i-phone and said, "But you did not send me a text."

In 2004 an unusual undertaking was a project endowed by Debra Miller, an executive at Unum Provident Corporation. It was a support system for non-traditional female students known as "Your Opportunities are Unlimited "(Y. O. U.)." Its primary feature was a clothes closet located on the campus. Miller was assisted in the endeavor by Cele Curtis, the college's Adult Services Coordinator, and community members Carol Rahne, Uneva Shaw, Nancy Casson and Jamie Hamby.

Another unique program was referred to as "SAILS" (Seamless Alignment and Integrated Learning Support). The college received almost one million dollars in grants in 2013-2014, and one of these was approximately $100,000 from the TBR Access and Diversity Grant for the SAILS program. The purpose of the project was to provide high school students their 4th year of high school math while making them college ready in math during their senior year of high school. After successful completion of the bridge math course, students were eligible to take their college math elective course at Cleveland State through dual enrollment. Sequoyah High School student Allison Young was the first person in the state to complete the SAILS program offered through CSCC. Karen Wyrick, Math Department Chair, said, "There are 11 community colleges in the state of Tennessee doing SAILS, but Allison is the first student in the state to mark off her competencies." John Squires, Regional SAILS Math Director, said, "As one of the original pilot programs, Cleveland State has helped pave the way for SAILS to spread across the state."

In another groundbreaking event Tracey Wright, Director of Special Programs and Community Relations, and Holly Vincent, Public Information Coordinator, were instrumental in organizing the college's "First Year Experience" (FYE) Program. Wright was a graduate of MTSU, where she received her Bachelor's and Master's degrees. She had also worked at Appalachian State University in North Carolina. Vincent was a Cleveland State graduate and she received her Bachelor's degree from Tennessee Tech University. The goal of the annual FYE project was to support first year students with New Student Orientation, New Student Advising and Registration, the First Year Seminar Course and the Advising and Early Alert program. In addition (as noted above) a "Freshmen Connection" event featured sessions to assist with the transition from high school to college. Information sessions were conducted for parents and non-traditional students, and prizes and tickets to venues such as Dollywood, the Tennessee Aquarium and Ruby Falls were available in drawings by the participants.

Service Learning was a major component of the First Year Seminar Course. Jamie Barks, a former Resource Development Coordinator for the city of Cleveland's Habitat for Humanity, was hired as a Service Learning Program Assistant. Barks noted that in the fall of 2013 more than 30 community agencies partnered with the college, and over 300 students participated in service learning by providing approximately 2,400 hours of service to the community. In 2014 Dr. Liz Moseley, CSCC Assistant Professor of Psychology and the First Year Seminar Coordinator, stated that, "The key word for FYS this year was growth. Dr. Seymour (Cleveland State President) and Dr. Brandon (Dean of Humanities and Social Sciences) were huge advocates of the program statewide which allowed us to grow to 18 sections in the fall and 4 sections in the spring, approximately 400 students." An important community agency partner for the college was the Museum Center at Five Points in Cleveland. In 2014 Cleveland State and the Museum entered into a partnership that allowed faculty to use the Museum as a teaching lab. In addition faculty, staff and students received free admission, access to member-only events and other special discounts.

The college continued to meet the workforce training and educational needs of its five-county service area. Equipment was purchased to enhance the Technology Department's Mechatronics Lab. The Lab provided state of the art robotics applications and performance-based assessment machines to identify and measure skills, competencies and training for mechanical, electrical, programmable logic control and computer numeric control. Rick Creasy, Director of Workforce Development, said, "Cleveland State is committed to developing workers for advanced manufacturing jobs through our 'OneSource' assessment and industrial readiness training center." Close relationships were formed by the college with companies such as Cormetech, Merck, Georgia-Pacific, Columbus McKinnon, RockTenn and Mueller. The Workforce Readiness Center assisted these companies in process consulting, training needs analyses, applicant selection, referrals, promotions, testing assessments and training. Other members of the CSCC team, in addition to Creasy, were Allan Gentry (Technology Department Chair), Bre LaMountain (Director of Workforce Training) and John Hannah (Technology Department Instructor).

The athletic teams continued to be competitive during the 2001-2016 years. Mike Policastro served as the college's Athletic Director during the era. The golf team won the state and region championships in 2003-2005, and the team was ranked in the top ten of the National Junior College Athletic Association (NJCAA) Division II in four straight years (2002-2005). Coached by Jason Sewell, the team members in 2002-2003 were Josh Coley, Ricky Honeycutt, Justin McMaster, Jacob Bennett and Wes Rackley. Coley was named a first team All-American in 2001-2002 and 2002-2003, Honeycutt was a first team All-American in 2002-2003, and Holton Freeman and Tyler Neff were first team All-Americans in 2003-2004. Golf team members in 2004-2005 were Nick Parker, Brandon Cissom, Tyler Nelson and Titus Osborne. Unfortunately the golf team, which was revived in 2000, was suspended in 2006 for economic reasons.

In 2014 and 2015 the Lady Cougar basketball team was runner-up in the Tennessee Community College Athletic Association (TCCAA) and the NJCAA Region. Kierra

Johnson was an All-American in 2010-2011, and Jamesha Mosley was an All-American in 2014-2015. Coach Dan Lumpkin was voted TCCAA Coach of the Year for 2015-2016. In men's basketball Coach Lee Cigliano's team was the runner-up in the TJCCAA and the NJCAA Region Tournaments in 2006-2007. The team also repeated the same feat in 2008-2009. Mykail Vibbert (2006-2007) and Nick Ross (2011-2012) were named NJCAA All-American Men's basketball players. In baseball, coached by Mike Policastro, Kenny Reed (2003-2004), Kevin Hammons (2005-2006) and Cody Hooper (2009-2010) were NJCAA All-Americans.

Several other athletes were Academic All-Americans during 2001-2016. These were: Andrew Hogan, Golf (2002-2003); Andrew Smith, Baseball (2002-2003); Jonathon Martin, Men's Basketball (2002-2003; Josh Sullivan, Men's Basketball (2002-2003); Travis Lee, Men's Basketball (2003-2004); and Holton Freeman, Golf (2003-2004). In 2012-2013 Colin Sullivan and Casey Griffin were named to the Academic All-American Team, and in 2014 Bobby Towne and Evan Speicher were named to the NJCAA Academic All-American Team. Recent recipients have been Jaclyn Griffith, Ryan Mahaffey, Brittany Arnold, Haley Hodgson, Madison Stiner, Catherine Davis, Rachel Goodson, Mikayla Teal, Christian Amos and Christian Burnett.

In 2012 the NJCAA recognized the Cleveland State Community College Softball Team as the 2012-2013 Academic Team of the Year. Qualification for the honor required a minimum grade point average (GPA) of 3.0 in a 4.0 scale. The team had a cumulative GPA of 3.05. Softball Coach, Katie Willingham, noted that the team "exceeded our expectations, and I couldn't be more thrilled as a coach." Members of the team were: Meghan Allen, Amber Covington, Maura Ditto, Kenzie Fish, Sarah Goza, Casey Griffin, Shelby Hanson, Sydney Howell, Kenly Lambert, Heather Lynn, Paige Mayer, Ashlen Mitchell, Meghan Smith, Kerstyn Stansberry, Kelly Sullins and Halen Weeks.

In 2005 the Cougar Booster Club played the lead role in the dedication of a "Cougar Room" in the gymnasium. It contained pictorial presentations of the college's history in athletics. The advisory committee members for the room were: Jim Cigliano, Vice-President of Student Services; Mike Policastro, Athletic Director and Baseball Coach; Hugh Walker, former Ladies' Basketball Coach; Jason Sewell, Golf Coach; and Tony Bartolo, Director of Marketing and Public Information.

In 2013 the college inaugurated a Sports Hall of Fame induction ceremony. Athletic Director Mike Policastro said, "We are celebrating 45 years of men's basketball this year, so we thought this would be a good time to recognize athletics at CSCC and people who have made an impact on athletics by beginning a Sports Hall of Fame." A 9-member selection committee was appointed to review nominees and make selections to the Hall. The committee included coaches and athletic directors from current and previous years at the college. These were: Policastro, Jim Cigliano, Lee Cigliano, Dan Lumpkin, Steve Longley, Jason Sewell, Tony Cavett, Tom Losh and Hugh Walker. Sixty athletes and individuals with meritorious service to athletics have been inducted since 2013.

Numerous faculty and staff members received recognitions during the years of 2001-2016. The co-chairs of the successful reaccreditation process in 2005 were Mary Evelyn Lynn, Director of Library Services, and Denice King, Associate Professor of Biology. Other campus leaders in the process were Dr. Ann Cunningham, Julie Fulbright, Pat Jenkins, Dr. David Watts, Susan Webb-Curtis, Dr. Michael Stokes, Karen Wyrick, Jean Crockett and Cele Curtis. Others receiving recognitions were: Associate Professor Bob Lantz received the "Solar Star Award" from the Southern Alliance for Clean Energy (for his development of a curriculum for Energy Efficient Residential Construction); and Karen Wyrick (Math Department Chair) and John Squires (former CSCC employee and Math Department Head at Chattanooga State Community College), co-authored an "eCourse" series that was recognized as a Pearson Higher Education Product of the Year.

In other recognitions, Dr. Neil Greenwood, Associate Professor of History, delivered a series of lectures on on the Civil War for both the campus and the community; Alejandra Hoffer, Associate Professor of Spanish, was recognized as a Service Learning Champion by the college; the Nursing Department faculty and staff (Joyce Chapman, Dawn Steele, Vickie Still, Judy Norton, Sonya Franklin, Nancy Labine, Nancy Herrig, Victoria Hight, Lisa Ste. Marie, Kelly Ford, Priscilla Simms, Nancy Thomas and Maureen Baksh-Griffin) won a Service Learning Team Champion designation; Barbara Aderhold was recognized for having been an outstanding part-time English instructor in the Athens service area for over thirty years; Nursing instructor Maureen Baksh-Griffin received national recognition for her research on emergency preparedness at the Eighteenth World Congress on Disaster and Emergency Medicine in Manchester, England; Karen Dale, Associate Professor of Music, was selected to serve as a PTK 2016-2017 Faculty Scholar (Dale was one of thirty community college instructors selected from among nearly 3,000 chapter advisors); and Director of Nursing, Nancy Labine, received the Tennessee Head Start 2015-2016 Community Volunteer of the Year Award.

Student organizations and individual students also remained active during the years of 2001-2016. PTK continued to win numerous regional and international awards and won Tennessee's Most Distinguished Chapter Award for several years in a row. Over one-hundred awards, on Awards Day, were presented annually to students who excelled in academic areas (such as Math, Chemistry, History, Psychology, Spanish and many others) and to those who made contributions to a multitude of student activities. From the earliest years of the college to the present, averages of approximately seventy students per year have been recognized in the annual edition of "Who's Who Among Students in American Junior Colleges."

An interesting student was Virginia Pauline Morgan (known as Miss Polly). She was Cleveland State's oldest student (age 89). She said she had been a life-long student for 50 of her 89 years, and sixteen of those years were at CSCC. She worked with the US Postal Service in Copperhill, Tennessee, until her retirement in 1990. Sadly, she was killed in a car wreck on March 28, 2006 on her way to the college from her home in Copperhill. During the May Commencement ceremony, College President, Dr. Carl Hite, proclaimed a special "Spirit of Learning Award" in her memory.

Spring Commencement speakers (secondary, smaller December Commencements began in 2014) since 2001 were: Joanne Walker, Plant Director of M & M Mars; Doyle Dykes, renowned performer and guitarist whose daughters attended CSCC; Margaret L. Callihan, President and CEO of Sun Trust Bank in Chattanooga; Lee Anne Carmack, former CSCC student; Tennessee Governor, Phil Bredesen; Congressman Zach Wamp; Dr. Lana Seivers, Tennessee Commissioner of Education; Ken Jones, Assistant Professor at Dyersburg Community College and "Abraham Lincoln Presenter;" Dr. Belle S. Wheelan, President of the Commission on Colleges and of the Southern Association of Colleges and Schools; Dr. Melinda Strickland, CSCC graduate and a Principal in Floyd County Education in Georgia; Peggy Crisp, Cody Browder and Casey McCullum's joint presentations on "Student Reflections;" Dr. Ingomar Kovar, President and CEO of Wacker Chemical Corporation; Larry Gatlin, Country Music Song Master; Chet Guthrie, Richard Patterson, Mark Partain, Jeffrey Lawson, Steve Cowan, and the Vocal Rhapsody and Chamber Choir's (directed by Karen Dale, CSCC Associate Professor of Music) joint presentations on "Student Reflections;" Tim Spires, President and CEO of the Tennessee Association of Manufacturers; Allan Jones, Businessman Owner and Philanthropist; Walter Presswood, Student President of the Class of 1969; and Anna McDade, Student Member of the Class of 2016.

The Foundation has continued to be an active supporter of the college and the two-year term Foundaton Presidents since 2000 have been: Gray Epperson, Don Lorton, Jeff Morelock, James O. Williams, Amy Card-Lillios, Matt Bentley, Coleman Fosse, Don Lorton (for a second term) and Amy Card-Lillios (for a second term). A few of the most recent Student Government Association's Student Senate Presidents have been: Marcie Webb, Katie Ward, Candace Burns, Kristine Blankenship, Brandon Hall, Jill Hilton, Aaron Reed, Josh Simpson, Casey McCullum, Kylie Sherlin, William Lunny, Alyssa Durham, Quentin Murray, Kevin Houk, Shadia Suarez and Haley Hodgson.

Distinguished Graduate Award recipients since 2001 have been: Dustin Adam Lane, Brenda Taylor, Josh Sullivan, Shantae Morris, Troy Cannon, Linda Howerton, Wesley Callahan, Landon Saffles, Diana Ballew, Casey McCullim, David St. Clair, Karleigh Bloomer, Steven Cowan, Rachel Burgess, Bo Marshall and Carolina Roman. Distinguished Staff Award recipients have been: Susan Rodriquez, Linda Henry, Laura Brogden, Alvin Beck, Brenda Ellis, Barbara Higgins Eaves, Alan Goslen, Joyce Brock, Sherry Miller, Jason Sewell, Tony Fox, Ashley Raburn, Suzanne Bayne, Mike Policastro, Ruth Kirkendall and Patricia Weaver. Distinguished Faculty Award recipients have been: Ann McCoin, Dr. Ken Adcock, Jere Chumley, Jean Crockett, Suzanne Wood, Amy Patten McGranaham, Judy Sheppard Norton, John Squires, Susan Webb-Curtis, Dr. Ann Cunningham, Dale Yates, Amy Fowler, Nancy Thomas, Ryan Thompson, Mark McLeod and Karmon Kingsley.

Although the titles of those in charge of Academics during the last fifty years have changed from Deans to Vice-Presidents, they have been: Dr. F. Dean Banta, Dr. L. Quentin Lane, Dr. Galen McBride, Dr. Charles Tollett, Dr. Mary Barker, Dr. Renate Basham, Dr. Barry Vann, Dr. Frank McKenzie (interim), Dr. Luba Chliwniak, Dr. Joan Fitch, Dr. Spencer Culbreth, Dr. Jerry Faulkner and Dr. Denise King. Titles for those in charge of Student Affairs have had similar changes from Deans to Vice-Presidents and they have been: Dr. George Mathis, Jim Cigliano, Jason Sewell (interim), Dr. Linda Croley and Dr. Michael Stokes. Business Managers or Deans or Vice-Presidents of Financial Affairs have been: McKamy Hall, Ronald Mason, James Morris, Jacky Liner, Dr. Charles Hurley and Dr. Tommy Wright. As has been noted, the Presidents through the years have been: Dr. David Adkisson, Dr. L. Quentin Lane, Ray Coleman (interim), Dr. James W. Ford, Dr. Peter Consacro (interim), Dr. Owen Cargol, Dr. Renate Basham (interim), Dr. Carl M. Hite and Dr. William A. Seymour.

Dr. Carl Hite retired in December 2013, after serving as college President for 17 years. He was honored at the 2014 International PTK Convention in Orlando, Florida, with the Michael Bennett Lifetime Achievement Award. The TBR also honored him by naming the campus Math and Science building for him. Hite's replacement was Dr. William Seymour. Seymour served as Vice President for Institutional Advancement and Vice President for Student Services at Jackson State Community College. He was previously the President of Lambuth University. He received his Bachelor's degree in Psychology from State University of New York College at Oswego, his Master's degree in Counseling and Personnel Services from the University of Missouri and his Doctorate in Higher and Adult Education from the University of Missouri.

Dr. Seymour announced that his guiding principles for the college would be what he called "The R Factor." This included recruitment, retention, reputation, revenue and reinforcing the college's mission. He unveiled a new strategic plan for the college named the "Cleveland State 2020 Community First Plan." A steering committee for the plan consisted of a broad spectrum of faculty, staff, students, community representatives and members of the Board of Trustees. Although the plan contained nine major goals and sixty-three objectives, its highlights included: enrollment growth, a new fund raising program, the construction of a new classroom building, growth in off-campus facilities and programs in Athens and Monroe County and a celebration of the college's 50th Anniversary.

Recent events at the college have been: the creation of a 30-member Advisory Board of college and community representatives to gain greater knowledge of educational and workforce needs and partnership opportunities throughout the service area; two annual celebrity roasts (featuring Jim Cigliano and Mayor Tom Rowland); annual Alumni and Friends celebrations; the development of the aforementioned "College is for Me" program; and the first annual "Community First Awards" program to recognize outstanding community citizens (the recipient of the first major award, presented in

2016, was Brenda Hughes, the former Director of Family Cornerstones); and the introduction of the college's Tennessee Valley Early College to enable students to work toward their high school diplomas and associate degrees at the same time.

The college officially kicked-off its 50th Anniversary celebration with a heavily attended Convocation on August 26, 2016. CSCC President Bill Seymour presided at the event and the other program participants were: Haley Hodgson, CSCC Student Senate Representative; Judy Crawley Robinson, member of the Class of '69 and vocalist for the national anthem; Angela McClure Mathis, former two-time President of the Student Government Association; the CSCC Choir, Vocal Rhapsody (directed by Karen Dale); Dr. Spencer Culbreth, former Vice-President of Academics; Dr. Denise King, the current Vice-President of Academics; David Gregory, interim Chancellor of the TBR; Amy Card Lillios, CSCC Foundation President; Mike Bell, Tennessee State Senator; Kevin Brooks, Tennessee State Representative; and Dan Howell, Tennessee State Representative. Tracey Wright, the college's Director of Special Programs and Community relations, played the lead role in organizing the event.

A 2012 study by the Southern Regional Education Board revealed that the enrollment in the community colleges and the four-year universities was equal in its sixteen state area. According to an article in the October 29, 2012 Chattanooga Times, community college enrollment had grown from approximately 500,000 in 1970 to 2.8 million in 2010. During the same time period, four-year college enrollment had grown from approximately 1.2 million to 2.8 million. CSCC, as noted earlier, is a member of the seventh largest system of higher education in the nation. Its administrative leader, the TBR, governs 13 community colleges, 6 universities and 27 technology centers. In 2010, in Tennessee, 407,599 students were enrolled in all of its colleges. Of these, 96,777 were in TBR community colleges and 96,669 in TBR universities. The average 2010 tuition was $6,190 at an in-state Tennessee University and only $3,121 at a Tennessee Community College.

From its modest beginnings in a small house on Broad Street, the college has made impressive progress that has included the construction of eleven major campus buildings, a steady enrollment of 3,500 students and a huge Endowment Fund. In 1967 the college had six administrators, sixteen faculty members and 65 course offerings. In 2015 there were 126 administrative and staff personnel, 76 full-time faculty members and a total of 867 course offerings at 17 different locations throughout the college's five-county service area. From 1976 until 2015 the College Foundation awarded 6,372 scholarships for a total of $5,296,404. As of 2015 the Foundation also had $5,013,113 Scholarship Endowment Funds. The results of the numerous Alumni Satisfaction Surveys throughout the years have indicated that Tennessee Valley citizens have been highly pleased with their education at Cleveland State. The college has been at the forefront of the nation's community colleges and has the resources and the qualifications to remain an educational leader for another fifty years.

ANNOTATED BIBLIOGRAPHY

The major sources for the book have been the Cleveland State Employee Newsletters (1968-2016) and the student newspaper, The Cherokee Signal (1968-2000). Two other college publications, published at various times through the years, were also useful: the "Cleveland State Update" and the "Cleveland State Profile." The college's annual "Fact Book" also contained important statistical information. The press releases from the college's marketing department, written by Holly Vincent and Tony Bartolo, and often appearing in the local newspaper, The Cleveland Daily Banner, were a valuable source of information for the years 2001-2016. Information about international and national events, as well as pop culture news, was found in the 2011 and 2014 editions of The World Almanac and Book of Facts and from the electronic source, www.thepeoplehistory.com (1967-2016). An occasional supplemental source was George Tindall's, America: A Narrative History, second edition, New York: W. W. Norton and Company, 1988, as well as Roy S. Nicks, editor, Community Colleges of Tennessee: The Founding and Early Years, Memphis, Tennessee: Memphis State University Press, 1979. A 1978 Cleveland State publication, and a valuable source for the early years of 1967-1978, was Sue Little, author, and Walter Presswood, editor, Morning Has Broken.

ABOUT THE AUTHOR

Spencer Culbreth was born and raised in Frog Level, North Carolina, near Sandy Mush and Shingle Hollow and close to the towns of Rutherfordton and Spindale. He majored in History at three different colleges. He received his Bachelor's Degree from Wofford College, his Master's Degree from the University of North Carolina at Chapel Hill and his Doctorate from Middle Tennessee State University. He served in Vietnam as a Captain in the U.S. Army during the Vietnam Conflict. He was a Professor and Administrator at Cleveland State Community College, Cleveland, Tennessee, for thirty-seven years. His wife, Ann, was an Elementary School Teacher, Principal and Supervisor in the Cleveland City School System for forty years.

www.ingramcontent.com/pod-product-compliance
Lightning Source LLC
Chambersburg PA
CBHW081344280526
45788CB00009B/2773